International Law and International Security

Soviet contributions translated by James S. Beaver

International Law and International Security

Military and Political Dimensions

A U.S.–Soviet Dialogue

Edited by
Paul B. Stephan III
and
Boris M. Klimenko

M. E. Sharpe, Inc.
ARMONK, NEW YORK
LONDON, ENGLAND

Available in the United Kingdom and Europe from M. E. Sharpe, Publishers, 3 Henrietta Street, London WC2E 8LU.

Library of Congress Cataloging-in-Publication Data

International law and international security : military and political dimensions: a U.S.-Soviet dialogue / edited by Paul B. Stephan III, Boris M. Klimenko.
p. cm.
Includes index.
ISBN 0-87332-887-6
1. International law.
2. Security, International.
3. United States—Foreign relations—Soviet Union.
4. Soviet Union—Foreign relations—United States.
I. Stephan, Paul B.
II. Klimenko, B. M. (Boris Mikhailovich)
JX3091.I6585 1992
341.7′2—dc20
91-4289
CIP

Printed in the United States of America
The paper used in this publication meets the minimum requirements of American National Standard for Information Sciences—Permanence of Paper for Printed Library Materials, ANSI Z39.48-1984.

∞

MV 10 9 8 7 6 5 4 3 2 1

This study, jointly conducted by the University of Virginia School of Law and the Diplomatic Academy of the USSR Ministry of Foreign Affairs, is being published simultaneously in the United States in the English language and in the Union of Soviet Socialist Republics in the Russian language. Its preparation and publication have been made possible thanks to the financial support of the John D. and Catherine T. MacArthur Foundation and the Soviet Fund for Peace. To the best of our efforts, the text is current as of May 1, 1991.

This book is dedicated to our families.

TABLE OF CONTENTS

Authors

Boris Mikhailovich Klimenko. Moscow State University '58, candidate of juridical science '62 (Institute of State and Law of the USSR Academy of Sciences), doctor of juridical science '72 (ISL). Professor of the Diplomatic Academy of the USSR Ministry of Foreign Affairs. Head of section of international law, Research Department of the Diplomatic Academy, 1975-90. Partipant in various diplomatic and non-governmental conferences. Main editor of DICTIONARY OF INTERNATIONAL LAW and COMPREHENSIVE INTERNATIONAL SECURITY.

Valerii Ivanovich Kuznetsov. Moscow State University '63, candidate of juridical science '68 (Moscow State Institute of International Relations), doctor of juridical science '81 (MSIIR). Professor, department head, Diplomatic Academy. Member of the UN committee for economic, social, and cultural human rights, member of the permanent chamber of the Court of Arbitration. Participant in various diplomatic conferences.

Bakhtiyar Raisovich Tuzmukhamedov. MSIIR '77, candidate of juridical science '83 (MSIIR). Docent in the department of international law, Diplomatic Academy. Participant in the UNIDIR project on "Confidence Building Measures for Maritime Security." Expert in the Soviet delegation for the Special Committee of the UN on the Indian Ocean in 1987. Member of the editorial board of the SOVIET YEARBOOK ON INTERNATIONAL LAW.

Ednan Tofikovich Agayev. MSIIR '79, candidate of historical science '85 (Diplomatic Academy). Head, branch for questions of international security in the UN, MFA Directorate for International Organizations. UN Secretariat in Geneva, 1980-86, UN Institute for Disarmament Research, 1982-86. Member of the Soviet delegation to UN General Assembly sessions.

Vladimir Nikolayevich Fedorov. MSIIR '56, candidate of juridical science '63 (MSIIR), doctor of juridical science '83 (Diplomatic Academy). Visiting professor, department of international law, Diplomatic Academy; Expert, branch for the Security Council and political and juridical issues in the General Assembly, MFA Directorate for International Organizations. Participant in diplomatic conferences, sessions of the UN General Assembly, Soviet deputy representative to a series of organs.

Sergei Nikolayevich Kiselev. Moscow State Pedagogical Institute for Foreign Languages, '81. Second secretary, MFA Directorate for Arms Control and Disarmament. Participant in the Soviet-American negotiations on limiting and banning nuclear arms tests, and in sessions of the Conference on Disarmament (ad hoc committee for chemical arms).

Sergei Vadimovich Kortunov. MSIIR '79, candidate of historical science '82 (MSIIR). Counselor, MFA Directorate for Arms Control and Disarmament. Participant in the Soviet-American negotiations on nuclear and space weapons, on the reduction of conventional forces in Europe and on confidence and security-building measures, and in sessions of the Conference on Disarmament.

Petr Gennadievich Litavrin. MSU '74, candidate of historical science '82 (Institute for the USA and Canada of the USSR Academy of Sciences). First secretary, MFA Arms Control and Disarmament Directorate. Member of the Soviet delegation to the Third Special Session of the UN General Assembly on Disarmament. Participant as a government expert of the USSR in the expert group conducting a comprehensive study of the arms trade under the direction of the UN General Secretary.

Aleksei Yur'evich Meshkov. MSIIR '81. First secretary, MFA Directorate for International Scientific and Technological Cooperation. Participant in the Soviet-American negotiations on limiting and banning nuclear arms tests, the Fourth Review Conference for the Nuclear Nonproliferation Treaty, and the 31st General Conference of the International Atomic Energy Agency.

Aleksei L'vovich Semeyko. MSIIR '81. Head of section, Political Department, RSFSR MFA. USSR MFA Directorate for International Organizations, 1981-90. Member of the Soviet delegation to sessions of the UN General Assembly, the Third Special Session of the UN General Assembly on Disarmament, and the Conference on the Interdependence of Disarmament and Development.

Nikita Petrovich Smidovich. MSIIR '75. Head of the prohibition of chemical and bacteriological weapons branch of the MFA Arms Control and Disarmament Directorate. Member of the Soviet delegation to the Conference on Disarmament in 1986, deputy head in 1989.

Mikhail Ivanovich Ul'yanov. Moscow State Institute for Historical-Archival Research '80. Member, USSR Mission to the United Nations. MFA Directorate for International Organizations, 1986-90. Member of the

Soviet delegation to the 1987 Conference on Disarmament, to the 1988 UN General Assembly Session, observor to the UN regional seminar on disarmament in the Universal Campaign for Disarmament.

Sergei Alekseyevich Yegorov. MSIIR '77, candidate of juridical science '85 (Diplomatic Academy). Docent in and deputy head of the department of international law, Diplomatic Academy. Senior staff member, executive committee of the Union of Soviet Societies of the Red Cross and Red Crescent, 1977-81.

Aleksandr Vladimirovich Zmeyevskii. MSIIR '79. First secretary, MFA International Law Directorate. Member of the Soviet delegation to the Fourth UN Congress on Crime Prevention and Treatment of Offenders, Sixth Session of UN Committee on Crime Prevention and Control, Rome Conference on Combatting Illegal Acts Directed Against Safety of Maritime Navigation, UN General Assembly Sessions, and Sessions of UN Commission on Human Rights.

Paul B. Stephan III. B.A. 1973, M.A. 1974, Yale University; J.D. 1977, University of Virginia. Percy Brown, Jr. Professsor, University of Virginia School of Law. Law clerk to Judge Levin H. Campbell, United States Court of Appeals for the First Circuit, 1977-78, and Justice Lewis F. Powell, Supreme Court of the United States, 1978-79. Chair, Forum for U.S.-Soviet Dialogue, 1986-89.

William D. Jackson. B.A. 1966, Florida State University; M.A. 1968, Ph.D. 1972, University of Virginia. Professor, Miami University Department of Political Science. Member, U.S. Commission on the United Nations, 1970-72. Vice Chair, Forum for U.S.-Soviet Dialogue, 1983-89.

Thomas Graham, Jr. A.B. 1955, Princeton; LL.B. 1961, Harvard. General Counsel and Special Advisor to the Director, U.S. Arms Control and Disarmament Agency, and lecturer, University of Virginia School of Law. Law clerk to Chief Judge of the United States Court of Appeals for the District of Columbia. Assistant general counsel, ACDA, 1970-73; Deputy General Counsel, 1973-76; General Counsel, 1976-81; Director, Congressional Relations and Public Affairs, 1981-83; General Counsel since 1983. Legal advisor to U.S. SALT II delegation, 1974-79; Legal Advisor to U.S. delegation to the Non-Proliferation Treaty Review Conference, 1980; ACDA Senior Representative to U.S. delegation, Intermediate Range Nuclear Forces Negotiations, 1981-83; Legal Advisor to U.S. delegation, Nuclear and Space Arms Negotiations, 1985-88; Legal

Advisor and Senior Representative, U.S. Conventional Armed Forces Delegations, 1989-90. Chairman, ABA Committee on Arms Control, International Law Section.

Harold G. Maier. B.A. 1959, J.D. 1963, University of Cincinnati; LL.M. 1964, University of Michigan. David Daniels Allen Professor and Director of Transnational Legal Studies, Vanderbilt University. Counselor on International Law, US Department of State, 1983-84. Consultant, Office of the Secretary of the Army, Panama Canal Negotiations, 1976; Study Group on Law Applicable to International Sales, US State Department, since 1984.

John H. McNeill. B.A. 1962, Notre Dame; J.D. 1965, Villanova; LL.M. 1970, Ph.D. 1974, London School of Economics; Diploma of the Hague Academy of International Law, 1973. Assistant General Counsel for International Affairs and Intelligence, United States Department of Defense; Charles H. Stockton Visiting Professor of International Law, U.S. Naval War College. Arms Control and Disarmament Agency, 1975-83.

John Norton Moore. B.A. 1959, Drew; LL.B. 1962, Duke; LL.M. 1965, University of Illinois. Walter L. Brown Professor and Director, Center for Oceans Law and Policy and Center for Law and National Security, University of Virginia. Counselor on International Law, US Department of State, 1972-73; Member, U.S. Delegation to the UN General Assembly, 1972-76; U.S. Representative, UN Seabeds Commission, 1973; Chairman, National Security Council Task Force on Law of the Sea and Deputy Presidential Special Representative, Law of the Sea Conference, 1973-75; U.S. Ambassador, Third UN Conference on Law of the Sea, 1975; Special Consultant for the U.S., Gulf of Maine Case, International Court of Justice, 1981; Chair, U.S. Institute of Peace, since 1985; Consultant, Arms Control and Disarmament Agency, since 1987.

John B. Rhinelander. B.A. 1955, Yale; LL.B. 1961, University of Virginia. Partner, Shaw, Pittman, Potts & Trowbridge, and lecturer, University of Virginia School of Law. Special Civilian Assistant to the Secretary of the Navy, 1966-68; Chief Counsel, then Acting Deputy Director, Office of Foreign Direct Investments, Department of Commerce, 1968-69; Deputy Legal Advisor, Department of State, 1969-71; Legal Advisor, U.S. SALT Delegation, 1971-72; General Counsel, Department of Health, Education, and Welfare, 1973-75; Under Secretary, Department of Housing and Urban Development, 1975-77. General Counsel, Arms Control Association.

Oscar Schachter. B.S.S. 1936, C.C.N.Y.; J.D. 1939, Columbia University. Hamilton Fish Professor Emeritus of International Law and Diplomacy, Columbia University. Principal Divisional Assistant, US State Department, 1942-44; Asssistant General Counsel, UNRRA, 1944-46; Deputy Director, UN General Legal Division, 1946-52, Director, 1952-56; Director, UN Institute of Training and Research, 1966-75. President, American Society of International Law, 1967-70. Chair, American Group, Institute de Droit Internationale. Arbitration Panel, International Center for Settlement of Investment Disputes, 1980-87.

Louis B. Sohn. Dip. Sc. M. 1935, LL.M. 1935, John Casimir University; LL.M. 1940, S.J.D. 1958, Harvard University. Woodruff Professor of International Law, University of Georgia; Bemis Professor Emeritus of International Law, Harvard Univeristy. Legal Officer, UN Secretariat, 1950-51; Counselor on International Law, US Department of State, 1970-71. President, American Society of International Law. Consultant, US Arms Control and Disarmament Agency, 1961-70; UN, 1969, 1984; US Department of State, since 1971.

Robert F. Turner. B.A. 1968, Indiana University; J.D. 1980, University of Virginia. Associate Director, Center for Law and National Security, University of Virginia, and Lecturer, University of Virginia Department of Government and Foreign Affairs. Special Assistant and Legislative Assistant to Senator Robert P. Griffin, 1974-79; Special Assistant to Under Secretary of Defense for Policy, 1981-82; Counsel, President's Intelligence Oversight Board, 1982-84; Deputy Assistant Secretary of State for Legislative and Intergovernmental Affairs, 1984-85; President, United States Institute of Peace, 1986-87; Chairman, ABA Standing Committee on Law and National Security.

Acknowledgments

This project has drawn on the resources and patience of numerous persons. Dean Thomas H. Jackson of the University of Virginia School of Law and Rector Oleg G. Peresypkin of the Diplomatic Academy have been stalwart in their support. The John D. and Catherine T. MacArthur Foundation and the Soviet Fund for Peace have provided financial assistance, without which we could not have gone forward. S. Neil MacFarlane and Jim Hayn of the University of Virginia's Center for Russian and East European Studies also supported our work in many ways. The preparation of the manuscript depended on the translation services of James S. Beaver, the research assistance of Christopher F. Clarke, and the typing of Diane Glasgow. Finally, Pamela Clark and Mariya Kabalevskaya are owed special thanks for opening up their homes to visiting editors, and for supporting their husbands throughout.

The authors wish to emphasize that the views expressed here are solely their own and are not necessarily shared by their employers or the other bodies with which they are associated.

Introduction

Paul B. Stephan III
Percy Brown, Jr. Professor, University of Virginia School of Law

This project had its genesis in a meeting held at the Diplomatic Academy of the USSR Ministry of Foreign Affairs in January 1989. Up until then the Academy had not been open to many visitors from the United States, but the fortuitous appearance of William Jackson and myself in Moscow at a time when this policy was changing led to a fascinating and valuable encounter with professors Boris M. Klimenko and Valerii I. Kuznetsov. Our discussion that day ranged over many topics, but we focused on the problem of developing a common methodology for the development of international law within the context of different ideologies and superpower competition. We agreed that it was unrealistic to expect our governments, founded on different social and economic assumptions, to accept a common precise definition of international norms and obligations, but we considered it feasible to build a consensus as to sources and methods of international law.

At that meeting we enthusiastically endorsed increased collaboration among Soviet and U.S. specialists in international law and international affairs. A few months later professor Klimenko and Dr. Bakhtiyar R. Tuzmukhamedov presented us with a proposal to implement this concept. After several months of discussions, we reached agreement on the scope and content of this project. Successful funding applications followed, the John D. and Catherine T. MacArthur Foundation generously supporting the U.S. side and the Soviet Peace Fund financing the Soviet side.

The implementation of our proposal has confirmed our initial intuition about the benefits of collaboration. Professionalism has predominated, and such minor problems as have arisen were solved easily and calmly. Collateral to the writing and editing, we were able to arrange seminars at both the Diplomatic Academy and the University of Virginia School of Law. Direct contacts among the authors supplemented the editors' coordination and supervision.

The period of this book's conception and production has encompassed a sea change in the international order. In January 1989 only a (somewhat demented) visionary could have contemplated the extent to which the bipolar superpower competition that still prevailed would be transformed into the international alliance that has opposed the Iraqi invasion of Kuwait. We do not know what shape the new structure of international relations will take, but it seems reasonably clear that the norms and principles of international law will take on a greater significance and attain a new level of effectiveness. The world remains a dangerous place, but we hope efforts such as ours will help to contain that danger. Due to the happy coincidence of timing, this book constitutes the first major statement of international law in the post-Cold War era.

One of the objectives of this project was to do more than engage in an academic exercise. The professoriat may have its views on international law, but unless governments take these norms and principles seriously their formulations have only moral significance. As a result, we have attempted to the extent possible to involve as contributors persons with significant government experience, either past or present. The writers in this book are not only learned (although certainly they are that), but, except for myself, they have held responsible positions involving the formulation of their government's approach to international law. The views expressed, of course, are entirely private, and are not meant in any way to be taken as the official view of either the United States or the Soviet Union. But it is our hope that the ideas and proposals found herein have been tempered by the fire of experience, and our belief that in the aggregate they constitute an important contribution to the development of international law in the new era of superpower cooperation.

B.M. Klimenko
Professor, USSR Diplomatic Academy

Principles and rules of international law are of great significance for the establishment of effective international security. International security in the broad sense of the term constitutes a specific system of intergovernmental relations, a system which will be observed only if it expresses mandatory rules of conduct by a state, while the latter is nothing other than the principles and rules of international law. The principles and rules of international law that enter into a system of international security indicate the boundaries of conduct by states, beyond which the actions of one state may do detriment to the security of others.

The traditional concept of international security applies only to the renunciation of military force and issues directly related to this, such as peaceful resolution of disputes, sovereign equality, territorial integrity, *etc.* Principles of international law of the same name are formally articulated in the UN Charter, which also contains specified powers of the UN Security Council pertaining to maintaining international peace and security.

The development of international relations provides a basis for a broader approach to international security. It is impossible today to discuss international security without addressing issues of disarmament and arms limitation. Economic, environmental, and humanitarian issues are also encompassed within the domain of international security, since the world cannot be safe if there occur hunger and disease, environmental disasters, and violations of fundamental human rights and freedoms. Limiting these phenomena is hardly of less significance than limiting arms.

The basic principles for such a broad approach to international security are contained in the UN Charter. In particular, the authorities of the UN General Assembly and Security Council in matters of disarmament and arms limitation are formally articulated in the UN Charter, while international economic and social cooperation contains a linkage with the need for establishment of peaceful and friendly relations between nations.

The fundamental principles contained within the UN Charter, however, do not resolve all the problems of a diversified reality and frequently constitute merely a point of departure for moving forward and for reaching new agreements on the road toward international security. UN practical efforts are proceeding precisely along the path of formulation of new agreements and recommendations on various specific issues pertaining to international security. The norms of these agreements and recommendations create a second, in relation to the UN Charter, more specific stratum of international legal order, which is grounded on the purposes and principles of the UN Charter.

The basic principles of the UN Charter, such as sovereign equality, renunciation of force, the territorial integrity of states, peaceful settlement of disputes, noninterference, self-determination of peoples and nations, and respect for human rights and fundamental freedoms are all directly related to international security. But almost all these principles are stated extremely tersely in the UN Charter, and subsequently have been further developed in a number of UN General Assembly resolutions as well as in other documents.

The powers of the UN General Assembly and Security Council pertaining to disarmament and arms limitation merely point out the importance of actions in this area but do not of themselves resolve these problems. It has been the practice of states to draw up various treaties in this area.

The central forum for the development of principles and rules of international law is the United Nations. Under the auspices of the United Nations and in its organs and institutions many international law instruments are undertaken. In addition, significant processes can go forward on a regional basis. The European process on security and cooperation embodies a new stage of development of international relations in Europe, characterized by a transition from conflict to cooperation. This process encompasses several spheres: the military, political, economic, ecological, and humanitarian. A component of this process is the development of fundamental principles of international law, the creation of new treaty norms, and the development of new legal norms. This is a multilateral arrangement, but as such it entails the creation of new structures and institutions of cooperation. For many issues of international security there may be a resolution even in bilateral agreements.

The process of development of the principles and rules of international law in the domain of international security can by no means be considered completed. The content of the basic principles of international law which are developed in UN General Assembly resolutions and in the Final Act of the Helsinki Agreement should be given precisely defined legal force. Analogous problems arise with the formulation and adoption of a general principle of environmental protection as well as a number of other matters connected with the content and legal force of the basic principles of international law.

The status of treaty norms in the domain of international security is of an even more varied nature. International treaties exist on some problems, and in these cases only the question of their effectiveness may arise. On a number of problems treaties are just at the formulation stage, while on others there exist only UN General Assembly declarations or resolutions, which often precede the formulation and adoption of international treaties. And finally, even a consensus of opinion has not yet been reached on some problems.

In the military area of international security there exist legal problems pertaining to increasing the effectiveness of a number of existing treaty norms, as well as the drafting and adoption of new international treaties. In particular, it is necessary to strengthen the effectiveness of such treaties currently in force as the Nuclear Nonproliferation Treaty, treaties on nuclear-free zones, *etc.* The process of drawing up new international treaties is today proceeding in such directions as the cessation of nuclear weapons testing, banning and elimination of chemical weapons, *etc.* Such problems as preventing an arms race in space, banning the development and production of new types and systems of weapons of mass destruction, *etc.*, are presently at the stage when the existing problem and the need for agreement on the necessity of concluding an international treaty are under discussion. Finally, there are also problems, discussion of which boils down to preliminary submission of initiatives and exchange of views by the interested parties: These include the problem of total banning and elimination of nuclear weapons, lowering levels of military potential to limits of reasonable sufficiency, limiting naval activity, limiting arms transfers, transformation of military-political alliances, and reduction of military budgets.

Resolution of the main item–arriving at a decision to draw up an international treaty on a specific problem–is the business of the top echelons of political power of each interested country. This is followed by the process of reaching a formal understanding on all specific items and formal articulation of these formal understandings in the articles of the treaty being drafted.

This process is rather complex from the standpoint of international law. Even in cases where states have an interest in settling various issues, their positions as a rule differ on individual aspects of these issues. Bringing such positions into agreement once again requires political solutions. At this phase, however, a solution can sometimes be reached by the purely legal technique of formulation of appropriate treaty articles, with which in any case the process of drafting a treaty ends.

Thus international law is of considerable importance for formally articulating attained understandings or agreements on all problems pertaining to international security. The science of international law is also called upon to play an important role in this. Inasmuch as the establishment of international law norms constitutes bringing the positions of interested states into agreement, study of these positions is of considerable importance for constructing possible variations of drawing them closer together, utilizing the means of international law.

In this study an attempt has been made by Soviet and U.S. specialists in international law at a joint investigation of the principles and rules of international law in the military and political domains of international security–the status of and prospects for development of these principles and rules. The views presented in this study are the personal views of the authors, which do not necessarily reflect the official positions of their country's government.

A Note on Translation

To avoid controversy and other pitfalls, the editors have chosen to follow what we hope will be understood to be a neutral principle of translation: Wherever a term discussed appears in an official document for which authentic Russian and English translations exist, we have accepted the translation used there.

PART I. INTERNATIONAL LEGAL PRINCIPLES AND RULES IN THE MILITARY SPHERE

1. RENUNCIATION OF MILITARY AGGRESSION AND THE THREAT THEREOF AS AN INSTRUMENT OF NATIONAL POLICY

THE UN CHARTER AND THE PROHIBITION OF AGGRESSION IN THE POST-COLD WAR ERA

William D. Jackson
Professor of Political Science, Miami University

With the adoption of a series of UN Security Council resolutions in response to the Iraqi invasion of Kuwait in August 1990, an important new precedent has appeared in the history of the effort to prohibit military aggression through the strengthening of international law. The Security Council's decisions represent a significant revivification of the mandate conferred on the Security Council by Article 39 of the Charter to "determine the existence of any threat to the peace, breach of the peace, or act of aggression" and "to decide what measures shall be taken in accordance with Articles 41 and 42 to maintain or restore international peace and security." In promptly condemning the Iraqi invasion of Kuwait (Resolution S.660), and in deciding, first, to impose sweeping economic sanctions against Iraq (Resolution S.661), and, subsequently, to authorize Members to use necessary means to end the Iraqi occupation of Kuwait (Resolution S.678), the UN Security Council assumed a role which its founding members had originally intended it to play in enforcing international legal prohibitions against the aggressive use of military force. With the single exception of its decision, under unusual circumstances, in the case of the Korean War, the Security Council had been unable to play its intended role throughout the Cold War. By its actions in the case of the Iraqi attack on Kuwait, which were possible only as a result of the cooperation of all the Permanent Members, the Security Council has demonstrated its potential to act effectively in the interpretation and enforcement of the provisions of the Charter regarding the use of force in the emerging "post-Cold War" world.

The purpose of the following essay is to suggest that the international law regarding the use of force that has come into existence since 1945 is clear and consistent in terms of the prohibition of military aggression. Notwithstanding some disputes concerning the interpretation of aspects of the law regarding the use of force, consensus on its basic principles has been in fact very substantial. The full potential of contemporary international law regarding the prohibition of the aggressive use of force has been unrealized not as a consequence of defects in the law itself, but as a result of unfavorable political circumstances of the Cold War that frequently rendered the application of the law to factual situations controversial. These circumstances are now rapidly disappearing. Far from needing major reform, or significant amendment or elaboration, this law requires for its enhanced effectiveness a prudential application based upon new efforts to coordinate the security policies and perspectives on the law regarding force of the Permanent Members of the Security Council, including especially the policies of the United States and the Soviet Union.

A. The Prohibition of Military Aggression

A central tendency in the development of international law in the twentieth century has been the growth of an international consensus in support of an increasingly restrictive set of international legal norms regarding the use of force in international relations. The Covenant of the League of Nations, the 1928 Treaty Providing for the Renunciation of War as an Instrument of National Policy, the Charter of the International Military Tribunal affirmed in the London Agreement, and the Charter of the United Nations represent steps in the development of an international legal regime regarding the use of force that represents an achievement of profound importance. The essence of the international legal regime regarding the use of force in the post-World War II world is contained in Article 2(4) of the UN Charter which provides:

> All Members shall refrain in their international relations from the threat or use of force against the territorial integrity and political independence of any state, or in any other manner inconsistent with the Purposes of the United Nations.

As a corollary to this broad prohibition on the threat or use of force, the Charter in Article 2(3) imposes on all members of the United Nations an obligation to settle international disputes "by peaceful means in such a manner that international peace and security, and justice, are not endangered." That these provisions of the Charter represented both a profound change in international law and possessed a character of overriding importance has been widely acknowledged by jurists and governments alike. Far from being an expression of unrealistic aspirations to transform international relations, the law concerning the use of force contained in Article 2 of the Charter reflected a profound and realistic appreciation of the destruction of modern war and the greatly increased interest governments had in preventing such war.

Though the Charter affirmed in Article 51 that members continued to have "the inherent right of individual or collective self-defense if an armed attack occurs," and "until the Security Council has taken measures to maintain international peace and security," nothing in the language of Article 51 was intended to diminish the comprehensive restriction of Article 2 of the Charter. Rather, the intention of the drafters of the Article, as reflected in Secretary of State Stettinius's report to the President on the work of the San Francisco Conference, was to affirm that as sweeping as the restraints on the use of force were under the Charter, they did not deny members the right to use force defensively if an armed attack occurred and until, as Stettinius stressed, the Security Council acted. The qualifying language of Article 51 itself reflected a view on the part of the government assembled at San Francisco that the nature of modern war required the establishment of restraints on the right to use force of a new and highly restrictive character.

Notwithstanding a subsequent degree of dissensus surrounding the interpretation of certain ambiguities in the Charter regime, *e.g.*, the meaning of "armed attack," the nature of the inherent right of self defense under the Charter, and the more general ambiguities of Article 2, which some have sought to argue implicitly legitimizes uses of force which are neither against the territorial integrity or political independence of states nor inconsistent with the purpose of the Charter, the legal norms contained in the Charter regarding the use of force were certainly, when compared to earlier international law, relatively unambiguous in their basic formulation. Members were obligated to refrain from the use of military force against the territorial integrity or political independence of states. Only armed attack could justify the use of force in self defense.

The same determination to condemn the aggressive use of military force in the Charter was reflected in the Charter of the International Military Tribunal, which declared the planning or participating in wars of aggression a crime under international law. Like the Charter's radical prohibition of military aggression, the Nuremburg Principles, it is well to recall, reflected a close identity of views between the Soviet and American governments. Together Washington and Moscow played a leading role at the close of World War II–at conferences in Washington, San Francisco, and London–in framing a set of international legal principles designed to both prohibit and deter the aggressive use of military force. Notwithstanding deep differences over many aspects of international law, both the U.S. and Soviet governments shared a common determination to establish international legal controls which would deter the types of military aggression that had provoked the devastating world war from which they had just emerged. The efficacy of this new regime to control the use of force would depend greatly, however, on the self-restraint of the Permanent Members of the Security Council, including of course the United States and the Soviet Union, who were protected from the threat of Security Council sanctions by the veto, and the willingness of the Permanent Members to cooperate in using the power granted to the Security Council to maintain international peace in general.

Though at the close of World War II the Superpowers had cooperated closely in framing a far-reaching set of legal prohibitions on the aggressive use of military force, the development of the Cold War led both to frequently conflicting claims of the "lawful" use of force and to a general ineffectiveness of the Security Council as a mechanism for maintaining peace.

The Superpowers themselves on numerous occasions sought to justify their own use of military force with claims to be acting within the framework of Article 51. Significantly, these claims were generally rejected by large majorities in the General Assembly. Such was the case, for example, with respect to Soviet claims regarding the introduction of Soviet forces into Hungary in 1956, Czechoslovakia in 1968 and Afghanistan in 1979. Similarly, it was the case with respect to U.S. claims regarding the introduction of U.S. troops into Cambodia in 1970, Grenada and Lebanon in 1983, and Panama in 1989, and the bombing of Libya in 1986. In the Case Concerning Military and Paramilitary Activities In and Against Nicaragua (*Nicaragua v. United States*), the International Court of Justice refused to sustain the U.S. claim that U.S. support for the Contras was a justifiable exercise of the right of collective self-defense on the grounds, *inter alia*, that evidence was lacking that the Nicaraguan government was engaged in activities that constituted an armed attack against its neighbors. Notwithstanding the general lack of endorsement that Superpower claims received in the international community, there can be little doubt that the Cold War contributed negatively to the development of the law regarding force, by nurturing dissensus between the Superpowers, and more generally East and West, on the meaning and application of the provisions of the Charter regulating the use of force.

A second principal respect in which the Cold War negatively affected the development and application of the restrictive regime regarding the use of force is to be found in the effect that Superpower conflict had on the operation of the Security Council. That the Security Council would be unlikely to play the role in the maintenance of peace assigned to it in the Charter was clear to the more perspicacious observer of international politics as early as 1946, and widely acknowledged by the mid-1950's. The prospect of effective collective sanctions organized by the Security Council under Chapter VII in response to a threat to the peace, breach of the peace, or act of aggression could not serve as a meaningful deterrent, as was intended under the Charter design, to states who might contemplate uses of military force unlikely to be viewed generally as consistent with Article 2 or 51 of the Charter. Nor, given its divisions, could the Security Council exert leadership in the application and interpretation of the Law of the Charter by acting and responding with a voice grounded in a consensus of view. By design, the Permanent Members of the Security Council had protection, in their right of veto, against collective sanctions of Chapter VII. It was hoped in 1945, however, that the Permanent Members would provide leadership through the Security Council in enforcing the norms that they had taken the lead in framing. The onset of the Cold War rapidly eliminated these expectations of cooperation among the Permanent Members.

Though the Cold War had a generally negative impact on the constructive application of the regime regarding the use of force grounded in the Charter, it is significant that nearly half a century after the adoption of the Charter, and notwithstanding a multiplicity of Cold War related conflicts, the centrality of the Charter norms prohibiting the aggressive use of military force as governing international law remains virtually universally acknowledged by governments as well as legal scholars. The International Court of Justice in its 1986 decision in *Nicaragua v. United States* affirmed and endorsed the view expressed by the UN International Law Commission that "the law of the Charter concerning the prohibition of the use of force in itself constitutes a conspicuous example of a rule in international law having the character of jus cogens." (Paragraph 190). Significantly, in almost all cases in which governments have resorted to the use of force since 1945, they have sought legally to justify their actions by referring to the right of self-defense in response to an alleged previous armed attack. Such a pattern further testifies to the widespread acceptance that, in principle at least, the use of force in international relations is generally deemed illegitimate except defensively in response to an armed attack.

The basic principles of the Charter regarding the use of force have been affirmed and elucidated, moreover, in a long series of resolutions by the General Assembly which have been adopted either unanimously or by consensus. Among these documents not least in importance have been the 1970 Declaration on the Principles of International Law Concerning Friendly Relations and Co-operation Among States in Accordance with the Charter of the United Nations and the 1974 Resolution on the Definition of Aggression. The former document is remarkably clear in its formulation regarding a state's obligation to refrain from the use of force. It affirms *inter alia*, "Every state has the duty to refrain from the threat or use of force to violate the existing international boundaries of another State or as a means of solving international disputes." The 1974 Resolution on the Definition of Aggression, the product of long and arduous discussions, though not itself wholly devoid of ambiguity, expresses a consensus on the nature of aggression which is of considerably political as well as legal significance. Of special importance in this respect is Article 2 of the Definition, which affirms that "[t]he first use of armed force by a State in contravention of the Charter shall constitute *prima facie* evidence of an act of aggression" unless the Security Council concludes that such a determination is not justified.

That a substantial general consensus on the general norms embodied in the Charter endured despite the Cold War is testimony to an overarching recognition that the unprecedented destructiveness of modern war gives all states an interest in supporting far-reaching international legal restraints on the aggressive use of military force. Even during the period of the Cold War, when the Superpowers disagreed over the application of the Charter's restraints regarding the use of force, they cooperated both tacitly and explicitly in the affirmation of its basic principles. It was a consensus that transcended the Cold War and included both Superpowers that produced the 1970 UN Declaration on Friendly Relations and the 1974 Resolution Defining Aggression. Outside the context of the United Nations, as Superpower relations improved beginning in the 1970's, both in bilateral negotiations and in the context of the multilateral Conference on European Security, the Superpowers did affirm and develop the commitment to refrain from the use of force in international relations. Of significance in this regard are the 1972 Agreement on Basic Principles of Relations and the 1975 Helsinki Final Act in which the Superpowers reaffirmed in a general and unqualified manner their commitment to refrain from the use of force commensurate with their obligations under the Charter.

The International Court of Justice in its decision in the Nicaragua Case attributed considerable significance to the elaboration and development of legal prohibitions on the use of force that occurred in the context of the East-West agreements of the 1970's. In particular, the Court referred to the Second Principle of the 1975 Final Act of the Helsinki

Conference in which the participating states undertake to "refrain in their mutual relations *as well as in their international relations in general* from the threat or use of force." (Emphasis added by the Court). The Court concluded that "acceptance of a text in these terms confirms the existence of an *opinio juris* of the participating States prohibiting the use of force in international relations." (Paragraph 189).

In "the long view" of the development of international law regarding the use of force over the last half century, it is evident that the restrictive regime which the Superpowers themselves had cooperated to frame at the end of World War II not only survived the Cold War, but continued to be developed and elaborated during the period of the Cold War itself. In this regard perhaps, the law has expressed an underlying rationality in the assessment of states' interests in the nuclear age.

B. Legal Restraints on Aggression in the Post-Cold War Era

If the Charter regime has survived the Cold War intact, the present decade offers new opportunities for its development. The emergence of a new and increasingly cooperative relationship between the United States and the Soviet Union on a growing range of international security issues in recent years provides a promising basis for enhancing the role of the United Nations in the maintenance of international peace and security, and more generally, for enhancing the effectiveness of international law in the regulation of the use of force. In pursuit of these ends, closer Superpower cooperation in several realms of policy is desirable.

First, in order to further the effectiveness of legal controls on the use of force in international relations, the United States and the Soviet Union should seek to develop a cooperative and coordinated approach to interpreting and applying the provisions of the Charter regarding the use of force. Often during the period of the Cold War the "discussion" of differing interpretations of Articles 2(4) and 51 took place around real conflicts, *e.g.* Czechoslovakia or Vietnam, Afghanistan or Grenada, in which the two governments sought to condemn each other's policies. Given the general climate of mistrust and the broad and deep-seated conflicts in the security policies and objectives of the two sides during the period of the Cold War, as well as the impact that ideological differences exerted on approaches to many questions of international law, a reasoned discussion of legal policy differences was not possible. In recent years this situation has changed significantly. The emergence of a new and cooperative relationship between the two governments, and the development of "new thinking" with respect to the use of the United Nations in the management of regional conflicts can be conducive to a less conflict-ridden approach to interpreting and applying the principles of the Charter. The close identity of the views of the two governments with respect to the interpretation and application of the relevant international law following the introduction of Iraqi troops into Kuwait in August 1990 itself suggests that the new political relationship has the potential to produce a more cooperative and beneficial impact on the interpretation and application of a critical area of law. As the disagreements over the legality of U.S. support of military action in Panama in December 1989 suggest, the Superpowers–even in an era of closer cooperation–can still differ over the necessity and legality of the use of military force. Given the new relationship, however, both governments have reason to take more seriously the perspectives and responses of the other side. The prospect that the Security Council can act effectively on a broader range of regional conflicts creates, moreover, new policy alternatives to unilateral action and in political terms diminishes the case of those who would argue in favor of unilateral resort to "defensive" force in circumstances that are controversial.

As the climate of political cooperation and greater trust between the United States and the Soviet Union develops, it should become possible to hold frank and constructive discussions over policy differences about the meaning and application of Charter provisions regarding the maintenance of international peace. There already exists a multilateral forum for such a discussion in the form of the forty-seven member UN Special Committee on the Charter of the United Nations and on the Strengthening of the Role of the Organization. Many of the issues under consideration in that forum, such as defining "threat to the peace," "threat of force," the legal status of military demonstrations, and the supplying of arms to parties in conflict, could profitably be discussed directly, as could other issues related to differences of interpretation surrounding Articles 2(4) and 51 of the Charter. In an era in which the Security Council, it is to be hoped, will be acting more often to maintain peace, it would be desirable also to reach closer understanding between the Superpowers on the effect of Security Council action on states' rights to take further action under Article 51. Beyond these issues, it would be perhaps desirable for the Superpowers to discuss directly a number of international legal policy issues of general import. These would include the interpretation of Article 2(4), especially regarding the ambiguity suggested by the reference to uses of force inconsistent with the UN Charter. Other items of the UN agenda bearing on the development of international law with respect to the prohibition of aggression, such as the Draft Code of Crimes Against the Peace and Security of Mankind–a continuation of a legal project which had its origin in Superpower cooperation in the framing of the Charter of the International Military Tribunal–could also become the subject of direct discussion between officials responsible for legal policy in the U.S. State Department and the Soviet Foreign Ministry.

It is well to recall that the greatest achievements in the development of international law concerning the use of force since 1945 occurred as a result of close cooperation of the United States and the Soviet Union in the formulation of the Charter, as well as the principles of the International Military Tribunal. Now, as a new century approaches, it is time, after a long and unfortunate hiatus, for the United States and the Soviet Union to resume their cooperation.

V.N. Fedorov
Expert, International Organizations Directorate,
USSR Ministry of Foreign Affairs, and
Visiting Professor, USSR Diplomatic Academy

The idea of the inadmissibility of settling disputes between states by means of war has been stated by thinkers and political leaders of many countries, since deep antiquity. This idea did not find embodiment in a treaty text, however, until the twentieth century. The resolve of states to renounce military aggression and the threat of military aggression as an instrument of national policy was formally articulated in international law in the Kellogg-Briand Pact, signed on August 27, 1928, which proclaimed a ban against resorting to war as a means of settling international disputes and as an instrument of national policy. The Soviet Union, which was the first to ratify the Kellogg-Briand Pact, typically proceeded from the position that not only a declared war but any de facto military actions initiated by any state should be considered a breach of the Pact, that is, any employment of military forces by one state against another should be considered unlawful, regardless of what motives it might give in justification. The principle of refraining from aggressive war was further developed in the UN Charter.

The principle of outlawing the use or the threat of force is embodied in the UN Charter, pursuant to which all UN Member States:

> shall refrain in their international relations from the threat or use of force against the territorial integrity or political independence of any state, or in any other manner inconsistent with the Purposes of the United Nations.

The principle of refraining from force embodied in the UN Charter is of an imperative nature, that is, its observance is mandatory for all states and imposes an absolute prohibition to the initiation of any and all wars. Certain exceptions from this prohibition are directly and clearly prescribed by the Charter, which allows for no other arguments or excuses to justify any state's departure from this principle. Thus the UN Charter does not leave open the possibility of resorting to war for the purpose of settling disputes between states.

The experience of recent years, especially the most recent past, confirms that the task of unconditional affirmation of the principle of refraining from force in international affairs has unfortunately not disappeared but, on the contrary, has become even more crucial. Mankind has traveled an enormous distance since the creation of the United Nations, and the world has undergone considerable change. These changes present at the same time both new opportunities and new dangers.

Resolution 21/2160, "Strict Observance of the Prohibition of the Threat or Use of Force in International Relations, and of the Right of Peoples to Self-Determination," adopted at the initiative of Czechoslovakia at the Twenty-first General Assembly Session, was essentially the first attempt by the General Assembly to deliberate this principle as applied to the changing conditions of international affairs. The content of the principle of refraining from the threat or use of force has taken on new elements pursuant to this Resolution. In particular, the Resolution states that an armed attack by one state on another or the use of force in any other form contrary to the UN Charter constitutes a breach of international law that evokes international responsibility. In addition to this, any direct or indirect coercive action that deprives peoples under foreign domination of their right to self-determination, freedom, and independence, as well as their right freely to determine their political status and to carry out their own economic, social, and cultural development, constitutes a violation of the UN Charter. Of particular significance is that point formulated in the Resolution to the effect that the use of force for the purpose of depriving peoples of the form of their national existence, which is prohibited by the Declaration on the Inadmissibility of Intervention in the Domestic Affairs of States and the Protection of their Independence and Sovereignty, constitutes a violation of their inalienable rights and the principle of noninterference. Proceeding from the above, the Resolution broadens the content of the principle stated in Article 2(4) of the UN Charter, augmenting it with an appeal to all states:

> To renounce and refrain from any action contrary to the above-stated fundamental principles and to assure that their activities in international relations are in full harmony with the interests of international peace and security.

In addition to so-called "negative" obligations of states pertaining to refraining from force, this Resolution, for the first time in UN practice, also prescribes a number of positive obligations that promote strengthening of the principle of refraining from the threat or use of force. It contains, for example, an urgent appeal to states:

> To exert every effort and to undertake all necessary measures with a view to facilitating the exercise of the right of self-determination of peoples under colonial rule, lessening international tensions, strengthening peace and promoting friendly relations and cooperation among States.

The principle of refraining from the threat or use of force underwent further development in the Declaration of Principles of International Law Concerning Friendly Relations and Co-operation Among States in Accordance with the Charter of the United Nations, adopted by consensus at the Twenty-fifth Session of the General Assembly in 1970. The Declaration denominates an aggressive war as one of the most dangerous acts of use of force. It constitutes a crime against the peace, for which international law prescribes liability. Among the prohibited acts, the Declaration lists propaganda of aggressive wars. It specifies a number of acts that fall under the general banning of the threat or use of force in international relations. It prescribes in particular that each state is obligated to refrain from the threat or use of force for the purpose of breaching the existing international boundaries of another state or as a means of settling international disputes, including territorial disputes, as well as issues pertaining to national boundaries. A prohibition against using or threatening force for the purpose of breaching international lines of demarcation, such as established truce lines or truce lines that are in conformity with an international agreement to which a given state is a party or which that state is obligated to observe on any other basis, also applies to such acts. Prohibition of acts of reprisal involving the use of force, as well as any violent actions that deprive peoples of their right to self-determination, freedom, and independence, a prohibition which is prescribed by the Declaration, also adds new content to the principle of refraining from the threat or use of force. The Declaration extends the ban on the use of force to the organization, or the encouragement of the organization, of irregular forces or armed bands, including mercenaries, by one state for the purpose of invading the territory of another state. The obligation of each state to refrain from organization, instigation, aid or participation in acts of civil war or terrorist acts in another state or connivance toward organizational activity on its soil, directed toward the perpetration of such acts, including when such acts involve the threat or use of force, also comes under the principle of refraining from the threat or use of force pursuant to this Declaration. Of particular significance is the organic linkage between the principle of refraining from force and disarmament and the enhancement of the effectiveness of the United Nations, which is established for the first time in this Declaration. In this regard provisions to the effect that all states must, on the basis of the generally recognized principles and rules of international law, conscientiously carry out their obligations in respect to maintaining international peace and security and endeavor to make more effective the UN security system grounded on the Charter, help reveal the content of this principle.

Developing the content of the principle of refraining from force, from the standpoint of imparting specificity to the term "force," constitutes one of the most important areas of effort by states to make this principle effective. This area of effort was first reflected in General Assembly Resolution 27/2936, "Non-Use of Force in International Relations and Permanent Prohibition of the Use of Nuclear Weapons," which was adopted on November 29, 1972, on the initiative of the Soviet Union. The Resolution deals with banning the use of force in its most dangerous expression—nuclear. In this Resolution refraining from the threat or use of force is formulated in an organic linkage with banning the use of nuclear weapons and is advanced as a law governing international affairs, which is to be fully observed by all states. The resolution contains the solemn declaration:

> on behalf of the State Members of the Organization, [of] their renunciation of the threat or use of force in all its forms and manifestations in international relations, in accordance with the Charter of the United Nations, and the permanent prohibition of the use of nuclear weapons.

The Resolution states that the actions of the two principal UN bodies are to be unified in order to ensure the effectiveness of the principle of renunciation of force, and it prescribes that the Security Council shall take appropriate measures as promptly as possible to ensure full implementation of this General Assembly declaration.

Toward this same end a draft Universal Treaty on Renunciation of Force in International Relations was drawn up and submitted by the Soviet Union for UN consideration in 1976. This draft states for the first time a spatial extent of application of the principle of renunciation of force and details the term "force." In this connection it is emphasized in Article I of the draft Universal Treaty that states shall refrain, in conformity with this principle, "from employment of armed forces, utilizing any type of weapon, including nuclear weapons and other kinds of weapons of mass destruction, on land, at sea, in the air and in space, as well as from threatening such use."

Adoption by the General Assembly in 1974 of a definition of aggression by a consensus vote led to further specification of the principle of refraining from the threat or use of force. In conformity with this definition, acts of employment by a state of military force which are prohibited by the UN Charter include the following:

> (a) The invasion or attack by the armed forces of a State of

the territory of another State, or any military occupation, however temporary, resulting from such invasion or attack, or any annexation by the use of force of the territory of another State or any part thereof;

(b) Bombardment by the armed forces of a State against the territory of another State or the use of any weapons by a State against the territory of another State;

(c) The blockade of the ports or coasts of a State by the armed forces of another State;

(d) An attack by the armed forces of a State on the land, sea, or air forces, or marine or air fleets of another State;

(e) The use of armed forces of one State which are within the territory of another State with the agreement of the receiving State, in contravention of the conditions provided for in the agreement or any extension of their presence in such territory beyond the termination of the agreement;

(f) The action of a State in allowing its territory, which it has placed at the disposal of another State, to be used by that other State for perpetrating an act of aggression against a third State;

(g) The sending by or on behalf of a State of armed bands, groups, irregulars or mercenaries, which carry out acts of armed force against another State of such gravity as to amount to the acts listed above, or its substantial involvement therein.

Concretization of the principle of refraining from force has been performed not only within a UN framework but also at the bilateral and regional levels. The principle of renunciation of the use of force was subjected to particularly detailed formulation in the Final Act adopted at the Helsinki Conference on Security and Cooperation in Europe in 1975. The Declaration of Principles by which the Parties shall be guided in their mutual relations prescribes further detailing of the principle of refraining from the threat or use of force. It specifies not only renunciation of force but also the obligation of states to refrain from any actions that constitute a threat of force or a direct or indirect use of force against another state. The Declaration also provides that states shall refrain from all manifestations of force aimed at compelling another state to give up full exercise of its sovereign rights. In like manner states shall refrain in their mutual relations from any acts of reprisal with the use of force.

One characteristic feature of this Declaration is the establishment of a close linkage between the principle of renunciation of force and other principles of international law, in particular the principle of peaceful resolution of disputes. The Declaration specifically states in this connection that no use or threat of force shall be employed as a means of settling disputes or issues which could cause disputes between states. Approval by consensus vote at the Forty-second Session of the General Assembly in 1987, at the initiative of the Soviet Union, of a Declaration on the Enhancement of the Effectiveness of the Principle of Refraining from the Threat or Use of Force in International Relations, marked a very important stage in the further development of the principle of renunciation of force. The Declaration constitutes a politically packed document of a multi-aspect nature, in which the basic aspects of the principle of refraining from force are reflected. The document's *leitmotif* is a banning of the threat or use of force by states under any pretext, in order to ensure correct and courteous relations between states in the aim of building a nuclear-free and violence-free world. One distinctive feature of the Declaration is the fact that the general principle of refraining from the threat or use of force is concretized in detail in this document and is bolstered by so-called "negative" political obligations of states to refrain from committing a number of specific actions. This makes it possible substantially to refine and detail the scope of this fundamental principle as applied to today's realities. The Declaration enumerates those actions from which states should refrain, which makes it possible to gain a much clearer understanding of the boundaries of what is permitted in the conduct of states in the international arena.

The potential of the ideas embodied in the 1986 New Delhi Declaration of Principles of a World Free of Nuclear Weapons and Violence is utilized in this Declaration. The ideas and principles formulated in the New Delhi Declaration, which expressed the interests of the entire community of peace-loving nations, served as a point of departure for a number of points in the declaration pertaining to strengthening the effectiveness of the principle of refraining from the threat or use of force in international relations. For example, the points of the preamble were formulated under the direct influence of the New Delhi Declaration, in particular Paragraphs 1 and 9, which state that:

> In today's international situation, in which nuclear weapons exist, there is no reasonable alternative to peaceful relations between states . . . that the question of general and complete disarmament is of paramount importance and that peace, security, basic freedoms, economic and social development are indivisible . . . .

Many of the provisions of the Political Declaration ratified at the Eighth Conference of Heads of State and Government of the Nonaligned Nations in Harare in September 1986 also found expression in this Declaration. For example, interest on the part of all states "in securing a stable and equitable world economic environment as an essential basis for world peace" is expressed in the preamble of the Declaration on Enhancement of the Effectiveness of the Principle of Refraining from the Threat or Use of Force in International Relations, and the conviction is expressed that states "should strengthen international co-operation for development and work toward a new international economic order."

A characteristic feature of the Declaration lies in the fact that in it the question of imparting maximum effectiveness to the principle of refraining from the threat or use of force is organically linked to the question of guaranteeing national security and international security as a whole. Security cannot be built on a policy of force. International security, especially in the nuclear age, can rest only on renunciation of the use of force, on peaceful coexistence of states with differing social systems, and on the right of free choice and independent development of each country.

The formal understandings reached in Stockholm at the Conference on Confidence- and Security-Building Measures and Disarmament in Europe exerted appreciable influence on the content and character of the Declaration. Many points of the Declaration were formulated under the influence of the Conference Document dated September 19, 1986, in particular those points pertaining to an affirmation that respect for, effective exercise of, and defense of all human rights and basic freedoms constitute important factors of international peace and security, as well as justice and the development of friendly relations and cooperation among all states.

Under present conditions the UN Organization, its bodies, and agencies constitute the most suitable international instrument for implementing, monitoring, and ensuring effectiveness of the principle of the inadmissibility of initiating wars. The Declaration also proceeds from this, stipulating in Paragraph 26 that:

> States should cooperate fully with the organs of the United Nations in supporting their actions relating to the maintenance of international peace and security and to the settlement of international disputes in accordance with the Charter of the United Nations.

The Declaration reflects the objective need to place a powerful barrier against the use of force in all its manifestations, and particularly in its most dangerous manifestation–nuclear, as well as the resolve of states, dictated by this necessity, fully to bring to bear the entire potential of the United Nations, particularly the Security Council, in the interests of ensuring universal security that is equal for all states. It specifies that states shall actively seek to strengthen the effectiveness of the system of collective security by means of rigorous observance of the provisions of the Charter, especially those that apply to the special responsibility placed upon the Security Council in this connection.

The Declaration consistently expresses the idea that international security is formed of the security in the various regions and points out that the states which are parties to regional agreements or members of regional bodies should consider the possibility of more extensive utilization of such agreements and bodies for resolving issues which pertain to maintaining international peace and security, in accordance with Article 52 of the UN Charter. Thus the idea that all international institutions and forms, and particularly such a universal body of cooperation among states as the UN Organization, should be brought to bear in the campaign for universal security and for the elimination of war from the experience of human society, an idea which is winning over all the peoples of the world to an ever increasing degree, is reflected in the Declaration.

Thus the Declaration constitutes not only a qualitatively new stage in development of the principle of refraining from the threat or use of force, but also a realistic program of concrete, practical actions by the community of states, directed toward eliminating the threat or use of force from the practice of international relations, and called upon to become an integral component of the formation of an all-encompassing system of international peace and security, grounded on the UN Charter, a foundation block of legal order and rule of law in the world.

In spite of the significance of this Declaration, one must acknowledge that from a legal standpoint it constitutes a recommendation, but at the same time it can be viewed as a unanimous interpretation of the principle of refraining from the threat or use of force in the conditions prevailing at the end of the twentieth century. In connection with this a question arises: Can the Declaration be considered to be a concluding phase in the revelation of the content of the principle and its practical affirmation in intergovernmental relations? Obviously it would be erroneous to consider the process of further development of the principle of refraining from the threat or use of force and the imparting of maximum effectiveness to this principle to be completed, considering in particular the fact that many problems, such as renunciation of first use of nuclear weapons, for example, are not encompassed by the Declaration, as well as the fact that the matter of the final legal form of the subsequent affirmation of this principle in the practice of international relations has not yet been settled. In addition, some important elements of the principle have not at all been examined (for example, renunciation of force in space, on the seas and oceans) or have only been mentioned in passing (for example, the problem of indirect use of force).

One should also bear in mind that the disposition of forces around this issue which has become established in recent years attests to the fact that the very term "force" continues to be one of the principal unresolved elements of the principle of renunciation of force. The United States and other Western countries continue to consider that, in conformity with the UN Charter, the term "force" signifies only direct military force. The developing countries believe that the term "force" encompasses not only armed or military force, but in addition economic coercion, political pressure, actions to destabilize governments, refusal to render food and financial assistance, utilization of mercenaries, *etc.* The matter of a definition of the term "force" was the subject of the sharpest debate and differences of opinion at all stages of consideration, both within and outside the United Nations, of ways to increase the effectiveness of the principle of refraining from the threat or use of force in international relations. Unfortunately these differences have not yet been fully resolved, and considerable effort will be required on the part of the international community of nations in order ultimately to reach a uniform, generally acceptable definition of the principle of refraining from force. Determination of the content and definition of the term "threat of force" is another very complex problem that is also virtually unresolved. While the scope of the term "force" more or less does not evoke particular doubt or question, especially following ratification in 1987 of the Declaration on the Enhancement of the Principle of Refraining from the Threat or Use of Force in International Relations, the term "threat of force" is viewed by practically all states as a highly ambiguous and indefinite term. The state of affairs as regards this term is further aggravated by the fact that for all practical purposes, both at the theoretical and practical level "threat of force" is often equated with interference in the internal and external affairs of states. It is evidently high time for the world community seriously to address these complex and urgent problems; the reaching of generally acceptable formal understandings on these problems could substantially strengthen the principle of nations' renunciation of war against one another.

The Soviet Union propounds the necessity of creating solid, reliable guarantees of international security. Implementation of a series of Soviet peace initiatives, particularly the program calling for eliminating weapons of mass destruction by the end of this century, contained in a Declaration by M.S. Gorbachev on January 15, 1986, and an all-embracing international security plan, which can and should function due to steadily increasing reliance on measures of a political, economic, and humanitarian nature with total renunciation of use of force, banning and physical elimination of nuclear, chemical, and space weapons, is taking on enormous importance in this connection.

Practical experience indicates that not one dispute between states ever has been or ever can be settled on a solid and fair basis with the aid of the threat or use of force. On the contrary, use of force for purposes of aggression, annexation of territory and oppression of other peoples has always sown nothing but the seeds of animosity and hatred, has laid the foundations for new conflicts, and has resulted in loss of lives and enormous material destruction. The appearance of nuclear weapons in the arsenals of the state and the accumulation of these weapons have radically changed the notion of the consequences that military conflicts can bring to peoples, while the probability of escalation of a given crisis or conflict into a nuclear conflict has increased by many orders of magnitude.

Major, fundamental Soviet foreign-policy initiatives are of exceptional importance for creating a qualitatively new situation in the world, particularly the initiatives presented in a September 17, 1987, article by M.S. Gorbachev entitled "Realities and Guarantees of a Safe World," in his speech at the United Nations on December 7, 1988, and in the documents of the First Congress of USSR People's Deputies and the USSR Supreme Soviet, which encompass all the major areas and domains of activity of states in the interest of disarmament, restoration of confidence, and strengthening of the prospects for a peaceful future and progress for all peoples.

A specific approach by the Soviet Union to certain aspects of ensuring comprehensive security, namely increasing the effectiveness of the United Nations and its principal bodies, more extensive utilization of UN operations to maintain peace, and affirming the primacy of international law in intergovernmental relations was laid out in a memorandum of the Soviet delegation at the Forty-third Session of the General Assembly, entitled "Toward Comprehensive Security by Enhancement of the Role of the United Nations."

The Soviet Union believes that it is impossible to guarantee one's own security without considering the interests of others. It is impossible in the nuclear age to build reliable security by military means, no matter how technologically sophisticated they may be. This prompted the Soviet Union to advance a fundamentally new conceptual plan for achieving comprehensive security. It is the firm conviction of the Soviet Union that the United Nations should become a center for reconciling nations' approaches toward forming a new security model.

Of great significance from the standpoint of further affirmation in international affairs of the principle of renunciation of the threat and use of military aggression as an instrument of government policy is the passage by a consensus vote at the Forty-fourth Session of the General Assembly, for the first time in the history of the United Nations, of Resolution 44/21, jointly submitted by the Soviet Union and the United States, dated November 15, 1989, entitled "Enhancing International Peace, Security and International Co-operation in All Its Aspects in Accordance with the Charter of the United Nations." This Resolution reconfirms support for the effectiveness and significance of the UN Charter and contains an appeal to all states to observe it and to respect the principles contained in it, and, particularly, "to refrain from the threat or use of force inconsistent with the Charter." The instrument focuses all nations on increasing their practical efforts toward accomplishing the task of strengthening international peace and security and on finding multifaceted approaches with the aim of more effective utilization of the United Nations' peacemaking potential.

Advocating demilitarization of international relations, the Soviet Union believes that political and legal methods should become dominant in resolving problems which arise. Our ideal is a world community of states governed by rule of law, with states also subordinating their external political activities to the law. Firm establishment in international affairs of the principle of the renunciation by nations of war against one another would constitute an important practical step in this direction.

A characteristic sign of the new times is the fact that scientists and politicians in both East and West are beginning to work on the problem of eliminating war from the practice of intergovernmental relations. And many approaches to resolving this historic problem are either close to or coincide with one another. This applies, for example, to a unanimous striving to observe fully and to the letter the principles and goals of the UN Charter, to resolve international disputes exclusively by peaceful means, and to seek generally acceptable formal understandings in resolving today's global problems. Also meriting attention are proposals, advanced by certain Western scholars, calling for formulation of a nonmilitary or neutral status of states, unconditional recognition of the mandatory jurisdiction of the United Nations' International Court of Justice in disputes between states, *etc.* It would seem useful in turn to study and attempt to reach generally acceptable understandings on certain other problems, which would help affirm the principle of renunciation of force and the primacy of international law in international relations. These include the following:

> the establishment of a global as well as regional security structures on the basis of a balance of interests of all parties in order to prevent conflicts and international instability;
>
> the ensuring of the security of each country primarily by political means, as a component part of general and equal security;
>
> the elimination of nuclear weapons in the course of a negotiation process focused toward disarmament and reduction of the defense potential of states down to levels of reasonable sufficiency;
>
> the achievement of generally acceptable understandings, within the framework of the United Nations, on a uniform interpretation of the principles and rules of international law;
>
> the assumption by states of additional unilateral international obligations, such as has been done, for example, by the Soviet

Union and the PRC, which have forsworn the first use of nuclear weapons;

the formulation and adoption, within the framework of the United Nations and other international organizations, of practical confidence-building measures and measures of international cooperation in all domains: military-political, economic, environmental, humanitarian, and others;

the progressive development and concretization of the general principles and rules of the UN Charter and international law, taking into consideration the realities of the nuclear and space age;

the formulation of principles and rules of international law for new areas of cooperation between states;

the full utilization of all means of peaceful settlement of disputes prescribed by the UN Charter, such as negotiation, mediation, conciliation, arbitration, judicial remedy, appeal to regional bodies or agreements, good offices, *etc.*;

the establishment of a broad arsenal of mechanisms and methods of investigation and collection of facts to be used by states and UN bodies in order to obtain the fullest and most reliable information on disputes and conflicts, their early prevention, political settlement and exercise of impartial verification of compliance with settlement agreements;

the elaboration, within a UN framework, of measures of a preventive nature, capable of effectively preventing the emergence of any threats and challenges in all areas of international relations: military-political, economic, environmental, and humanitarian;

the elaboration of effective international guarantees, including coordinated collective measures adopted by the United Nations and particularly by the Security Council, ensuring that states fulfill the provisions of the UN Charter and the principles and rules of international law.

Joint efforts by all states, and by the Soviet Union and the United States in particular, to reach mutually acceptable formal understandings and agreements on these and other proposals would unquestionably help bring the world community of nations closer to realization of an age-old dream of mankind: a world without weapons, a world without wars.

2. The Scope of Legitimate Self-Defense

Oscar Schachter
Hamilton Fish Professor Emeritus of International Law and Diplomacy, Columbia University

The right of self-defense recognized expressly in Article 51 of the UN Charter and by customary law allows every state to respond with force to an illegal armed attack on it provided such force is necessary and proportionate. Legitimate self-defense also embraces collective self-defense, a concept expressly included in Article 51. Collective self-defense allows any state to use armed force in response to an armed attack on another state if the attacked state requests such assistance. The requirements of necessity and proportionality apply to collective self-defense as to individual self-defense. Article 51 also imposes an obligation on States to report immediately to the UN Security Council any measures taken in the exercise of the right of self-defense. That Article provides that the right of self-defense shall not be impaired "until the Security Council has taken the measures necessary to maintain international peace and security."

Self-defense is referred to in Article 51 as an "inherent right" (in French as *droit naturel*, in Russian as *neot"yemlemoye pravo*). The reference to "inherent" or "naturel" is generally considered to affirm the customary law basis of self-defense, a view also expressed by the International Court of Justice in its 1986 Judgment in *Nicaragua v. United States*. In that case the Court applied the customary law of self-defense, noting that the content of that law has developed since 1945 under the influence of the Charter. Recognition of self-defense as a legal right implies that the legitimacy of its exercise is not a matter left entirely and exclusively to the state claiming the right. See Judgment of the International Military Tribunal at Nuremberg, 208 (1946). A state may–and often must–decide in the first instance whether it may use force in self-defense but it cannot be the ultimate judge. The validity of the claim of self-defense must in the final analysis be determined by the authorized bodies of the international community, that is, by the United Nations or the International Court of Justice. The International Court has held, in *Nicaragua v. United States*, that a claim of self-defense is a justiciable matter. Judgment at Paragraph 34.

A. The Requirement of Armed Attack

Article 51 authorizes self-defense "if an armed attack occurs." The majority of governments and scholars consider that this means "only if an armed attack occurs." Some commentators, such as Derek Bowett and Stephen Schwebel, have argued to the contrary, mainly on the ground that customary law allowed force in response to a threat of attack and that this was safeguarded as the "inherent right" referred to in Article 51. This interpretation would render the phrase "if an armed attack occurs" redundant, which is not likely to have been intended. It would have made no sense to include it if it were not a limitation. The Judgment of the International Court in *Nicaragua v. United States* accepts the requirement of armed attack and both parties presented their arguments on that basis. See Judgment at Paragraph 195.

Questions have arisen as to the precise meaning of "if an armed attack occurs." One problem concerns the precise moment an attack has begun, thus justifying counter-force as legitimate defense. Obviously such attacks may be begun before the target country is actually penetrated; the latter may then rely on self-defense to fire the first shot. Situations may also occur in which the imminence of an attack may be so clear and the danger so great that defensive action is clearly necessary to avoid irreparable injury of grave consequence and no choice is left to use other means. A strong case can be made to allow self-defense in response to such imminent attack.

Not all uses of force against a state constitute armed attacks. In *Nicaragua v. United States*, the International Court distinguished between an armed attack and a "mere frontier incident," noting that an armed attack must have greater "scale and effects." See Judgment at Paragraph 195. The Court recognized that an armed attack included the sending of armed bands and "irregulars" into the territory of another state to carry out hostile acts. Assaults of this kind must be of "sufficient gravity," to constitute armed acts. The Court held that assistance to rebels in the form of the provision of weapons or logistical or other support does not amount to an armed attack. A contrary view expressed in a dissenting opinion is that "substantial involvement" in support of an insurgency can amount to armed attack and justifies individual and collective self-defense in response. Schwebel, dissenting opinion, Paragraph 176; Jennings, dissenting opinion, Page 543.

While Article 51 does not quality armed attack and on its face may apply to armed attacks from non-State entities (such as terrorist bands), it is generally accepted that self-defense applies only against a state that had itself wrongfully used force. However, where a state is responsible for organizing and supporting armed bands that have attacked another state, the latter may rely on self-defense to use force against the culpable state.

The obvious targets of armed attack are the territory of a state or its military units. An attack on diplomatic premises or on the persons of diplomats, officials or military personnel would also amount to an armed attack on a state, justifying self-defense. See Judgement in the Case Concerning United States Diplomatic and Consular Staff in Tehran (United States v. Iran). It has also been maintained that a state may use force in self-defense to protect or rescue private persons who are nationals of that state when such persons are attacked because of their nationality. The United States took this position, for example, with respect to the Entebbe hostage rescue operation by Israel.

B. Necessity and Proportionality

"Necessity" and "proportionality" are conditions of self-defense that depend largely on the particular circumstances of the situation in question. In principle, armed force should not be necessary until peaceful measures have been found inadequate or when they clearly would be futile. But this cannot mean that a state must allow an invasion or bombardment to continue until a peaceful solution is found. It suffices that an armed attack has occurred to justify the proportionate use of counter-force as an immediate response. Similarly, in a situation involving an imminent danger to the lives of hostages, it may be unreasonable to preclude the state of nationality from an armed rescue action on the ground that peaceful measures should first be exhausted.

The question of "necessity" becomes more complicated if a significant period of time has elapsed after an aggressor has succeeded in capturing and occupying foreign territory: Necessity involves an element of immediacy. Thus, the International Court in *Nicaragua-United States* observed that the condition of necessity was not fulfilled when the United States began its collective defensive measures many months after the alleged attack by Nicaragua on El Salvador had begun. Judgment at Paragraph 237. The argument against the applicability of self-defense is even clearer when the presumed attack occurred a long time ago, resulting in continued occupation of conquered territory. Such occupation would not be an adequate ground for self-defense; it would not be a continued armed attack. This is indicated by the failure of Argentina to obtain significant support for its self-defense claim to "recover" the Falkland-

Malvinas Islands. On the other hand, the right of self-defense would not be forfeited solely because the victim state first sought peaceful solutions through negotiation or UN measures and then found it necessary to employ armed force.

However, if the Security Council adopts measures to maintain or restore peace and security in the particular case, that action may, by virtue of Article 51, "impair" (*i.e.*, override) the right of self-defense. This point is discussed below in the section on the Security Council.

Proportionality, like necessity, is a requirement difficult to define in terms of general criteria. In spite of this difficulty, it is an important factor in judging the lawfulness of acts of self-defense and it has been referred to in judging many incidents involving use of force and self-defense claims. The absence of a definition has not prevented governments from recognizing a clearly disproportionate use of force. UN organs have condemned the bombings of civilian areas as illegal even though they are responses to an armed attack—*e.g.*, UN General Assembly Resolution 41/38 (1986) (censuring the United States for the bombing of Libya); Security Council Resolution 509 (1982) (condemning Israel for the invasion of Lebanon). The International Court ruled in *Nicaragua v. United States* that placing mines by the United States in Nicaraguan harbors and territorial waters was illegal because, *inter alia*, it was disproportionate to any aid Nicaragua might have illegally given the insurgents in El Salvador. Paragraph 237.

Proportionality does not mean that a defending state must limit its counterforce to the same force as the attacker used. Rather the defensive act must be judged in relation to the legitimate end. Thus, a defensive retaliatory response may substantially exceed the force of the attack when the response is appropriate to deter future attacks and, if there is a good reason to expect such attacks. However, this would not justify retaliatory actions that result in indiscriminate killing of noncombatants forbidden by the humanitarian laws of war.

C. Collective Self-Defense

Collective self-defense allows a state to come to the aid of another state that has been illegally attacked. It is explicitly recognized in Article 51. The conditions of necessity and proportionality are applicable as is the requirement of Article 51 to report the exercise of the right immediately to the Security Council. Collective self-defense is referred to in the North Atlantic Treaty, the Inter-American Treaty of Reciprocal Assistance of 1947 (Treaty of Rio), and in many bilateral defense pacts. However, a treaty is not a necessary condition of the right of collective self-defense. It is generally recognized today that any state may use force to assist a victim of aggression to repel an armed attack. Thus, the Security Council acknowledged the right of collective self-defense as applicable to any state coming to the aid of Kuwait when the latter was invaded by Iraq in 1990.

The International Court ruled in *Nicaragua v. United States* that collective self-defense did not apply unless the victim of an alleged illegal attack declared itself to have been attacked and requested aid from a third state. Paragraphs 195-99. Dissenting views of some judges questioned this position, noting that an armed aggression violates a fundamental obligation owed to the community of states. Jennings, dissenting opinion, Pages 545-46. On that view, each state has an independent right to use counter-force when necessary, even if asked not to do so by the victim state.

Collective self-defense also provides a legal basis for a state to use force in an internal conflict where such use of force is a response to a prior illegal armed intervention. The legal premise is that in case of a civil war, an outside state may not use force to help either side. Such use of force would violate Article 2(4) inasmuch as it would be against the political independence of the country—that is the right of the people freely to choose their government. Counter-intervention against the prior illegal attack then becomes permissible as collective self-defense. The International Court recognized this legal principle in *Nicaraguan v. United States*, but the majority of judges did not consider it applicable to the facts in that case. They held that Nicaragua's aid to insurgents in El Salvador, though illegal, did not amount to an armed attack and consequently collective self-defense did not apply to the counter-intervention by the United States. Paragraph 211. (This question is considered further in the chapter on Internal Conflict.)

D. The Security Council and the International Court

As already noted, Article 51 provides a role for the Security Council in respect of the exercise of self-defense. It imposes a duty on members exercising the right of self-defense to report their action immediately to the Security Council. This requirement, though categorical and unambiguous, has rarely been observed by states using force under a claim of self-defense. The failures to report have not prevented the Council from considering, and in some cases passing judgment on, such claims when the matter was raised by other states. The Council has rejected claims of self-defense in several cases but, more often than not, has been precluded by the veto from reaching decisions on such claims. Most of those cases were then considered by the General Assembly which unfettered by the veto, generally condemned the alleged self-defense action as a violation of the Charter.

Article 51 also provides that the right of self-defense shall not be impaired "until the Security Council has taken the measures necessary to maintain international peace and security." It is thus envisaged that Security Council measures would supplant self-defense. While the Council clearly has the authority to bar self-defense measures, the question has arisen whether the sole fact that measures have been taken by the Council should *ipso jure* terminate self-defense. The issue arose for the first time in regard to the Council's actions against Iraq for its invasion of Kuwait in August 1990. The Council adopted a series of measures against Iraq, but it did not expressly state that the right of self-defense was "replaced" or pre-empted by those measures. However, it resolved the issue in November 1990 by adopting a decision under Chapter VII authorizing UN Members to take necessary measures to repel the aggressor. It was understood that such measures included the use of force. UN Security Council Resolution S.678, November 29, 1990.

It has been argued that "ineffective" measures should not be given the effect of terminating self-defense. On the other hand, the Council's deliberations may show that the Council's intent was to replace self-defense rights by the Council actions; if so, the Council's authority should prevail even if its measures did not achieve their aim. In case of a division of views within the Council so that it could not adopt a decision on the issue of preemption, one could reasonably conclude that the right of self-defense remains unimpaired. A Council resolution authorizing Members States to use force in aid of a victim of aggression could be regarded as both an endorsement of collective self-defense and as UN action under Chapter VII. To take the Iraq case as an example, inasmuch as the Council did not establish a UN command or call upon the Military Staff Committee for assistance and advice, its decision to call on members to take necessary measures against Iraq appears to be more consonant with collective defense than with the conception of a UN armed force taking enforcement measures.

The fact that the Security Council has the responsibility under Article 51 to consider claims of self-defense does not preclude the International Court of Justice from adjudicating issues of self-defense when it has the jurisdiction to do so under Article 36 of its Statute. Contentious cases involving self-defense may be decided by the Court even in situations that have also been before the Security Council. The Court's decision would be binding on the parties to the case. It would in all probability be taken into account by the Council. However, the Council would still be free to take such measures as it chooses in accordance with the Charter. The Council could issue an order under Chapter VII that would be obligatory on the states involved even if it required a state to act in a manner inconsistent with the Court's binding decision. As a matter of Charter law, the Council's decision would require compliance irrespective of the Court's responsibility. However, the Council's authority should not have the effect of depriving member states (and the Council itself) from receiving an authoritative judicial clarification of the respective legal rights of the parties concerning the use of force and self-defense. This would serve the common interest in strengthening the rule of law and the responsibility of states under the UN Charter.

V.N. Fedorov
Expert, International Organizations Directorate,
USSR Ministry of Foreign Affairs, and
Visiting Professor, USSR Diplomatic Academy

From remote antiquity virtually up to the present day the right of self-defense has been viewed by states as inalienable, as coming exclusively within the competence of a state's supreme agencies of government, and exercised entirely at their discretion, without any outside pressure or interference. Each state considers itself alone empowered to determine the degree of threat to its security and the time of the exercise of the right of self-defense, as well as the nature and types of means of self-defense. And in the opinion of the majority of states, virtually all means at a state's disposal could be used for the purpose of self-defense, including war, employment of reprisals, both with and without the employment of military forces, application of political pressure, economic pressure, *etc.* In other words, the right of self-defense was interpreted by states entirely arbitrarily, and many states believe to this day that there do not exist any restraints of international law. Some states have not even entertained doubts about the unlawful nature of certain of the most repugnant instances of self-defense. States have refused to accept any and all attempts even to regulate in some manner exercise of the right of self-defense, to determine at least the general limits of this right, to prescribe any elements of commensurability of measures of self-defense to the nature and extent of unlawful actions or degree of threat to security in response to which such measures were undertaken. The result was that virtually any self-defense measures taken by a state were considered permissible, just as it was considered acceptable, in spite of the clearly stated provisions of Article 51 of the UN Charter, to resort to any pretexts in order to exercise the right of self-defense. As we know, the list of pretexts included the threat to the lives of citizens, rescue of hostages, protection of property and establishments in a foreign country, bringing pressure to bear on a government that is supplying arms or providing technical assistance to rebels in a third country, defense of the national interests of a state or states, *etc.* As a result the right of self-defense began to be viewed by some as virtually an "absolute" right, subject to no restrictions or limitations by the UN Charter or international law.

The right of self-defense became firmly embodied in the practices of mutual relations between states, and reference to this right was perhaps utilized most frequently by states as a convenient pretext for the use of force, and frequently also for taking unlawful actions involving the bombing of populated localities, seizure of foreign soil, intervention, *etc.* In the estimate of Western scholars, just since the end of World War II alone the armed forces of approximately 100 states of the 170 states that currently exist have invaded the territory of other sovereign states for hostile purposes, at a frequency of once every seven or eight weeks. And in almost every one of these instances of incursion or invasion by military forces, Article 51 of the UN Charter would be cited to justify the legitimacy of the position taken by the country in question. All this cannot help but draw close attention to the question of whether the right of self-defense is in fact totally under the control of a given state or whether there in fact exist certain limits to the application of this right, limits defined by the UN Charter and by international law.

The question of the limits of legitimate self-defense is one of the most complex issues not only in the theory of international law, but also, and in particular, in practical intergovernmental relations. Some scholars claim that there can be no limits regarding a state taking response measures to turn back aggression carried out against that state. No matter how attractive this point of view may be, it nevertheless is not fully in conformity with reality and existing norms of contemporary international law, and particularly with the provisions of such a unique international document as the UN Charter, which all the world's presently existing states have pledged to observe. To permit the contrary would signify, like it or not, negating the results of the struggle by the peoples of all countries, a struggle that has been in progress for many years, to eliminate the threat or use of force from international relations practice, and would constitute connivance with forces acting against the establishment of firm legal order and stability in the world, which in conditions of the existence of nuclear and other types of weapons of mass destruction could result in the demise of human civilization.

Many Western countries interpret extremely broadly the concept of self-defense, essentially prescribing no limits whatsoever to response actions. Western theorists even allow for the employment of military force as self-defense in response to indirect use of force. The Japanese representative on the Special Committee to Define Aggression, for example, stated that:

> One can scarcely deny to a state which is the victim of actual aggression carried out by indirect means the right to exercise its right to legitimate self-defense under the pretext of the indirect nature of employment of aggressive means.

The Soviet position on this issue is that armed attack alone provides grounds, according to the intent of Article 51 of the UN Charter, to exercise the right of individual or collective self-defense. And no matter how difficult the task of defining the limits of self-defense in the present nuclear missile age may seem to be, the Soviet Union considers that the establishment of well-defined legal limits to the exercise of the right of self-defense is becoming an urgent necessity, especially in conditions whereby there exist unprecedented means of death and destruction, when weapons of mass destruction can be employed virtually within minutes, and when the continued existence of human civilization is essentially in question.

The limits of legitimate self-defense are clearly spelled out by the UN Charter. Pursuant to Article 51, every state possesses the inalienable right of individual or collective self-defense, but a state may exercise this right only if an armed attack occurs, and until such time as the Security Council takes measures essential to maintain international peace and security. This is a very substantial limitation to the right of self-defense. For the first time the UN Charter takes away from the state the possibility of determining for itself whether or not the specific conditions of the situation and the actions of another state require that measures of self-defense be taken, and it clearly points out that a state is entitled to take such measures only in case of armed attack on the state itself. Consequently, if self-defense measures are undertaken, for example, in response to attempts at economic intervention or political pressure, or in connection with some minor border incident, such measures will not be recognized as legitimate and shall be subject to condemnation by the world community of nations. In like manner self-defense measures in response to an imminent attack, that is, so-called preventive self-defense, cannot be acknowledged as legitimate.

Close linkage between self-defense measures and activities by the United Nations and its Security Council, prescribed by the UN Charter, constitutes a very substantial element limiting the right of self-defense. The means at the disposal of the United Nations, and particularly of the Security Council, as well as collective influence that the Organization can exert on a given situation, directly influence the nature and scope of responsive measures in self-defense. The state that has been subjected to armed attack may put these measures entirely at the discretion of the Security Council or General Assembly. The list of steps that can be undertaken by the Security Council in this case is quite extensive and in practice frequently proves to be quite effective. They include, in particular, sanctions of an organizational-political nature. In conformity with the UN Charter (Article 5), if actions of a preventive or coercive nature have been taken against any member of the Organization, the General Assembly is empowered, on a recommendation by the Security Council, to suspend the exercise of rights and privileges possessed by that state as a member of the Organization. Exercise of these rights and privileges can be restored by the Security Council. It follows quite clearly from this that exercise of rights and privileges by any state, including the right of individual or collective self-defense, is "overseen" by the world community, and any abuse of this right may bring appropriate response on the part of the Security Council and General Assembly, in the form of direct limitation of the rights enjoyed by said state. In addition, if a given state attempts to persist in abuse of the rights and privileges it has been given, including the right of self-defense, and has the intention of ignoring the provisions of the UN Charter, such state may find itself outside the system of legal order and rule of law established by the UN Charter, with all consequences proceeding therefrom. Pursuant to Article 6 of the UN Charter, a UN member that violates in a systematic manner the principles contained in the Charter may be expelled from the Organization by the General Assembly, on recommendation of the Security Council. It is quite obvious that any state planning to exercise the right of self-defense must consider this extremely serious deterrent factor, which is capable of bringing upon it an adverse reaction by the entire world community of nations.

Some scholars are of the opinion that the obligation of states to exercise their right of self-defense "until the Security Council has taken the measures necessary to maintain international peace and security," an obligation prescribed in Article 51 of the UN Charter, constitutes a substantial temporal limiting factor to the unchallenged exercise of the right of self-defense. Thus the Charter establishes a clearly defined time limit for a state to exercise its right of self-defense by its own means, and as soon as the Security Council commences taking measures necessary to maintain international peace and security, a state may no longer undertake additional self-defense measures solely at its own discretion. As for the term "measures," which the Security Council is to undertake, there is no unanimity of opinion on the nature and scope of such measures.

Some Western scholars question the very existence of a limitation of this kind in exercise of the right of self-defense. They assert that the right of a state to resort unilaterally to self-defense is limited only at the moment when "the United Nations takes collective actions against the aggressor." But since a "standing UN army," as prescribed by Chapter VII of the Charter, has not been established to date, then the very existence of this limitation is questionable. One can hardly agree with such assertions. First of all, it would obviously be incorrect to boil down all the diversified Security Council "measures" solely to coercive measures connected with the use of UN military forces, as prescribed in Articles 42 and 43 of the UN Charter. It is well known that the term "measures" is interpreted essentially to mean any action undertaken by the Security Council, including actions on the basis of Chapter VI of the UN Charter, as well as "provisional measures" undertaken pursuant to Article 40 of the UN Charter.

In addition, in accordance with Chapter VII the Security Council is empowered to decide what collective measures not involving the use of military forces are to be taken in order for it to implement decisions, and it can require that UN members take such measures. These measures may include total or partial severing of economic relations, interruption of rail service, maritime shipping, air transportation, postal and telegraph service, radio or other means of communication, as well as the breaking off of diplomatic relations. And as practical experience indicates, such measures often prove to be highly effective. Finally, although the provisions of Chapter VII of the UN Charter that prescribe that military forces needed for maintaining international peace and security shall be placed at the disposal of the Security Council at its request and in accordance with a special agreement or agreements have not been implemented to date, the practice of Security Council conduct of UN peacekeeping operations has been established on the basis of Chapter VII, involving the employment of UN military forces and UN military observers. As experience has shown, UN peacekeeping operations are a highly effective instrument of UN peacemaking activities, and such operations can unquestionably be assigned to the category of those "measures necessary to maintain international peace and security" undertaken by the Security Council, measures to which reference is made in Article 51 of the UN Charter. Of course the above does not exclude, but on the contrary presupposes, the need for further study and reconciliation of views on this complex issue of international law and world politics.

The requirement that "[m]easures taken by Members in the exercise of this right of self-defense shall be immediately reported to the Security Council," which is contained in Article 51 of the UN Charter, constitutes a highly effective deterrent factor, which unquestionably affects the nature and scope of self-defense measures undertaken by a state. This requirement places the exercise of a nation's right of self-defense within a certain framework and compels a state to bring already undertaken or planned self-defense measures into harmony with the provisions of the UN Charter and the generally recognized principles and rules of international law, to weigh the legitimacy of and justification for its actions, and to consider the possible negative reaction on the part of the world community of nations to undertaken measures. Unfortunately postwar history abounds in instances of failure to observe this requirement. Many states, including the Soviet Union and the United States, although citing Article 51 in carrying out their foreign-policy actions, have preferred not to inform the Security Council immediately on measures taken by them in exercise of this right.

A provision embodied in Article 51, pursuant to which measures undertaken by states in self-defense "shall not in any way affect the authority and responsibility of the Security Council under the present Charter to take at any time such action as it deems necessary in order to maintain or restore international peace and security," constitutes an important legal and political "blocking mechanism" to a state's exercise of the right of self-defense. A very significant limitation of a state's right of self-defense proceeds quite definitely from this provision, a limitation which consists in the fact that a state may not unilaterally determine and carry out self-defense measures, but is virtually obligated to place the execution of such measures under the supervision of the Security Council. Furthermore, self-defense measures undertaken by a state must not only not be in conflict with but even may not affect, that is, diminish to any degree whatsoever, the jurisdiction and responsibility of the Security Council. In addition, the Security Council may, in accordance with Article 39 of the Charter, determine the existence of any threat to peace, any breach of the peace or act of aggression and, as a result, reach a decision to take its own self-defense measures. The unique nature of such measures lies in the fact that in this instance the Security Council is acting not only on behalf of the state which is exercising its right of self-defense but also on behalf of all members of the UN Organization, while the effectiveness of the measures proper is bolstered by the great prestige of the United Nations and the aggregate will and power of the UN member states which, pursuant to Article 25 of the UN Charter, have accepted the obligation to submit to and carry out the decisions of the Security Council.

At the same time there is also possible a development that is undesirable to a state carrying out self-defense measures, when the Security Council, having considered the merits of an issue, may reject as unfounded a state's claim of the right of self-defense, and consequently may adjudge the measures taken by said state to be unlawful. In this case the "blocking mechanism" operates fully: A state's right of self-defense is essentially denied, and its actions are condemned by the world community of nations.

It should be emphasized that the limiting nature of the exercise of the right of self-defense is also confirmed by the fact that provisional measures undertaken by the Security Council, for example, "shall be without prejudice to the rights, claims, or position of the parties concerned," while the Security Council shall merely "duly take account of failure to comply with such provisional measures."

In addition, self-defense measures undertaken by the Security Council are also subject to very strict limitations. Beginning with the establishment of UN Emergency Force II in 1973, UN forces, employed with Security Council approval, have invariably followed a practice whereby they could use light arms only for self-defense and to resist violent attempts to prevent UN forces from performing their functions. This means that weapons cannot be used by UN troops for purposes of coercion, but may be used only to turn back or repel armed encroachments and attacks.

It is obvious that many states presently do not recognize the noted limits to the exercise of the right of self-defense. Painstaking, persisting efforts both at a bilateral and regional level, as well as within the framework of the UN Organization, are needed in order to gain their international acceptance. There is no doubt that this "gap" in international law, which has existed up to the present time, can be filled through the joint efforts of all nations. It would seem that implementation of some highly interesting and detailed proposals and observations stated by a number of prominent Western researchers and scholars would promote understanding of the significance, content, and nature of the right of self-defense. Particularly meriting attention are proposals by Western experts, including H. Hagland, to draw up a clearly defined code of conduct of states pertaining to the exercise of the right of self-defense, and to draft rules and procedures for employment of weapons by UN military forces in all types of situations, from incidents of limited violations at checkpoints to armed attacks on patrols and UN troop deployment sites. Also of considerable interest is an approach to resolving the problem of due and proper use of the right of self-defense proposed by U.S. scholar Oscar Schachter, in conformity with which states could agree to limitations in exercise of the right of self-defense by entering into treaties, drawing up political declarations, reaching gentlemen's agreements and understandings, or by reaching a tacit understanding. The Declaration on Establishment of Facts presently being drafted by the Special Committee on the UN Charter and on Strengthening the Role of the Organization, as well as work by the Special Committee on UN Peacekeeping Operations, which has recently been stepped up, would also constitute an important contribution toward resolving the problem of regulated exercise of the right of self-defense, in conformity with the UN Charter.

Also promising are efforts by states at the regional level, in particular in the process of forming all-European security and cooperation structures, when generally acceptable formal understandings could be reached to impart maximum effectiveness to the principle of renunciation of the threat or use of force, including agreement on a precise manner and procedure of nations' exercise of the right of self-defense and on the establishment of multinational peacekeeping forces in Europe.

Practical realities are placing on the agenda the task of laying forth the content and significance of formulating and reaching agreement on a generally acceptable definition of the right of self-defense, taking into account established practice and the realities of the present day. Accomplishment of this task would be not only of great theoretical significance but of the most direct practical significance as well, and would constitute a substantial contribution toward strengthening general and equal security for all states. As is indicated by the experience of drafting a definition of aggression at the United Nations, such a task is fully within the capabilities of the UN Organization. It would also seem desirable, if for any reason formulation of a definition of the right of self-defense is acknowledged as inappropriate at the present time, to proceed as proposed by M.S. Gorbachev in his well-known speech before the United Nations on December 7, 1988, in which he, speaking about the importance of resolving problems that arise not by force but exclusively by political and legal methods, emphasized that an agreement within the framework of the United Nations on a uniform understanding of the principles and rules of international law would help achieve this. It would seem entirely possible to examine all aspects of the right of self-defense and to reach agreement on a generally acceptable interpretation of the right of self-defense and the boundaries of its practical implementation. Such a formal understanding could be articulated in the form of both a declaration and a memorandum of understanding or in some other manner, and could be approved on the basis of a consensus vote by the General Assembly, which would be a valuable help in the activities of the Security Council.

3. Internal Conflicts and International Law

Oscar Schachter
Hamilton Fish Professor Emeritus of International Law and Diplomacy, Columbia University

Internal conflicts as a general rule are outside of the province of international law, but there are important exceptions. The exceptions fall broadly into two categories. The first comprises the limits imposed by international customary and treaty law on the conduct of hostilities–the *jus in bello*–and on acts contrary to international human rights law. The second category relates to the involvement of foreign powers in the internal conflicts and is centered on the principle of non-intervention in internal affairs. These exceptions will be discussed below. They will be considered mainly in respect of internal conflicts involving armed force but reference will also be made to non-violent conflicts that raise questions of international law.

The proliferation of civil wars and lesser acts of internal violence have presented grave challenges to the international legal order. However, it cannot be said that international law is opposed in principle to internal conflicts, violent or peaceful. Indeed, the legal principles of sovereign equality, political independence, and self-determination, enshrined in the UN Charter, recognize not only that peoples everywhere have the right to choose their government and political structure, but implicitly accept their right to resort to force to achieve those ends. At the same time, it has become an acknowledged fact of life that internal armed conflicts almost always have international repercussions and that they rarely can be fully contained in the state where they occur.

A. The International Law of Armed Conflict and of Human Rights Law

Although internal conflicts, per se, are generally outside of the scope of international law, the law of armed conflict—the *jus in bello*—applies in some important respects to internal armed conflicts. The principal treaties that prescribe the humanitarian rules of war, the four Geneva Conventions of 1949 for the protection of war victims, include a common provision, Article 3, which reads:

> In the case of armed conflicts not of an international character occurring in the territory of one of the High Contracting Parties, each Party shall be bound to apply, as a minimum, the following provisions . . . .

The provisions that follow require generally that persons taking no active part in the hostilities shall be treated humanely. They also specifically prohibit a number of acts such as murder, hostage-taking, torture, and cruel or degrading treatment. It is also forbidden to impose sentences or executions "without previous judgment pronounced by a regularly constituted court, affording all the judicial guarantees which are recognized as indispensable by civilized peoples." Article 3(1)(d). Article 3 is binding treaty law for virtually all the states of the world. A majority of judges in the International Court have also suggested that Article 3 lays down a "common yardstick" for non-international conflicts derived from "elementary considerations of humanity." *Nicaragua v. United States*, Paragraph 218. Conflicts of a non-international character are also the subject of Additional Protocol II to the Geneva Conventions, to which a substantial number of states have adhered. The Protocol goes beyond Article 3 in adding requirements of humane treatment of persons who do not take part in hostilities or have ceased to do so.

The expression "armed conflict not of an international character" is not defined in Article 3 beyond indicating that it is a conflict within the territory of a contracting Party other than an armed international conflict. An authoritative commentary of the International Committee of the Red Cross states that it must be a "genuine armed conflict" and that it does not apply to internal disturbances, such as riots and sporadic acts of violence. The commentary also suggests that for Article 3 to apply in a civil war, the insurgents must possess an organized military force and an authority responsible for its acts with means of carrying out the requirements of Article 3. Additional Protocol II includes similar conditions in its Article 1.

Governments engaged in internal conflicts, even on a large scale, tend to deny the applicability of Article 3. In the 1980's for example, the civil wars in Afghanistan, El Salvador, and Nicaragua were not regarded by the governments of those countries as within Article 3. However, the International Court of Justice in *Nicaragua v. United States* did recognize that the conflict between the Nicaraguan government and the insurgent Contras was subject to Article 3, whereas the actions of the United States in and against Nicaragua were subject to the rules applicable to international conflicts.

The status and obligations of insurgents under Article 3 and Additional Protocol II have been uncertain in some respects. It is clear that insurgents remain subject to the criminal law of the State except as qualified by the obligations of Article 3. They do not become privileged combatants but they do receive a legal status from Article 3 as soon as the threshold of conflict meets the minimum standard. The question arises whether they, on their part, can be bound by a treaty they have not accepted. One answer has been that they must be bound by the obligations of the state when they purport to be the rightful government. If they do not claim governmental authority, it is at least arguable that they may be regarded as subject to the obligations on the basis of their claim that they are not mere brigands but a responsible body pursuing legitimate ends. As a practical matter, their compliance with the obligations is more likely to be motivated by their interest in reciprocal compliance by the government.

International treaties and customary law prescribing human rights may also apply to internal armed conflicts. There is no doubt that the prohibition of genocide, slavery and torture would apply. It is clear that these obligations are non-derogable under the relevant treaties. The fact that internal armed conflict would plausibly be a valid ground for derogation as a "public emergency which threatens the life of the nation" would not legitimize violation of non-derogable rights guaranteed by the treaties. In addition to those prohibitions mentioned above, such non-derogable rights would include the prohibition against retroactive penal measures and the right to life (a right that is qualified in the relevant treaties).

B. The Prohibition Against Armed Intervention in Internal Conflicts

The basic international law principle prohibiting armed intervention by foreign states in internal conflicts is Article 2(4) of the UN Charter. It reads:

> All Members shall refrain in their international relations from the threat or use of force against the territorial integrity or political independence of any state, or in any other manner inconsistent with the Purposes of the United Nations.

The principle is also accepted as a rule of customary international law and as a peremptory norm (*jus cogens*) from which no derogation is permitted. Customary international law also includes a general principle of non-intervention in internal affairs, formulated by the UN General Assembly as follows:

> No state or group of States has the right to intervene, directly or indirectly, for any reason whatever, in the internal or external affairs of any other State. Consequently, armed intervention and all other forms of interference or attempted threats against the personality of the State or against its political, economic and cultural elements, are in violation of international law.

UN General Assembly Resolution 25/2625 (1970); see also UN General Assembly Resolution 20/2131 (1965). It is obvious from these principles that a foreign state may not use force to support insurgents or opposition elements against the government of a state.

Notwithstanding the sweeping character of the foregoing prohibitions, foreign states have used armed force, on one side or another, to influence the outcome of most internal conflicts that have occurred since 1945. These apparent departures from the general principles on non-use of force and on non-intervention have been justified by the intervening states on various legal grounds. The issues raised by these interventions and the accompanying legal claims were considered in most of the cases by the UN General Assembly or Security Council. While the resolutions adopted by these bodies were generally non-binding, they are indicative of the attitudes of states and their legal positions. In addition, the International Court of Justice passed upon some of the controversial issues in its 1986 Judgment in *Nicaragua-United States*. These decisions, supplemented by commentary of authoritative international legal bodies, have greatly clarified the law on armed intervention in internal conflicts. A significant factor is that most of the cases have involved critical differences on the facts rather than on the law. The following summary avoids taking positions on disputed issues of fact. It presents legal conclusions on the basis of the legal positions taken by the parties to the conflicts and by competent international organs and recognized legal authority.

A prominent justification for armed intervention has been the request or agreement of the government of the state in which the internal conflict has occurred. Approval by the territorial sovereign, it is argued, should refute any implication that the foreign intervention is "against the territorial integrity or political independence of any state" in question or contrary to UN purposes. Hence Article 2(4) would not apply. Nor does the general customary norm of non-intervention apply when the de jure government requests military assistance. It has long been recognized that foreign states may extend military aid to other states when invited to do so and that such assistance may be employed to maintain internal law and order.

While these conclusions are generally accepted, they do not dispose of some situations that have arisen. One such case is presented when there is reason to believe that the government or official extending the invitation to intervene or assenting to it lacks the authority to do so. Important examples of such spurious authority have been cases where the invitation or consent to the intervention has come from officials who were unlawfully imposed by the intervening power. The alleged invitations to the Soviet Union by the Hungarian government in 1956 and the Afghanistan government in 1979 are well-recognized examples. A somewhat difference case of spurious claim of authority could arise when a request is made by an official lacking constitutional authority to bind the state. This issue was considered in regard to the request of the Governor-General of Grenada for U.S. intervention in 1983. The UN General Assembly implicitly denied the authority of the Governor General when it condemned the U.S. action. UN General Assembly Resolution 38/7 (1983).

The authority of a government to request foreign intervention and the right of a foreign state to intervene may also be questioned when the internal conflict has assumed the dimensions of a civil war in which the insurgents are supported by a substantial part of the population. A government thus beset by civil strife the outcome of which is in doubt has weak authority to speak for the state as a whole. Moreover, foreign military intervention impairs the right of the people to decide their political destiny. In those circumstances, the foreign state may be held to violate the prohibition of the Charter on the use of force against the political independence of a State. In sum, foreign armed intervention on either side in a civil war is illegal under the Charter unless such intervention can be justified as collective self-defense in response to a prior unlawful armed attack. This exception is discussed above in the chapter on legitimate self-defense.

Military assistance to a government requesting such aid may also be legally questionable when the aid is to be used for purposes incompatible with the principles of the Charter or of international law such as genocide, slavery or apartheid.

While governments and legal authority generally agree that foreign military intervention against a government is forbidden except in self-defense, exceptions to this rule have been suggested by some international lawyers and government officials. The general argument presented has been that the rule against force should not apply where the objective of external intervention is to achieve an important, generally accepted aim of the UN Charter or of the international community. Examples of such aims have been self-determination, basic human rights, democratic rule, and protection against massacres and degradation. It is argued that armed intervention for such aims could not constitute the use of force against territorial integrity or political independence, or be in any way inconsistent with the purposes of the United Nations.

A short answer to this argument is that such armed intervention would indeed be inconsistent with a Charter purpose—namely, the primary aim of international peace. The fact that force may serve other Charter purposes would not override its inconsistency with that primary objective. Nor can it be denied that sending armed forces into another state would violate the territorial integrity of that state. Beyond these legal arguments, it has been observed that to allow unilateral intervention for reasons other than self-defense would go a long way to nullify Article 2(4). The governments of the world have rejected such far-reaching exceptions to the prohibition against use of force. Indeed, even the governments that have intervened with armed force have invariably based their position on a claim of self-defense against a prior attack or a claim of consent by the government of the state in which the intervention occurred. Whether or not these claims were well-founded, the reliance upon them by the governments that have used force are indications that the other exceptions have not been accepted by governments or by authoritative international bodies. It does not seem likely that this will change in the near future. Governments are not generally prepared to support a principle that would legitimize armed interventions for "good causes" that might threaten the overthrow of their regimes.

However, this does not mean that governments are immune to censure or international measures of a non-forceful character for violations of basic human rights and freedoms that occur in internal conflicts.

C. Intervention of a Non-Forcible Character

The prohibition against intervention in internal affairs is not limited to acts of armed force. Two major UN Declarations—each adopted by consensus—prohibit "all other forms of interference . . . against the personality of the state or against its political, economic and cultural elements". They expressly declare that no State "shall interfere in civil strife in another State." Many multilateral and bilateral treaties also include general obligations to refrain from interference in domestic affairs. They often include, as do the UN Declarations, recognition of the right of all peoples to determine freely, without external interference, their political, economic, cultural, and social systems.

The general rule against interference in civil strife is accompanied by a more specific prohibition namely, "No State shall organize, assist, foment, finance, invite or tolerate subversive, terrorist or armed activities directed toward the violent overthrow of the regime of another State."

This provision would appear to bar foreign states from any forms of assistance or even "toleration" of violent opposition movements. As thus stated, the rule against "interference" in internal conflict is not intended to require equal treatment of both sides. No limitation is imposed on the political or economic relations between outside states and the recognized government during an internal conflict, even if it is a large-scale civil war. Moreover, under customary law a foreign state may not extend *de jure* recognition to an insurgent group during the civil war, at least not as long as the recognized government is able to carry on resistance.

An outside state may, however, extend *de facto* recognition and recognize belligerent rights of the insurgency. De facto recognition is permissible where an insurgent force exercises effective authority over an area of the country. Agreements with such de facto regimes may be concluded when required by the facts of their effective control. Recognition of acts of de facto regimes in domestic courts of a foreign state have not been regarded as violations of the international law rule against intervention. If the insurgents succeed in achieving effective control over a country (or nearly all of its territory), other states may extend de jure recognition without violating the principle of non-intervention. On the other hand, if a foreign state should consider the new government as illegitimate and refuse de jure recognition, it would not violate the non-intervention rule solely because of such non-recognition.

However, if the non-recognized regime exercises effective authority and if it has not achieved power in violation of international law, other states have a duty to treat that regime as a government in regard to its international relations. They cannot, for example, ignore its international rights to territorial integrity and they must accept its acts in respect of adherence to treaties or other obligations. Thus, while a foreign state may legally withhold formal recognition, the refusal to treat a regime exercising effective authority as the government for international relations would amount to impermissible intervention.

The general principle of non-intervention in internal strife has been complicated by UN declarations and governmental statements concerning the right of self-determination. In particular, the UN declarations assert that peoples are entitled to seek and receive support in their actions against forcible measures by states which deprive such people of their right to self-determination. This principle has been construed to allow states, and perhaps oblige them, to support self-determination movements provided that such support does not include use of force contrary to the UN Charter. On this interpretation, it would appear that foreign states may assist national liberation movements with non-forcible action against the government in power. Consequently when a national liberation movement has been recognized as such by the United Nations, it would be difficult to maintain that foreign assistance to it, short of armed force, violates the rule against non-intervention.

D. UN Intervention in Internal Conflicts

The UN Charter declares in Article 2(7) that nothing in the Charter "shall authorize the United Nations to intervene in matters which are essentially within the domestic jurisdiction of any state . . . ." It adds that this principle shall not prejudice the application of enforcement measures under Chapter VII. In fact, the United Nations has played a role in numerous internal conflicts quite apart from applying enforcement measures. The prohibition of Article 2(7) was not applied in these cases on the ground that the internal conflicts were not essentially domestic. This was mainly evidenced by the actual or likely involvement of outside states in the internal conflict to a degree that appeared to endanger international peace and security. Other reasons for denying the essentially domestic character of an internal conflict were also given in some cases. For example, wars of national liberation against colonial powers were not treated as internal. Examples include Greece (1946-47), Lebanon (1958), Congo (1960-65), Cyprus (since 1964), and Nicaragua (1984). Some governments also maintained that internal conflicts resulting from large-scale racial or ethnic discrimination should not be regarded as domestic, as in the case of Rhodesia and Southwest Africa (Namibia). It was also argued in some cases that situations are no longer domestic when treaty or customary law obligations have been violated in the internal conflict.

UN involvement in internal conflicts has taken various forms. It has been most evident where UN peacekeeping forces have been sent to maintain order and security in the area of conflict. The largest such operation occurred in the former Belgian Congo, now Zaire, at the invitation of the Central Government faced with rebellion and a breakdown of public order. Recent examples occurred in Namibia in the transition to independence and in Nicaragua to assist in disarming the rebels.

In summary, it may be said that where an internal conflict is no longer essentially domestic, the competent UN organ (Security Council or General Assembly) may act by: (1) making recommendations to the parties involved or to other states; (2) offering the parties pacific means of settlement; (3) placing observers or peacekeeping forces to police cease-fire or buffer zones, with the consent of the government; (4) giving relief and refugee assistance, with the consent of the government; and (5) imposing sanctions of a non-military character or authorizing armed force to restore peace and security under Chapter VII. In all these cases, the United Nations would be subject to its Charter. Consequently, it would not have the right to contravene the principles of sovereign equality and political independence by imposing constitutional or other domestic policies on a state.

S.A. Yegorov
Docent and Deputy Head of Department,
USSR Diplomatic Academy

An internal, that is a noninternational, armed conflict, which as a rule is defined as a civil war constituting an organized armed struggle for political power between classes, ethnic, religious or other social groups within a single state, differs from an international armed conflict. Particular contributing factors include the use of specific forms and methods of combat actions by the opposing sides, extreme uncertainty regarding the composition of the opposing sides, and frequently the impossibility of making a clear-cut delineation between "combatants" and "noncombatants," that is, between those who are taking direct part in the armed struggle and those who are not directly participating in this struggle.

A difference between an international and an internal armed conflict lies in the fact that, while as a rule the former constitutes a sequential phase in the development of an international dispute, the latter does not. In an internal armed conflict, attributes of an international dispute are lacking from the very outset, and internal socioeconomic events occur, which exert revolutionary effect on the nature and character of power and authority relations within a single state. In spite of the internal character of the latter conflict, it can present a serious threat to international security, and by virtue of this cannot be ignored by the community of nations.

More than half a century of experience in codification and the progressive evolution of international law applied during a period of armed conflicts attests to the fact that states, while being principal participants in processes of creating and applying laws, have invariably shown particular restraint and caution in drafting provisions aimed at regulating the complex aggregate of relations arising in the course of armed conflicts of a noninternational nature. The above-noted restraint is due on the one hand to a disinclination by states to limit through norms of international law the freedom of action on the part of a central government *vis-à-vis* an opposition that is waging an armed struggle against it, and on the other hand is due to the fear of legalizing intervention in the internal affairs of a state, on the territory of which a conflict is occurring, by another state or group of states, *i.e.*, intervention which leads to internationalization of an internal conflict, which is undesirable to the central government.

The relatively modest share of legal norms in the overall mass of legislative material that comprises the legal foundation of the law of armed conflicts or international humanitarian law applicable in a period of armed conflicts, is due in large measure to the above-named reasons. For example, of the approximately twenty sources presently existing in this area of international law, sources containing a total of more than 600 articles, only one agreement, containing twenty-eight articles, is directly related to the problem of internal armed conflicts. This document is the Additional Protocol, adopted in 1977, to the Geneva Conventions of August 12, 1949. This Protocol deals with protecting the victims of armed conflicts of a noninternational nature (Protocol II), further developing and supplementing Article 3, which is common to all four 1949 Geneva Conventions.

Article 3 of the Geneva Conventions of 1949, the first international law provision designed to be applied "[i]n the case of an armed conflict not of an international character," remained for almost three decades, right up to the time when Protocol II entered into force, the sole requirement under international law of humane treatment, by each of the parties to a conflict, under all circumstances and without any discrimination, of "[p]ersons taking no active part in the hostilities, including members of armed forces who have laid down their arms, and those placed *hors de combat* by sickness, wounds, detention, or any other cause." Article 3 introduces into current international law a legislative prohibition against carrying out the following actions against the persons listed above:

> (*a*) violence to life and person, in particular, murder of all kinds, mutilation, cruel treatment and torture;
>
> (*b*) taking of hostages;
>
> (*c*) outrages upon personal dignity, in particular humiliating and degrading treatment;
>
> (*d*) the passing of sentences and the carrying out of executions without previous judgment pronounced by a regularly constituted court, affording all the judicial guarantees which are recognized as indispensable by civilized peoples.

These prohibitions, the primary purpose of which is to ensure observance of the basic rights of the civilian population as well as other persons who do not take direct part in an armed struggle, are in effect for the more than 160 states which are Parties to the 1949 Geneva Conventions.

Article 3 specifies that the International Red Cross Committee (IRCC) may offer its services to the parties to a conflict. This provision constitutes to a certain degree a legal attempt to create a mechanism the purpose of which is to guarantee observance of the norms contained in Article 3. The content of this provision, however, does not support the conclusion that the parties to a conflict are automatically and unconditionally obligated to accept the services of the IRCC. It is apparent that in all cases a state retains the right either to permit or to prevent the IRCC from performing its humanitarian and monitoring functions.

The Geneva Conventions contain other provisions that also can serve to guarantee observance of the rules of conduct set out in Article 3. Article 1, for example, common to all four 1949 Geneva Conventions, reads: "The High Contracting Parties undertake to respect and to ensure respect for the present Convention in all circumstances." The pledge "to ensure respect" of the convention can in practice be expressed in the form of a diplomatic demarche against the state on the territory of which a conflict is taking place and in a request to the IRCC that it perform the functions prescribed in Article 3. States obviously have a right, acting in concert, to apply against a violator measures of an enforcement nature that do not involve the employment of military force, such as suspending a treaty, *etc.*

One should evidently consider as one form of guarantee the obligation of states that are Parties to the Geneva Conventions to seek out and prosecute, on the basis of appropriate domestic laws, persons accused of having carried out or having ordered the carrying out of an action stipulated by the conventions as "serious violations" of the conventions. In our opinion violation of Article 3 constitutes such a "serious violation."

The final provision of Article 3 reads: "The application of the preceding provisions shall not affect the legal status of the Parties to the conflict." This provision obviously means that application of Article 3 shall not result in the opposition acquiring the status of a subject of international law. At the same time the assertion that Article 3 imposes corresponding obligations in equal measure on each of the parties to a conflict would not be in conflict with the spirit and letter of this Article.

Complexity and a certain element of conflict, however, lie in the fact that the Geneva Conventions were signed by sovereign states, while insurgents rebelling against the governments of Parties do not as a rule constitute full and equal Parties to these Conventions.

In spite of repeated violations of the provisions of Article 3, one should acknowledge its on the whole positive influence on the process of humanization of armed conflicts of a noninternational nature. The deficiencies and gaps in Article 3, which diminish its practical significance, are well known. For example, it does not contain even an approximate listing of objective criteria which characterize a noninternational armed conflict. It also lacks clearly formulated provisions which directly prohibit armed attack on the civilian population, civilian property and installations.

Considering, alongside other circumstances, the degree of protection of parties to noninternational armed conflicts, which fails to meet the demands of the time, in 1968 the UN General Assembly adopted Resolution 23/2444, in which it appealed to the members of the international community to apply basic humanitarian principles in all armed conflicts and called upon the UN Secretary General, jointly with the IRCC, to study "[t]he need for additional humanitarian international conventions or for other appropriate legal instruments to ensure better protection of civilians, prisoners and combatants in all armed conflicts . . . ."

Additional Protocol II to the 1949 Geneva Conventions, adopted in 1977, covers armed conflicts taking place on the territory of any Protocol II Party, between its armed forces or other organized armed groups which, being under responsible command, exercise control over part of its territory, control that enables them to conduct continuous and coordinated military operations and to apply the provisions of Protocol II. This Protocol applies, without any adverse distinction whatsoever, to all persons affected by conflicts of this type.

Endeavoring strictly to limit the sphere of application of Protocol II, its authors established that it shall not apply to cases of disruption of domestic order and the occurrence of a state of internal tension, such as riots, isolated and sporadic acts of violence, as well as other acts of a similar nature, since they do not constitute conflicts.

Article 3 of Protocol II is of considerable importance for understanding the content of the Protocol. According to this Article, nothing in Protocol II shall, first of all, be interpreted as affecting the sovereignty of a state or the obligation of a government, using all legal means, to maintain or restore law and order in the state or to defend the state's national unity and territorial integrity; secondly, it shall not be interpreted as justification for direct or indirect intervention, for any reason whatsoever, in an armed conflict or in the internal or external affairs of a Party to Protocol II on the territory of which said conflict occurs.

Just as Article 3 of the 1949 Geneva Conventions, Protocol II comprises a document of a humanitarian nature, intended to protect human rights in conditions of an armed conflict of a noninternational nature. Further developing the content of Article 3 of the Geneva Conventions, Protocol II extended the domain of the principle of protection of the civilian population to the conditions of a domestic armed conflict. Pursuant to Article 13 of Protocol II, even in a period of armed conflicts of a noninternational nature, the civilian population and individual civilians shall enjoy general protection against the dangers that arise in connection with military operations, by virtue of which they shall not constitute a target of attack, and acts or threats of violence the main purpose of which is to terrorize the civilian population are prohibited. Article 17 prohibits the compulsory displacement of civilians, unless the need for displacement is dictated by the requirement that civilians be provided safety or by urgent reasons of a military nature. Protocol II prohibits the use of hunger or starvation among the civilian population as a method of conduct of military operations, and in connection with this prohibits attack on, destruction of, removal or disabling of items and facilities that are essential for survival of the civilian population, such as stocks of food supplies, crops, livestock, drinking water supply facilities, and irrigation facilities. Installations and facilities containing dangerous forces, namely dams, dikes, and levees, as well as nuclear power generating plants, may not be the target of attack in a period of internal armed conflict. Protocol II specifies that cultural assets and religious facilities shall be protected.

Protocol II does not, however, contain a formal prohibition of those types of weapons the use of which is prohibited in a period of armed conflict of an international nature (toxic chemical agents, defoliants, boobytraps, napalm, explosive bullets, *etc.*). In this connection we feel that it is appropriate to cite the well-known Martens qualification, according to which, in cases not provided for by corresponding international agreements, civilians and combatants shall remain under the protection and effect of principles of international law that proceed from established customs, from humanitarian principles, and from the demands of social conscience.

The granting-of-permission procedure of conduct of an operation to aid the civilian population, even in a case when it is experiencing excessive privations due to inadequate supply of goods that are quite important for its survival, such as food and medical supplies, does not fully meet the requirements of humanization of an internal armed conflict. Pursuant to Paragraph 2 of Article 18, the consent of the interested Party to Protocol II is required for the performance of these humanitarian operations, in spite of the fact that they are of an impartial nature and are carried out without any adverse distinction.

On the whole one can state that Protocol II, which has taken a step forward in comparison with Article 3 of the Geneva Conventions in the area of protection of the rights of various groups of persons affected by an armed conflict of a noninternational nature, has proven to be much less effective than Additional Protocol I in matters of articulating the rights of parties to a conflict to resort to various means and methods of conduct of combat operations, duly regulating the conduct of operations to render humanitarian, impartial aid to the civilian population, and further improving the international and internal mechanisms that guarantee observance of the corresponding provisions of the norms and principles of international law by the parties to a conflict.

Examination of the international-law aspects of internal armed conflicts would be incomplete without mentioning Article 4 of the International Covenant on Civil and Political Rights. According to this Article, during a state of emergency in a country, when the nation's existence is in peril (such a situation can quite possibly arise as a consequence of an internal armed conflict) and the existence of which is officially declared, states which are Parties to this Covenant may take measures departing from their obligations under this Covenant only "to the extent strictly required by the exigencies of the situation," with the proviso that such measures cannot be incompatible with their other obligations under international law and do not cause discrimination exclusively on the basis of race, skin color, sex, language, religion, or social origin.

It is prohibited thereby to depart from provisions that formally articulate the inalienable right of each individual to life, that prohibit all types of slavery and servitude, that prohibit torture, cruel treatment or treatment which demeans the individual, and that guarantee each individual the right to freedom of thought and belief, conviction and religion.

Within the context of the requirement contained in Article 4 that measures departing from the obligations under the Covenant be compatible with other obligations of states under international law, departures by states from the obligations articulated in both Article 3 of the Geneva Conventions and Additional Protocol II to these Conventions can be characterized as unlawful.

The provision of Article 4 that states may depart from their obligations under the Covenant only in proportion to the exigencies of the situation is of considerable importance. In practice, however, the uncertainty of the term "exigencies of the situation" makes possible extensive subjective interpretation of this term on the part of an interested state.

The question of the legal status of armed opposition by rebels against a central government is an extremely complex issue and without question requires further elaboration in international law. In particular, the questions of the procedure of recognition of an armed opposition as a belligerent and the consequences in international law that proceed from the fact of such recognition seems to be insufficiently clear. The most precise possible determination of that boundary (the sum total of legal facts) beyond which an armed conflict of a noninternational nature assumes the attributes of an international armed conflict is needed.

Considerable difficulties in determination of an internal armed conflict arise when the central government of a state on whose territory the conflict is taking place does not recognize the rebels as a "belligerent." In practice insurgents can count on recognition as a "belligerent" both by the central government and by third countries if they: a) possess a specific degree of organization; b) are led by agencies that bear responsibility for the actions of the rebels; c) have established power and authority over a portion of the territory of the state in question; and d) observe the laws and customs of war in their actions.

The question of recognition as a belligerent has to date not been uniformly resolved, either in international law doctrine or in the legislative practice of states. On the whole recognition as a generic concept constitutes a legal institution with a clearly marked political thrust. As regards recognition as a belligerent, it also contains a certain ideological thrust. It is precisely this factor that in the postwar period determined to a considerable degree the aggravation of confrontation between states with opposing socioeconomic systems.

However, an examination of the institution of the recognition of belligerency through the prism of the new political thinking, from the position of the primacy of international law in politics, enables one to classify it as one of the means of reducing the level of ideologization of intergovernmental relations in connection with internal social conflicts and preventing their internationalization by means of unlawful intervention in the internal affairs of a state.

The institution of recognition can perform this function if, first of all, the criteria of defining an internal conflict (civil war) gain general acceptance, criteria on the basis of which a central government and third countries will be obliged to recognize an armed opposition as a belligerent. The attributes of an international armed conflict as set forth in Article 1, Paragraph 1, of Additional Protocol II to the 1949 Geneva Conventions could constitute the basis of such criteria. Second, if such recognition results, in particular, in the following legal consequences:

> the renunciation by states of any and all intervention in the internal affairs of states on the territory of which a civil war is being fought, including armed intervention in a direct or indirect form, and further, the renunciation of the rendering of military-technical assistance to the parties to a conflict;
>
> responsibility by the parties to a conflict for actions contrary to standards of international law;
>
> conformity of domestic legislation and the actions of the law-enforcement agencies of the central government to the requirements of the standards of contemporary international law;
>
> capability by the opposition to take part in the negotiation process and to be a party to agreements aimed at a fair and just political settlement of a conflict;
>
> recognition as a belligerent should not give the opposition full status as a party to international law, inasmuch as, for example, by virtue of the principle of nonintervention, third states shall not enter into treaty or other relations with a domestic opposition entity that are aimed at rendering assistance to the latter in one form or another; and
>
> persons taking part in an armed struggle on the side of the opposition are under the protection of international law norms

applicable during a noninternational armed conflict.

This is in conformity with the standards of contemporary international law, and in particular Article 2(7) of the UN Charter, pursuant to which this organization may not "intervene in matters which are essentially within the domestic jurisdiction of any state." At the same time one should note that contemporary international law does not contain an exclusive list of matters possessing this attribute. In addition, in recent years there has been noted a tendency toward narrowing of the sphere of so-called "domestic jurisdiction" of states. Attesting to this, in particular, is the process of internationalization, which is encompassing areas of activity that have traditionally been considered domestic domains, such as military, human rights, environmental protection, *etc.* An internal armed conflict can hardly be totally and entirely removed from the domain of domestic jurisdiction of states. In connection with this it is appropriate to make reference to the first principle of the 1970 Declaration of Principles of International Law, which states that:

> Every State has the duty to refrain from organizing, instigating, assisting or participating in participating in acts of civil strife . . . in another State or acquiescing in organizing activities within its territory directed towards the commission of such acts.

An explicitly formulated provision in this regard is also contained in the above-mentioned Article 3 of Additional Protocol II to the 1949 Geneva Conventions.

Violation by states of the above-cited norms leads to internationalization of an internal armed conflict and to loss of its character as a noninternational conflict because of the increasing complexity of its structure, particularly in the case of armed intervention by a third party.

Radical and revolutionary changes within individual countries and societal structures have occurred and will occur in the future. The task facing international legal science and diplomatic practice with respect to ensuring international peace and security consists in the creation of political and legal mechanisms that, in the first place, would eliminate the possibility of these processes going beyond national borders and being transformed into a factor of aggravation of intergovernmental relations on a regional and global level. Second, they would ensure an international legal order that would promote effective resolution of existing and prevention of new armed conflicts, both of an international and noninternational character.

The new political thinking and action, thanks to which in recent years it has been possible to accomplish positive changes in settling conflict situations by peaceful means in a number of regions of the world, constitutes an important condition for successful accomplishment of this task.

4. LIMITATIONS ON NUCLEAR WEAPONS

Thomas Graham, Jr.
General Counsel, U.S. Arms Control and Disarmament Agency

The United States tested its first nuclear device in Alamogordo, New Mexico, in July of 1945 and then exploded nuclear weapons over Hiroshima and Nagasaki the next month at the close of World War II. This culminated the vast, secret wartime project that was code-named the Manhattan Project. It also exhausted the United States arsenal and no more weapons were fabricated for several years. None have been used in war since 1945.

The effort to control nuclear weapons began almost with their creation. The proposal in the Baruch Plan in 1946 to create an international authority to control nuclear weapons proved to be ill-fated with the onset of the Cold War. Thereafter, efforts have been by means of international regulation of national programs.

With the first test of a Soviet nuclear device in September of 1949, the nuclear weapons race, with the Cold War already well underway, began in earnest. After a lengthy debate, the United States decided to proceed with the "super weapon," the hydrogen bomb, first tested in November of 1952. The Soviet Union followed suit in August of 1953. The United Kingdom tested its first atomic weapon in 1952, France in 1960, and China in 1964. The five nuclear powers, coterminous with the five victorious powers in World War II, are also the permanent members of the Security Council of the United Nations. These five states are defined as the Nuclear Weapon States Parties pursuant to the terms of the Treaty on the Non-Proliferation of Nuclear Weapons (NPT), which provides that any state that manufactured and exploded a nuclear weapon or other nuclear explosive device before January 1, 1967, is to be so considered.

As the nuclear arms race intensified, more and more tests were conducted, principally by the United States and the Soviet Union. In March 1954, in the process of its testing program, the United States carried out a test at Bikini Atoll in the Pacific of a hydrogen device with a planned explosive yield of eight megatons, the equivalent of eight million tons of TNT. By contrast, the atomic bomb detonated over Hiroshima in 1945 had a yield of fourteen kilotons or the equivalent of 14,000 tons of TNT. However, the designers miscalculated and the device came in at fifteen megatons, thus causing the radioactive "fall out" from the test to appear far outside the quarantined area. A Japanese fishing boat, the *Lucky Dragon*, found itself in the path of this radioactive "fall out." The result was radiation poisoning causing serious illness to the crew. In another such incident, radioactive rain containing debris from a Soviet hydrogen bomb test fell on Japan. About the same time, articles began to appear in the press alleging that radioactive elements that were by-products of nuclear tests, in particular strontium-90, were being found in the food chain in all regions of the world. Environmental contamination and resultant genetic damage were widely feared. Thus began the worldwide pressure from the public to cease nuclear weapon tests.

A. Steps Toward a Nuclear Test Ban

Responding to this pressure, the first negotiations on an international agreement to end all nuclear tests began in the Subcommittee of Five (the United States, the United Kingdom, Canada, France and the Soviet Union) of the UN Disarmament Commission in May 1955. In 1956, the Democratic candidate for President of the United States, Adlai Stevenson, proposed a moratorium on nuclear tests as part of his campaign. He was severely criticized for this suggestion by the incumbent Eisenhower Administration, but by 1958 such a moratorium, declared by the United States, the Soviet Union, and the United Kingdom, was part of U.S. government policy.

In 1955, the Soviet Union had included the termination of nuclear weapons tests in its disarmament proposal. On June 14, 1957, the Soviet Union for the first time offered test ban proposals that included some form of international control. In March 1958, the Soviet Union announced that it would terminate nuclear testing and appealed to the other nuclear powers to take similar action. In the summer of 1958, the Geneva Conference of Experts (the United States, the United Kingdom, the Soviet Union, Canada, France, Poland, Czechoslovakia, and Romania) announced agreement on a comprehensive monitoring system for a nuclear test ban to include 170 to 180 land control posts and ten on ships.

The United States and the United Kingdom supported the Experts' report and announced that they were prepared to suspend nuclear weapon tests from the beginning of negotiations, and that suspension could continue on a year-to-year basis, provided that: the Soviet Union likewise refrained from testing; the control system agreed upon by the Experts was functioning; and satisfactory progress was being made on major arms control efforts. Soviet Premier Khrushchev reversed course, criticized the United States and the United Kingdom for linking a nuclear weapon test ban to other issues, and announced the Soviet Union was releasing itself from its moratorium and resumed testing. Nevertheless, by the end of 1958 all three nuclear testing states had entered into a testing moratorium.

This test moratorium lasted for approximately three years. In December 1959, President Eisenhower stated that the United States was no longer bound by the "voluntary" moratorium but would give notice of any plans to resume testing. The Soviet Union announced twice in 1959 that it would not resume testing if the Western powers did not. France conducted its first atomic test in February of 1960, two more in 1960, and a fourth in April of 1961. In May of 1961 the Soviet Union announced that it might have to resume testing if France continued to test. In August 1961 the Soviet Union stated that it would resume nuclear weapon testing, even though the United States and the United Kingdom had not, and there had been no further tests by France. Shortly thereafter the Soviet Union did resume testing with a massive test series culminating in the largest nuclear detonation conducted before or since, an estimated 59 megatons. The United States began testing again two weeks later. The moratorium had ended.

Negotiations in Geneva, Switzerland, among the then-nuclear-weapon powers, the United States, the United Kingdom, and the Soviet Union, on the termination of nuclear weapon tests began in earnest in October 1958, remaining in almost continuous session through January 1962. This followed consideration by the UN General Assembly and by the Subcommittee of Five (later Ten) of the UN Disarmament Commission. The principal issue was verification, more importantly how many on-site inspections on each Party's territory would be permitted in a year. The Soviet Union was willing to agree to three per year, the United States finally was willing to settle for seven. Also, the number of automatic seismic detection stations, the so-called "black boxes" that would be placed on the territory of each country, was a significant question.

The Three-Power negotiation ended in frustration in early 1962 with the Soviet Union claiming that "national means" of detection (that is, devices under the control of the verifying state outside the territory of the verified state) would be sufficient for the monitoring of a nuclear test ban. A new forum for the negotiations was the recently formed eighteen-nation Disarmament Committee created under the auspices of the UN General Assembly. Negotiations continued in this body in Geneva into 1963. However, the same basic issues, particularly the insistence of the Soviet Union that it would agree to no more than three on-site inspections per year on its territory, prevented any forward progress toward a treaty banning all nuclear weapon tests. In June 1963, President Kennedy announced in a commencement speech at American University in Washington that the three testing powers had agreed to resume meetings on the test ban in Moscow and that the United States would not be the first to resume testing in the atmosphere. This was taken to be a proposal to conclude a treaty banning nuclear tests in the atmosphere and all other environments except underground (the one environment where verification was an issue). Premier Khrushchev promptly accepted this proposal. Three-Power negotiations began in July in Moscow and were concluded in ten days.

Verification of atmospheric tests had never been a problem. The concern had always been over cheating through undetectable underground nuclear tests. Further, the public was exorcised about atmospheric tests and the damage they did to the environment. The Treaty Banning Nuclear Weapon Tests in the Atmosphere, in Outer Space and Under Water, known as the Limited Test Ban Treaty (LTBT), was signed on August 5, 1963, and entered into force later that year. Largely as a result of the LTBT (even though France and China have never joined), nuclear tests are no longer conducted anywhere except underground. France began testing in 1960 and for some years thereafter it tested in the atmosphere, but since 1974 has conducted its tests underground at its testing facilities in the South Pacific. The same was true of China, which began testing in 1964, but underground since 1980. The only other country that has conducted a declared nuclear test, India, conducted its sole test underground in 1974. An incident took place in 1979 over the South Atlantic that some believed was a nuclear test involving Israel or South Africa, but no conclusive determination of an actual test was ever made.

Although the LTBT ultimately had the effect of eliminating aboveground nuclear weapon testing, vigorous U.S. and Soviet test programs continued. Beginning in 1964, the United States, for example, conducted an extensive underground nuclear test program as part of the safeguards that Senator Jackson insisted upon as a condition of Senate advice and consent to ratification of the LTBT.

A complete abolition of nuclear testing, the first and for some the central goal of nuclear arms control, has proved to be illusive ever since. With the lessening of public pressure since nuclear tests were no longer conducted in the atmosphere, political support favoring a complete ban on nuclear testing slackened. In a bi-polar world dominated by the Cold War where the West relied upon nuclear deterrence to keep the peace, many viewed it as essential to continue to conduct nuclear tests in order to ensure the reliability of the stockpile of nuclear weapons, to improve existing types of nuclear weapons, and to develop new types to be associated with new types of delivery systems (*e.g.*, missiles and bombers).

In general, the LTBT has been successful as far as it went. It has well over 100 Parties. Its text is simple and straightforward. Only the first Article is substantive. Paragraph 1 of Article I commits each of the Parties "to prohibit, to prevent and not to carry out any nuclear weapon test explosion, or any other nuclear explosion" (thus making clear that no distinction should be made between nuclear devices detonated as part of a weapons program and those utilized for so called peaceful purposes, such as the construction of a canal):

> at any place under its jurisdiction or control: (a) in the atmosphere; . . . [in] outer space. . . , or under water. . . or [additionally] (b) in any other environment [*i.e.*, underground] if such explosion causes radioactive debris to be present outside of the territorial limits of the State under whose jurisdiction or control such an explosion is conducted.

Paragraph 2 prohibits the Parties from "causing, encouraging or . . . participating" in the carrying out of a nuclear test by another state which would contravene paragraph 1.

The prohibition in Paragraph 1(b) of conducting underground nuclear tests in a way that causes "radioactive debris" to be present outside the borders of the testing state has given rise to many charges of violations made by the United States and the Soviet Union against each other. In part this is a result of careless testing practices, primarily by the Soviet Union, concerning the depth of burial of the device being tested underground, and in part a result of a dispute between the two Parties over the proper interpretation of the word "debris." The United States has always taken the position that this term includes gaseous matter. The Soviet Union has interpreted the word to be limited to particulate matter or "fall out" (which was the principal concern of those who wished to ban atmospheric testing for reasons of environmental safety).

Desultory negotiations on a comprehensive test ban treaty continued in the 1960's and early 1970's in Geneva at the Conference of the Committee on Disarmament, the successor to the Eighteen-Nation Disarmament Committee. The United States and the Soviet Union had in effect agreed to disagree on whether on-site inspection was needed to verify a ban on underground nuclear tests. The Soviet Union insisted that remote seismic stations and national means of verification were sufficient to detect any explosion and to distinguish nuclear tests from natural phenomena such as earthquakes.

In 1974, a new effort was undertaken to limit underground nuclear testing. President Nixon was searching for a new nuclear arms treaty that would be signed at the forthcoming Summit in Moscow in July of 1974. Scrutiny turned to the nuclear testing area. The alternatives considered were a limit on the number of underground nuclear tests or a limit on their yield or explosive power. The U.S. government decided to propose a yield limitation of 150 kilotons, slightly over ten times the yield of the Hiroshima explosion. The United States judged that such a limit would not hinder its basic program to support nuclear deterrence and would limit the Soviet Union high yield programs associated with their very large, or "heavy," intercontinental ballistic missiles. The proposal to limit underground nuclear weapon tests to 150 kilotons was made to the Soviets and a treaty codifying this constraint was negotiated at Moscow in June of 1974.

The Treaty Between the United States of America and the Union of Soviet Socialist Republics on the Limitation of Underground Nuclear Weapon Tests, known as the Threshold Test Ban Treaty (TTBT), was signed in Moscow on July 3, 1974. The first Article contains the operative provision, limiting underground nuclear tests to 150 kilotons after March 31, 1976. This date was chosen to allow time to negotiate a companion treaty limiting underground nuclear tests for peaceful purposes which were regarded as indistinguishable. The Protocol to the TTBT calls for the exchange of certain verification information and also defines nuclear weapon tests as those conducted at designated nuclear weapon test sites.

The second Article provides that the TTBT will be verified by national technical means of verification. The United States believed—in 1974—that the 150 kiloton limit was high enough so as to be verifiable by remote seismic facilities under the control of the verifying Party. This belief was to be severely tested in future years, although the technical problems associated with the verification of a nuclear yield limitation were recognized to some degree by the Parties at the time. During the negotiations, the Soviet Union suggested a "mistakes" understanding concerning occasional, minor, unintended breaches. Discussions of such an understanding were held in the fall of 1974 after signature of the TTBT and again in 1976. The understanding, as finally agreed upon, stated that the Parties would attempt to comply fully with the terms of the Treaty. However, uncertainties did exist with predicting the precise yields of nuclear weapon tests. Thus, one or two "slight, unintended breaches per year would not be considered a violation" but would, upon request, be the subject of consultations. This understanding, sent to the Senate as part of the transmittal documents accompanying the Treaty, in effect sanctions one or two minor violations of the 150 kiloton limit by each Party each year.

The third Article of the TTBT calls for the negotiation of an associated agreement to limit underground nuclear explosions for peaceful purposes. Immediately after the conclusion of the TTBT negotiations, the work on this companion treaty began. The Treaty Between the United

States of America and the Union of Soviet Socialist Republics on the Limitation of Underground Nuclear Explosions for Peaceful Purposes, known as the Peaceful Nuclear Explosions Treaty (PNE Treaty), was signed on May 28, 1976.

The PNE Treaty applies the 150 kiloton limit of the Threshold Test Ban Treaty to all nuclear explosions not conducted at designated weapon test sites. By definition, these are underground nuclear explosions for peaceful purposes. The PNE Treaty also places a 1.5 megaton limit on all group nuclear explosions, defined as nuclear explosions conducted at an interval of five seconds or less within a short distance of one another. Group explosions were permitted in 1976 because the Soviet Government still believed that nuclear explosives could be used for public works projects, such as digging canals. Verification of the PNE Treaty is by national technical means, supplemented pursuant to the Protocol to this Treaty by on-site inspection since (unlike weapon tests) many peaceful nuclear explosions are conducted in areas not well known as far as their seismic qualities are concerned. Also special, very intrusive on-site measures are provided for in the Protocol whenever the aggregate of a group explosion exceeds 150 kilotons. The Treaty also creates a Joint Consultative Commission to address questions of compliance with the PNE Treaty and, by implication, with the TTBT. This body is now the Bilateral Consultative Commission pursuant to the new Protocol to the TTBT.

Since the PNE Treaty was not completed by March 31, 1976, the stated date of operation of the TTBT, both signatories issued statements that it was in their interest to abide by the 150 kiloton testing limit of the TTBT until the completion of the negotiations of the PNE Treaty. This exchange of statements had larger implications than were foreseen in 1976. The two Treaties were sent to the Senate in July 1976. The Committee held hearings in 1977 and reported them to the full Senate by a wide margin. However, they became involved in the acrimonious debate over the abortive 1977-1979 attempt of the Carter Administration to negotiate a comprehensive test ban treaty and neve came to a vote in the Senate. The TTB and PNE Treaties were returned to Committee at the end of the Congress in 1978, where they languished for twelve years.

Successive Administrations, relying on the 1976 statement, continued to informally observe the 150 kiloton ceiling. The 1961 Act of Congress which established the Arms Control and Disarmament Agency provides that the Executive Branch is not empowered to enter into an international agreement that would "obligate" the United States to:

> disarm or to reduce or to limit the Armed Forces or armaments of the United States, except pursuant to the treaty making power . . . or unless authorized by further affirmative legislation. . . .

Informal observance of the TTBT and the PNET was never challenged within the United States. However, informal observance of the SALT I Interim Agreement, discussed below, which began upon its expiration in 1977, was immediately challenged in the U.S. Senate, albeit ultimately ineffectively. Likewise, informal observance of the SALT II Treaty, also discussed below, came under challenge as well. Subsequently, with respect to the testing Treaties, the two Parties expressed their adherence to the obligation in Article 18 of the Vienna Convention on the Law of Treaties not to defeat the "object and purpose" of a treaty pending ratification.

After 1976, in reliance on data from remote seismic stations, the United States believed that an increasing number of Soviet nuclear weapon tests exceeded the 150 kiloton limit. Further, dissatisfaction grew within the United States with reliance on national means of verification of the two Treaties because of broad uncertainties. It argued that remote seismic monitoring could measure underground nuclear explosions only by a factor of two. This meant that if a given event registered at 150 kilotons, it was equally likely that the actual yield was at any point between 75 and 300 kilotons.

In November of 1987 the United States and the Soviet Union began new negotiations to reach agreement on additional verification provisions that would make it possible for the United States to ratify the two Treaties. New protocols to replace the existing TTBT and PNET Protocols were developed that provided for intrusive on-site verification, including the down hole yield measuring system that the United States uses at its Nevada Test Site as well as on-site seismic monitoring. These two Protocols were signed on June 1, 1990. Advice and consent to ratification of the Treaties with the two new Protocols was given by the U.S. Senate in September of 1990 by a vote of 98-0. The Supreme Soviet approved the two Treaties shortly thereafter. The TTB and PNE Treaties finally entered into force in the fall of 1990, approximately fifteen years after their signature.

Therefore, thirty-five years after negotiations on limiting nuclear weapon tests began, a comprehensive test ban treaty remains elusive. Through October 24, 1990, the United States has conducted 929, and the Soviet Union 714 nuclear tests. Achieving a negotiated cessation of nuclear testing remains for some the basic goal of nuclear arms control and in a sense the many other efforts to prohibit nuclear weapons in various environments and to limit their delivery systems could be described as derivative of this objective. A comprehensive test ban is seen by others as less important as it is possible for additional states to acquire a nuclear capability (at least for atomic if not hydrogen weapons) without testing. And there remains the question of ensuring the reliability of nuclear weapons through testing as long as they are relied upon to keep the peace. Nevertheless, a decision whether or not to seek a comprehensive test ban by the 1995 Non-Proliferation Treaty Conference, which will determine for how long in the future the Treaty will be extended, will be an important political issue for many states. A number of countries attempted unsuccessfully to conclude a comprehensive test ban by amendment of the LTBT at a LTBT Amendment Conference called by the Parties in January 1991.

B. Efforts to Prevent Nuclear Proliferation

In the years immediately after the conclusion of the Limited Test Ban Treaty in 1963, arms control efforts turned to prohibiting the spread of nuclear weapons to environments where they were not yet found.

The Antarctic Treaty of 1959 had prohibited military bases, fortifications and maneuvers as well as nuclear explosions on that Continent. In January 1967, the negotiation of the Treaty on Principles Governing the Activities of States in the Exploration and Use of Outer Space, Including the Moon and Other Celestial Bodies, known as the Outer Space Treaty, was completed. The Outer Space Treaty followed the precedent of the Antarctic Treaty in prohibiting the establishment of military bases and fortifications as well as military maneuvers and weapon testing in outer space. It went a step further, however, in that in Article IV it prohibited the stationing of nuclear weapons in outer space as well as placing such weapons in orbit around the earth. It is worth noting that later, in 1967, the Soviet Union conducted a test of its fractional orbit bombardment system, a delivery system for nuclear weapons that utilized a fractional orbit. Because a complete orbit was not utilized, the United States judged this as not being inconsistent with the Outer Space Treaty.

In 1968, a major step in nuclear arms control was achieved with the signing of the Treaty on the Non-Proliferation of Nuclear Weapons. It entered into force on March 5, 1970. Under the NPT, a Nuclear Weapon State Party is defined as one of the five states that had manufactured and exploded a nuclear weapon or other nuclear explosive device before January 1, 1967, that is, the United States, the United Kingdom, the Soviet Union, France and China. Non-Nuclear Weapon States Parties are all the other Parties. Article I of the NPT provides that each of the Nuclear Weapon States Parties undertakes not to transfer nuclear weapons or any other nuclear explosive devices "to any recipient whatsoever" nor to assist any state in acquiring nuclear weapons or any other nuclear explosive devices. Article II contains the companion commitment that no Non-Nuclear Weapon State Party will receive nuclear weapons or other nuclear explosive devices from any other state, manufacture such devices itself, or seek or receive assistance in developing such devices from any other state.

These obligations do not run just between Parties. A Nuclear Weapon

State Party may not transfer a nuclear device to any other state whether or not it is a Party to the NPT, and likewise a Non-Nuclear Weapon State Party cannot receive such a device from any other state. Another point to note is that the definition of a Nuclear Weapon State Party would exclude India, should India ever become a party to the NPT, because it tested its device in 1974. Further, it might be asked, what if Israel should ever decide to become a Party? It is suspected by many of possessing nuclear weapons even though it has never conducted a test.

Article III is a central part of the NPT, providing for "full scope" safeguards by the International Atomic Energy Agency (IAEA) of all declared nuclear facilities of Non-Nuclear Weapon State Parties. This is the all-important verification regime of the Treaty.

Article IV of the NPT contains the commitment of the Nuclear Weapon State Parties to share the technology for the peaceful uses of nuclear energy. Article VI provides that the Parties undertake to pursue negotiations in good faith toward an early cessation of the nuclear arms race. At NPT Review Conferences held every five years pursuant to Article VIII, this provision is often argued by Non-Nuclear Weapon States Parties to be a commitment by the Nuclear Weapon States Parties to a comprehensive nuclear test ban treaty in exchange for the commitment of the Non-Nuclear Weapon States Parties not to possess nuclear weapons. Article VII of the Treaty preserves the right of the Parties to negotiate nuclear-free areas (such as the regime established by the Treaty for the Prohibition of Nuclear Weapons in Latin America signed the year before on February 14, 1967).

Like the Antarctic and Outer Space Treaties, the Treaty for the Prohibition of Nuclear Weapons in Latin America is designed to establish a nuclear-free zone in the Latin American area, and when it comes fully into force will include adjacent ocean areas as well. Unlike the NPT, it makes a distinction between nuclear weapons and nuclear devices for peaceful purposes, although the latter are strictly regulated. It has two Protocols. Protocol I applies the Treaty regime to territories under the jurisdiction of a state located outside the Latin American area. This Protocol has been signed by the relevant states—the United States, the United Kingdom, the Netherlands, and France. All have ratified except France. Protocol II is a vehicle by which the five nuclear-weapon states agree to respect the Treaty regime. All are Parties to this Protocol.

The Treaty has an elaborate structure for the application of its obligations. The Treaty Zone only comes into full effect after all Latin American States are Parties to the Treaty, both Protocols are fully subscribed, and IAEA safeguards have been agreed to be applied by all Latin American states. Such safeguards are also required of all Non-Nuclear Weapon States Parties by Article III of the NPT. For an individual Latin American State to be actually obligated (even if it is a Party), it must not only sign and ratify, but must also formally declare that it waives the above requirements and is prepared to assume the obligations of the Treaty. Only Cuba has not signed the Treaty. However, only a few Latin American states have negotiated IAEA safeguards and some of the major Latin American states have either not ratified or not waived.

The next treaty in this series is the Treaty on the Prohibition of the Emplacement of Nuclear Weapons and Other Weapons of Mass Destruction on the Seabed and the Ocean Floor and in the Subsoil Thereof, or the Seabed Arms Control Treaty. This Treaty was signed in February 1971, and entered into force on May 18, 1972. It provides in Article I a prohibition on the emplacement of nuclear weapons or associated structures, launching installations, or other facilities designed for storing, testing, or using of nuclear weapons on the seabed beyond a zone coterminous with the twelve mile territorial limit. Article III permits observation of activities on the seabed for purposes of verification, with the right of an appeal to the UN Security Council if consultations concerning a suspected violation should fail.

Finally, the South Pacific Nuclear-Free Zone Treaty, known as the Treaty of Raratonga, which established a nuclear-free zone in the South Pacific region, was signed in February, 1986, and entered into force on December 11, 1990. Under the Treaty, Parties undertake not to acquire nuclear weapons, assist another state to acquire them, permit their stationing on their territory, or test a nuclear explosive device or assist another state to do so. There are three Protocols to the Treaty open to the nuclear weapon states. Protocol 1 would have the Parties to the Protocol not manufacture, station, or test nuclear explosives on the territory of a Party to the Treaty. Protocol 2 provides an undertaking by the parties to the Protocol that they will not use nuclear explosives against Parties to the Treaty. Protocol 3 provides that its Parties will not test such explosives anywhere in the South Pacific zone. None of the Protocols is fully subscribed.

The Outer Space Treaty permits visits to national installations to verify the constraints of the Treaty, as does the Antarctic Treaty. The NPT addresses the verification problem by means of the intrusive IAEA safeguards required by Article III of all Non-Nuclear Weapon States Parties. The Nuclear Weapon States Parties to the NPT have signed voluntary agreements with the IAEA permitting certain facilities to be subject to safeguards. The Treaty on the Prohibition of Nuclear Weapons in Latin America utilizes a generally stated verification regime as well as IAEA safeguards.

C. SALT I—The ABM Treaty and Initial Limits on Strategic Offensive Weapons

In 1969 negotiations began on the central delivery systems of strategic nuclear weapons of the United States and the Soviet Union. The efforts were bilateral and conducted in secrecy.

The Treaty Between the United States of America and the Union of Soviet Socialist Republics on the Limitation of Anti-Ballistic Missile Systems (ABM Treaty) is the most important of the two principal documents negotiated during the SALT I negotiations. The other is the Interim Agreement Between the United States of America and the Union of Soviet Socialist Republics on Certain Measures with Respect to the Limitation of Strategic Offensive Arms (Interim Agreement). SALT I was the first attempt through bilateral negotiations to attempt to limit the delivery vehicles of nuclear weapons. The objective of the SALT I negotiations was to place initial limits on the strategic nuclear offensive and defensive systems of the two superpowers.

There are three basic types of strategic offensive nuclear weapons. First, intercontinental ballistic missile systems (ICBMs) are land-based ballistic missiles with a sufficient range to enable them to strike targets at intercontinental distances. (As defined in an Agreed Statement associated with the Interim Agreement, ICBMs are missiles with a range in excess of the shortest distance between the northeastern border of the continental United States and the northwestern border of the continental Soviet Union, or as later defined in the Treaty Between the United States of America and the Union of Soviet Socialist Republics on the Limitation of Strategic Offensive Arms (SALT II Treaty), more than 5500 kilometers.) Second, submarine launched ballistic missiles (SLBMs), although of shorter range and launched from under the sea, are considered capable of striking intercontinental targets. Third, certain heavy bombers are recognized by the two sides as being capable of operating at intercontinental distances. Starting in the mid-1970's, long-range cruise missiles, highly accurate air-breathing systems that can be based at sea, on the ground or in the air, were a fourth type added to this list of strategic nuclear delivery vehicles.

On the defensive side, the key systems are anti-ballistic missiles (ABMs) that are designed to intercept strategic ballistic missiles (ICBMs and SLBMs) in flight trajectory. (Air defense systems, including surface-to-air missiles (SAMs), have tactical and conventional in addition to strategic and nuclear roles, and have not been the subject of direct limitations.)

The SALT I negotiations began in November 1969 and culminated at the Moscow Summit in May 1972. The two Agreements were signed on May 26 and entered into force on October 3, 1972. As the negotiations evolved, it became apparent that a relatively complete approach to strategic defense, but only a partial coverage for strategic offense, was possible. There was some discussion of a prohibition on multiple independently targetable reentry vehicles (MIRVs), which are devices carried on ballistic missiles capable of directing a number of nuclear warheads at widely dispersed targets. MIRV systems first began to be deployed by the United States in 1970. Negotiation of such a ban, however, was never seriously attempted. The Soviet Union commenced testing MIRVs in 1975. With the advent of MIRVs on both sides, a first-strike capable of destroying the other side's strategic weapons became theoretically conceivable.

Pursuant to the terms of the Interim Agreement, the United States was permitted launchers of 1054 deployed ICBMs and 656 deployed SLBMs, and the Soviet Union launchers of 1608 deployed ICBMs and 740 deployed SLBMs. The limitations on ICBMs were achieved indirectly by a ban on construction of additional fixed land-based ICBM silo launchers in Article I. The Interim Agreement and later the SALT II Treaty utilized missile launchers as the unit of account because the agreements as a result could be verified by national technical means. This term "national technical means of verification" includes photographic satellites that the Soviets had claimed, in the 1960's, were violative of international law, but which were implicitly recognized in the ABM Treaty and the Interim Agreement as operating in accordance with "generally recognized principles of international law". Both agreements contained further commitments not to interfere with nor deliberately conceal activities from such satellites. Launchers were also considered appropriate limits because neither ICBM silo launchers nor SLBM launch tubes were viewed as reloadable with sufficient speed to affect the outcome of a strategic exchange. Unlike the treatment of ICBMs, the SLBM limitations were explicitly set forth in the Protocol to the Interim Agreement. The initial limits, of 656 and 740, respectively, could be increased if certain older ICBM launchers (*i.e.*, Titan II for the United States and SS-7s and SS-8s for the Soviet Union) were dismantled in what was described as a one-way freedom to mix.

Article II provided a ban on the conversion of "light" ICBM launchers, or certain older ICBM launchers, to modern "heavy" ICBM launchers, thus fixing the number of deployed modern heavy ICBMs at zero for the United States and 308 for the Soviet Union. The sides were never able to negotiate a legal definition of heavy ICBMs—which, amidst much controversy, was left for SALT II—but the only modern heavy ICBM in existence in 1972 was the Soviet SS-9 missile system. In addition, as indicated, each side had a number of certain older ICBMs, defined as those deployed prior to 1964. These were the 54 Titan II missiles for the United States and 210 SS-7 and SS-8 missiles for the Soviet Union.

Pursuant to the terms of Article III of the Interim Agreement and the Protocol, these older missile launchers could be exchanged for SLBM launchers. However, President Nixon, at the Summit, gave General Secretary Brezhnev a secret side letter stating that the United States had no plans to exchange its launchers of Titan missiles for SLBM launchers.

Thus, the numbers were 1000 ICBM launchers (plus 54 old Titan IIs) and 656 SLBM launchers for the United States and 1398 ICBM launchers and 950 SLBM launchers for the Soviet Union. The Interim Agreement had a five-year term. The United States considered acceptable the Soviet Union's approximately 50 percent advantage in strategic missile launchers in view of two factors: the ongoing U.S. MIRV deployment program, and the fact that the Interim Agreement did not limit heavy bombers where the United States had a significant lead (approximately 450 to 150). Land-mobile ICBM launchers were not limited by the Interim Agreement; the United States made a unilateral statement at the close of the negotiations that it "would consider the development of land-mobile ICBM launchers during the period of the Interim Agreement as inconsistent with the objectives of that Agreement." Neither Party deployed land-mobile ICBM launchers during the term of the Interim Agreement.

The reason for the indirect delineation of numbers in the Interim Agreement was Soviet unwillingness to disclose or even discuss its numbers of deployed ICBM and SLBM launchers. While the development and acceptance of the legality of photographic satellites under the rubric of "national technical means" made SALT I possible, this Soviet penchant for secrecy in military matters under negotiation made the agreements more controversial in the United States.

The achievement of equal numbers of treaty-limited strategic systems, a definition of heavy ICBMs, some limits on MIRVs, and the attainment of an agreed statement on data all became major objectives for the United States in the SALT II negotiations. There was also concern in the United States over the greater size and lifting capability, or "throw-weight," of Soviet missiles once the Soviet Union began to deploy MIRVs due to the theoretical capability of Soviet ICBMs to carry many more warheads than U.S. ICBMs. This disparity was due to the fact that the United States preferred to concentrate on light, miniaturized systems from the earliest days of the ICBM programs whereas the Soviet Union preferred larger, more crude systems. "Throw-weight" was a controversial issue during SALT II, but even in these negotiations only initial steps were taken—a definition of heavy ICBMs in terms of throw-weight (and launch-weight) and a ban on increasing the throw-weight of heavy ICBMs, thus preventing any further growth in capability of such missiles. Negotiations to eliminate the "throw-weight" disparity were left to the Strategic Arms Reduction Talks, or START, negotiations in the 1980's.

The ABM Treaty, unlike the Interim Agreement, is an agreement of indefinite duration. It originally limited strategic defense systems and components in ABM deployment areas to two sites for each Party. For purposes of the Treaty, the three current ABM components are listed as ABM launchers, ABM missiles, and ABM radars. Article III limits the number of ABM interceptor missile launchers to 100 per site, or 200 for each Party, and contains strict limits on the ABM radars deployed at each site. One site may be located to defend the national capital and one may be located to defend one ICBM deployment area. The two sites must be at least 1300 kilometers apart to prevent them from working together to create a base for a national or territorial defense.

Article I of the ABM Treaty includes the fundamental obligation not to create an ABM defense of the national territory nor the base for such a defense, and the creation of an ABM defense of a region is prohibited except for such deployment as is permitted by Article III. An Agreed Statement provides that if ABM systems based on future technology ("other physical principles" in the terms of the agreed statement referred to as Agreed Statement D), such as lasers or particle beams, should be created in the future, such systems cannot be deployed absent amendment of the Treaty. Article IV provides an exception to the deployment limitations of Article III for ABM launchers at ABM test ranges.

Article V of the ABM Treaty prohibits the development, testing, and deployment of ABM systems or components that are not fixed land-based (*i.e.*, sea-based, air-based, space-based or mobile land-based). This sweeping prohibition on ABM systems or components except fixed land-based is designed to reinforce the constraints of Article I.

Further to the same objective are two constraints in Article VI. One prohibits the upgrade, or improvement, of air defense systems to ABM capability. The second, in conjunction with another Agreed Statement applicable to the deployment of large phased array radars (the relevant modern technology), covers radars that are not ABM radars but that are deployed in the future for the purpose of early warning of ballistic missile attack (as opposed to an ABM role of directing missiles to intercept the incoming weapons). They must be located on the periphery of the national territory and oriented outward so as not to contribute to the creation of a base for a nationwide defense by means of the location of large ABM-capable radars throughout the country. This provision was the subject of a much-discussed Soviet violation when a large phased array radar with early warning capabilities began to be constructed near Krasnoyarsk in Siberia. It is neither located on the periphery nor is it oriented outward. After years of argumentation the Soviet Union has finally agreed to dismantle the radar in the near future.

The objective of the ABM Treaty, in essence, is to eliminate the deployment of a large-scale ABM strategic defense, making each Party a hostage of the other. The ABM Treaty was amended in 1974 by a Protocol reducing the two permitted deployment areas for each Party to one, thereby reducing strategic defense deployments to a level just short of abolition. The entire structure of the ABM Treaty is designed to interact so that all provisions operate so as to reinforce the fundamental goal set forth in Article I.

In 1985, an interpretation dispute arose within the U.S. Government over the meaning of Article V, Paragraph 1, of the ABM Treaty, which provides that "Each Party undertakes not to develop, test or deploy ABM systems or components which are sea-based, air-based, space-based, or mobile land-based."

One side of this debate argued that a "broad" interpretation of the language of this provision is legally permissible. Such an interpretation would limit the application of this provision to ABM technology actually in being at the time of signature of the Treaty in 1972. Thus, it was argued that the only limitation on ABM systems employing future technology is the deployment ban in Agreed Statement D. In this view, the definition of ABM systems set forth in Article II, Paragraph 1, limits all the subsequent Articles of the Treaty to existing technology.

Article II, Paragraph 1, the key definitional section of the Treaty, is critical to this dispute. It reads as follows: "For the purpose of this Treaty, an ABM system is a system to counter strategic ballistic missiles or their elements in flight trajectory, currently consisting of: (a) ABM interceptor missiles . . . (b) ABM launchers . . . and (c) ABM radars . . . ." Further, Agreed Statement D provides that:

> In order to insure fulfillment of the obligation not to deploy ABM systems and their components except as provided in Article III of the Treaty, the Parties agree that in the event ABM systems based on other physical principles and including components capable of substituting for ABM interceptor missiles, ABM launchers or ABM radars are created in the future, specific limitations on such systems and their components would be subject to discussion in accordance with Article XIII and agreement in accordance with Article XIV of the Treaty.

The "broad" interpretation argument is that there was no agreement in 1972 to limit the testing of ABM devices that use future technologies. Thus the "currently consisting of" language in Article II means that the list of ABM components in Article II is intended to be complete, and thus all subsequent Articles limit only ABM launchers, ABM missiles, and ABM radars. Therefore, there are no Treaty limits on ABM systems based on future systems except in Agreed Statement D, which contains only a deployment limitation. Because there are no testing limits on ABM systems based on future technology, the testing of future technology ABM systems, whether based on the ground, in the air, or in space, is allowed.

The other side of this debate adhered to the traditional interpretation of Article V, which was that it applies to all types of mobile ABM systems, regardless of technology. This came to be known as the "narrow" interpretation. Those arguing for this interpretation asserted that the "broad" interpretation is inconsistent with the structure and purposes of the Treaty, starting with the basic obligation of Article I not to deploy a nationwide ABM defense or to "provide a base" for such a defense. Future ABM systems based on technology such as lasers and particle beams are capable of much wider area coverage than 1972 vintage ABM launchers, ABM missiles, and ABM radars. Article V, containing a ban on development and testing, as well as on deployment, of all mobile-type systems thereby reinforces Article I.

The proponents of the "narrow" or "traditional" interpretation maintain that an ABM system is defined as a system to counter strategic ballistic missiles or their elements in flight trajectory, with the Treaty noting that it only *currently* consists of ABM launchers, ABM missiles, and ABM radars. Future ABM systems were contemplated by both Parties to be included within this definition of an ABM system. Agreed Statement D reinforces the limitations on the deployment of fixed land-based ABM systems that are set forth in Article III and is intended to ensure that these strict limits cannot be undermined by the deployment at one of these sites of, for example, ABM laser interceptors covering a wide area in lieu of conventional ABM interceptor missiles.

This dispute was never resolved. The U.S. Executive Branch adopted the "broad" interpretation, but the U.S. Congress enacted legislation that in effect has denied any funding for tests inconsistent with the "narrow" or "traditional" interpretation. After this debate became public the Soviet Union publicly stated that it adhered to the "narrow" interpretation.

D. SALT II—The Treaty That Was Never Ratified

The SALT II Treaty has as its objective the completion of the limitations on strategic offensive systems begun with SALT I. The Interim Agreement had, as have all arms control agreements beginning with the Limited Test Ban Treaty (excepting only the Outer Space Treaty, which permits withdrawal on one-year notice for any reason), a provision permitting withdrawal if an "extraordinary event" related to the subject matter of the Agreement should "jeopardize the supreme interests" of a Party. At the close of SALT I, the United States stated that if a more complete agreement limiting strategic offensive arms were not achieved in the five year term of the Interim Agreement, U.S. supreme interests could be jeopardized. The more complete agreement referred to in this statement was what the SALT II Treaty was intended to be.

When the SALT II Treaty had not been completed by 1977, the Interim Agreement, as indicated above, was extended indefinitely by parallel policy statements of the Parties at the time of its expiration. This arrangement, unlike the similar step taken with the Threshold Test Ban Treaty, was objected to by many Senators as being violative of U.S. domestic law, specifically Section 33 of the Arms Control and Disarmament Act. After a tumultuous debate, the Senate passed a resolution approving the informal extension of the Interim Agreement. The SALT II Treaty, which was signed in 1979 but never ratified, was similarly observed through an informal arrangement, this time by an exchange of oral statements between the U.S. Secretary of State and the Soviet Foreign Minister. The United States said it would not "undercut" existing agreements. This informal arrangement for both agreements was terminated by President Reagan in 1986, citing Soviet violations, some six months after the SALT II Treaty would have expired had it been ratified and nine years after the expiration of the Interim Agreement. Since 1986 there have been no limitations on strategic offensive arms, although the START negotiations, which began in 1982 and were suspended in 1983, resumed in 1985.

The SALT II Treaty was signed in June of 1979, two years after the formal expiration of the Interim Agreement. By its terms it was to continue in force until the end of 1985. It implemented the Vladivostok Accord of 1974 in which the United States and Soviet Union agreed on the principle of equal aggregate limitations on ICBMs, SLBMs, and heavy bombers. The SALT II Treaty established an aggregate limitation of 2400 ICBM launchers, SLBM launchers, and heavy bombers. This aggregate was to be reduced to 2250 eighteen months after entry into force. Consistent with the Vladivostok Accord, limitations were placed on multiple warhead systems ultimately to include heavy bombers carrying long range (in excess of 600 kilometers) air-launched cruise missiles and launchers of ICBMs and SLBMs equipped for MIRVs. The Treaty established a limit of 1320 on all such multiple warhead systems, 1200 on launchers of ICBMs and SLBMs equipped for MIRVs, and 820 on launchers of ICBMs equipped for MIRVs (viewed as the most threatening of strategic systems).

A definition of heavy ICBMs was achieved in terms of launch-weight and throw-weight. A heavy ICBM is an ICBM greater in either of these two measures than the largest light ICBM, by now the Soviet SS-19, a MIRVed, substantially larger and much more capable replacement for the less accurate single warhead SS-11, which had been the largest light ICBM in 1972. The provision codifying the Soviet monopoly in heavy ICBMs was carried over from the Interim Agreement. In Paragraph 7 of Article IV, a cap in terms of launch-weight and throw-weight was placed on missile growth beyond the parameters of the SS-18, a heavy ICBM that was a MIRVed and much more capable replacement for the SS-9.

Two important verification counting rules were achieved. By national technical means, it is not possible to determine how many individual warheads, below a maximum capacity for a particular type, are actually deployed on specific missiles tested with MIRVs. Likewise, it is not possible to determine what type of missile, MIRVed or non-MIRVed, is actually deployed in a particular launcher. Hence, the "type" rules set forth in Paragraph 5 of Article II of the Treaty, *i.e.*, once a missile of a particular type has been tested with MIRVs, all missiles of that type are considered to be equipped with MIRVs, and once a launcher of a particular type has had a missile equipped with MIRVs flight tested from it, all launchers of that type shall be included in the MIRV launcher aggregate total, regardless of the type of missile that is actually deployed in any such missile launcher.

Article IV of the SALT II Treaty contains many provisions that are important to the operation of the Treaty. Paragraph 3 is the above-mentioned provision codifying the Soviet monopoly of heavy ICBMs and indirectly fixing their number for the Soviet Union at 308. This provision takes the form of a ban on the conversion of a launcher of a light ICBM to a launcher of a heavy ICBM and makes necessary the definition of heavy ICBMs found in Paragraph 7 of Article II. Article IV also contains the upper limit, in terms of launch-weight and throw-weight, on heavy ICBMs. In Paragraph 8, there is a prohibition on the conversion of medium range ballistic missiles to ICBMs, which is accompanied by a Common Understanding banning the Soviet SS-16 ICBM. Since the Soviet SS-20 medium range ballistic missile was simply the first two of the three missile stages of the SS-16 ICBM, this provision was designed to prevent breakout from the SALT II limitations by the deployment of a third stage on the unregulated SS-20. A Protocol to the Salt II Treaty of three years duration prohibited the flight-testing of land-mobile ICBMs and the deployment of land-mobile ICBM launchers, after which, pursuant to the Treaty, such systems would be permitted and included in the limitations unless further constraints should be agreed. The Protocol also provided for a three-year ban on the deployment of long-range sea- and ground-launched cruise missiles.

Article IV of the Treaty, in Paragraphs 9 through 11, contains elaborate provisions designed to limit growth in ICBM capability. Each Party is limited to one new type of light ICBM, and new type is measured by a change in the propellant (liquid to solid) or a change (of more than five percent) in the length, largest diameter, or throw-weight of the missile.

The one permitted new type can have no more than ten reentry vehicles and each existing type of ICBM cannot be tested with more than the maximum number of reentry vehicles with which it had been tested. These numbers are listed for each ICBM type. An exception is made for the U.S. Minuteman III, which was tested with seven very small reentry vehicles and it is capped at three. In addition, there is a prohibition on the testing or deploying of an SLBM with more than fourteen re-entry vehicles.

The SALT II Treaty was to be verified by national technical means. In a Common Understanding associated with Article XV, encoding (encryption) of telemetry signals from an ICBM to the ground during a test flight that impedes (not prevents, but impedes) verification is prohibited. The Treaty also contains in Article XII a prohibition on the circumvention of the limitations of the Treaty through a third state or states or in any other manner. This provision, in a vague and general way, was designed to reduce the potential of the United States to evade the limitations of the Treaty by transferring systems limited by the Treaty to its Allies, although the United States made clear its existing programs of cooperation would not be affected.

The SALT II Treaty was never ratified and strategic offensive nuclear arms negotiations were begun again in 1982 under the rubric of the START negotiations. Verification of START will be not only by national technical means but also by extensive and intrusive on-site inspection. The limitations will be placed on warheads directly as well as on missiles and associated launchers. These are legacies of the arms control breakthrough codified in the INF Treaty described below.

E. INF Treaty—Total Elimination and Verification Breakthrough

The negotiations on Intermediate Range Nuclear Forces (INF) were begun in November 1981. The principal U.S. objective of these negotiations was the limitation of the growing Soviet modern, highly accurate road-mobile, MIRVed, medium-range ballistic missile force (the SS-20s), which replaced its older, less accurate, single-warhead, silo-based, medium-range ballistic missiles (SS-4s and SS-5s). The Soviets finally agreed to eliminate all SS-20s (as well as all SS-4s and SS-5s) in exchange for elimination of the U.S. Pershing II missiles and the U.S. Ground Launched Cruise Missiles, which began to be deployed in Europe in 1983 to counter the SS-20. These deployments were made pursuant to a NATO decision in 1979 to deploy the missiles unless, by 1983, an arms control alternative to deployment could be found. The INF Treaty contains a ban on intermediate-range missiles (ranges 1000 to 5500 kilometers) worldwide (including beyond the Urals outside of European Russia). In the INF Treaty the Soviet Union also agreed to ban, worldwide, shorter-range missiles (ranges 500 to 1000 kilometers), in particular the Soviet SS-12 and SS-23 ballistic missiles and the U.S. Pershing I ballistic missile.

At the Reykjavik Summit meeting in 1986, the Soviet Union agreed to the principle of intrusive on-site inspection in the INF Treaty. This was a true breakthrough in nuclear arms control agreements. Ironically in 1990, almost two years after the entry into force of the INF Treaty, it was learned that the Soviet Union in the mid-1980's had transferred SS-23 missiles to the German Democratic Republic, Czechoslovakia and Bulgaria, creating a serious diplomatic problem. The Soviet side maintained that the transfer did not involve an INF Treaty violation, because these missiles were not "possessed" (the Treaty term) by the Soviet Union as of the time of its entry into force. However, given the fact that the Soviet Union had made much of the United States Pershing I missiles transferred to the Federal Republic of Germany and had insisted on their elimination, not to have mentioned that it transferred SS-23 missiles during the negotiations was, in the view of the United States, indefensible.

The United States did not want to agree to a non-circumvention provision in this negotiation as the lack of clarity of the meaning of such an obligation in the SALT II Treaty had received much criticism in the U.S. Senate. However, the issue of the 72 Pershing I missiles that the United States had transferred to the Federal Republic of Germany was strongly asserted by the Soviet Union to be a problem which needed to be addressed by the INF Treaty in some way. The United States did not want these missiles included under the Treaty as they belonged to a sovereign third state even though the United States controlled the nuclear warheads. Eventually, the Federal Republic of Germany unilaterally announced that it would destroy these missiles prior to the completion of missile elimination under the INF Treaty, and the United States agreed to destroy the associated reentry vehicles after these missiles had been eliminated. A similar arrangement, in the view of the United States, should have been developed for the transferred Soviet SS-23 missiles. This problem to date remains unresolved.

The Treaty Between the United States of America and the Union of Soviet Socialist Republics on the Elimination of Their Intermediate-Range and Shorter-Range Missiles (INF Treaty) was signed on December 8, 1987, and entered into force on June 1, 1988. In addition to the complete elimination of a whole class of nuclear weapon delivery systems, the most notable feature of the INF Treaty is the far-reaching on-site inspection regime.

Article IV of the INF Treaty provides that all intermediate-range missiles, launchers of such missiles, and all support structures and support equipment of the Parties shall be eliminated within three years of entry into force in two phases, the first of twenty-nine months duration and the second, the remaining period to thirty-six months. Article IV provides for the elimination of all shorter-range missiles, launchers of such missiles, and associated support equipment of the parties within eighteen months of entry into force.

Article VI was regarded during the negotiations as, in fact, the strongest bulwark of verification in the Treaty. This Article prohibits the production and flight testing of the missiles to be eliminated under the Treaty. Thus, even if the national technical means and on-site inspection verification regimes miss a significant number of covert missiles, their value will dramatically decline over time due to the lack of flight testing that is verifiable by national technical means.

Article VIII, Paragraph 1, of the INF Treaty requires that all intermediate-range missiles and launchers of such missiles (including stages), after entry into force, may be located only at deployment areas or missile support facilities or be in transit. Paragraph 6 further requires that thirty days after entry into force, intermediate-range and shorter-range missiles (including stages) and launchers of such missiles may not be located at missile or launcher production facilities or at test ranges.

Article IX provides for a comprehensive exchange of data on systems subject to the Treaty to be contained in the Memorandum on Data. It is provided that this data shall be updated, as of the date of entry into force, thirty days after entry into force and thirty days after the end of each six-month period thereafter. The data to be exchanged includes the number of missiles, launchers, support structures, and equipment for all missile systems subject to the Treaty. In addition, Article IX, Paragraph 5, requires notification of: the elimination of a deployment area, missile-operating base, or missile support facility thirty days in advance; changes in the number and location of elimination facilities and of the scheduled date of elimination (except launches for purposes of elimination) thirty days in advance; a launch or series of launches for purposes of elimination ten days in advance; changes in the number of missiles, launchers, support structures, and support equipment as the result of elimination pursuant to the Protocol on Elimination forty-eight hours after they occur; and transit of intermediate-range or shorter-range missiles or launchers of such missiles, as well as training missiles and launchers of these types, no later than forty-eight hours after it has been completed. "Elimination" is the INF Treaty term meaning removal from the aggregate numbers covered by the Treaty. Elimination is to be accomplished primarily by destruction. However, in limited numbers and for a limited period SS-20s could be launched to destruction under the Treaty. Elimination could also be effected by accidents and in small numbers under strict regulation by static display in museums.

Article X requires that missile systems subject to the Treaty be eliminated in accordance with the Protocol on Elimination, with on-site inspection thereof pursuant to the Protocol on Inspection. The Protocol on Elimination in general provides for elimination by explosive demolition, cutting, crushing, or flattening depending on the nature of the piece of equipment being eliminated. Paragraph 5 of Article X permits a party in the first six months after entry into force to eliminate by launching up to 100 intermediate-range missiles. The purpose of this provision was to permit the Soviet Union to meet the time schedules set forth in the Treaty given the large number of SS-20s it possessed. Experimental missiles, never deployed, of which each Party had one type must be eliminated within six months after entry into force. Paragraph 7 provides that missile systems are considered to be eliminated under the Treaty once all the requirements of the Protocol on Elimination are met and notification given pursuant to Article IX.

Article XI, along with the greatly detailed Protocol on Inspection, sets forth the on-site inspection regime of the Treaty, truly a new beginning in arms control. Paragraph 2 provides that such inspections may be conducted on the territory of the Parties as well as within the territories of third party basing countries (permitted by an associated Basing Country Agreement). Paragraph 3 of Article XI provides that no later than thirty days after entry into force each Party shall have the right to conduct on-site inspections at all missile operating bases and missile support facilities (other than missile production facilities) listed in the Memorandum on Data, and at all missile elimination facilities contained in the first data update called for in Paragraph 3 of Article IX. These inspections must be completed thirty days after entry into force. This is the so-called baseline inspection for the purpose of verifying the initial data.

Paragraph 4 provides for on-site inspection of the elimination of missile operating bases and support facilities, which inspections must be conducted within sixty days of the scheduled date thereof. This has been termed the close-out inspection. Paragraph 5 contains the right to conduct inspections, beginning ninety days after entry into force, of missile operating bases, missile support facilities (other than elimination sites), and missile production facilities to verify the numbers of missiles, launchers, support structures, and support equipment located at such sites, as well as former missile operating bases and support facilities that have been eliminated. This right is to exist for thirteen years under the INF Treaty, the three-year elimination period and for ten years thereafter. A declining number of inspections is provided, that is, twenty per calendar year during the first three years after entry into force, fifteen such inspections during each of the subsequent five years, and ten per year in the last five years. No more than half of these inspections by each Party in any one year may be in the territory of one basing country.

During the negotiations, the United States learned that the first two stages of the SS-25 land-mobile ICBM are identical ("outwardly similar" in the language of the Treaty) to the two stages of the SS-20. The United States insisted upon the right of continuous inspection of the one SS-25 final assembly plant, the Votkinsk Machine Building Plant, located in the town of Votkinsk in the Ural Mountains, to assure itself that covert SS-20s are not produced there. Paragraph 6(a) of the Protocol on Inspection grants the United States this right. A reciprocal right is granted the Soviet Union at a former U.S. Pershing II production facility at Magna, Utah in Paragraph 6(b). The parameters of the inspection are governed by the Protocol which, in summary, establishes a perimeter with portals through which the missiles must leave the plant and, in appropriate cases, imaging of the missile canisters and the right to open up to eight missile canisters a year. (Unlike U.S. ballistic missiles, Soviet ballistic missiles leave the final assembly facility and are subsequently deployed inside canisters.) This right is effective six months after entry into force and will terminate at any time after the end of the second year after entry into force if there has been no final assembly at such plant for a previous period of twelve months.

Paragraph 7 sets forth the right of on-site inspection of the process of elimination, including elimination by means of launching pursuant to Article X, Paragraph 5. Inspectors conducting these inspections are required to confirm that the process of elimination has been completed in each specific case before the data may be changed.

The final principal part of the verification regime is Article XIII, Paragraph 3, termed national technical means enhancement. Up to six times a year, for the three-year reduction period, the United States may, upon six hours notice, request cooperative measures at deployment bases of SS-25 ICBMs that are not former SS-20 operating bases (where a right to inspect would already exist under Paragraph 5 of Article XI) whereby the roofs of all fixed structures for SS-25s shall be opened and all missiles displayed on launchers in the open.

F. Conclusions

In conclusion, the nuclear arms control regime can be summarized as follows.

Nuclear testing is, in effect, prohibited in all environments except underground, where all testing has been conducted since the early 1980's. The two principal testing powers over the years, the United States and the Soviet Union, have recently brought into force, after a long wait, two

Treaties that place an upper limit on their underground testing at 150 kilotons.

The testing and deployment of nuclear weapons is prohibited in Antarctica, outer space and on the seabed outside the territorial limit. When the Treaty for the Prohibition of Nuclear Weapons in Latin America comes into full operation, there will be comparable treaty restrictions on that continent. A South Pacific nuclear-free zone has been established by the Treaty of Raratonga.

The Nuclear Non-Proliferation Treaty has as its objective the prohibition of the spread of nuclear weapons beyond the five original nuclear weapon states. The NPT has been a success in that it converted the initial acquisition of a nuclear weapon capability by a state from an act of national pride to one of international outlawry. There are far fewer nuclear weapon states in the world than was predicted in the years prior to the signing of the NPT. However, it has not been wholly successful. Important states remain outside the regime while one of them, India, has tested a nuclear device. At least two others (Israel and Pakistan) allegedly have become nuclear weapon capable without testing. Some states within the NPT regime (Libya and Iraq) have evidenced an interest in acquiring nuclear weapons. On the other hand, South Africa, which is suspected of possessing a nuclear weapon capability, may join the NPT regime in the near future. France and China have never become Parties but they both have declared that they will act as though they are Parties. For the first time both these states attended the fourth NPT Review Conference held in Geneva in August-September 1990.

There is no agreement presently in force limiting strategic offensive nuclear delivery vehicles. The Interim Agreement and the SALT II Treaty are not in force. A third even more comprehensive agreement, the START Treaty, eight years in the negotiation, hopefully will be completed in the near future. The ABM Treaty continues to limit strategic defensive systems to a very low level just short of a complete ban. Land-based ballistic and cruise missile nuclear delivery vehicles of the United States and Soviet Union which are below strategic range (5500 kilometers) down to 500 kilometers are completely prohibited by the INF Treaty. There is no agreement limiting ballistic and cruise missile nuclear delivery vehicles of ranges below 500 kilometers, although negotiation of such may begin at some point in the future. There are no agreements directly limiting either nuclear-capable aircraft that are not defined as strategic, nor air defenses, in part because of their predominantly conventional roles. Combat aircraft that are deployed on land in Europe (defined as from the Atlantic Ocean to the Ural Mountains), however, are limited by the Treaty on Conventional Armed Forces in Europe as part of that Treaty's general limitations.

Some of the agreements referred to above rely on national means of verification, either implicitly as in the case of the Limited Test Ban Treaty, or explicitly as in the ABM Treaty. Others rely on intrusive inspections conducted by IAEA inspectors. With the new departure created by the INF Treaty, recent nuclear arms control agreements are relying on intrusive on-site inspection regimes created by the agreements themselves, *i.e.*, the INF Treaty and the new Protocols to the Threshold Test Ban Treaty and the Peaceful Nuclear Explosions Treaty.

Finally, it should be noted that most of the treaties discussed above are of indefinite duration. An important exception is the Nuclear Non-Proliferation Treaty. It has a twenty-five year duration at the expiration of which in 1995 a Conference of the Parties must be called which will determine whether the NPT is to be extended indefinitely or for a fixed period or periods. Thus, 1995 will be an important decision point for nuclear arms control.

S.N. Kiselev
Second Secretary, Arms Control and Disarmament Directorate, USSR Ministry of Foreign Affairs

A. Nuclear Testing

The cessation of nuclear weapons testing is of considerable importance for reducing nuclear arms, preventing the proliferation of nuclear weapons, and, ultimately, accomplishing the complete elimination of nuclear weapons, as well as for the environmental safety of all states.

In spite of the fact that the question of ceasing the testing of nuclear weapons first arose in the mid-1950's, this problem has not yet been fully resolved. There exist a number of international treaties that prohibit the testing of nuclear weapons in certain environments (the atmosphere, space, and under water) and in certain regions (nuclear-free zones and the Antarctic). Recently the Soviet Union and the United States have reached an agreement on limiting underground nuclear testing. The total banning of underground testing of nuclear weapons and the inclusion of testing of nuclear weapons by all states with an all-embracing ban remains a problem.

At the present time 117 states are Parties to the 1963 Treaty Banning Nuclear Weapon Tests in the Atmosphere, in Outer Space, and Under Water. The nuclear states France and China are not Parties to this Treaty. Pursuant to Article I, each Treaty Party pledges to prohibit, prevent, and to refrain from conducting any and all test explosions of nuclear weapons as well as any other nuclear explosions at any location under its jurisdiction or control. The Treaty bans the testing of nuclear weapons in the atmosphere and beyond the atmosphere, including in space and underwater, comprising territorial waters and the high seas. The Treaty also prohibits nuclear explosions in any other environment if such explosion will cause radioactive fallout debris beyond the territorial boundaries of states under the jurisdiction or control of which an explosion is performed. Parties to the Treaty shall not cause, encourage, or participate in the conduct of such explosions. The Treaty is nonexpiring. It is stated in Article IV, however, that each Party has the right to withdraw from the Treaty if it decides that exceptional circumstances connected with the content of this Treaty have placed that country's higher interests under threat. The Moscow Treaty of 1963 was the first major achievement in efforts to limit the nuclear arms race. Underground nuclear explosions, however, were not covered by the ban.

In order to resolve this problem and as a result of talks between the Soviet Union and the United States held in Moscow in June-July 1974, a Treaty was drafted that banned the conduct of underground testing of nuclear weapons with a yield exceeding an agreed-upon maximum level. The Soviet Union and the United States pledged, commencing March 31, 1976, to prohibit, prevent, and refrain from conducting any underground testing of nuclear weapons with a yield in excess of 150 kilotons, at any site under their jurisdiction or control. In addition, the parties pledged to limit their underground nuclear tests to a minimal number, as well as to continue talks aimed at achieving resolution of the problem of all underground nuclear weapons testing. For the purpose of monitoring compliance with the Threshold Test Ban Treaty, signed in Moscow on July 3, 1974, each party agreed to use, in conformity with generally recognized principles of international law, national technical means of verification at their disposal and not to interfere with or impede the other party's means of verification. The parties also agreed to consult with one another when necessary, to make inquiries, and to provide information in connection with such inquiries. A Protocol to the Treaty contains a list of data subject to exchange for the purpose of ensuring reliability of verification, as well as a procedure for exchanging these data.

The Treaty and Protocol did not go into effect at that time, because the United States, following signing, refused to ratify them, citing inadequacy of the prescribed verification system. At the same time, in accordance with a formal understanding reached in 1976, the Parties agreed to observe de facto the provisions of the Treaty and Protocol. This Treaty, which prohibited the conduct of highest-yield underground nuclear testing, and the Protocol, which contains an understanding on exchange of information on test sites of the parties, which had previously been considered classified information, demonstrated the possibility of finding, if the political will is present, mutually acceptable solutions to the most complex problems. These agreements also pointed to the possibility and effectiveness of gradually reducing the permitted yield of nuclear tests, down to a level at which they will lose their military significance.

The Treaty Between the United States of America and the Union of Soviet Socialist Republics on the Limitation of Underground Nuclear Weapon Tests called for drawing up a separate agreement on a special regime for peaceful nuclear explosions. Pursuant to this, on May 28, 1976, there was signed in Moscow and Washington the Treaty Between the United States of America and the Union of Soviet Socialist Republics on the Limitation of Underground Nuclear Explosions for Peaceful Purposes, as well as a Protocol to the Treaty. The Treaty and Protocol were drawn up as a result of talks held in Moscow from October 1974 through March 1976.

This Treaty was to regulate all underground nuclear explosions for peaceful purposes, conducted by the parties subsequent to March 31, 1976. The Soviet Union and the United States pledged to prohibit, prevent, and refrain from conducting, at any location under their jurisdiction or control, as well as to refrain from conducting, not to take part in and not to assist in the conduct of, at any location whatsoever: any individual nuclear explosion for peaceful purposes with a yield in excess of 150 kilotons; any series of explosions with an aggregate yield in excess of 1.5 megatons; any explosion conducted not for peaceful applications; any explosion not in accordance with the provisions of the Treaty Banning Nuclear Weapon Tests in the Atmosphere, in Outer Space and Under Water, the Treaty on the Non-Proliferation of Nuclear Weapons, as well as other international agreements. Each of the Parties reserved the right: to conduct such peaceful nuclear explosions at any location under its jurisdiction or control, beyond the geographic boundaries of test sites and ranges designated pursuant to the provisions of the Treaty on the Limitation of Underground Nuclear Weapon Tests; and to conduct, take part in, and assist in the conduct of such peaceful explosions on the territory of another state at the request of that state. The Parties also agreed additionally to consider the question of conduct of individual explosions with a yield in excess of 150 kilotons.

In order to guarantee assurance of compliance with the Treaty, the Parties agreed to utilize national technical means of verification in conformity with generally accepted norms of international law, as well as to provide each other with information and access to explosion sites, and to provide assistance in conformity with the Protocol to the Treaty. The Parties agreed to establish a Joint Consultative Commission to assist in implementation of the Treaty. They also agreed to develop bilateral cooperation and cooperation with the IAEA in the area of peaceful nuclear explosions.

The Treaty prescribes that it shall remain in force for a period of five years and shall be subject to ratification in conformity with the constitutional procedures of each of the Parties. Upon the termination of this period, the Treaty will be automatically extended for subsequent five-year periods if one of the Parties does not decide to withdraw from the Treaty. Neither Party shall have the right to withdraw from the Treaty, however, as long as the Treaty Between the United States of America and the Union of Soviet Socialist Republics on the Limitation of Underground Nuclear Weapon Tests remains in force.

The 1976 Treaty and Protocol, just as the 1974 Treaty and Protocol, did not enter into force, due to U.S. refusal to ratify them. The United States has not conducted peaceful nuclear explosions since 1973.

The significance of the Treaty and Protocol lies in the fact that a mechanism of nuclear explosion on-site verification was formulated in a treaty for the first time, a mechanism that can serve as a basis for drafting effective measures of verification of cessation of nuclear testing. The verification mechanism which was formulated in the Protocol signed in 1976 was used as one of the points of departure in subsequent talks between the Soviet Union and the United States on drafting improved underground nuclear explosion monitoring measures.

The signing of the Soviet-U.S. Treaties of 1974 and 1976 by no means ended the issue of a comprehensive nuclear test ban. Soviet-U.S. consultations on this problem began in Washington in 1977. These consultations were resumed in Geneva in July of that same year, with the participation of Great Britain. Official three-way talks commenced in Geneva on October 3, 1977. In the course of these talks the parties succeeded in hammering out practically all the provisions of a future treaty on a total and universal ban on nuclear weapons testing, but the United States unilaterally broke off the talks in 1980.

Seeking to get moving stalled efforts to resolve this problem, on August 6, 1985, the Soviet Union announced a unilateral moratorium on all nuclear explosions and appealed to other nuclear powers to follow this example. This appeal met no response, in spite of the fact that the Soviet Union extended the moratorium on five separate occasions.

Realizing that the problem of banning nuclear testing could not be resolved without due participation by the United States, in March 1986 the Soviet Union declared that it was also prepared to hold talks on a total nuclear test ban on a bilateral basis with the United States. These talks commenced in Geneva on November 9, 1987. As a first step, both parties were to agree upon effective verification measures, which would make it possible to ratify the 1974 Treaty on the Limitation of Underground

Nuclear Weapon Tests and the 1976 Treaty on Underground Nuclear Explosions for Peaceful Purposes, and subsequently to proceed with hammering out additional intermediate nuclear testing limitations on the way toward the ultimate goal of a total ban on nuclear testing as part of an effective disarmament process.

In the course of the negotiations a text was drawn up of an agreement on conducting a Soviet-proposed joint verification experiment (JVE), for the purpose of providing a practical demonstration of the strong points and deficiencies of the verification methods proposed by the parties. The agreement was signed by Eduard Shevardnadze and George Shultz on May 31, 1988. Conduct of the JVE made it possible to obtain requisite information on estimating the effectiveness and practical applicability for verification purposes of the Soviet-proposed seismic method of measuring yield and the U.S.-proposed hydrodynamic method of measuring the yield of underground nuclear explosions. On the whole the experiment made it possible better to understand how these methods could be implemented in the 1974 Treaty compliance verification mechanism. The JVE demonstrated that the remote seismic verification method can be employed as an effective method of determining the yield of explosions. At the same time the experiment demonstrated that such drawbacks as complexity, high cost, intrusiveness (acquisition of data not connected with determining the yield of an explosion), and the need for the presence of a large number of monitoring personnel at the other party's test site for extended periods of time are inherent in the hydrodynamic method. In addition the JVE demonstrated that this method also provides a sufficiently high degree of accuracy so that it can be used as a 1974 Treaty verification mechanism. This experiment also was an unprecedented undertaking from the standpoint of openness and mutual confidence-building.

In the course of six rounds of talks, the most recent of which ended on May 26, 1990, the Parties reached agreement on new verification protocols to the 1974 and 1976 Treaties, replacing the protocols agreed upon in 1974 and 1976. The new Protocols specify a system of verification of the 1974 and 1976 Treaties, consisting of a combination of the hydrodynamic and seismic methods of measuring yield, as well as on-site inspection. In specific terms the mechanism of verification of these treaties is as follows.

For purposes of verifying compliance with the 1974 Treaty on the Limitation of Underground Nuclear Weapon Tests, the verifying Party has the right to employ the hydrodynamic and seismic methods of measuring yield for any test by the other party with a planned yield exceeding fifty kilotons, as well as to perform on-site inspection in the case of any test by the other Party with a planned yield exceeding thirty-five kilotons, whereby on-site inspection may be performed for a test with a planned yield exceeding fifty kilotons only if the verifying Party does not employ the hydrodynamic method of measuring yield. In addition, for purposes of improving the Parties' national technical means, the Protocol stipulates the right of the verifying Party to perform hydrodynamic measurement of the yield of tests with a planned yield of fifty kilotons or less, and it introduces the concept of calibration test, conduct of which may be demanded by the verifying side. For purposes of implementation of the Treaty and Protocol, the latter provides for the establishment, immediately after the Treaty enters into force, of a Bilateral Consultative Commission and specifies its functions.

For purposes of verification of compliance with the 1976 Treaty on Underground Nuclear Explosions for Peaceful Purposes, the verifying side is entitled to employ the hydrodynamic method of measuring the yield of each of the other Party's explosions, including each explosion in a group explosion the planned yield of which exceeds fifty kilotons, and to employ, alongside the hydrodynamic method of measuring yield, a local seismic network for each group explosion the planned aggregate yield of which exceeds 150 kilotons, as well as to perform on-site inspection for each explosion with a planned yield exceeding thirty-five kilotons, and for each explosion with a planned yield exceeding fifty kilotons only if the verifying side has decided not to employ the hydrodynamic method of measuring yield. The Protocol governs procedures of consultation and coordination within the framework of the Joint Consultative Commission prescribed in the Treaty.

The Protocols to the 1974 and 1976 Treaties stipulate in detail the procedure of presenting notifications and information pertaining to nuclear testing and peaceful nuclear explosions, the specific types of activity and monitoring procedures, as well as the equipment that may be used in monitoring and verification, plus the rights and obligations of both Parties connected with the performance of verification. The Protocols on verification shall constitute an integral part of the 1974 and 1976 Treaties. They shall enter into force on the date on which the Treaties enter into force, and they shall remain in force as long as the corresponding Treaties remain in force. The Protocols were signed in Washington on June 1, 1990, by Presidents Bush and Gorbachev. The Protocols, together with the corresponding Treaties, have been ratified by the legislative bodies of the two countries.

One can scarcely exaggerate the significance of the Protocols to the 1974 and 1976 Treaties that were signed in Washington. They formulate an exceptionally firm and detailed mechanism of verification of limitation of nuclear explosions, grounded on a combination of monitoring methods that differ in their scientific and technical nature. Also of considerable significance here is the possibility of employing verification procedures that are extremely "sensitive" to the monitored party, namely the performance of hydrodynamic measurements, and to a certain degree on-site inspection as well. It would seem that this would constitute a quite effective inhibitor to the testing programs of the Soviet Union and the United States. This became obvious as early as the negotiation stage, when the Soviet Union announced a substantial decrease in its nuclear test yields and a reduction in the number of tests. And the Soviet Union has been conducting virtually no nuclear testing since the fall of 1989. The U.S. testing program was also radically cut back in 1990.

An important result of the work done on the Protocols to the 1974 and 1976 Treaties is the fact that the verification procedures worked out in the course of negotiations, and particularly employment of the seismic method of measuring yield and performance of on-site inspection, with minimal additional work could be applicable to future radical limitations on nuclear explosions, right up to the total cessation of testing.

The efforts of only two nations, however, even the most powerful nations in the nuclear domain, are not enough in order to achieve a worldwide and total cessation of all nuclear weapons testing. This can be achieved only through cooperation and joint efforts of a large number of nations, particularly all nuclear powers. This will require multilateral negotiations. Nevertheless, in spite of annual UN General Assembly resolutions presented at the only presently existing international forum of talks in the area of disarmament–the Geneva Conference on Disarmament–efforts to establish a special committee for the holding of multilateral talks on the total and universal banning of nuclear testing have not yet been successful.

At the same time it would seem that genuine advances in the area of monitoring and verification, achieved within the framework of bilateral contacts between the Soviet Union and the United States, could become a basis for commencing practical discussion and debate on the problem of banning nuclear testing on a multilateral basis. The mechanism of seismic monitoring and on-site inspections formulated within the framework of the new Protocols of the 1974 and 1976 Treaties constitutes an indisputable contribution by the Soviet Union and the United States toward future talks.

The "Basic Provisions of a Treaty on Total and Universal Banning of Nuclear Weapon Testing" (Document CD/756, dated June 17, 1987), presented on June 9, 1987, by a group of socialist countries at the Conference on Disarmament, a document that summarizes the entirety of positive achievements from preceding discussions of the problem of banning nuclear testing, could constitute a framework for discussion at future talks.

This document places main emphasis on monitoring measures to verify that nuclear testing is not being conducted. In addition to using national technical means of verification, this document prescribes the establishment of an international seismic monitoring system, exchange of data on radioactivity of air masses, regular verification with the assistance of international inspectors, and the possibility of conducting mandatory on-site inspections on demand, without right of refusal. There is one provision according to which treaty ratification by an agreed-upon number of states, which for a beginning would contain only two of the five nuclear powers—the Soviet Union and the United States—would be sufficient for the treaty to enter into force.

The Soviet Union proposed establishing within the framework of the Conference a group of scientific experts to draft scientifically validated recommendations on the structure of monitoring and verification for any possible agreement on refraining from the conduct of nuclear weapons testing, to determine verification methods and their feasibility, and to work out a procedure for their implementation. The Soviet Union also proposed instituting an international worldwide radiation danger monitoring system utilizing satellite communications links.

Unfortunately none of these proposals has as yet evoked response on the part of the Western countries.

It would be erroneous to assume, however, that no work whatsoever is being done at the Conference on Disarmament to prepare for future talks on a nuclear test ban treaty. A special working group of scientific experts was formed in 1976 within the framework of the Conference to consider international joint measures pertaining to detection and identification of seismic events. The group consists of seismology experts designated by the Disarmament Conference member states, as well as by non-member states, plus a representative of the World Meteorological Organization (WMO). The group meets twice each year and reports on the results of its work to the Conference on Disarmament. The group's job includes drawing up detailed instructions for experimental testing of a global system of international joint measures to detect and identify seismic events, as well as the scientific and technical aspects of such a global system.

Since the group has been in existence it has successfully conducted a number of international experiments on exchange of level I seismic data (normal representation, with minimal delays, of the principal parameters of detected seismic signals), via World Meteorological Organization Global Telecommunications System (GTS/WMO) channels, and they have begun phased conduct of experiments on exchange of level II seismic data (the initial record of a seismic signal of specified duration, including a small noise region prior to signal onset).

For the present realistic prospects for reaching future agreements in the area of limitation and cessation of nuclear testing are determined in considerable measure by the degree of agreement on this matter between the Soviet Union and the United States and depend directly on the success of the two parties in seeking mutually acceptable practical agreements.

Unfortunately there continues to be a lack of clarity here, although successful achievement of the tasks of the first phase of Soviet-U.S. nuclear test talks and the obligation of the parties, stated in their mandate, to proceed with discussion of subsequent limitations on nuclear testing along the way toward the total cessation of testing is a prerequisite for further bilateral progress. In spite of this fact, in the course of the Washington summit at the end of May and beginning of June 1990, the U.S. side avoided responding to a Soviet proposal to resume bilateral talks in the fall of 1990. Apparently this situation was a consequence of the diametrically opposite approaches of the Soviet Union and the United States to the problem of limitation and cessation of nuclear testing.

While the Soviet Union is for an immediate ban to nuclear testing and set this goal among the priorities of the program of nuclear disarmament up to the year 2000, which it proposed on January 15, 1986, the United States is against the total cessation of nuclear testing, viewing achievement of this task merely as a "long-range" goal, and has expressed its willingness to accept a total cessation of nuclear testing only under conditions whereby, as was stated in U.S. President Ronald Reagan's address to Congress on August 27, 1988,

> It will not be necessary for the United States to depend on nuclear deterrents to ensure international security and stability and when an agreement is reached on extensive, deep, and verifiable arms reductions, substantial improvement in verification capabilities, more extensive confidence-building measures, and a firmer balance of conventional forces.

Under these conditions a sharp reduction in the permitted nuclear test yield threshold with an equally substantial limitation in the number of nuclear tests could become the subject of the next stage of bilateral talks. The Soviet Union has repeatedly stated its willingness to reach an agreement on reducing nuclear test yield to one kiloton and the number of tests to two to three per year. Similar proposals have been suggested by a fair number of U.S. lawmakers, particularly in the House of Representatives, as well as by many U.S. public figures. It would seem that if the White House were also willing to consider the possibility of adopting such further nuclear test limitation measures, these measures would become a natural continuation of the bilateral dialogue begun in Geneva in November 1987.

There is considerably less certainty over the prospects for multilateral test ban talks. Certain possibilities are opened up by a conference of parties to the 1963 Moscow Treaty, to be held in January 1991 and called at the initiative of a group of nonaligned nations for the purpose of introducing an amendment to the Treaty that would extend the Treaty to cover underground nuclear explosions. In accordance with the Treaty, however, any amendment to the Treaty will be considered adopted if a majority of Treaty Parties votes in favor of it, with mandatory support by all three depositaries–the Soviet Union, the United States, and Great Britain. Two of the depositaries–the United States and Great Britain–have already voiced a negative position toward the proposed amendment. At the same time, preparation for and conduct of a conference in a nonconfrontational spirit could create the necessary political climate for considering on a positive note the problem of a total ban on nuclear weapons testing. The conference, for example, could provide impetus to commence corresponding multilateral efforts either at the Conference on Disarmament in Geneva or within the framework of a body specifically formed for this purpose.

The political situation developing in the world around the problem of nuclear weapons testing suggests that one might hope for positive development of events in this area.

A.Yu. Meshkov
First Secretary, International Scientific and Technical Cooperation Directorate, USSR Ministry of Foreign Affairs

B. Nonproliferation and Limitations on Deployment

Ensuring the nonproliferation of nuclear weapons is one of the key factors of international security and stability. This problem became particularly acute at the beginning of the 1960's, when there occurred an increase in the number of countries which would be capable, on the basis of their scientific-technical and economic potential, of manufacturing their own nuclear weapons.

In these conditions the international community clearly felt the need to prevent a possible course of events that would threaten to become an uncontrollable and irreversible process, drawing an increasing number of countries into a highly dangerous nuclear arms race. There appeared a profound awareness of the inseparability of one's own security from the security of all other states, which created the political and moral-psychological preconditions for the birth of a Treaty on the Non-Proliferation of Nuclear Weapons and the establishment of a corresponding international regime.

The Soviet Union was one of the initiators and firm supporters of extensive discussion of the problem of nonproliferation in the United Nations and in other international forums. A draft Treaty on the Non-Proliferation of Nuclear Weapons was prepared as a result of complex, painstaking negotiations within the framework of the Committee on Disarmament. The Treaty was approved at the Twenty-Second Session of the UN General Assembly and opened for signature on July 1, 1968, in the capitals of the three depositary states (the Soviet Union, United States, and Great Britain), and entered into force on March 5, 1970.

At the present time the Non-Proliferation Treaty has the largest number of Parties—141 states—of any international legal document in the area of arms limitation. It constitutes an extensive, multifaceted international document, in which the principle of nonproliferation of nuclear weapons is established. The heart of the Treaty is comprised of so-called counterpledges by its Parties, in conformity with which the nuclear powers pledged not to hand over to any other nation nuclear weapons or other nuclear explosive devices as well as control over such weapons and devices, while non-nuclear states pledged not to produce or acquire such weapons. The International Atomic Energy Agency (IAEA) was entrusted with verification of compliance with these basic pledges. In execution of Article III of the Treaty, which prescribes that nuclear materials and equipment shall be provided to non-nuclear nations for peaceful purposes only under the condition that such materials and equipment are monitored by the IAEA, Party countries that do not possess nuclear weapons shall enter into guarantee agreements with the IAEA, drawn up on the basis of a corresponding standard draft agreement. This standard draft agreement legally constitutes an international agreement, although technically it was formulated by the Agency and was not drawn up in the form of an international treaty.

Pursuant to such an agreement, the IAEA performs inspection functions in regard to all a country's peaceful nuclear activities, in order to prevent nuclear energy from being transferred from peaceful uses to the production of nuclear weapons and other nuclear explosive devices. More than 2000 inspections were performed in 1989, involving forty-two non-nuclear Party countries. It is notable that analysis of the results of past work enables the IAEA to state in its reports year after year that nuclear material placed under safeguard has continued to be used solely for peaceful nuclear activities. The credibility of this conclusion is bolstered by the fact that the Agency employs thoroughly detailed and specific scientific and technical standards and safeguard procedures, taking into account the specific features of design and construction of installations of various stages of the nuclear fuel cycle. Another important factor ensuring the functioning of the mechanism of safeguards is the fact that IAEA monitoring is carried out with full respect for the sovereign rights of states and does not hinder or impede their peaceful nuclear activities and international cooperation in the area of peaceful use of nuclear energy. As of the beginning of 1990 safeguard agreements with the Agency were in effect in eighty-two of the 138 non-nuclear Treaty Party countries. However, as cited data indicate, a number of countries have not as yet entered into the required monitoring agreements. And although the majority of these countries are not engaged in any nuclear activities, the IAEA Secretariat is engaged in persisting efforts aimed at correcting this abnormal situation.

The nuclear activities of nations possessing nuclear weapons are not subject by the Treaty to monitoring by the IAEA, although the Nuclear Power States Parties (the Soviet Union, the United States, and Great Britain), as well as France and the PRC, which are not Parties to the Treaty, have signed with the Agency agreements on employment of guarantees and safeguards as an act of good will and for the purpose of improving safeguard methods and procedures.

The extensive development of international dealings in the area of peaceful use of nuclear energy predetermined the creation and strengthening of an additional element in the nuclear weapons nonproliferation regime—control of nuclear export. In 1974 the Non-Proliferation Treaty States Parties that export nuclear materials reached an understanding pertaining to implementation of Article III, Paragraph 2, of the Non-Proliferation Treaty. It prescribes IAEA safeguards in regard to nuclear material and equipment transferred to Non-Nuclear States Parties, that is, such transfers may be carried out only under the condition that the receiving nation makes its entire nuclear activities available to Agency monitoring. The main thing in this formal understanding is an agreed-upon list of such material and equipment, which was published in the form of an IAEA document. At the present time twenty-three states are parties to this formal understanding.

An understanding on the guiding principles of nuclear export, hammered out in London in 1975-1977, became another important element ensuring subsequent strengthening of control over nuclear export. The parties to this agreement declared their intention to implement a joint policy regarding the export of nuclear materials, equipment, and technology, grounded on these guiding principles, as well as a common "initial list" of such materials and equipment. These principles govern the possibility of providing such materials, equipment, and technologies to non-nuclear countries, by the latter pledging not to utilize them for building nuclear explosive devices, and by providing shipments with IAEA guarantees, safeguards, and requisite physical protection measures. The same conditions are prescribed in the case of reexport. Twenty-four countries are parties to this agreement.

The authors of the Treaty were clearly aware that it is extremely important to halt the spread of nuclear weapons across the planet, but that this is insufficient to ensure the world a peaceful and safe future. But the safety valve created by the treaty will be subjected to steadily increasing pressure if the channels of qualitative and quantitative growth of nuclear arms, regardless of their ownership, are not cut off. For this reason the treaty forms an integral element of the disarmament effort. Article VI of this Treaty states that every Party is pledged to negotiate in good faith on effective measures to bring the nuclear arms race to an end in the near future and to accomplish nuclear disarmament, as well as to engage in negotiations for a treaty on total and universal disarmament under rigorous and effective international verification. The preamble to the Treaty notes the need to achieve a permanent cessation of all nuclear arms testing and to continue talks toward this end. Naturally progress in achieving these provisions of the Treaty has been and continues to be an object of close attention on the part of the States Parties, particularly the non-nuclear nations. In addition, many countries, both States Parties and non-Parties, in appraising its effectiveness take into consideration specific changes occurring in the domain of disarmament, particularly as a result of Soviet-U.S. disarmament talks. Sharing these concerns and proceeding from its treaty obligations, the Soviet Union proposed a program of phased elimination of nuclear weapons by the year 2000 and the building of a nuclear-free and violence-free world.

There has occurred a major breakthrough in this area in recent years. The Treaty Between the United States and the Union of Soviet Socialist Republics on the Elimination of Their Intermediate-Range and Shorter-Range Missiles has been concluded and is being successfully implemented, the basic provisions of a future treaty on reducing strategic offensive arms by fifty percent have been agreed upon by the Soviet Union and the United States, and Protocols to the Treaties on the limitation of underground nuclear weapon tests and on underground nuclear explosions for peaceful purposes have been signed, which ensures the possibility of ratification of these instruments.

These important steps by the Soviet Union and the United States confirm their firm adherence to the goals and purposes of the Nuclear Non-Proliferation Treaty and create realistic prerequisites for accession to the Nonproliferation Treaty by those countries that have refrained from doing so, justifying their position in particular by the fact that the principal Parties to the Treaty have not yet proceeded with carrying out obligations contained in the Treaty pertaining to nuclear disarmament.

A special place in this Treaty is occupied by Article IV, pursuant to which all Parties pledge to foster and promote the fullest possible exchange of equipment, materials, scientific, and technical information on the use of nuclear energy for peaceful purposes and are entitled to participate in such an exchange. During the years the Treaty has been in existence the Parties have become convinced in a practical manner that it creates both the necessary legal basis for ensuring the effectiveness of such cooperation and corresponding confidence-building measures that encourage these ties.

The Parties to the Treaty devote serious attention to the problem of its effectiveness. Pursuant to Article VIII, conferences are regularly convened (once every five years) to review how the Treaty is operating and to assure that the goals set forth in the preamble and the provisions of the Treaty are being carried out. Four such conferences have been held.

The 1985 Conference produced important positive results, which made it possible significantly to strengthen the international nonproliferation regime. The viability of the Treaty was reaffirmed in the Conference Final Declaration. It was noted that the main task of the Treaty—the prevention of the emergence of new nuclear states—has been successfully accomplished. The Declaration emphasized determination to achieve further strengthening of the nonproliferation regime and an increase in the number of Parties to the Treaty which, the declaration states, "plays an important role in maintaining international peace and security."

The Fourth Conference to review the effect of the Non-Proliferation Treaty was held in August-September 1990. The States Parties came to the conference with substantial results. The international nonproliferation regime had become stronger and more stable, and the Treaty had taken on greater authority, as a result of the fact that eighteen additional countries had acceded to the Treaty over the preceding five years. The overall world situation had undergone qualitative change, and genuine progress has been achieved in the area of nuclear disarmament. All this was expressed in the course of the general discussion at the Fourth Conference. Although no consensus Final Declaration was adopted at the Conference, it unquestionably helped further strengthen the Treaty and reaffirmed the adherence of its Parties to its goals and principles.

At the same time, appraising the situation in a realistic manner, one should assume that collisions in the area of nonproliferation will continue to occur in coming years. This is due in large measure to the fact that a group of countries that possess the requisite scientific potential and technology to produce nuclear weapons, as well as two nuclear powers, remain outside the Treaty. And although the countries that are not parties to the Treaty proper do not as a rule oppose the principles set forth in it and generally act in conformity with these principles in their policies and trade and economic activities, certain facts attest to an endeavor by a number of countries, and particularly Israel, the Republic of South Africa, and Pakistan, to acquire military nuclear technology and to obtain access to materials and equipment which can be used to build nuclear explosive devices. Also cause for concern are tendencies toward a certain joining of efforts on the part of certain "near-nuclear" countries in attempts to acquire a nuclear status.

The problem of universalization of the Treaty takes on imperative significance in these conditions. Progress in this area would make it possible to guarantee the international community against spread of the nuclear threat, to raise confidence-building measures in the nuclear domain to a qualitatively new and higher level, to stabilize the situation in a number of regional conflicts, and, finally, to ensure that the process of nuclear disarmament will continue without a halt. The year 1995 will be an important landmark in the history of the Treaty. A conference will be convened that year, pursuant to Article X, to decide the matter of Treaty extension. It is quite obvious that the period of time during which the Treaty should remain in effect should be determined solely by one factor–by how long nuclear weapons continue to exist. Considering this, the most logical step would be to make the Treaty nonexpiring. It could be replaced only by a comprehensive international agreement on the nonreemergence of nuclear weapons following their total and final elimination.

B.R. Tuzmukhamedov
Docent, USSR Diplomatic Academy

Nuclear-free zones and zones of peace are for the purpose of promoting achievement of the goals of nonproliferation and limitation of deployment of nuclear weapons; the regime prescribed by such zones is more stringent regarding nuclear weapons than a nonproliferation regime.

Taking into account presented initiatives and already adopted treaty measures, one can give the following general description of the elements of a nuclear-free zone and the basic fundamentals of its regime. Territory on which the testing, manufacture, and deployment of nuclear weapons are prohibited on the basis of an international treaty between interested states, as well as within the boundaries of which and against which the use of nuclear weapons is prohibited, is considered a nuclear-free zone. Both groups of states and individual states can comprise a nuclear-free zone; such a zone may also be established in common-use space. The fact that it must be totally free of any and all nuclear weapons is a mandatory condition for forming such a zone. This means that, in addition to the above-enumerated elements, the zone regime should preclude the transit of nuclear weapons across its boundaries, no matter how brief such transit might be. States comprising the zone pledge not to manufacture, stockpile, import for their own needs, or permit the deployment of nuclear weapons on their territory as well as not to install and not to permit installation on their territory of equipment and devices connected with nuclear weapons. On the other hand states possessing nuclear weapons pledge not to permit such weapons by any manner or means on the territory of states within the zone, not to transfer such weapons to the possession or control of these states, and not to use or threaten to use nuclear weapons against the zone.

Plans to establish zones of peace, more extensive in content than nuclear-free zones, began to be presented in large part taking into account initiatives and initial experience in the establishment of nuclear-free zones. Synthesis of UN materials, materials of the nonaligned movement, and specific initiatives enables one to give the following general description of the elements that comprise a zone of peace. These elements include: prohibition of the deployment of nuclear weapons in the zone; limitation and reduction of conventional forces; employment of confidence-building measures; reduction and elimination of the military presence of states that are not part of the given area; elimination of foreign military bases; provision of the security of states by means of confirmation and concretization of international legal principles of renunciation of the use and the threat of force, peaceful settlement of disputes, *etc.*

Nuclear-free zones and zones of peace should be a means of spatial limitation of proliferation of arms, nuclear arms within the former and both nuclear and conventional arms within the latter. Both categories of zones seek to promote international security; while the direct effect of nuclear-free zones is felt primarily in the military domain of international security, zones of peace also exert influence on the political domain; both combine certain elements of demilitarization and neutralization. One should stipulate, however, the conditional nature of nuclear neutralization, since by virtue of the inevitable catastrophic consequences of the use of nuclear weapons and the global consequences of such employment, it is scarcely possible to remove any given region of the world from the sphere of effect of nuclear weapons.

Two nuclear-free zones have been established by special treaty agreement to date: in Latin America and in the South Pacific. The effectiveness of both Treaties, however, is limited by the permissibility of nuclear weapons transit across the territory to which the effect of these Treaties extends. In addition, the 1967 Treaty for the Prohibition of

Nuclear Weapons in Latin America does not exclude the possibility of conduct of nuclear explosions for peaceful purposes by the Parties and, in addition, in determining the spatial extent of Treaty application, it refer to the extent of territorial waters established by a number of Latin American states, which exceeds by a considerable extent that recognized by international law. Correspondingly, not all states within and outside the region, including nuclear nations, are parties to the Treaties and Protocols. Only the Soviet Union and China of the nuclear powers, for example, are Parties to the corresponding Protocols to the South Pacific Nuclear-Free Zone Treaty.

A nuclear-free zone in Africa, as proclaimed by the Organization of African Unity in 1964 and supported by a UN General Assembly resolution in 1965, first of all was not put into the proper legal form as prescribed by the resolution and, second, cannot become a full-fledged nuclear-free zone until suspicions are removed regarding the nuclear status of the Republic of South Africa.

A number of proposals for the establishment of nuclear-free zones (in the Near East, on the Korean and Balkan peninsulas, in the Mediterranean, in Southeast Asia, *etc.*), some of which are being considered by the UN, have not been implemented due to the fact that there is lacking agreement on their content among the potential participating nations or, in the case of Europe, due to disagreement with such proposals by the NATO nations, which continue to pursue a strategy of "flexible response" that was officially adopted by this alliance during the years of confrontation between East and West. In particular, a proposal to establish such a zone in Northern Europe is not being carried out for this reason.

Alongside specific-purpose treaties, UN resolutions, and initiatives calling for the establishment of nuclear-free zones, there are a number of broader-purpose Treaties that formally articulate elements of nuclear-free zones in the Antarctic, in space and on celestial bodies, and on the seabed beyond the 12-mile limit. As experience indicates, it has not been considered feasible or necessary to reach formal agreements on the establishment of nuclear-free zones or on the establishment of a regime containing elements of such zones. Establishment of such zones is most likely in areas in which at the time of concluding the Treaty there are no nuclear weapons or nuclear weapons deployment, including transit. From this point of view early establishment of full-fledged nuclear-free zones encompassing substantial regions of the world, where such weapons are presently deployed or in which there are states suspected of possessing or seeking to possess such weapons, is not an easily attained goal. However, this does not exclude a realistic possibility of one state or a limited group of states declaring themselves a nuclear-free zone.

At the same time, successful progress in arms limitation talks may in the future lead to the de facto establishment of such zones. For example, the attainment of formal agreements on radical reductions in conventional forces in Europe, simultaneously with agreement on encompassing and profound confidence-building and security measures, will once and for all greatly diminish the NATO argument calling for reliance on nuclear weapons as a means of deterrence. This argument has already been placed in question by positive trends in relations between East and West. Thus conditions would be created for the elimination of tactical nuclear weapons and, considering the effect of the INF Treaty, for establishing a nuclear-free area in Central Europe. The prospects for expanding this area are linked to establishment of a Balkan and a Northern European nuclear-free zone, as well as elimination of nuclear weapons from the Baltic Sea. As regards the latter problem, the preconditions for resolving it are being created in the process of unilateral elimination by the Soviet Union of certain categories of sea-based nuclear weapons from Baltic waters.

As regards zones of peace, the Antarctic regime is close to the proposed regime of such zones, but there exist as yet no zones of peace formally established by treaty. In addition, the demilitarized and neutralized zone in the Antarctic was established on uninhabited territory that is not under anybody's sovereignty and that is little used for purposes of transportation and communication. It was a result of a compromise among the interested states, reached in the course of negotiations.

Above-listed attributes are lacking in the case of existing initiatives calling for the establishment of zones of peace. As regards the most strongly proposed initiative, for example—to establish a zone of peace in the Indian Ocean—there is a lack of agreement among the nations of the region on the content of such a zone, and many problems between these nations, including territorial, have not been settled; and the proposal is opposed by some Western nations, which view it as an attempt to limit capability to deploy strategic and general-purpose naval forces and to control lines of communication. For several years now the UN Ad Hoc Committee on the Indian Ocean, which was commissioned to perform preparatory work on this question, has been unable to carry out its mandate. As of 1990 representatives of the United States and a number of other Western countries that had previously declared their refusal to take part in a conference are declining to take part in the work of the committee.

Implementation of all proposed elements of a zone of peace by embodying them in a uniform treaty appears unlikely. One possible approach would be the gradual development of cooperation at the regional, subregional, and bilateral levels in such areas as trade, exploitation of resources on the continental shelf, fisheries, environmental protection, the campaign against infectious diseases, recovery from natural disasters, *etc.*, with simultaneous establishment of appropriate organizational structures. On this foundation, in time it would be possible to make a transition to cooperation in the political domain. As regards the military presence of powers from outside the region, against which initiatives to establish zones of peace were originally directed, initially agreement should be reached on stabilization of this military presence, with an eye toward the possibility of reducing military presence in the future, depending on development of the situation in the region and in relations between these powers.

E.T. Agayev
Head of Branch, Directorate for International Organizations, USSR Ministry of Foreign Affairs

C. Quantitative and Qualitative Limitations

Nuclear arms limitations are legally embodied in a number of bilateral Soviet-U.S. agreements that prescribe the establishment of limits on precisely defined types of weapons. The Treaty Between the United States of American and the Union of Soviet Socialist Republics on the Limitation of Anti-Ballistic Missile Systems (ABM Treaty) is the key document that laid down the basis for strategic stability in relations between the Soviet Union and the United States.

This Treaty was signed in Moscow on May 26, 1972, and entered into force on October 3, 1972. It contains specific limitations on Soviet and U.S. ABM systems. Pursuant to this Treaty, each of the Parties is permitted to deploy ABM systems only in two areas: a) within one area 150 kilometers in radius with its center located in the capital of the given Party; and b) within a single ABM area with a radius of 150 kilometers from a site at which intercontinental ballistic missile (ICBM) launch silos are deployed. The limitation of individual ABM system components (number of antiballistic missile launchers and antiballistic missiles, number and capability of radar facilities) is prescribed in each of these areas. The Parties to the Treaty pledge not to build, test, or deploy sea-launched, air-launched, space-based or mobile-based ABM systems or components, as well as launchers for launching more than one antiballistic missile simultaneously and devices for antiballistic missile launcher automatic reload.

ABM systems or components above and beyond the numbers or outside the zones specified by the Treaty, as well as systems prohibited by the Treaty, must be destroyed or dismantled within the shortest possible agreed-upon time. The Soviet Union and the United States pledge not to transfer to other states and not to deploy outside their national territory Treaty-limited ABM systems or their components. Compliance with Treaty obligations shall be verified by national technical means, with observance of generally recognized norms of international law. The Treaty prescribes establishment of a Standing Consultative Commission to assist in implementation of Treaty provisions. The Soviet Union and the United States pledge "to continue active negotiations for limitation on strategic offensive arms." The Treaty is of unlimited duration, but it contains a provision that each of the Parties has the right to withdraw from the Treaty if it decides that exceptional circumstances connected with the content of the Treaty threaten its higher interests.

In the Agreed Statements of May 26, 1972, in connection with the ABM Treaty, the Parties noted that in case ballistic-missile defense systems based on different physical principles and containing components capable of substituting for antiballistic missiles, antiballistic missile launchers, or ABM radars are created in the future, specific limitations on such systems and their components would be subject to discussion in conformity with Article XIII and to agreement pursuant to Chapter XIV of the Treaty. It was also stipulated that the Parties shall proceed from the understanding that Article V of the Treaty includes pledges not to build, not to test, and not to deploy antiballistic missiles carrying more than one independently targetable warhead per missile. The Parties agreed not to deploy phased-array radars with a power-aperture product exceeding 3 million, except as provided under Articles III, IV, and VI of the Treaty, or except for purposes of tracking space objects or for use as national technical means of verification.

In 1974, as a result of the Moscow Summit Talks, the Soviet Union and the United States signed a Protocol to the ABM Treaty, according to which each of the parties would have only one instead of two ABM system deployment areas. In the Soviet Union this is the Moscow ABM system, and in the United States the Grand Forks missile base (North Dakota).

The ABM Treaty established an international legal norm prohibiting the deployment of strategic defense weapon systems. An entire system of strategic mutual relations between nuclear powers, particularly the Soviet Union and the United States, was formed on the basis of this norm. This by no means ideal system can be variously assessed, but one cannot deny that success was achieved in removing at least one very substantial component from the arms race and from the complex balance of forces. The ban on ABM systems is still in force and continues to remain an actually operating legal norm regulating strategic stability.

In parallel with the drafting of the ABM Treaty, efforts were in progress to limit offensive strategic arms. In contrast to the "prohibitory" principle on which the ABM Treaty is based, the principle of "permission" was applied in regard to strategic offensive arms. In other words, from the very outset the parties did not have in mind eliminating or reducing anything. In addition, it was not even proposed to "freeze" levels existing at the moment of treaty signing. Establishment of "permitted ceilings" was selected as the optimal way to search for and reach an agreement.

On May 26, 1972, an Interim Agreement Between the United States of America and the Union of Soviet Socialist Republics on Certain Measures with Respect to the Limitation of Strategic Offensive Arms was signed in Moscow. It entered into force on October 3, 1972. The limits prescribed by this instrument (SALT I) apply to the following types of strategic offensive arms:

1) not to commence after July 1, 1972, the construction of additional land-based intercontinental ballistic missile (ICBM) fixed-site launchers;

2) not to convert land-based light ICBM launchers as well as launchers of old-type land-based ICBMs deployed prior to 1964 into launchers for land-based heavy ICBMs of types deployed subsequent to this time;

3) to limit submarine-launched ballistic missile launchers and modern ballistic missile submarines to the number in operational service and under construction as of the date of signing of the Agreement.

Pursuant to the Protocol to the SALT I Agreement the Soviet Union may have not more than 950 submarine-launched ballistic missile (SLBM) launchers and not more than sixty-two modern ballistic missile submarines. The United States may have not more than 710 SLBM launchers and not more than forty-four modern ballistic missile submarines. Placement of additional SLBM launchers into operational service, above 740 SLBM launchers for the Soviet Union and above 656 SLBM launchers for the United States in operational service and under construction, may be carried out as replacement for an equal number of launchers of ballistic missiles of old types, deployed prior to 1964, or ballistic missile launchers of old submarines.

In the agreed declarations in connection with the SALT I Agreement, the Parties reached an understanding that land-based ICBM launchers shall be defined as launchers for strategic ballistic missiles with a range capability exceeding the shortest distance between the northwestern boundary of the continental Soviet Union and the northeastern boundary of the continental United States.

The SALT I Agreement did not resolve all problems. The Parties proceeded from the position that this constituted only a first phase of joint efforts to limit nuclear potentials, and soon after this Agreement entered into force they resumed talks aimed at working out additional and more substantial limitations. The new talks were called SALT II. They were held under rather difficult circumstances: quite fierce political battles raged around these talks. The situation was frequently such that it seemed that they would not produce any results. Nevertheless both sides, displaying flexibility and an endeavor to reach a mutual understanding, to the extent this was possible in those years of rollback to ideological confrontation and "cold war," ultimately reached compromise positions.

The Treaty Between the United States of America and the Union of Soviet Socialist Republics on the Limitation of Strategic Offensive Arms (SALT II) was signed in Vienna on July 18, 1979. This Treaty did not enter into force due to the fact that, following the bringing of Soviet troops into Afghanistan, the United States considered the international situation to have become aggravated and not conducive to continuing the process of nuclear disarmament.

The Treaty specifies for both parties equal maximum levels of nuclear delivery systems; in order to begin the process of reduction, it prescribes reduction of existing nuclear arms; and in order to lessen the threat presented by the arms race, the Treaty imposes substantial limitations on the modernization of strategic offensive systems and the development of new systems.

Each of the Parties pledges:

> to limit strategic offensive arms in both a qualitative and quantitative respect, and to show restraint in the development of new types of strategic offensive arms;
>
> after the Treaty enters into force, to limit ICBM launchers, submarine-launched ballistic missile (SLBM) launchers, heavy bombers, and air-to-surface ballistic missiles (ASBM) to an aggregate total not to exceed 2,400 units;
>
> from January 1, 1981, to limit strategic offensive arms (ICBMs, launchers of SLBMs, heavy bombers, and ASBMs) to an aggregate total not to exceed 2,250 units, and to proceed with reduction of those arms in excess of this aggregate total as of that date;
>
> to limit launchers of ICBMs and SLBMs fitted with multiple independently targetable reentry vehicles (MIRV) and MIRVed ASBMs, as well as heavy bombers fitted to carry cruise missiles with a range capability in excess of 600 km, to an aggregate total not to exceed 1,320 units.

The Parties agreed to use national technical means of verification to ensure compliance with the provisions of the Treaty. The Treaty was to remain in force through December 31, 1985, unless superseded prior to that date by an agreement on further limitation of strategic offensive arms.

The Treaty contains an obligation for the Parties:

> to begin, promptly after the entry into force of this Treaty, active negotiations with the objective of achieving, as soon as possible, agreement on further measures for the limitation and reduction of strategic arms.

Concurrently with the Treaty a Protocol was signed, plus a Joint Statement of Principles and Basic Guidelines for Subsequent Negotiations on the Limitation of Strategic Arms, as well as a document entitled "Agreed Statements and Common Understandings Regarding the Treaty Between the United States of America and the Union of Soviet Socialist Republics on the Limitation of Strategic Offensive Arms." Pursuant to the Protocol, the Parties pledged not to deploy mobile ICBM launchers and not to conduct ICBM flight tests from mobile launchers. Limitations were also specified for cruise missiles. The Parties pledged not to deploy cruise missiles capable of a range in excess of 600 km on sea- or land-based launchers. In addition, flight tests of cruise missiles fitted with multiple independently targetable warheads and with a range capability of greater than 660 km from sea- and land-based launchers were prohibited.

Following the signing of SALT II in 1979, there ensued a fairly lengthy pause in bilateral efforts in the area of nuclear disarmament. This was caused by aggravation of the international situation and the unwillingness of both parties to make a genuine effort to understand one another's interests. Concurrently an extensive debate commenced on the problem of so-called "Euromissiles," in other words U.S. plans to deploy in the countries of Western Europe the new Pershing II intermediate-range missiles and Tomahawk intermediate-range cruise missiles in response to the SS-20 missiles earlier deployed by the Soviet Union. The debate had the clearly marked character of a propaganda war. The Soviet leadership of that time was seeking to keep the SS-20 missiles and at the same time to persuade the West Europeans not to agree to the deployment of new U.S. intermediate-range weapons.

The talks, originally begun under the title "Limitation of Nuclear Arms in Europe," became literally mired down in positions that would not budge. Efforts by diplomats to find a compromise encountered the rock-hard positions of the military and political leadership. A radically new approach, a resolute freeing from old stereotypical notions of security was needed in order to resolve the problem.

The Soviet-U.S. Geneva Summit Meeting in November 1985 provided a powerful impetus for forward movement in negotiations. In the course of this summit meeting the two sides succeeded for the first time in reaching an understanding of the need for a total elimination of intermediate-range and shorter-range nuclear missile weapons. Negotiations, resumed following the Geneva Summit, proceeded at an accelerated pace, and in the course of the next two years the countries succeeded in reaching agreement on an entire aggregate of issues.

A Treaty Between the United States of America and the Union of Soviet Socialist Republics on the Elimination of Their Intermediate-Range and Shorter-Range Missiles (INF Treaty) was signed in December 1988. This Treaty constitutes a qualitatively new stride forward in the area of nuclear disarmament, since this Treaty, in contrast to SALT I and SALT II, for the first time provides for the elimination of specific types of nuclear weapons. Thus the INF Treaty shifts nuclear disarmament from the level of limitations to the level of reductions.

As M.S. Gorbachev noted in his speech at the United Nations on December 7, 1988, the Soviet Union and the United States, which have built massive nuclear missile arsenals, becoming aware of their responsibility in a practical and substantive manner, have succeeded in becoming the first to conclude an agreement on the reduction and physical elimination of a portion of these arms, which threatened both themselves and all others.

The INF Treaty is unique both in the nature and scope of obligations assumed by its Parties, and in the mechanism of carrying out these obligations. It prescribes not only the total elimination of intermediate-range and shorter-range nuclear missile weapons in the possession of the parties but also a ban on the manufacture and testing of such weapons. Soviet and U.S. missiles with a range capability of from 500 to 5,500 kilometers, their launchers, and associated support structures and equipment are to be physically eliminated.

Pursuant to the INF Treaty, all Soviet and U.S. intermediate-range missiles and launchers for these missiles, as well as all auxiliary structures and all support equipment associated with these missiles and launchers, are to be destroyed.

The Treaty contains the clarification that the term "intermediate-range missile" shall mean a ground-launched ballistic missile (GLBM) or a ground-launched cruise missile (GLCM), the range capability of which is equal to or greater than 1000 kilometers but does not exceed 5,500 kilometers.

Also to be eliminated are all Soviet and U.S. shorter-range missiles and launchers for such missiles, as well as all support equipment associated with such missiles and launchers. The term "shorter-range" missiles shall mean a GLBM or GLCM, the range capability of which is equal to or greater than 500 km but not greater than 1,000 km.

The following types of intermediate-range missiles are to be eliminated in the course of the first three years the Treaty is in force: Soviet RSD-10 (SS-20), R-12 (SS-4), and R-14 (SS-5), as well as the U.S. Pershing II and BGM-109G missiles. As for shorter-range missiles, within a period of one and a half years the Soviet Union shall eliminate OTR-22 (SS-12) and OTR-23 (SS-23) missiles, while the United States shall eliminate Pershing IA missiles. Soviet RK-55 and U.S. Pershing IB ground-launched cruise missiles, which are considered to come under the category of "tested but not deployed," are also to be eliminated.

The nuclear warheads of all the above-listed missiles, including seventy-two U.S. warheads for West German Pershing IA missiles, are also to be eliminated.

The Treaty stipulates that neither Party shall produce any intermediate-range or shorter-range missiles in the future, shall not conduct flight tests of such missiles, and shall not build any stages of such missiles or any launchers for such missiles.

As of the date the Treaty entered into force (June 1, 1988), 889 deployed and undeployed intermediate-range missiles were to be eliminated in the Soviet Union, and 677 in the United States. As for shorter-range missiles, 957 were to be eliminated on the Soviet side, and 169 on the U.S. side. The total number of missiles to be eliminated was 1,846 for the Soviet Union and 846 for the United States.

The Protocol on Procedures Governing the Elimination of the Missile Systems Subject to the Treaty specified the missile system components to be eliminated and the procedure and methods of elimination of missiles, launchers, and associated support equipment and structures.

It is permitted to use former mobile launchers and transport vehicles (prime movers) for civilian purposes. In connection with this, in the course of implementation of the INF Treaty, more than 1,000 pieces of special automotive equipment for hauling large loads will be transferred into the Soviet civilian economy.

Intermediate-range missiles are to be eliminated over the course of three years, in two stages, the first of which runs twenty-nine months. This process shall commence simultaneously for both the Soviet Union and the United States.

The United States shall eliminate all types of missiles on a proportional basis, in such a manner as to observe the initial ratio of ground-launched ballistic missiles and cruise missiles to be eliminated. Shorter-range missiles are to be eliminated over the course of eighteen months.

The Treaty provides for effective monitoring and verification measures. It is appropriate to note that in drawing up the Treaty the Soviet side expressed willingness to proceed further in the area of monitoring and verification than the U.S. side. Ultimately, thanks to the constructive attitude displayed by both sides, a mutually acceptable, optimal solution to this problem was worked out. As a result the INF Treaty constitutes a genuine advance in the area of monitoring and verification and provides assurance that all obligations prescribed in the

Treaty will be strictly observed.

The system of verification applying to the INF Treaty provides for utilization of national technical means of verification, conduct of on-site inspections both on a continuing and occasional basis, exchange of data, and notification of weapons coming under the Treaty.

A total of five types of inspection are prescribed: to verify initial data, to confirm the fact of elimination of missile operating bases and missile support facilities, inspection to verify that missiles are not being built at missile production facilities, inspections at intermediate-range and shorter-range missile elimination facilities, and inspections on a quota basis.

The Protocol contains general obligations of the Parties pertaining to the procedure of notification of intention to conduct inspection, obligations of the inspecting and inspected party in connection with such notifications, procedure of entry, receiving and delivery of inspectors to an inspection site, including the manner and procedure of use of monitoring equipment, general rules and procedures of conduct of inspection, *etc.*

The manner of conduct of inspections on the territories of basing countries shall be determined by agreements with them in implementation of corresponding Soviet-U.S. agreements on the matter of inspections.

In addition to continuous monitoring at the exits of missile production plants in the town of Votkinsk (Udmurt ASSR) and in the town of Magna (Utah), the Treaty prescribes inspections to verify the initial data of inspections of missile operating bases and missile support facilities, and inspection of the processes of eliminating missile systems covered by the Treaty.

On-site inspections are conducted both on the territory of the Soviet Union and the United States, as well as on the territory of countries basing missiles to be eliminated: the GDR and Czechoslovakia on the one hand, and the FRG, Great Britain, Italy, Belgium, and the Netherlands on the other. The total number of inspections that the Soviet Union may conduct on the territory of the United States and in the respective basing countries of Western Europe over the period of thirteen years covered by the inspection mechanism is approximately 240; the United States may conduct a total of approximately 400 inspections. The U.S. right to a larger number of inspections is due to the fact that a larger number of missile systems is to be eliminated in the Soviet Union, and a greater number of facilities covered by the Treaty is to be eliminated on the territory of the Soviet Union, Czechoslovakia, and the former territory of the GDR.

The experience of implementation of the INF Treaty since it entered into force enables one to draw a firm conclusion that its mechanism is functioning effectively. The provisions of the Treaty are being carried out by the parties in conformity with the obligations they have assumed, and this process is being rigorously monitored, for which inspection agencies have been established in the Soviet Union and the United States.

A regular exchange of data, notifications, and reports is being conducted between the two countries' nuclear risk reduction centers. Inspections on short notice are conducted, monitoring of the elimination process is being performed, and inspections on a continuous basis have been organized at the missile plants in Votkinsk and Magna.

A Special Verification Commission, tasked with resolving matters pertaining to the performance of obligations by the parties and with reaching agreement on measures to increase the effectiveness and viability of this international legal enactment, was established for the purpose of helping to achieve the goals and to implement the provisions of the INF Treaty in conformity with its provisions and is in operation. Matters of a legal, administrative-procedural, and technical nature pertaining to fulfillment of the Treaty, in particular its provisions on verification, are discussed and resolved within the framework of the Commission, and concerns arising with the parties in this connection are resolved.

The INF Treaty created preconditions for moving forward in other directions in the area of disarmament. The value of the experience of its conclusion and implementation is obvious for the draft treaty on Limitation and Reduction of Strategic Offensive Arms.

Work on a treaty on limitation and reduction of Soviet and U.S. strategic offensive arms has been in progress since March 12, 1985, at the bilateral Soviet-U.S. talks on nuclear and space-based weapons in Geneva. Progress in this area has been achieved as a result of the subsequent six meetings between Soviet and U.S. leaders (Geneva (1985), Reykjavik (1986), Washington (1987), Moscow (1988), Malta (1989), and Washington (1990)).

Since the commencement of the START talks, substantial changes have occurred in execution of Soviet and U.S. military programs in the direction of reduction in the volume of deployment of corresponding arms and postponement of entry of new weapons into service. The number of new military programs has also sharply decreased.

If a Soviet-U.S. treaty on limitation and reduction of strategic nuclear arms is concluded, this will mean that for the first time in the history of development of the strategic triad there will be a break in the persisting trend toward a buildup of all three of its components, and over the course of a seven-year period there will be a reduction both in the number of strategic nuclear delivery systems (ICBMs, SLBMs, and heavy bombers) and of nuclear warheads.

Thus the process of actual reduction of strategic arms will finally begin, and a very large reduction, involving hundreds of delivery systems and thousands of warheads. Even more important is the fact that these reductions will be aimed at making a first strike less probable. As a result stability will be strengthened and the threat of war lessened.

In assessing the significance of a future treaty on strategic offensive arms it is also important to bear in mind that, in the absence of such a treaty, the Soviet Union and the United States could possess more than twice as many ICBMs and SLBMs and could appreciably increase the number of heavy bombers carrying both nuclear-tipped and conventional-warhead ALCMs. Nor would the program of deployment of nuclear SLCMs be limited.

The principal agreed provisions of the proposed treaty are as follows:

The total number of deployed ICBMs and associated launchers, deployed SLBMs and associated launchers, and heavy bombers will be reduced to a level not exceeding 1,600 units. Within the framework of this total quantity, the number of deployed heavy ICBMs and associated launchers will be reduced to a level not exceeding 154 units.

The total number of warheads counting against deployed ICBMs, deployed SLBMs, and heavy bombers will be reduced to a level not exceeding 6,000 units. Of that, there will be not more than 4,900 warheads on deployed ICBMs and deployed SLBMs, not more than 1,540 warheads on heavy ICBMs, and not more than 1,100 warheads on mobile ICBMs.

The aggregate throw-weight of deployed ICBMs and SLBMs of each party will be limited to an agreed level, comprising approximately fifty percent of the existing level of the aggregate throw-weight of deployed ICBMs and SLBMs of the Union of Soviet Socialist Republics as of a date to be agreed upon. This maximum limit shall not be exceeded during the entire period in which the treaty remains in force.

Heavy bombers fitted to carry long-range nuclear-tipped air-launched cruise missiles (ALCM) shall be distinguishable from other heavy bombers. Heavy bombers fitted to carry nuclear weapons other than long-range nuclear-tipped ALCMs shall count as one delivery system to a maximum level of 1,600 units, and one warhead shall be counted against them, counted against a maximum level of 6,000 units.

Heavy bombers fitted to carry long-range nuclear-tipped ALCMs shall count as one delivery system to a maximum level of 1,600 units, and an agreed number of warheads, counting against a level of 6,000 units, shall be counted against them. Ten warheads apiece shall be counted against existing and future U.S. heavy bombers fitted to carry long-range nuclear-tipped ALCMs. Eight warheads apiece shall be counted against existing and future Soviet heavy bombers fitted to carry long-range nuclear-tipped ALCMs.

The United States shall be able to possess, within the maximum aggregate level of 1,600 delivery systems, not more than 150 heavy bombers fitted to carry long-range nuclear-tipped ALCMs, against which ten warheads apiece shall be counted. The Union of Soviet Socialist Republics may possess forty percent more than this number of heavy bombers. If the United States exceeds a level of 150 units, that number of long-range nuclear-tipped ALCMs for which it is actually equipped will be counted against each additional heavy bomber fitted to carry long-range nuclear-tipped ALCMs. If the Union of Soviet Socialist Republics exceeds a level of 210 heavy bombers fitted to carry long-range nuclear-tipped ALCMs, that number of long-range nuclear-tipped ALCMs for which it is actually equipped shall count against each such heavy bomber.

Existing and future U.S. heavy bombers may be fitted to carry not more than 20 long-range nuclear-tipped ALCMs. Existing and future Soviet heavy bombers may be fitted to carry not more than 12 long-range nuclear-tipped ALCMs.

ALCMs with a range capability of more than 600 kilometers shall be considered to be long-range air-launched cruise missiles. Future long-range conventional-warhead ALCMs shall not be considered as nuclear if they are distinguishable from long-range nuclear-tipped ALCMs. No limits shall be applied to the deployment of such ALCMs carried by aircraft not limited under this treaty.

Reductions shall be carried out in three stages over the course of seven years. Specific equal intermediate levels shall be achieved for the agreed categories of strategic offensive arms by the end of each stage of reductions.

Achievement of and compliance with the quantitative limitations prescribed by the treaty shall be accomplished by means of conversion or elimination, in conformity with agreed-upon procedures.

Sea-launched cruise missiles (SLCMs) will not be limited under the strategic offensive arms treaty. Each of the parties shall submit to the other party a unilateral statement of its policy regarding nuclear-tipped SLCMs, and shall subsequently, on an annual basis throughout the entire time during which the treaty remains in force, submit unilateral statements pertaining to that party's planned deployment of long-range (that is, with a range capability of more than 600 kilometers) nuclear-tipped sea-launched cruise missiles. These statements shall be of a politically binding nature. These annual statements shall specify the maximum number of deployed nuclear-tipped SLCMs for each of the subsequent five years of the treaty, and the stated number shall not exceed 880 units. Policy statements shall include the statement that the Soviet Union and the United States will not produce or deploy sea-launched cruise missiles with multiple independently targetable warheads. The parties confirmed their Joint Statement at the Washington Summit in December 1987 pertaining to continuation of the search for "mutually acceptable and effective methods of verification."

The verification regime being drafted includes the following:

On-site inspections: For purposes of verification of treaty compliance, each of the parties shall conduct, in accordance with agreed-upon procedures and on the basis of reciprocity, twelve types of on-site inspection as well as continuous monitoring of mobile ICBM production facilities. Included in the above, each of the parties shall conduct inspections on short notice at strategic offensive arms-related sites, including inspections to verify the number of warheads on deployed ballistic missiles, inspections to confirm the fact of elimination of strategic offensive arms and associated facilities, inspections "on suspicion," and various viewings.

National technical means of verification: For purposes of verification each of the parties shall use the national technical means of verification at its disposal in such a manner as to be in conformity with generally recognized principles of international law. The treaty shall prescribe an aggregate of measures based on cooperation, aimed at increasing the effectiveness of national technical means of verification. Interference with or jamming of such means of verification shall be prohibited.

Prohibition of impeding access to telemetry data: The parties have agreed to perform onboard measurements of technical parameters on ICBMs and SLBMs and to transmit all telemetry obtained as a result of such measures. With the exception of certain strictly limited exceptions, any actions, including use of encryption, encapsulation, and jamming, hindering full access to telemetry data shall be prohibited.

Exchange of information: Before signing the treaty, the parties shall exchange data on numbers, locations, and technical characteristics of their strategic offensive arms. These data shall be regularly updated during the entire time during which the treaty remains in force.

A comprehensive agreement will be reached on the manner and procedure of deploying mobile ICBM launchers and the missiles associated with them and on corresponding limitations on their movement in such a manner as to ensure effective verification of compliance with the quantitative limits established under this treaty. As an additional provision, the number of undeployed ICBMs for mobile launchers shall be limited, while mobile ICBMs shall be subject to the application of specific identifying markings.

To assist in carrying out the purposes of this treaty, the parties shall establish a Joint Commission for Monitoring and Inspection.

The parties have agreed that the treaty shall remain in force for a period of fifteen years, unless it is superseded by a subsequent agreement prior to that time. On agreement between the parties, the treaty may be extended for additional five-year periods if it is not superseded.

At the same time the Soviet Union and the United States agreed, based on the results of negotiations in progress, to hold new talks on strategic offensive arms and the linkage between strategic offensive and defensive arms. This was formally articulated in the joint statement pertaining to future talks on nuclear and space-based arms and further strengthening of strategic stability, announced during M.S. Gorbachev's visit to the United States in June 1990. The purpose of these talks will be to reduce to an even greater extent the risk of outbreak of war, especially nuclear war, and to ensure strategic stability, transparency, and predictability by means of further stabilizing reductions in the strategic arsenals of both countries. This will be achieved by seeking agreements that increase survivability, that eliminate incentives to deliver a nuclear first strike, and that embody a suitable linkage between strategic offensive and defensive systems.

To reach these goals, the parties have agreed to the following:

First. Following the signing of the strategic offensive arms treaty, the parties will without delay hold consultations pertaining to future negotiations, and these important negotiations will commence as soon as is possible from a practical standpoint. Both parties will be entitled to raise at these future talks any and all matters pertaining to any strategic offensive arms.

Within the framework of the existing structure of the talks on nuclear and space-based arms in Geneva, the parties will continue without delay talks on ballistic missile defense and space.

Thus in the course of future talks the parties will discuss matters of strategic stability of interest to them, including a linkage between strategic offensive and defensive arms, taking into consideration stabilizing reductions of strategic offensive arms and the development of new technologies. The parties will proceed in the direction of accomplishing an important task of achieving the earliest possible results at these talks.

Second. The Soviet Union and the United States, just as in the case of the treaty on strategic offensive arms that is presently being drawn up, shall at the new talks seek to achieve a reduction in their strategic offensive arms in such a manner as to be in conformity with the task of increasing strategic stability. Both parties agree to place emphasis in the course of these new talks on eliminating first-strike incentives, on reducing concentration of warheads on strategic delivery systems, and on giving preference to weapons possessing enhanced survivability.

In particular, the parties will seek measures that will reduce the concentration of warheads on strategic delivery systems as a whole, including measures pertaining to heavy ICBMs and MIRVed ICBMs.

Effective verification will be provided by national technical means, cooperative measures, and on-site inspection.

Third. Having agreed to the need to ensure predictability of the strategic ratio between the Soviet Union and the United States throughout the entire period during which the strategic offensive arms treaty remains in force, the parties shall exchange information at the beginning of each calendar year on planned changes in quantities of strategic offensive arms as of the end of the current year.

Fourth. The parties shall endeavor to adopt additional confidence-building measures and measures to ensure predictability in the military activities of the Soviet Union and the United States, reducing the possibility of outbreak of nuclear war as a result of chance, miscalculation, terrorism, or an unanticipated technological breakthrough, and preventing the possibility of occurrence of incidents between them.

Fifth. The parties believe that reducing the risk of outbreak of nuclear war is the responsibility not only of the Soviet Union and the United States, and that other states should also make a contribution toward achieving this goal, in particular in the area of nonproliferation of nuclear weapons. They call upon all states to consider new possibilities for participation in common efforts by mankind directed toward eliminating throughout the world the danger of outbreak of nuclear war.

D. Long-Range Goals of Nuclear Arms Control and the Question of Complete Elimination

The problem of nuclear disarmament has long held the attention of the international community and has been regularly discussed at UN General Assembly sessions. Deliberation on an aggregate of nuclear disarmament issues, taking place in the United Nations, is accompanied by an increasing inclination on the part of the majority of states to internationalize specific actions aimed at promoting genuine reduction and phased elimination of nuclear weapons.

The Final Document of the Tenth Special Session of the General Assembly, the first special session devoted to disarmament, held in New York from May 23 through June 30, 1978, a Document that was adopted by a consensus vote by all UN member states, points out that:

> Nuclear weapons pose the greatest danger to mankind and to the survival of civilization. It is essential to halt and reverse the nuclear arms race in all its aspects in order to avert the danger of war involving nuclear weapons. The ultimate goal in this context is the complete elimination of nuclear weapons. (Paragraph 47).

The Document goes on to emphasize that:

> The process of nuclear disarmament should be carried out in such

> a way, and requires measures to ensure, that the security of all States is guaranteed at progressively lower levels of nuclear armaments, taking into account the relative qualitative and quantitative importance of the existing arsenals of the nuclear-weapon States and other States concerned. (Paragraph 49).

The international community has reached a consensus regarding ways to wind down the nuclear arms race. In particular, Paragraph 50 of the Final Document notes:

> The achievement of nuclear disarmament will require urgent negotiation of agreements at appropriate stages and with adequate measures of verification satisfactory to the States concerned for:
>
> (a) Cessation of the qualitative improvement and development of nuclear-weapon systems;
>
> (b) Cessation of the production of all types of nuclear weapons and their means of delivery, and of the production of fissionable material for weapons purposes;
>
> (c) A comprehensive, phased programme with agreed time-frames, whenever feasible, for progressive and balanced reduction of stockpiles of nuclear weapons and their means of delivery, leading to their ultimate and complete elimination at the earliest possible time.

The priority nature of nuclear disarmament consistently finds expression in resolutions of UN General Assembly sessions. For example, Resolution 41/59F, "Nuclear Disarmament" (based on a draft resolution presented by the PRC), was adopted by a consensus vote. This Resolution states that the governments and peoples of various countries expect the Soviet Union and the United States to reach a formal understanding on ending the nuclear arms race and on reducing stockpiles of nuclear weapons, in order to proceed with the process of nuclear disarmament, bearing in mind that the total elimination of nuclear weapons is the ultimate goal of this process. The Resolution also recognizes the responsibility of all states possessing nuclear weapons to foster and promote nuclear disarmament.

The consensus on nuclear disarmament was formally articulated at subsequent sessions. Resolutions entitled "Nuclear Disarmament" were adopted by the General Assembly without a vote at the Forty-second, Forty-third, and Forty-fourth sessions. There is no reason to believe that this consensus will change in the future.

The convergence of nations' approaches to resolving the problems of elimination and banning of nuclear weapons and preventing nuclear war finds expression in resolutions adopted by the General Assembly. The level of mutual understanding rises year by year, and new foundations for cooperation are created. The number of nations that are actively advocating the immediate commencement of multilateral actions and more specific debates at the United Nations on the problem of nuclear disarmament is growing at the same time.

Over a period of a number of years, for example, the GDR and Argentina conducted active efforts in the United Nations on nuclear disarmament issues. Corresponding resolutions were adopted year after year at their initiative. Resolutions entitled "Nuclear Weapons in All Their Aspects," adopted at the GDR's initiative, contained an appeal to the Conference on Disarmament to proceed without delay with talks on ending the nuclear arms race and on nuclear disarmament and to begin drafting practical measures in this area in conformity with Paragraph 50 of the Final Document of the UN General Assembly's First Special Session on Disarmament, including a program of nuclear disarmament, establishing a special committee for this purpose. The Resolutions also noted that any hope for victory in a nuclear war is senseless, and expressed the conviction that nations must discard all military doctrines and concepts that could lead to the initiation of nuclear war.

This proposal was successfully integrated for the first time at the Forty-first Session with a proposal by Argentina and a number of other nonaligned nations that traditionally have held similar views. Resolution 41/86F, adopted on the basis of the joint proposal, refers to the Final Document of the First UN General Assembly Special Session on Disarmament and the Conferences in New Delhi and Harare, as well as the Mexican Declaration, stresses the importance of nuclear disarmament, condemns the doctrine of nuclear deterrence, welcomes proposals calling for the elimination of nuclear weapons worldwide, and notes the need for ceasing all testing, manufacture, and deployment of nuclear weapons. An appeal was addressed to the Conference on Disarmament to establish at the commencement of its 1987 Session a special committee to develop further the provisions of Paragraph 50 of the Final Document. It is emphasized thereby that the purpose of talks should be to bring to an end the qualitative improvement and development of nuclear weapon systems, the manufacture of all types of nuclear weapons and delivery systems, and the production of fissionable materials for weapons purposes, as well as to achieve a substantial reduction in existing stockpiles of nuclear weapons with the goal of achieving their complete elimination.

At subsequent sessions this fruitful cooperation was formally articulated in General Assembly resolutions, which for the most part restate the provisions of Resolution 41/86F.

For many years now the United Nations has been considering, at Indian initiative, the question of banning the use of nuclear weapons. India was the first to propose initiation of talks for the purpose of drafting an international convention banning the use of nuclear weapons or the threat of use of nuclear weapons under any circumstances whatsoever, in the course of the UN General Assembly's Second Special Session on Disarmament in 1982. Since that time resolutions have been regularly adopted at General Assembly sessions, affirming requests to the Conference on Disarmament that talks be initiated on drafting the text of a convention on a priority basis, using as a basis the text of the draft convention submitted by India at the UN General Assembly Second Special Session on Disarmament. Commencement of practical work at the Conference on Disarmament has been opposed, however, by the United States and its NATO allies.

For a number of years now the attention of the General Assembly has been focused on the question of renunciation of nuclear weapons and the prevention of nuclear war. The most recent Resolution on this matter, Resolution 44/119, was adopted in 1989 at the Forty-fourth UN General Assembly Session. The Resolution cites the Final Document of the Ninth Conference of Heads of State and Government of Nonaligned Nations in Belgrade and expresses the conviction that renunciation of first use of nuclear weapons is one of the most urgent measures aimed at preventing the occurrence of nuclear war and stresses the need to make military concepts and doctrines strictly defensive in nature. The General Assembly expressed the hope that those nuclear states which have not yet done so will consider making declarations against first use of nuclear weapons. The Resolution also contains a request that the Conference on Disarmament commence talks on drafting an international document of a legally binding nature in which a no-first-use of nuclear weapons pledge would be formulated.

A "Prevention of Nuclear War" Resolution is regularly adopted on the basis of a draft resolution by Argentina and other nonaligned nations. This Resolution contains a request that the Conference on Disarmament commence talks on a priority basis aimed at reaching an agreement on appropriate and practical measures to prevent nuclear war and to form for this purpose a special committee to deal with this matter.

Many UN member countries view a nuclear arms freeze as an important measure leading to reduction and ultimately to the complete elimination of nuclear weapons. A Resolution on this matter that is regularly adopted at General Assembly sessions on Indian and Mexican initiative emphasizes that a freeze would "provide for a simultaneous total stoppage of any further production of nuclear weapons and a complete cut-off in the production of fissionable materials for weapons purposes."

The General Assembly has adopted a Resolution entitled "Prohibition of the Production of Fissionable Materials for Weapons Purposes," based on a draft resolution submitted by Canada and a number of other Western countries. It requests the Conference on Disarmament to continue examination, at the appropriate stage of its work on the agenda item "Nuclear Weapons in All Aspects," of the question of adequately verifiable cessation and prohibition of the production of fissionable materials for nuclear weapons and other nuclear explosive devices.

The character of the Resolutions adopted by the UN General Assembly on nuclear disarmament reflects the principled approaches of the various parties in this area.

The Western countries firmly insist on the need to maintain nuclear potential in the foreseeable future, as they fail to see any realistic alternative to the nuclear deterrence component. At the same time this concept is no longer as monolithic as it was several years ago. Processes of genuine disarmament, particularly nuclear disarmament, and radical changes in East-West relations, which have placed in question the need for Soviet-U.S. nuclear confrontation, have sparked intensive debate within the Western alliance regarding the quantitative and qualitative parameters of nuclear deterrent forces. As a result problems of tactical nuclear weapons soon appeared on the negotiating table, and the taboo on the discussion of naval nuclear weapons was removed.

On the other hand, one can clearly trace in the General Assembly Resolutions the position of the countries of the Nonaligned Movement, which calls for an immediate and radical solution to all aspects of nuclear disarmament. This position clearly fails to consider the specifics of the problem, leads multilateral dialogue off in the direction of mere declaration, and diminishes the significance of bilateral understandings reached in the area of nuclear disarmament.

In this situation it is important to make a practical search for points of contact between positions and to develop a dialogue directed to globalization of disarmament, encompassing all categories of arms in negotiation processes and involving an adequate contribution by all states toward securing the goals of disarmament. Constructive mutual supplementation of bilateral and multilateral efforts in this area would help achieve concrete results.

Evidently the United Nations should concentrate its attention on those nuclear disarmament issues that require multilateral participation and are close to solution. This would include, for example, the problem of banning the production of fissionable materials for weapon purposes. Active UN involvement in efforts to reach an agreement on such a ban would lead to reduction of the industrial base for manufacture of key nuclear weapon components. Priorities also include matters pertaining to the nonproliferation of nuclear weapons, banning of nuclear weapon testing, guarantees for nations not possessing nuclear weapons, and a number of other items. The problem of nuclear deterrence, upon which the entire nuclear "pyramid" essentially rests, requires detailed examination in the United Nations.

The Soviet Union pursues an active policy seeking internationalization of the process of nuclear disarmament and moving of the nuclear debate at the United Nations to a practical level. Beginning with its first proposal to ban atomic weapons in 1946, the Soviet Union has to this day inalterably advocated the need for priority resolution of the problem of nuclear disarmament.

At the UN General Assembly Second Special Session on Disarmament in June 1982, the Soviet Union presented a memorandum entitled "Ending the Growing Nuclear Threat, Holding the Arms Race in Check," which contained a proposal for drafting, adoption and phased implementation of a program of nuclear disarmament, and unilaterally pledged not to be the first to use nuclear weapons. This pledge went into effect on June 15, 1982.

A comprehensive program of general security through disarmament, presented by the Soviet Union in a statement by M.S. Gorbachev on January 15, 1986, provided strong new impetus to move to specifics in the UN debate on nuclear disarmament. This program constituted a concentrated expression and further specific development of the firm, principled Soviet policy in the area of disarmament.

At the Forty-first Session of the General Assembly the Soviet delegation, guided by the goals and tasks of the Program of January 15, 1986, presented a specific proposal: To proceed immediately with a multilateral exchange of views on nuclear disarmament issues among all nuclear powers, parallel with Soviet-U.S. talks on nuclear and space weapons (NST), in the course of which a number of important specific issues could be examined: in particular, cessation of the production of fissionable and fusionable nuclear materials for the purpose of developing and producing weapons; the procedure of eliminating nuclear arms; fundamental approaches to monitoring and verification of multilateral nuclear disarmament measures; and as a timetable for nuclear powers to enter the process of nuclear disarmament. This new Soviet proposal proceeds from the position that practical implementation of nuclear disarmament measures affecting other nuclear powers would take place following radical reduction of Soviet and U.S. nuclear arsenals.

Ideas pertaining to increasing the effectiveness of multilateral approaches to guaranteeing international security, set forth in an article by M.S. Gorbachev entitled "Realities and Guarantees of a Safe World," helped arouse heightened interest on the part of the international community in nuclear disarmament issues. It is emphasized in this article that we view nuclear weapons not as an unavoidable element of stability but rather as a destabilizing factor that undermines security, as the main obstacle on the way toward genuine democratization of interrelations between states, toward their actual equality and equal responsibility. The idea stated by the Soviet Union that problems of nuclear disarmament cannot be fully resolved solely at the level of Soviet-American bilateral talks, and that productive participation by the governments and the public in all countries is needed, evoked considerable interest at the United Nations. Proceeding from the position that utilization of the capabilities of the Security Council would promote more effective UN participation in nuclear disarmament, the Soviet Union introduced a proposal at the Forty-second Session of the UN General Assembly calling for the convening—following necessary preparations—of a special session of the General Assembly or the Security Council, possibly at the foreign minister level, for the purpose of discussing goals and tasks in the area of nuclear disarmament. It was noted therein that in the course of the forthcoming exchange of views specific measures could be proposed, leading to freeing the world of nuclear weapons, as well as provision of universal guarantees against the return of nuclear weapons. The Soviet Union's firm position in favor of commencing without delay, at the Conference on Disarmament, talks on drafting a nuclear disarmament program, talks being blocked by the United States and its allies, was reaffirmed at the same time.

In the course of the Third General Assembly Special Session on Disarmament the Soviet Union expressed the conviction that a non-nuclear guarantee of security was possible. The principles of sufficiency of defense potential, totally excluding the presence of weapons that could be used for a surprise attack, should constitute the basis of such security.

At the Forty-fourth Session of the UN General Assembly the Soviet Union maintained that it was possible to formulate specific parameters of minimum nuclear deterrence as a phase on the way to complete elimination of nuclear weapons. The idea of gradual transition from relations based on mutual nuclear deterrence to transparent and verifiable deterrence was advanced at the same time.

5. Limitations on Chemical and Biological Weapons

Thomas Graham, Jr.
General Counsel, U.S. Arms Control and Disarmament Agency

Chemical and biological weapons are two types of weapons of mass destruction that are closely linked historically and to which similar constraints were initially applied. The Protocol for the Prohibition of the Use in War of Asphyxiating, Poisonous or Other Gases, and of Bacteriological Methods of Warfare, signed in Geneva on June 17, 1925, known as the Geneva Protocol, in effect banned the first use in war of both chemical and biological weapons. The Convention on the Prohibition of the Development, Production and Stockpiling of Bacteriological (Biological) and Toxin Weapons and on Their Destruction, signed on April 10, 1972, known as the Biological Weapons Convention, prohibits the possession of biological weapons. A multilateral convention banning the possession of chemical weapons has been under active negotiations in Geneva since 1983 but is as yet without conclusion, although the United States and the Soviet Union have agreed on interim bilateral reductions.

Chemical weapons are essentially gas weapons, that is chemical compounds which are in the gaseous state when activated, and which are contained in shells, bombs, or spray tanks and are delivered by aircraft, artillery or ballistic missiles. During World War I, both chlorine and mustard gas weapons were used. Prior to World War II, the far more deadly nerve gases were developed, but gas weapons were not used between major combatants in that conflict. Toxins are chemical compounds which are the product of processes involving biological organisms. Botulinus toxin that causes botulism is an example. Even though toxin weapons are inert like chemical weapons, they are considered to be biological weapons because they are the product of biological processes. Biological weapons are essentially types of bacteria that are intended to be delivered in such a way as to cause disease among enemy troops. An example of a biological weapon agent is anthrax bacteria.

A. The Geneva Protocol

At the invitation of Tsar Nicholas II, an international peace conference was convened at the Hague in 1899 with the avowed purpose of limiting the ever more destructive nature of warfare. This first Hague Conference resulted in a signed declaration outlawed the use in war of asphysixiating gases. The second Hague Conference in 1907 prohibited the use of poison or poisoned weapons. Thus poison gas was declared to be an illegal weapon prior to World War I. Nevertheless, it was put to widespread use in that war beginning at Ypres, Belgium, in 1915. Before the war was over, the use of this weapon had caused over 100,000 deaths and in excess of one million casualties. It was regarded as a particularly noxious weapon by the public and this led to further efforts to ban it in the 1920's.

At the end of World War I, the victorious Allies reaffirmed in the Versailles Treaty the prewar ban on the use of poison gas in war and prohibited Germany from manufacturing such weapons. At the Washington Naval Disarmament Conference in 1922, the United States proposed that similar language prohibiting the use of poison gas in warfare be included in a treaty limiting submarines. The U.S. proposal was adopted and the U.S. Senate subsequently approved the Treaty without a dissenting vote. It never came into force, however, because the requisite French ratification was never obtained. In 1925, at a conference in Geneva on the supervision of the international arms trade, the United States proposed a ban on the export of gas for use in war. At the suggestion of France, it was decided to negotiate a Protocol prohibiting the use in war of poison gas and, at the suggestion of Poland, this was broadened to ban biological methods of warfare as well.

The result was the Geneva Protocol. By its terms, it prohibits the use in war of chemical and biological weapons among parties. Being a rule of warfare rather than an arms control agreement, it does not contain verification provisions. Because of reservations adopted by many Parties upon ratification, the Geneva Protocol is generally an agreement prohibiting the first use in war of chemical and biological weapons among Parties. The reservation, adopted by France upon ratification in May of 1926, is instructive in this regard. France declares that it is bound to the strictures of the Protocol only as regards relations with other Parties and it is released from its obligations under the Protocol with respect to any enemy state or states whose armed forces or allies do not observe its provisions. The Netherlands, in 1930, and the United States, when it finally did ratify in 1975, limited this first use feature only to chemical weapons. In other words, the Netherlands and the United States are bound by the Protocol never to use biological weapons against a Party in any situation and not to use chemical weapons as long as such weapons are not employed against them. Other countries such as Germany (1929), Switzerland (1932), and Mexico (1932) entered no reservations at all.

Ratification of the Geneva Protocol by the United States was a special matter, however. Unlike the Washington Naval Agreement, the Protocol encountered serious difficulties in the Senate, perhaps in part because in 1922 there had been representation from the Senate on the U.S. Delegation but not in 1925. The Senate Foreign Relations Committee reported the Protocol favorably but because of strong lobbying against it, the Protocol was not brought to a vote on the floor of the Senate. Thus, although a significant number of countries, including most of the great powers, ratified the Protocol in the late 1920's and the early 1930's, by the time of World War II, the United States had not. Nevertheless, President Roosevelt announced on June 8, 1943, that with respect to the weapons covered by the Geneva Protocol, their use had been "outlawed by the general opinion of civilized mankind" and that the United States would never be the first to use them. This statement by President Roosevelt could be interpreted to mean that the United States believed that the first use constraint established by the Protocol had, by 1943, become part of customary international law in view of the widespread recognition of this rule over almost twenty years. However, the United States still did not ratify the Protocol and in 1949, the Senate returned to President Truman a number of older treaties that had not been ratified, including the Geneva Protocol.

In 1966, the United States was criticized in the United Nations for the use of riot control agents (tear gas) and chemical herbicides in the war in Vietnam. The practice with riot control agents was to use them in part to force the enemy from protected hiding places so that he could be attacked, and the practice with herbicides was to defoliate forest areas so as to eliminate the enemy's cover. Hungary charged that the use in war of tear gas and chemical herbicides was prohibited by the Geneva Protocol, the obligations of which President Roosevelt had said the United States would respect. The United States argued that the Protocol did not apply to nontoxic gases and herbicides. In its final form, the Hungarian resolution simply called for strict observance by all states of "the principles and objectives" of the Protocol and for universal adherence to it.

The debate over the interpretation of the Protocol continued in 1969. In that year, in a foreword to a UN report on chemical and biological weapons, the Secretary General of the United Nations appealed for a "clear affirmation" that the Protocol prohibits the use in war of all chemical and biological agents. Discussion in the Conference of the Committee on Disarmament in Geneva indicated that most countries represented there supported the view of the Secretary General on the interpretation of the Protocol, although the United Kingdom argued that only the Parties to the Protocol had the right to interpret it.

This led to the introduction in the General Assembly of a resolution proposed by twenty-one countries asserting that the use in war of all chemical and biological agents was contrary to international law. The United States argued its interpretation and also that it was inappropriate for the General Assembly to use resolutions to interpret treaties. Nevertheless, the resolution was adopted by a vote of eighty to three (the United States voting no) with thirty-six abstentions (including France and the United Kingdom).

While this debate was underway, President Nixon announced on November 25, 1969, that he would resubmit the Geneva Protocol to the Senate and request advice and consent to ratification. He reaffirmed the U.S. policy of renunciation of the first use in war of lethal chemicals (adding to this renunciation incapacitating chemicals but not riot control agents). He also announced the unilateral renunciation of biological weapons. Some support for the U.S. interpretation on chemical weapons appeared. In 1930, during a discussion in Geneva, the United Kingdom asserted that the Geneva Protocol covered tear gas. In 1970, however, the British Foreign Secretary stated in Parliament that this remained the British position but that the riot control agent CS (which was what the United States had been using in Vietnam) was not harmful to man, unlike older tear gases, and therefore was not covered by the Protocol. In the same year, during the debate in the Diet on ratification of the Protocol, the Foreign Minister of Japan asserted that the Protocol did not cover tear gas and herbicides. Japan was the first militarily significant state to ratify the Protocol after the debate over its interpretation and it did so with the U.S. understanding as to its coverage.

In the Transmittal Documents accompanying the Protocol back to the U.S. Senate, the Secretary of State under date of August 11, 1970, set forth a reservation which provided that the United States retained the right to retaliate in the case of a chemical weapon attack and asserted an interpretative understanding that riot control agents and chemical herbicides are not covered by the Protocol. The Senate Foreign Relations Committee, however, refused to accept the interpretation of the Protocol as set forth in Secretary Rogers' letter. Chairman Fulbright stated that, in his view and that of many members of the Committee, it would be in the interest of the United States to either ratify the Protocol without "restrictive understandings" or to defer action until this became possible. The Committee, as a result, took no action on the Protocol and also held in abeyance approval of the Biological Weapons Convention that was before it as well.

As to the merits of this debate, they are unclear. There is no question but that it was the use of poison gas in World War I that caused the Protocol to be negotiated and that it was the prohibition on the use of poison gas in the Hague Conventions that the negotiators had in mind. Chemical herbicides were unknown in 1925 so the negotiators could not have had them in mind. Riot control agents and chemical herbicides were not used in Vietnam as weapons themselves, but as adjuncts to other weapons since used alone they are generally not lethal. There is a distinction between the two in that the use of tear gas in conjunction with other weapons could lead to immediate casualties, somewhat akin to the direct effect of poison gas, but the use of herbicides normally would only cause casualties over time after cover had been reduced. On the other hand, the Protocol, by its title, prohibits "poisonous, asphyxiating and other gases" and the UK, in 1930, took the position that tear gas was covered (while later exempting CS). On balance, it would appear that the Protocol is ambiguous on riot control agents, but that it is difficult to sustain the argument that chemical herbicides are covered.

In 1971, the Senate Foreign Relations Committee was responding to the politics of the day and the unpopularity of the Vietnam war. The Administration was concerned that if it conceded the point to the Committee, the United States could be accused of violations of international law in Vietnam. In 1974, the Ford Administration began a new effort to obtain ratification of the Geneva Protocol (and of the Biological Weapons Convention). A compromise was painstakingly worked out by the Arms Control and Disarmament Agency, acting as a mediator between the Committee and the Department of Defense. In summary form, this compromise was that the Committee would not rebut the interpretation of the coverage of the Protocol set forth by the Administration, and the Administration by Executive Order would "renounce as a matter of national policy" the first use in war of riot control agents and chemical herbicides. The first use of chemical herbicides in war was renounced except to control vegetation on U.S. bases and around their immediate defensive perimeters. The first use in war of riot control agents was barred except in defensive military modes to save civilian lives such as: controlling rioting prisoners of war; in cases where civilians are being used by the enemy as a screen; in rescue missions, for example where a pilot is downed behind enemy lines; and in rear echelon areas to protect convoys from civil disturbances, terrorists, and paramilitary organizations. In a carefully worked out question and answer before the Committee, the Director of the Arms Control and Disarmament Agency was asked what legal impediment there would be to subsequent presidents broadening the permissible use of riot control agents and chemical herbicides. The Director responded that there would be none, but this policy is "inextricably" linked to Senate consent to ratification of the Protocol. Therefore, such a change would be "inconsistent with the history of the ratification, and could have extremely grave political repercussions and, as a result, is extremely unlikely to happen."

This testimony was on December 10, 1974 and on December 12, the Committee, by unanimous vote, reported favorably on the Geneva Protocol and the Biological Weapons Convention. The Committee in its report indicated that it attached particular importance to this exchange between the Committee and the Director. The full Senate voted its approval, also unanimously, on December 16, 1974. The Geneva Protocol and the Biological Weapons Convention were ratified by the President on January 22, 1975, and the United States' instrument of ratification was deposited with France on April 10, 1975, just two months shy of 50 years after signature.

Thus, ratification by the United States in 1975 of the Geneva Protocol raised but did not settle some of the interpretive questions related to the now worldwide prohibition on the use in war of chemical and biological weapons. As foreshadowed by the statement of President Roosevelt in 1943, because of widespread and longstanding adherence to the principles of the Geneva Protocol, the constraints of the Protocol, at least the constraints on first use, have become part of customary international law binding on all states without regard as to whether they are Parties to the Protocol.

This is not to say that there have not been violations. Italy became a Party in 1928, but it used poison gas against Ethiopia (a Party) in 1936. Egypt also became a Party in 1928, but it used poison gas against Yemen (a Party) in 1967. Iraq has been a Party since 1931, but this did not stop it from the use of poison gas in its war with Iran (a Party), in the 1980's. Iraq also used poison gas in internal struggles against the Kurdish people, but there is no evidence that the negotiators intended that the Protocol apply to civil war, only international armed conflicts. On the other hand, it should be noted that the Protocol did work effectively during World War II even though all the warring great powers possessed chemical weapons, including nerve agents.

B. Biological Weapons Convention

In the long effort to ban the use of chemical and biological weapons, progress in prohibiting the manufacture and possession of such weapons has come slower. During the 1932-1937 Disarmament Conference, unsuccessful attempts were made to negotiate an agreement prohibiting the production and stockpiling of chemical and biological weapons. In the negotiations after World War II, chemical and biological weapons continued to be closely associated in various proposals. One hindrance to progress over the years was whether, in considering a ban on production and possession, they should continue to be linked. A British draft convention banning biological weapons only was submitted to the Eighteen Nation Disarmament Committee in July of 1969, while a similar convention proposed by the Soviet Union and other Eastern European countries two months later covered both chemical and biological weapons. The Soviet representative argued that negotiation of a biological weapons convention separately could serve to intensify the chemical weapons arms race.

The United States supported the British proposal and argued that the two types of weapons are inherently different. Biological weapons have never been used in war, but chemical weapons have been so used. Without reliable assurance that other states are observing the ban, many countries, including the United States, would be reluctant to eliminate chemical weapons from their arsenals since such weapons are used to deter the use of chemical weapons against them and to provide a retaliatory capability if deterrence fails. Meanwhile, the U.S. Administration had been conducting a comprehensive review of U.S. policy toward chemical and biological warfare. On November 25, 1969, President Nixon made the above-discussed announcement concerning chemical weapons and the Geneva Protocol, and coupled it with a unilateral renunciation of biological weapons. The President asserted that biological weapons were inherently unreliable and declared that the United States would unconditionally eliminate from its arsenal all types of biological agents for use in war. In the future, the U.S. program would be confined to research on strictly defined measures of defense, such as immunization. The Department of Defense was directed to draw up a plan for the destruction of existing stocks and on February 14, 1970, toxin weapons were added to this unilateral renunciation.

The U.S. example was welcomed internationally and followed by several other states. Canada, Sweden, and the United Kingdom announced that they did not have any biological weapons and did not plan to produce any. However, conversion of these unilateral policy renunciations into a legally binding international agreement continued to be blocked by the insistence of the Soviet Union and other countries that chemical and biological weapons could not be considered separately. The Eighteen Nation Disarmament Committee in August of 1969 became the Conference of the Committee on Disarmament with twenty-six members. Discussion in the Committee in 1970 produced no agreement until the Soviet Union and the states associated with it changed their position and, on March 31, 1971, introduced a draft convention prohibiting biological and toxin weapons. This shift permitted the co-chairmen of the Committee, the representatives of the United States and the Soviet Union, to develop an agreed draft convention and table separate but identical texts on August 5, 1971.

The Biological Weapons Convention was opened for signature at Washington, London, and Moscow on April 10, 1972. In submitting it to the Senate, President Nixon described it as "the first international agreement since World War II to provide for the actual elimination of an entire class of weapons from the arsenal of nations." The Senate Foreign Relations Committee delayed action on the Convention however, holding it for consideration after resolution of the debate over the interpretation of the Geneva Protocol. When this dispute was resolved in late 1974, it opened the way for ratification of the Biological Weapons Convention as well as the Geneva Protocol. The U.S. instrument of ratification of the Convention was deposited on March 26, 1975.

Article I of the Convention provides that the parties "never in any circumstances" will develop, produce, stockpile, or otherwise acquire or retain "biological agents, or toxins" "of types and in quantities" that cannot be justified for "prophylactic, protective or other peaceful purposes" as well as weapons, equipment, or means of delivery to use such agents or toxins "for hostile purposes or in armed conflict." Thus, the intent of the Convention is to bind the Parties not to acquire biological weapons "in any circumstances," for example, even if attacked by a hostile state with such weapons. There are no reservations to the Convention, thus its effect is to reverse the no-first-use regime of the Geneva Protocol for biological weapons for those Parties that are also Parties to the Protocol with a second use reservation for biological weapons. Whether or not an agent qualifies as a biological weapon is judged on the basis of whether it exists in types and amounts that have no apparent justification for peaceful purposes. Weapons, equipment, or means of delivery for such agents cannot be acquired if they are designed to use such agents in "armed conflict" or even for "hostile purposes"; therefore an international armed conflict is not necessarily required to trigger this provision. The effect of this Article is to eliminate such agents and weapon systems from the arsenals of the Parties except where the agents can be shown to have a justifiable laboratory research purpose.

Article II requires destruction or conversion to peaceful purposes of such agents within nine months of entry into force. Article III prohibits the transfer to any recipient whatsoever, or to any way induce or assist any third state or international organization to acquire, any of the items proscribed by Article I. As in the Nuclear Non-Proliferation Treaty of 1968, assisting any third state (and the Convention adds any international organization), whether or not a Party, to acquire biological weapons is prohibited.

Article IV obligates the Parties to adopt implementing legislation to the extent this is required by their constitutional processes. In the United States, there was a lively debate for many years as to whether this was necessary in view of existing regulatory legislation, but after fifteen years it was finally resolved in the affirmative. Legislation was passed in 1990 making it a criminal act for a private person to possess biological weapons in contravention of the Convention.

Articles V, VI, and VII provide the verification mechanism of this Agreement. The Parties are required to consult with one another in solving any problems that may arise as to the application of the Convention. A Party has the right to lodge a complaint of violation with the Security Council of the United Nations and all Parties are required to cooperate with any investigation that the Security Council may order. If the Security Council decides that a Party has been exposed to danger as a result of a violation of the Convention, upon request, all Parties are required to provide assistance to the Party so endangered.

Article VIII makes clear that the constraints of the Geneva Protocol are in no way derogated as a result of the total and unconditional ban on the possession of biological weapons. Article IX reaffirms the objective of an agreement prohibiting chemical weapons and Article X, again as in the Nuclear Non-Proliferation Treaty, requires all Parties to share scientific information and technology relative to the peaceful use of biological agents and toxins. The remaining provisions are procedural, but the provisions of Article XIII providing for an unlimited duration, but permitting withdrawal in case a Party's supreme interests are jeopardized (a standard clause in arms control agreements since the Limited Test Ban Treaty of 1963), should be noted.

The U.S. Executive Branch, in the ratification hearings for the Convention before the Senate Foreign Relations Committee in 1974, stated that the Convention was not verifiable, but remained in the interest of the United States in view of its unilateral renunciation. Nevertheless, at the first Review Conference of the Convention in the 1980's, held as called for by Article XII, the United States charged that an explosion that took place in the city of Sverdlovsk in the Soviet Union in 1979 revealed that an illegal biological weapons plant was in operation at that site. This issue has never been satisfactorily resolved. This issue was discussed again at the Second Review Conference held in 1986. At that Review Conference, the United States also alleged Soviet involvement in the production, transfer, and use of mycotoxins (the so-called poisonous "yellow rain" in southeast Asia) and that the Soviet Union maintained an offensive biological warfare program in violation of Article I. The Conference agreed on certain measures to strengthen the implementation of Article V, and to increase confidence it agreed on measures to prevent or reduce ambiguities, doubts, and suspicions. These included: (1) exchange of data on activities, research centers and laboratories; (2) exchange of information on outbreaks of infectious diseases caused by toxins; (3) publication of results of biological research; and (4) promotion of scientific research.

An additional, and perhaps central issue after a chemical weapons Convention is signed with its intrusive on-site inspection, is whether the Parties to the Biological Weapons Convention should adopt a protocol calling for similar on-site inspection.

C. Chemical Weapons Convention and Interim Agreement

A companion convention prohibiting chemical weapons has been under active negotiation at the Conference on Disarmament, the successor to the Conference of the Committee on Disarmament, in Geneva since 1983. The most difficult problems are verification and the proclivity of some states in the Third World, *e.g.*, Iraq, to retain chemical weapons.

Effective verification of a chemical weapons convention is recognized as being virtually impossible in the classical sense, but nevertheless intrusive verification is important as chemical weapons have actually been used in war. However, in the United States there could be significant Fourth Amendment problems if international inspectors were to have the right to look for chemical weapons on private property without first obtaining a court-ordered search warrant. Nevertheless, some right to searches without warrants may be necessary if a complete ban on possession is to have any hope of being verified. On the other hand, it is argued, clandestine chemical weapons stockpiles are useless to the armed forces of a state if troop training for such weapons, which can be monitored, is not conducted.

On June 1, 1990, the United States and the Soviet Union concluded a bilateral Interim Agreement limiting chemical weapons stockpiles and banning the production of chemical weapons. The purpose of this Agreement, as indicated by its title, is to "facilitate" the conclusion of the multilateral convention banning chemical weapons. However, this Interim Agreement will not be ratified by the United States until detailed inspection procedures, the negotiation of which began in the summer of 1990, are completed.

Article III of the Interim Agreement provides that upon entry into force and thereafter, neither the United States nor the Soviet Union shall produce chemical weapons. Thus, the chemical weapons production programs of the two Parties will be terminated. Article IV, Paragraph 1, calls for the destruction of most of the existing stocks of the Parties. It provides that by the end of 2002, some twelve years after signature, each Party will have reduced its stocks to 5000 metric tons of chemical weapon agents. Destruction under the Agreement must begin no later than December 31, 1992. By nine years after entry into force, December 31, 1999, each Party must have eliminated fifty percent of its existing stock of chemical weapons with the numbers based on a data exchange carried out six months before signature of the Agreement (or declared thereafter).

Article IV, Paragraphs 4 and 10, contain an arrangement whereby if a Party cannot reach a destruction rate of 1000 agent tons per year by 1995, it must notify the other Party and consult concerning ways to improve the situation. Meanwhile, the other Party need not destroy its chemical weapons at a rate exceeding that of the first Party. Pursuant to Paragraph 9, each Party must reduce its chemical weapon storage facilities to eight by December 31, 2002, the end of the reduction period under the Agreement. There is also reference to saving each Party's rights and obligations, specifically those under the Geneva Protocol.

Article V sets forth the principles of intrusive on-site inspection to verify the cessation of production by monitoring production facilities and to verify destruction by giving access to storage facilities and destruction sites. Detailed provisions for the implementation of these inspection rights are to be negotiated. As stated, the Interim Agreement will not be brought into force until it can be accompanied by the inspection procedures.

When the inspection procedures have been completed, this Agreement likely will not be sent to the Senate in the United States for advice and consent to ratification by a two-thirds vote. Rather, it probably will be sent to both Houses of Congress, which would involve a majority vote in each House. This is permitted by the Arms Control and Disarmament Act of 1961, which requires that international agreements containing limitations on the armed forces or armaments of the United States either must be approved by the Senate pursuant to the treaty-making process or by affirmative legislation passed by both Houses of Congress. The latter is the same process followed in ratifying the SALT I Interim Agreement on strategic nuclear weapons.

Article VI of the Interim Agreement on chemical weapons sets forth the measures to facilitate the multilateral Convention. The Parties commit themselves to have stocks no larger than 500 agent tons by eight years after entry into force of the multilateral Convention. At that time, the United States and the Soviet Union will consult and propose a special conference to determine whether adherence to the multilateral Convention is sufficiently widespread (that is, whether enough chemical weapon states such as Iraq have become Parties) to justify proceeding to zero. This special conference would make its determination by majority vote and the majority must include those states that had declared they possessed chemical weapons, signed the convention within thirty days after it was opened for signature, and become a Party no later than one year after entry into force. Therefore, any state that has made the declaration (which must be made by December 31, 1991, at the Conference on Disarmament) and has joined the Convention in a timely fashion, has a veto on proceeding to zero.

N.P. Smidovich
Head of Branch, Arms Control and Disarmament Directorate, USSR Ministry of Foreign Affairs

A. Chemical Weapons: Limitations on Stockpiling and Use and the Feasibility of Complete Elimination

The removal of chemical weapons from national arsenals and destruction of these weapons is a priority task in the military-political area of international security. Successful accomplishment of this task will make it possible sharply to reduce the threat of consequences of military conflicts that would be catastrophic to mankind and to the environment. Military operations involving the use of chemical weapons, especially in densely populated areas, would be extremely lethal. According to some estimates, the employment of chemical weapons for a period of twenty-four hours in a conflict on the European continent could lead to 12 million fatalities, chiefly among civilians. The proliferation of chemical weapons introduces a new and dangerous factor into areas of regional conflict.

Many years of experience in negotiations, in the course of which various approaches toward eliminating the threat of chemical weapons have been discussed, have led to the conclusion that this goal is attainable only on the basis of a special legal document–a multilateral universal convention that would guarantee the elimination of both stockpiles of chemical weapons and the industrial base for their manufacture, and would also safeguard against the reemergence of chemical weapons anywhere. Contemporary trends in international politics would be embodied in such a convention: Its adoption would demonstrate a high sense of responsibility of states in the military-political domain and their willingness to resolve problems of guaranteeing security in present-day conditions not by military means–by the stockpiling of weapons of mass and total destruction–but by political means–through disarmament agreements. Such a convention unquestionably will constitute a major, in many respects unprecedented step in the evolution of international law in the military-political domain of relations among states.

Many years of efforts in the area of chemical weapons disarmament have to date resulted in forming a political consensus on the necessity of complete and final elimination of chemical weapons. The very fact of such a consensus is in itself unique, for no such agreement exists in respect to any other category of weapons. As regards nuclear weapons, a large number of countries that possess such weapons advocate keeping them, at least as a "weapon of last resort"; Consequently, up to the present time only the possibility of limiting such weapons is being considered for the most part on a bilateral Soviet-U.S. basis. In the area of conventional arms only questions of arms limitation are being seriously discussed, and that only on a regional level, primarily in Europe. The fact of a consensus in favor of the total elimination of chemical weapons highlights this weapon category in international disarmament efforts and creates a solid political foundation for formulating a global international legal norm prescribing a final and total ban on these weapons.

A special role in reaching this consensus was played by a special Conference on Chemical Weapons that was held in Paris in 1989. This Conference, with the participation of 149 states, unanimously acknowledged the necessity of concluding in the very near future a convention prohibiting the development, production, stockpiling, and use of all types of chemical weapons and on their elimination. The principal parameters of the future Convention were also defined: It should be nonexpiring, global, comprehensive, and effectively verifiable. The resolutions of the Paris Conference contain an appeal to all states to become party to the Convention without delay, immediately after it is concluded.

Another distinctive feature of preparations for the Convention on chemical weapons disarmament is the fact that the use of chemical weapons has already been outlawed by the 1925 Geneva Protocol for the Prohibition of the Use in War of Asphyxiating, Poisonous or Other Gases, and of Bacteriological Methods of Warfare. The ban established by this Protocol is one of the most important international legal norms of contemporary international law in the military-political domain. The existence of this norm has in many respects deterred the employment of chemical weapons in military conflicts. The participants in the 1989 Paris Conference formally affirmed the "enduring value" of the 1925 Geneva Protocol.

There is a widespread opinion that the regime initially established by a treaty document—the 1925 Geneva Protocol—has now been transformed into a norm of customary international law, binding on all states without exception, regardless of whether or not they are a Party to the Protocol.

There have recently been successful efforts substantially to increase the effectiveness of the prohibition established by the 1925 Geneva Protocol.

For a long time the lack of a mechanism of verification of compliance was considered to be a serious deficiency of this Protocol. In 1989 the UN General Assembly, for the first time, approved by consensus special procedures for investigating reports of instances of violation of the Geneva Protocol. These procedures invest the UN Secretary General with sufficient authority promptly to dispatch, at the request of any UN member state, a team of experts to investigate on the spot reports of instances of use of chemical weapons. He is also empowered to hold consultations with any UN member state on matters pertaining to the possible use of chemical weapons. The Secretary General is to inform all UN member states of the results of such investigations.

Of considerable importance from the standpoint of increasing the effectiveness of the Geneva Protocol is UN Security Council Resolution S.620 (1988), in which the Security Council resolved to consider without delay, taking into consideration an investigation by the Secretary General, appropriate and effective measures in conformity with the UN Charter. These UN resolutions urge states to take adequate measures at the national level. A government enactment adopted in the Soviet Union in 1989, dealing with export of dual-use chemicals, states clearly and explicitly that such chemicals may not be exported from the Soviet Union to states that violate the prohibition of use of chemical weapons established by the 1925 Geneva Protocol. National legislative and administrative measures in response to possible violations of the 1925 Geneva Protocol are also being discussed in other countries.

Resolutions adopted by the General Assembly and Security Council have transformed the prohibition of use of chemical weapons established by the Geneva Protocol into a verifiable ban that is materially reinforced by a mechanism of sanctions against violators of the Protocol.

Reservations to the 1925 Geneva Protocol made by Parties to the Protocol, including the Soviet Union and the United States, constitute a component part of the present regime of the 1925 Geneva Protocol. In these reservations certain states retained the right to use chemical weapons in retaliation to the use of such weapons against them. This serves as grounds to assert that the norm established by the Geneva Protocol prescribes prohibition only of first use of chemical weapons. On the other hand, one should note that such reservations retaining the right to retaliatory use of chemical weapons were made by less than one third of the parties to the Geneva Protocol, and the overwhelming majority of these countries declared that they did not possess chemical weapons, which removes material foundation from their reservations. As a result, there arises the question of whether one can consider as general or universal a norm to which a minority of states party to a given agreement adhere on a de jure or de facto basis.

The view that a complete ban on any use of chemical weapons must apply from the moment the Convention enters into force is unquestionably predominant at the talks on the chemical weapons disarmament Convention. Objections to such a solution are for the most part heard from those who view chemical weapons as a means of "deterrence" against the use of such weapons. Patently evident in such an approach is the incompatibility of the very purpose of the Convention–the elimination the threat of chemical weapons by political means–and retention of the concept of "deterrence" through the aid of chemical weapons. The Soviet Union's position is unequivocal: the Convention should prescribe an absolute and unconditional ban on the use of chemical weapons. The Soviet Union is also prepared to move more rapidly toward this goal: without waiting for the international Convention to enter into force, to establish right today a global norm under international law prohibiting the use of chemical weapons. Such a measure merits discussion in the United Nations. One way to establish such a norm would be a mutual renunciation by all states of the reservations to the 1925 Geneva Protocol that allow for retaliatory employment of chemical weapons.

The chemical weapons disarmament Convention will be a comprehensive code of international legal norms governing the conduct of states that pledge not to develop, produce, stockpile, or use chemical weapons (states possessing stockpiles of chemical weapons or facilities for the manufacture of such weapons will also have to destroy these stockpiles and facilities).

Provisions on international verification of compliance with the Convention provisions constitute a most important feature of such a convention. Although no final formal understandings have yet been reached on specific wordings, one can state at the present time that, as regards degree of comprehensiveness and intrusiveness of verification methods, this Convention will be the most far-reaching of multilateral agreements in the area of arms limitation and disarmament.

The draft Convention calls for regular international monitoring, which may include the permanent presence of inspectors at appropriate sites, as well as utilization of monitoring and measuring devices at such sites. This applies particularly to chemical weapons storage facilities, chemical weapons production facilities, chemical weapons elimination facilities, and those facilities that will be manufacturing for permitted purposes those chemicals that are most dangerous from the standpoint of the Convention. At the initial phases of talks, IAEA procedures in the area of nonproliferation of nuclear weapons were adopted as a point of departure for drawing up corresponding provisions. These procedures have subsequently been expanded, however, and they presently appear to be much broader: They take into consideration not only the specific features of operations at facilities to be monitored under the convention but also modern scientific and technological advances in the area of instrumentation and communications devices. The newness of the technical solutions to problems of monitoring that are embodied in the draft Convention will require the formulation of a number of special legal norms, including provisions pertaining to safeguarding the confidentiality of information and military and trade secrets, and the transmission, dissemination, and storage of information obtained in the course of performance of inspection activities.

Provisions pertaining to so-called inspections on request would seem to be particularly important from the standpoint of international law. This special variation of on-site inspection is provided where suspicions arise regarding compliance with the Convention at installations that are not subjected to regular international monitoring pursuant to the provisions of the Convention. A generally acceptable concept of inspection on request essentially took form at the talks, following a long and difficult search for the most effective approaches toward solving this problem. This concept is grounded, on the one hand, on the possibility of conducting inspection of any site or installation without right of refusal, and, on the other hand, on recognition of the need to avoid abuses of such inspections via agreed-upon procedures of conduct that would prevent the disclosure of sensitive information unrelated to the ban on chemical weapons. Reaching agreement on provisions pertaining to mandatory inspections on request in regard to any site or installation will require revision of traditional legal concepts of the national sovereignty of states, since such inspections imply that states will give up in advance the right not to permit international inspection at their facilities.

One of the difficult problems faced at the talks, particularly from a legal standpoint, is that of ensuring compliance with the Convention by legal entities and natural persons of the Parties. We are dealing here primarily with extraterritorial jurisdiction. In view of the fact that the future Convention will apply not only to military activities but, in contrast to other disarmament agreements, to many other sectors of civilian industry, it will be necessary to find solutions to questions of jurisdiction that would guarantee compliance with the provisions specified by the Convention not only on the territory of a Party but also by its natural persons and legal entities, no matter where they might be. Otherwise ways to circumvent the Convention may appear, which will undermine its effectiveness. Efforts to find a generally acceptable approach have not been successful to date, due to profound differences in national positions regarding the permissibility of extraterritorial jurisdiction.

Just the above-enumerated problems connected with jurisdiction attest to the fact that passage of special domestic laws by the Convention Parties will be required in order to implement the Convention. In view of the specific features of the future Convention, a simple act of ratification by national parliaments will not be sufficient, as has been the case in the past in regard to other disarmament agreements. Very little has been done as yet, however, in the area of drafting the required domestic legislation. Meriting attention in this connection is the idea of interparliamentary coordination on matters connected with the legal underpinnings for implementation of the Convention, which will make it possible from the very outset to harmonize the approaches of the various states.

The chemical weapons ban talks have brought forth new approaches toward the matters of openness and confidence-building measures. In the past openness essentially boiled down to exchange of data as a result of entering into a specific agreement on limitation of a given type of arms, while confidence-building measures were as a rule implemented in a sporadic manner, most often unilaterally. While not denying the usefulness of these measures, nevertheless one should acknowledge their limited nature. The following important step was taken at the talks on banning chemical weapons. Exchange of data and confidence-building measures began to be carried out not as a result of negotiations but at the negotiation stage proper. The participants in the talks are presenting data on their chemical weapons arsenals and chemical industry pertaining to the future convention, are exchanging visits to corresponding facilities, *etc.* In many instances the Soviet Union has initiated such undertakings and is taking active part in them. As an example we could cite the Soviet Union's proposal on the possibility of conducting inspections for the purpose of removing doubts regarding its statements on the non-deployment of Soviet chemical weapons abroad. A test inspection on request, which took place in August 1990, conducted by FRG representatives at one of the Soviet storage sites selected by them on the territory of the GDR, confirmed the absence of chemical weapons.

The new quality in openness is making it possible to lay down a solid factual basis for the future Convention and to make it more realistic and reliable at the very outset. This approach received the support of the UN General Assembly which, acknowledging the need for exchange of data and welcoming the specific confidence-building steps that had been taken, appealed for:

> Member States to take further initiatives to promote confidence and openness in the negotiations and to provide further information to facilitate prompt resolution of outstanding issues, this contributing to an early agreement on, and universal adherence to, a convention for the prohibition of the development, production, stockpiling and use of all chemical weapons and on their destruction. General Assembly Resolution 43/74.

One can foresee that this new quality in openness and confidence-building measures will soon become customary practice at disarmament talks and will become the norm. This will be a certain safeguard against attempts to outfox the other side, to deceive one's negotiating partner. Openness will thus become transformed into a factor of acceleration of the pace at talks, since it will in many respects diminish the value of "bargaining" in negotiations, and it will avert attempts to go into negotiations with the intention of taking an exaggerated opening position. Verifiable exchange of data will create a healthy basis for establishing at the negotiating table an honest and adjusted balance of interests without detriment to anyone's security.

The current and future generation of agreements in the area of arms limitation and disarmament is inconceivable without an extensive system of international verification of compliance. This imposes heightened demands on the practicability of those provisions on inspections that are incorporated into the draft texts of corresponding agreements. It is probably impossible to achieve this without practical testing of corresponding monitoring procedures in the course of negotiations proper. Guided by these considerations, the Soviet Union presented at the chemical weapons ban talks an initiative calling for the conduct of experiments to test international verification procedures. This initiative evoked a positive response on the part of the participants in the talks, and several dozen test inspections of various kinds have been performed in the last two years. Practical experience amassed in the course of these inspections is being actively utilized to refine, detail, and make more specific provisions on inspection procedures hammered out at the negotiating table.

It is important to note that it has been possible to embody as legal norms many positive elements in the area of openness and confidence-building measures, which have become characteristic of the talks on banning chemical weapons, although at the present stage this has been done only on the basis of Soviet-U.S. agreements. Without waiting for a multilateral convention banning chemical weapons to enter into force, the Soviet Union and the United States have concluded two bilateral agreements: a September 23, 1989, Memorandum of Understanding on a bilateral verification and data exchange experiment in connection with the elimination of chemical weapons, and a June 1, 1990, Interim Agreement Between the United States of America and the Union of Soviet Socialist Republics on the Elimination of Chemical Weapons Stockpiles and the Prohibition of Their Production and on Measures to Encourage a Multilateral Convention on Banning Chemical Weapons.

The Agreement of June 1 contains pledges by the Soviet Union and the United States to cease the production of chemical weapons and to reduce the chemical weapons inventory by December 31, 2002, to a level of 5000 tons of toxic chemical agent by weight. Corresponding verification and openness measures are also prescribed. Formal understandings on exchange of data on the chemical warfare potential of the Soviet Union and United States, on visits to military and civilian chemical facilities, and on verification of the correctness of the presented data by means of inspections at declared sites and inspections on request (even before a multilateral convention enters into force) are articulated in the Memorandum. There is an agreement calling for the conduct of joint test inspections to work out inspection procedures. Implementation of the Soviet-U.S. agreements will enable both countries to amass valuable experience in practical implementation of measures connected with the banning and elimination of chemical weapons.

Recently there have appeared alarming trends involving the proliferation of chemical weapons. This is prompting the international community to take measures to counteract the growing threat of employment of these weapons. The 1989 Paris Conference, noting the threat to international peace and security presented by the risk of use of chemical weapons, as long as such weapons continue to be possessed and to proliferate, acknowledged the need for every state to show restraint and to act responsibly.

One can state that the process of emergence of an international legal norm against the proliferation of chemical weapons is presently under way. This norm can be finally and formally articulated only by the universal Convention on the banning and elimination of chemical weapons, which will provide the only long-term solution to the problem of proliferation of chemical weapons, while efforts presently being undertaken constitute merely intermediate steps toward this goal.

National legislative enactments regulating the export of a large number of chemicals that have peaceful uses but that also can be used to manufacture chemical weapons form the basis of the existing chemical weapons nonproliferation regime. This regime also includes bilateral and multilateral consultations between states for the purpose of containing the spread of chemical weapons.

The Soviet Union resolutely opposes the proliferation of chemical weapons. The Soviet Union has not transferred chemical weapons or equipment for the manufacture of chemical weapons to other countries, and it has not deployed chemical weapons on the territory of other states. In the Soviet Union there are regulations controlling the export of dual-use chemicals and technologies that can be used to produce them.

One can cite as an example of a chemical weapons nonproliferation regime the Soviet-U.S. Joint Declaration on Nonproliferation, adopted in Washington at the summit meeting held in May-June 1990. The agreed-upon approaches of the two countries are set forth in a special section of this Declaration dealing with the nonproliferation of chemical weapons. In this document both parties declare in particular that they will not disseminate chemical weapons, pledge to conduct bilateral discussions and to participate in multilateral efforts to expand cooperation for the purpose of preventing the spread of chemical weapons, including efforts in the area of export regulation, and express the intention to undertake political and diplomatic steps in those specific cases where concern arises in connection with the manufacture, use, and proliferation of chemical weapons. The Soviet Union and the United States called upon all the world's countries to join them in taking effective measures aimed at ending the proliferation of chemical weapons.

B. Biological Weapons: Effectiveness of the Ban on Possession and Use

Contemporary international law prescribes a comprehensive ban on the possession and use of bacteriological (biological) and toxin weapons (henceforth called "biological weapons" for brevity). This norm of international law was introduced and codified in the form of two multilateral agreements: the Protocol for the Prohibition of the Use in War of Asphyxiating, Poisonous or Other Gases, and of Bacteriological Methods of Warfare, which was signed in Geneva in 1925 and went into effect in 1926, and the Convention on the Prohibition of the Development, Production and Stockpiling of Bacteriological (Biological) and Toxin Weapons and on Their Destruction, which was signed in 1972 and entered into force in 1975.

These multilateral agreements, which banned at one stroke an entire category of weapons of mass destruction, are still today in their scope unique among the international treaties in the military domain of international security. This is essentially the first measure of genuine disarmament. Confirmation of the effectiveness and strengthening of the norm of international law they established against biological weapons is an important task, especially in the face of new advances in biotechnology. New sociopolitical realities in the world and movement from confrontation to partnership in the military-political areas of international security have made it possible in the latter half of the 1980's to proceed with the practical accomplishment of this task.

For a long time the lack of a mechanism of verification of compliance was considered to be one of the shortcomings of the 1925 Geneva Protocol. In 1989 special procedures for investigating reports of instances of violation of the Geneva Protocol were approved for the first time by consensus in the UN General Assembly. These procedures invest the UN Secretary General with sufficient authority to dispatch promptly, at the request of any UN member state, a team of experts to conduct an on-site investigation of cases of employment of biological weapons. He is also empowered to hold consultations with any UN member state on matters pertaining to the possible use of biological weapons. The Secretary General is to inform all UN member states of the results of such investigations. Of considerable significance is UN Security Council Resolution S.620 (1988), in which the Security Council resolved to consider without delay, taking into consideration investigations by the Secretary General, appropriate and effective measures pursuant to the UN Charter.

As an aggregate the procedures of investigation under the auspices of the UN Secretary General and Security Council Resolution S.620 (1988) create the basis under international law for effective actions against violators of the Geneva Protocol. Thus the 1925 Geneva Protocol has now been de facto supplemented by provisions on international verification of compliance and on international actions in response to violations of the Protocol.

First steps also have been taken to increase the effectiveness of the Biological Weapons Convention. The initial step was taken at the Second Biological Weapons Convention Review Conference (Geneva, September 1986), at which a number of measures for confidence-building among the parties to the Convention were agreed upon for the first time.

Measures include, first of all, exchange of data on installations with a biological protection level of P4 and installations with a protection level of P3, which specialize in activities pertaining to protection against the hostile use of biological agents or toxins; second, submission of information on unusual outbreaks of infectious diseases; and third, contacts between scientists and publication of the results of scientific studies pertaining directly to the Convention.

Resolutions adopted at the Second Biological Weapons Convention Review Conference created the first precedent for further development of the provisions of the Convention through the adoption of consensus agreements. Although they are not of a legally binding nature, they nevertheless constitute important political obligations of states. These formal understandings can be viewed as a new component part of the international-law regime of prohibition of biological weapons.

The next, Third Biological Weapons Convention Review Conference will be held in 1991. This will be an extremely important forum from the standpoint of efforts to strengthen the ban on biological weapons established by this international agreement. By decision of the preceding Conference, the forthcoming forum will consider, in particular, matters pertaining to the need for additional actions on cooperation measures by the Convention Parties or the need to add legally binding improvements to the Convention. This Conference agenda focuses on the search for ways to increase the effectiveness of the Biological Weapons Convention. In particular, elaboration of a special verification mechanism for the Convention and additional, more extensive measures of openness, as well as horizontal and vertical extension of the international law norm against biological weapons, could become the principal direction of movement toward this goal.

The lack of a system of effective international verification of compliance constitutes a weak point of the Biological Weapons Convention. The Convention in its present form prescribes only "consultations and cooperation" among its Parties in resolving any matters which may arise in regard to purposes or in connection with fulfillment of the Convention, in particular by using appropriate international procedures within the framework of the United Nations. Although these provisions underwent certain development in the resolutions of the Second Biological Weapons Convention Review Conference, which called for the immediate convening of consultative meetings of experts to consider any problems connected with fulfillment of the Convention at the request of any party to the Convention, there exists to date no mechanism of on-site inspections for the purpose of verifying compliance with the Convention.

The lack of such a mechanism is due in large measure to the time at which the Convention was drafted and to the contemporary approaches to matters of monitoring and verification. Indisputably a great deal has changed since those times: Monitoring and verification matters no longer appear to be the main obstacle in the way of reaching an agreement on arms limitation and disarmament. It is high time to implement new approaches and new thinking also with respect to the Biological Weapons Convention.

Talks on banning chemical weapons provide an adequate picture on how a system of international verification within the framework of a multilateral treaty might look in present-day conditions. Sometimes the opinion is stated that there is no sense in discussing verification within the framework of the Biological Weapons Convention until such time as a convention banning chemical weapons enters into force. One can hardly agree with this view, since this postpones for quite some time the commencement of meaningful consideration of matters pertaining to monitoring and verification for the Biological Weapons Convention. It would probably make more sense to commence such a discussion right now, and in the process of negotiations to reach more specific agreement on a time frame for putting new formal agreements on monitoring and verification into effect. Of course, one could also take into consideration the timetable for the chemical weapons ban Convention to enter into force.

As for verification within the framework of the Biological Weapons

Convention, it could incorporate such elements as exchange of agreed-upon data on activities and installations pertaining directly to the Convention and declared installations, as well as inspections on request for those sites and installations about which suspicions of Convention violation may arise. Measures to strengthen the verification system could be formally set forth in an additional protocol to the Convention, which would give them legally binding force. Adequate resolution of matters connected with ensuring inspectors access to installations, safeguarding of confidentiality of information, *etc.*, will be difficult without this.

One variation of a verification mechanism for the Convention could prescribe that Parties provide lists of appropriate biological facilities, so-called "national biological registers." These registers would list all installations with a P4 biological protection level, as well as all biological facilities with a lesser degree of protection if they, for example, are engaged in any projects dealing with protection against biological weapons or other projects for the ministry of defense. Initial visits could be made at installations included in the National Biological Register, for the purpose of confirming the declared information about these facilities, as well as for determining the danger presented by these facilities and their infrastructure to the goals of the Convention. Subsequently such installations would be subject to on-site inspections at any time without right of refusal. In order not to place anyone in a disadvantageous position, a system of quotas for inspections of this kind could be elaborated, which would prescribe, for example, both the number of inspections that would be conducted each year at facilities of the participating state and the number of inspections that would be conducted at the request of that state.

Inspections on request are becoming an integral element of disarmament agreements. The main purpose of such inspections is to verify compliance at installations that have not been declared by the parties within the framework of the agreement. Such mechanisms are discussed at talks on banning chemical weapons, talks on limiting arms in Europe, and at Soviet-U.S. strategic offensive arms reduction talks. If things reach the point of formal understandings on establishing a verification mechanism for the Biological Weapons Convention, it too will probably provide for the right of states to request inspections of undeclared installations whose activities arouse suspicions concerning Convention compliance.

A viable international monitoring and verification system should provide not only for effective procedures for establishing facts of violation but also reliable safeguards against disclosure in the course of inspection of information unrelated to the agreement in question. Corresponding procedures should also be drawn up applicable to the Biological Weapons Convention.

As precise as possible a delimitation of activities prohibited and permitted by the Convention would be of great importance in order to reach agreement on effective verification procedures. For this purpose it would make sense to refine the definitions of terms contained in the Convention, including those pertaining to prohibited (development, production, and stockpiling of weapons) and permitted (preventive, protective, and other peaceful purposes) activities, as well as to discuss the matter of lists and quantities of microorganisms and toxins and, possibly, lists of equipment that would require special attention from the standpoint of the danger of development of biological weapons. As a result one could determine "critical points" of corresponding activities in the field of biology, monitoring of which would prevent the development, production, and stockpiling of biological weapons. Agreed-upon interpretations across the entire spectrum of these issues could be incorporated into a supplementary verification protocol within the framework of the Convention. At the same time, in view of their immediate importance for the Convention in its present form, during the first phase they could be formally embodied in the resolutions of the Third Biological Weapons Convention Review Conference.

Without question the establishment of a system of effective verification for the Biological Weapons Convention is a difficult task, requiring the solution of a number of complex technical problems. At the same time it is indisputable that such solutions can be found only through talks between the Parties to the Convention. The Third Biological Weapons Convention Review Conference is to initiate the process of such talks.

In its original form the Biological Weapons Convention did not prescribe regular exchange of information among its Parties on activities connected with this agreement. This had a negative effect; lack of scrutiny of activities gave rise to and fed suspicions of Convention violations.

Initial agreements on exchange of information within the context of the Convention were reached in 1986 at the Second Biological Weapons Convention Review Conference. Although they were of a limited nature, these agreements created an important precedent, pointing to a possible way to correct the deficiencies of the Convention. This is particularly important since precisely in the area of banning biological weapons openness can play an important role in overcoming such past concerns as well as concerns that may arise in the future.

New and more profound measures of openness could be considered at the Third Biological Weapons Convention Review Conference in 1991. For example, such measures could include the following agreements:

First, exchanges of visits to installations that are declared within the framework of the agreed-upon exchange of data. Such visits could promote familiarization with the infrastructure of the facilities in question and the principal areas of their activities, could help gain assurance about the correctness of the information declared on these installations and, possibly, could help in drafting agreements on verification procedures for on-site inspections within the context of the Convention.

Second, encouragement to declassify projects relating to the Convention. One could introduce the practice of annual publication by the Parties of lists of projects carried out at declared installations or with the participation of personnel of these facilities.

Third, an exchange of scientists, including those working at declared installations, and field training exchanges. Such an exchange could promote the establishment of direct scientific contacts between counterpart installations, foster a better understanding of the work they are doing, *etc.* Thus this would become a major confidence-building factor. Conducting such exchanges not only on a short-term basis but including invited scientists working at a facility for a comparatively long period of time seems an interesting idea.

Fourth, organization of joint research, particularly in the area of prevention and treatment of natural diseases caused by pathogens that are potentially dangerous from the standpoint of biological weapons. Conduct of such research would, on the one hand, help bolster assurance that activities prohibited by the Convention are not being carried out under the pretext of research in this field and, on the other hand, would promote the solving of critical problems in combating the most dangerous epidemics.

Of course, the effectiveness of openness measures depends largely on the extent to which they become firmly embodied in practical implementation of the Convention by the Parties. Unfortunately, we must admit that participation by states in the first generation of agreed-upon measures in this regard is patently inadequate at the present time. One can hardly consider effective implementation of new, more profound measures in this area without general participation in already agreed-upon measures and meticulous fulfillment of initial agreements reached in this area. In this connection repeated appeals by the UN General Assembly for all states to take part in agreed-upon measures of openness within the context of the Biological Weapons Convention seem warranted.

Unquestionably prohibition of the development, manufacture, and stockpiling of biological weapons should become a provision of general international law. The shortest route toward this objective is participation by all nations without exception in the Biological Weapons Convention, that is, "horizontal" extension of its established provision of international law. To date already approximately 120 states are parties to the Convention. The protracted refusal of some countries to accede to the Convention cannot but arouse concern. Accession to the Convention without delay by all those states that have not yet done so would be in keeping with the interests of the entire international community.

Transformation of those Convention provisions which prohibit the development, production and stockpiling of biological weapons into provisions of national law would also help strengthen the ban on biological weapons. Such "vertical" extension of the effect of the provisions of the Convention would substantially bolster the legal force of the prohibitions it has established. Obligations on the part of Parties to take necessary measures on this score in conformity with their constitutional procedures are directly specified in Article IV of the Convention. A number of states already have corresponding laws in this area, and it would be useful to make this a general practice.

Analysis of current norms of international law pertaining to biological weapons suggests the unequivocal conclusion that contemporary international law prescribes a total and unconditional prohibition of the possession and use of biological weapons. Strengthening the Convention on the Prohibition of the Development, Production and Stockpiling of Bacteriological (Biological) and Toxin Weapons and on Their Destruction constitutes a principal way to increase the effectiveness of this ban in present-day conditions. The Third Biological Weapons Convention Review Conference, to be held in 1991, should make an important contribution toward the accomplishment of this task.

6. Limitation on the Development and Use of New Systems and Weapons of Mass Destruction and the Question of a Total Ban

Thomas Graham, Jr.
General Counsel, U.S. Arms Control and Disarmament Agency

At the Thirtieth Session of the UN General Assembly in 1975, the Soviet Union submitted for consideration a draft agreement on banning the development and production of new weapons of mass destruction. A resolution was adopted requesting that the Conference of the Committee on Disarmament (CCD) commence drafting the text of an international agreement prohibiting such systems. In ensuing years discussions were held on this subject in the CCD, but little progress was made on the development of such an agreement. In 1977 at the CCD some delegations expressed the view that there was a need to ban new types of weapons of mass destruction; however, there were differences as to the means of achieving this goal.

In August of 1948, at the United Nations, a resolution had been agreed upon that defined weapons of mass destruction. Such weapons were defined as including "weapons operating by atomic explosions, weapons operating with the aid of radioactive materials, lethal chemical and biological weapons" as well as any weapons to be developed in the future that possessed comparable characteristics. The Soviet Union, both at the United Nations and the CCD, urged that an agreement be reached specifically banning such weapons and offered a more precise definition of such weapons. The Western view has been that a definition of such weapons would be difficult to formulate with the specificity needed to develop an agreement that was verifiable, and that it was preferable in any case to address this problem by means of specific negotiated constraints on particular weapon systems.

The definition of weapons of mass destruction set forth in the UN resolution has been important over the years in the arms control process. For example, Article IV of the Treaty on Principles Governing the

Activities of States in the Exploration and Use of Outer Space, Including the Moon and Other Celestial Bodies (the Outer Space Treaty) of 1967 prohibits the placing in orbit around the earth of any objects carrying nuclear weapons or "any other kinds of weapons of mass destruction." The Treaty also prohibits the installation of such weapons on celestial bodies and the stationing of such weapons in outer space in any other manner. Also, the Treaty on the Prohibition of the Emplacement of Nuclear Weapons and Other Weapons of Mass Destruction on the Seabed and the Ocean Floor and in the Subsoil Thereof (the Seabed Treaty) of 1971 prohibits the deployment on the sea-bed beneath international waters of "any nuclear weapons or any other types of weapons of mass destruction."

There are many other international arms control agreements that provide specific limitations on certain weapons of mass destruction. The Protocol for the Prohibition of the Use in War of Asphyxiating, Poisonous or Other Gases, and of Bacteriological Methods of Warfare (the Geneva Protocol) of 1925 in effect prohibits the first use in war of chemical and biological weapons. The Treaty Banning Nuclear Weapon Tests in the Atmosphere, in Outer Space and Underwater (the Limited Test Ban Treaty) of 1963 prohibits the testing of nuclear explosive devices anywhere except underground. The Antarctic Treaty of 1959 prohibits the testing of nuclear weapons on that continent and in effect makes Antarctica a nuclear-free zone. The Treaty for the Prohibition of Nuclear Weapons in Latin America (the Latin American Nuclear-Free Zone Treaty) of 1967, when it comes into full force, will prohibit nuclear weapons in Latin America. The South Pacific Nuclear Free-Zone Treaty (the Treaty of Raratonga) of 1986, which entered into force on December 11, 1990, prohibits nuclear explosives in the South Pacific area.

The Treaty Between the United States of America and the Union of Soviet Socialist Republics on the Limitation of Underground Nuclear Weapons Tests (the Threshold Test Ban Treaty) of 1974 and the Treaty Between the United States of America and the Union of Soviet Socialist Republics on Underground Nuclear Explosions for Peaceful Purposes (the Peaceful Nuclear Explosions Treaty) of 1976, taken together, limit underground nuclear explosions conducted by the United States or the Soviet Union to 150 kilotons. The Nuclear Non-Proliferation Treaty of 1968 limits the spread of nuclear explosive devices to states other than the original five Nuclear-Weapon States Parties, *i.e.*, France, China, the United Kingdom, the United States, and the Soviet Union. The Convention on the Prohibition of the Development, Production and Stockpiling of Bacteriological (Biological) and Toxin Weapons and on Their Destruction (the Biological Weapons Convention) of 1972 prohibits the possession in any circumstances of biological and toxin weapons.

The Treaty Between the United States of America and the Union of Soviet Socialist Republics on the Limitation of Anti-Ballistic Missile Systems (the ABM Treaty) of 1972 limits strategic defensive systems, which can be nuclear systems, to a very low level. The Treaty Between the United States of America and the Union of Soviet Socialist Republics on the Elimination of Their Intermediate-Range and Shorter-Range Missiles (the INF Treaty) eliminates the entire class of medium range missiles which serve as nuclear delivery systems.

Thus, there already are many limitations on weapons of mass destruction. Nuclear weapons may only be tested underground and by the United States and the Soviet Union at yields not to exceed 150 kilotons. Nuclear weapons are to be prohibited in Latin America and are prohibited in Antarctica, in outer space and in the South Pacific region. Delivery systems for nuclear weapons are limited by the ABM Treaty and the INF Treaty, and soon will be by the Treaty Between the United States of America and the Union of Soviet Socialist Republics on the Reduction and Limitation of Strategic Offensive Arms (the START Treaty) that is still under negotiation. Chemical weapons cannot be used in war except in retaliation, and biological weapons are prohibited in any circumstances. A comparable prohibition on chemical weapons is currently under active negotiation. A bilateral agreement between the United States and the Soviet Union limiting chemical weapons was signed on June 1, 1990.

At the Thirty-first Session of the UN General Assembly, the U.S. delegation urged the negotiation of an international agreement banning radiological weapons. In 1977, this issue was discussed between the United States and the Soviet Union, and in 1979 it was submitted for consideration by the CCD in Geneva. Much work has been done in developing draft basic provisions of a convention prohibiting the development, stockpiling, and use of radiological weapons. However, considerable work on this subject, the remaining unregulated type of mass destruction weapons, still must be completed in Geneva. Should any new type of weapon of mass destruction that is not addressed by existing agreements or negotiations ever appear, undoubtedly it would be the subject of a new negotiation to develop precise limitations on such weapon systems.

In conclusion, weapons of mass destruction should be limited by negotiation of specific agreements covering specific weapon systems or types of weapons, as has been the practice for many years, rather than attempt to negotiate a broad-gauged agreement prohibiting weapons of mass destruction. It is most unlikely that a broad, general agreement on weapons of mass destruction is achievable or even desirable in the foreseeable future.

M.I. Ul'yanov
Member, Mission of the USSR to the United Nations

Scientific and technological progress, which appreciably accelerated in the postwar decades, has been attended by the acute danger of a qualitative arms race. It is becoming increasingly obvious that using the latest advances in science and technology for military purposes can destabilize the international situation, introduce an element of unpredictability, and to a significant degree can nullify already reached disarmament agreements and disarmament efforts currently being undertaken. And, as experience shows, it is extremely difficult to halt the development of new weapons once such a process has begun. For this reason an optimal procedure from the standpoint of the interests of general security would be to reach an agreement in advance at the international level on preventive measures that would make it possible to place reliable legal barriers in the path of a qualitative arms race, and particularly the most dangerous aspect of the arms race: development of new weapons of mass destruction (WMD) and WMD systems.

The question of banning the development and production of new WMD and WMD systems was first addressed from the aspect of international law in 1975, when the Soviet Union submitted a draft agreement on these issues for consideration at the Thirtieth Session of the UN General Assembly. A resolution was adopted at this session, containing an appeal to the Conference of the Committee on Disarmament (CCD) to draft the text of an international agreement prohibiting new weapons of mass destruction and WMD systems. Several unofficial sessions of the Conference of the Committee on Disarmament were held in April 1976, at which experts from the Soviet Union, GDR, and Hungary presented their view on ways and means to achieve this goal. The urgency of banning new types of WMD and WMD systems found expression in one form or another in official communiques released in 1976-1977 announcing the results of talks between the USSR Minister of Foreign Affairs and the foreign ministers of Belgium, Italy, Portugal, Turkey, Finland, and a number of nonaligned countries. In 1978 corresponding points were also included in the Final Document of the UN General Assembly First Special Session (Paragraph 77). During this same period, riding the wave of international detente, Western states also engaged in a substantive discussion of the Soviet initiative. Soviet-U.S. consultations on banning new weapons of mass destruction and WMD systems were held in 1977-1979. This issue was regularly deliberated on a multilateral basis at unofficial sessions of the CCD, accompanied by business-like discussion. At the 1977 summer session of the CCD, representatives of all groups of states observed that there was a consensus on the need to ban new types of weapons of mass destruction and that differences pertained chiefly to the means of achieving this goal. These differences were manifested most strongly during discussion of four issues of fundamental importance: determination of new kinds of weapons of mass destruction; the specific area to be covered by a possible agreement; and certain organizational and procedural matters.

The draft agreement on banning new types of weapons of mass destruction and WMD systems presented by the Soviet Union at the Thirtieth Session of the UN General Assembly proposed that the items to be covered by such a ban would be determined through negotiations. The Soviet Union presented its observations on this matter in Working Document SSD/514 dated August 10, 1976, in which it was proposed to proceed from the position that weapons based on qualitatively new principles of action, the effectiveness of which were commensurate with or exceeded that of the traditional types of WMD, should be considered new types of weapons of mass destruction. New modes and methods, targets, and nature of weapon effect were defined thereby as qualitatively new operating principles. Assignment of a given type of weapon to the classification of new type of WMD could be performed on the basis of newness of at least one of the three named attributes. Modes of effect were to be defined as variations of physical, chemical, and biological effects. Targets of effect were to be defined as varieties of targeted items: These would include vitally important elements of the human organism and elements of man's ecological and geophysical environment, as well as structures and systems of vital importance for man's existence. Nature of effect was to be defined as new variations of destructive effect, which either lead immediately to mass deaths or to the gradual dying off of large population groups.

Western experts, voicing a number of objections to the Soviet approach, proposed proceeding from the resolution agreed upon in August 1948 in the UN Commission for Conventional Armaments, according to which:

> Weapons of mass destruction shall be defined in such a manner as to include weapons operating by atomic explosion, weapons operating with the aid of radioactive materials, lethal chemical and biological weapons, as well as any weapons to be developed in the future which possess characteristics comparable in destructive effect to an atomic bomb and the other weapons mentioned above.

Adopting as a point of departure this definition, known as the "1948 UN formula," Western representatives also expressed doubts about the validity of classifying a number of potential types of weapons as new types of

WMD, as proposed by the Soviets. In the opinion of Western representatives, the majority of these types of weapons are variations of presently known types of weapons of mass destruction (nuclear, chemical, bacteriological, and radiological) and, consequently, should be considered only in this context.

Considering the position taken by its negotiating partners, the Soviet Union proposed a revised version of a definition in Working Document SSD/511, dated August 8, 1977:

> Weapons which may be developed in the future on the basis either of presently known scientific and technical principles which to date have not found application in the development of weapons of mass destruction, either individually or as an aggregate, or scientific and technical principles which may be discovered in the future and which possess properties which are similar or more powerful in destructive and/or casualty effect than presently known types of weapons of mass destruction, shall be considered new kinds of weapons of mass destruction and WMD systems.

The following were named in an annex to the working document as specific potential types of WMD: 1) radiological weapons of a nonexplosive type, operating with the aid of radioactive materials; 2) technical means of inflicting radioactive damage, based on the use of charged or neutral particles to affect biological targets; 3) infrasonic weapons, using acoustic emissions to affect biological targets; and 4) weapons utilizing electromagnetic radiation to affect biological targets. Even this definition, however, was judged by Western experts to be insufficiently precise.

In its Working Document SSD/514 the Soviet Union suggested proceeding from the position that systems that acquire the properties of a weapon of mass destruction as a result of application of new technical components of weapons—or of supporting means—should also be classified as new WMD systems (in addition to those that may be developed in the future upon completion of research and development of new types of WMD). It was proposed that the following be considered as a determining attribute of transition by a traditional weapon system into a new WMD system: the appearance of a new character of effect (mass human deaths) as a result of application of a new technical element of weapons or supporting means. Cited as an example were missile, artillery, air, and other traditional weapon systems that may acquire the properties of a new WMD system with utilization of a new technical element, such as fuel-air munitions to produce powerful pressure-effect explosions. The Western countries virtually refused to discuss the question of banning new WMD systems, and attention gradually shifted away from this matter.

Sharp differences of opinion were also voiced on the matter of the scope of a possible international agreement. The Soviet Union maintained that a comprehensive ban on the development and production of new types of weapons of mass destruction and WMD systems would be the most effective. The Western nations, however, adhered to the view that such an approach would lead to terminological confusion and constant disagreements on the matter of classification of new types of weapons as WMD, and would inevitably exert a negative effect on scientific and technological advance, since new scientific ideas are almost always of a dualistic nature at the development stage, that is, they can be used both for peaceful and military purposes. In addition, Western delegations pointed out that a comprehensive international agreement would not lend itself to effective verification. Therefore the most realistic approach to the question of banning new types of WMD, as they saw it, would consist, in the first place, in keeping this problem under continuous scrutiny and, second, in considering the possibility of concluding separate agreements on potential new types of WMD if such weapons, grounded on new scientific principles, were identified. It was emphasized thereby that, as experience indicates, there is a considerable span of time between the appearance of new types of WMD and their military production, in the course of which any necessary prohibitory measures could be agreed upon. Taking this point of view into consideration, at the 1977 summer session of the CCD the Soviet Union proposed a compromise solution, according to which, alongside a general comprehensive agreement, the possibility of concluding special agreements on prohibiting specific types of WMD would be considered, and the Soviet Union proposed to append to a general agreement a list of types of weapons and weapon systems subject to prohibition, a list which could subsequently be expanded. The Western countries, however, stuck to their previous position.

One more debatable issue pertained to the organizational forms of joint work. On March 28, 1978, the Soviet Union proposed the establishment, under the auspices of the Committee on Disarmament, of a special group of qualified government experts to examine the question of possible areas and directions of development of new weapons of mass destruction and WMD systems subject to inclusion in an initial list of prohibited types of WMD in a comprehensive agreement. In the Soviet view, this would ensure more effective study and determination of potentially dangerous areas and directions of development of new kinds of weapons of mass destruction. Such a group could continuously monitor the development of events in this area and present appropriate recommendations to the Committee on Disarmament at the earliest stage of potential development of new barbaric weapons. The Western countries stated in this connection that the creation of such a group would be premature inasmuch as, in their opinion, there did not exist an immediate threat of development of any new kinds of WMD in the near future. In order to monitor the state of affairs in this area, in the opinion of the NATO member nations, it would be quite sufficient to hold from time to time unofficial sessions of the Committee on Disarmament, when necessary with the participation of experts (such sessions were held up to 1982).

The next attempt to reconcile the positions of the parties and to work out a common approach was undertaken at the Thirty-third Session of the UN General Assembly, but it proved unsuccessful, chiefly due to disagreements over its scope. Two Resolutions on the question of prohibiting new types of WMD were approved at the session (33/66A and 33/66B): These were based on a British and on a Soviet draft proposal, which received approximately equal support. The following year the Western countries declined to submit their own draft resolution. This decision revealed a decline in interest in this problem on the part of the NATO countries, which became appreciable from the end of the 1970's.

In the subsequent period the Soviet Union repeatedly modified its position, endeavoring to overcome existing disagreements. For example, a new element was included in a draft resolution at the Thirty-sixth Session of the General Assembly: it was proposed that the permanent members of the Security Councils as well as other militarily important states, as a first step toward concluding a comprehensive agreement, make declarations, similar in content, renouncing the development of new types of weapons of mass destruction and WMD systems, with the understanding that such declarations could be approved by the UN Security Council. A new, major step toward the position of the Western countries was taken in July 1985, when the Soviet Union made the decision not to insist on its original proposal calling for conclusion of a comprehensive agreement and appealed to the states participating in the Conference on Disarmament to pledge (in a joint declaration or in the form of unilateral statements) to commence talks immediately following the appearance of a new type of weapon of mass destruction, aimed at prohibiting such a weapon and simultaneously to announce a moratorium on its practical development. The job of determining and identifying new types of WMD, according to this proposal, would be assigned to a periodically meeting group of qualified experts, which would keep these matters under continuous scrutiny, when necessary making recommendations on the holding of specific talks on new types of WMD.

New progress toward bringing the opposing positions closer together was made at the Forty-second and Forty-third sessions of the UN General Assembly. The Belorussian SSR delegation, for example, which in recent years has initiated the adoption of resolutions on new types of weapons of mass destruction and WMD systems, dropped its insistence on preserving in the text of the resolution provisions calling for the formation of a group of experts and adoption of a moratorium on the production of new types of WMD immediately after they are identified, and also included in the preamble reference to the 1948 UN formula. General Assembly Resolution 43/72 contains a request to the Conference on Disarmament that matters pertaining to prohibiting the development and production of new types of WMD be kept under scrutiny by enlisting appropriate assistance of experts, when necessary to advance recommendations on holding specific talks dealing with newly revealed types of WMD. The resolution also contained an appeal to all nations to consider these recommendations without delay in a receptive spirit. This resolution was passed with the largest majority in all the years this issue was under consideration: 152 votes in favor, with two abstentions (United States and Israel). Thus the groundwork was laid for achieving in the General Assembly a consensus on the inadmissibility of the development of new types of WMD. This would constitute an extremely important political statement.

At the same time there remains the need for further work on specific international legal aspects of this problem, in particular refinement of the definition of new types of WMD. In its present form the 1948 UN formula, although constituting a reliable methodological basis for identifying a given new type of weapon as a WMD, nevertheless allows for an arbitrary interpretation of the "criterion of commensurability" of casualty effect embodied in it, because the effects of nuclear, chemical, and bacteriological weapons differ from one another and depend on nuclear warhead yield, designation of chemical component, *etc.* The vagueness of the term "commensurability" could substantially weaken a political statement of the inadmissibility of development of new types of WMD, as, upon the emergence of a new barbaric type of weapon, sharp debates might arise over the question of whether it possesses "sufficient" killing power to be identified as a WMD. Agreement on and specification of the parameters of commensurability would make it possible to avoid such a danger. These same purposes could be served by refinement of the term "destruction," including reaching of agreement on whether, in addition to human deaths, it also includes destruction of the environment, as well as long-term effects of negative effect on man's health, his physical and mental abilities.

In conditions of initiated movement toward genuine disarmament, it would also seem advisable to return to consideration of the question of prohibiting new WMD systems. Reaching agreement on a definition which would make it possible to draw a clear-cut line between allowable modernization of existing and development of new WMD systems could serve as a point of departure for multilateral efforts in this area.

In addition it is important to establish an effective monitoring system to observe the development of trends in the area of military use of scientific and technological advances, in order to initiate talks in advance. It would seem that a promising way to accomplish this task is outlined in UN General Assembly Resolution 43/77A, adopted on Indian initiative. It contains a request to the UN Secretary General to keep an eye on advances in science and technology and to evaluate their effects on international security, when necessary with the assistance of qualified expert consultants. It was proposed that the UN member nations establish national groups of experts with similar functions. In implementation of this recommendation, the Soviet Union has already established a group of experts to make assessments and forecasts in the area of military application of scientific and technological advances, the reports of which will be submitted annually to the UN Secretary General. Establishment of similar groups in other countries, especially in the militarily most important countries, would make it possible substantially to increase the predictability of situation development in the military-political domain.

It would seem that the political determination of the inadmissibility of development of new types of WMD and WMD systems, in the form of a UN General Assembly resolution approved by consensus, in combination with an effective system of monitoring of the utilization of scientific and technological advances, with legally precise definitions, would make it possible to close off one of the most dangerous channels of the qualitative arms race.

A serious dialogue on the problems of new types of WMD and WMD systems was apparently one of the reasons that motivated the United States to come forth with its own initiative on a related matter. At the Thirty-first Session of the UN General Assembly, the U.S. delegation spoke out in favor of drafting a multilateral convention on banning radiological weapons (RW), which, incidentally, the United States viewed not as a new but as a "traditional" type of weapon of mass destruction, which had been mentioned in the 1948 UN formula. In 1977 this question was placed on the agenda of Soviet-U.S. consultations on new types of WMD, which ended in 1979 with submission for consideration by the Committee (Conference from 1984 on) on Disarmament, of joint draft basic provisions of a convention prohibiting the development, production, stockpiling, and use of radiological weapons (SD/31). Since then the problem of prohibiting RW and new types of WMD has been deliberated at the Conference within the framework of a single agenda item.

While the socialist and Western countries welcomed the Soviet-U.S. joint initiative and expressed willingness to complete work on the basis of the draft proposal at the earliest possible time, many members of the "Group of Twenty-One" (particularly Sweden, Brazil, Argentina, India, and Pakistan) let it be known that they considered the specific question of banning RW to be of little relevance. To justify their position they stated that such weapons are not in service with any country and are unlikely to enter operational service in the future, since the storage and use of such weapons involves a number of extremely difficult problems of a technical nature. In their opinion the problem of prohibiting attacks on nuclear facilities and installations, the destruction of which is fraught with immensely harmful consequences to people's health, lives, and the environment as a result of radioactive contamination, is becoming a much more relevant issue. Therefore, while not objecting in principle to a ban on RW, many nonaligned countries spoke out resolutely in favor of broadening the scope of a future convention by prohibiting the use of radioactive materials for hostile purposes, having in mind first and foremost the establishment of an effective international legal regime to protect nuclear installations.

Presenting arguments in support of their position, experts from Sweden and a number of nonaligned countries pointed in particular to the inadequacy of current legal provisions in this domain, established in 1977 by Additional Protocol I to the Geneva Conventions of August 12, 1949, on the Protection of Victims of International Armed Conflicts. Article 56 of this Protocol specifies that:

> Works or installations containing dangerous forces, namely dams, dykes and nuclear electrical generating stations, shall not be made the object of attack, even where these objects are military objectives, if such attack may cause the release of dangerous forces and consequent severe losses among the civilian population.

It is pointed out in that same Article, however, that in the case of nuclear power plants general protection from attack terminates if they produce electric power "in regular, significant and direct support of military operations and if such attack is the only feasible way to terminate such support." For all intents and purposes this means that Additional Protocol I allows for the possibility of military considerations outweighing humanitarian considerations and leaves the question of attacking nuclear power generating plants "to the discretion of the military on the battlefield," which is unacceptable to many states. Additional Protocol I, while introducing certain protective provisions pertaining to nuclear power generating plants, also leaves open the question of other types of nuclear installations with a high concentration of radioactive materials.

Agreeing on the need for a substantial strengthening of the regime for protection of nuclear installations, the socialist and majority of Western states spoke out in favor of separate consideration of this problem, realizing that otherwise, in the process of considering the matter of RW, substantial difficulties of a political, legal, and technical nature would be introduced. The "Group of Twenty-One," however, insisted on concurrent consideration of the problems of the prevention of attack on nuclear installations and a ban on radiological weapons in the "traditional" sense within the framework of the Special Committee on Radiological Weapons formed at the Conference on Disarmament. These issues are regularly considered in parallel at UN General Assembly sessions. Every year a consensus resolution is adopted on the basis of a Hungarian proposal, which contains a request to the Conference on Disarmament to continue talks on the issue of RW, taking into consideration all proposals in this regard presented to the Conference. In addition, at recent General Assembly sessions a resolution submitted at Iraqi initiative was passed by a majority vote. It contained a request that the Conference on Disarmament step up efforts to reach an agreement on prohibiting attacks on nuclear installations at the earliest possible time.

Many years of debate revealed a diversity of opinions on a broad range of issues, including matters of a purely technical nature, but the principal disagreements deal primarily with the form of linkage of problems pertaining to banning RW and prohibiting attacks on nuclear installations (whether they should be settled simultaneously and within the framework of a single agreement), as well as the question of categories of nuclear installations subject to protection. On the whole the Western countries oppose rigid linkage of questions pertaining to banning RW and prohibiting attacks on installations, preferring separate and phased resolution of these issues. The majority of countries in this group are in favor of protecting only installations involving peaceful nuclear uses (for example, installations under IAEA safeguards). The United States and France are totally unwilling to engage in talks on protection of nuclear installations. The "Group of Twenty-One" insists on concurrent banning of RW and prohibition of attacks on installations. Many of the members of this group are in favor of prohibiting attacks on agreed types of nuclear installations, without dividing such installations into peaceful and military.

The Soviet Union takes a flexible position on these issues. While preferring separate resolution of the problems of banning RW and prohibiting attacks on nuclear installations, it is also willing to settle these matters within the framework of a single agreement. Seeking to accommodate the position of the leading neutral and nonaligned states, the Soviet Union has declared its willingness for both peaceful and military nuclear installations to be subject to protection, with the exception of installations involved with weapon systems.

Serious differences between the Western and nonaligned countries, as well as disagreements within each of these groups, have led to a situation where for a number of years now the activities of the Special Committee on Radiological Weapons have essentially been at an impasse. At the same time, in the opinion of the majority of participants in the Conference on Disarmament, possibilities for finding generally acceptable solutions have not yet been exhausted. The urgency of these problems, which lie at the intersection of the interests of general security in the military and environmental domains, impels one to seek compromises.

It would seem that at the present stage concentration of attention on the form of linkage of problems pertaining to banning RW and prohibiting attacks on nuclear installations, as well as on reaching agreement on categories of installations subject to protection, would help to enhance solution of these problems, since many other debatable issues derive to one degree or another from these two issues. For example, signing a single convention prohibiting the use of radioactive materials for hostile purposes and two binding protocols to the convention (on banning RW and on protecting nuclear installations), or else two separate conventions, with the understanding that they will enter into force simultaneously, might be a possible compromise solution to the question of the form of linkage.

7. LIMITATIONS ON THE MILITARY USE OF SPACE

John B. Rhinelander
Partner, Shaw, Pittman, Potts & Trowbridge

In the United States, arms control is part of overall national security policy, and does not stand alone. Arms control policy reflects a net assessment of U.S. security interests, is consensual by nature (that is, resting on agreement and not sources such as UN statements or declarations), and is based on the premise that the United States may withdraw from a particular agreement if and when it no longer remains in the U.S. net interests. These general observations are especially applicable to limitations on military use of space. In addition, policy differences within the U.S. government are greater in this field than in any other aspects of arms control.

There has been much discussion of prohibitions on military activities in space over the past two decades, but there are only three treaties which substantially impact military space activities—the Treaty Banning Nuclear Weapon Tests in the Atmosphere, in Outer Space and Under Water (LTBT) of 1963, the Treaty on Principles Governing the Activities of States in the Exploration and Use of Outer Space, Including the Moon and Other Celestial Bodies (Outer Space Treaty) of 1967, and the Treaty Between the United States and the Union of Soviet Socialist Republics on the Limitation of Anti-Ballistic Missile Systems (ABM Treaty) of 1972. There are also only two significant space powers, the United States and the Soviet Union.

A. THE THREE BASIC TREATIES

The LTBT confines nuclear tests by states parties to the Treaty to those conducted underground. One hundred and seventeen (117) states are now parties to the LTBT, but some nuclear-weapon and nuclear-weapon-capable states are not. Above-ground nuclear tests were common in the 1950's and early 1960's, but no atmospheric tests have been conducted since 1980. Some critics of any type of test ban once claimed that tests could be conducted behind the moon or a planet and, therefore, even a test ban in space was not verifiable, but there has been no serious comments of this kind in recent years. As a result of the LTBT, even if the United States had wanted to test in space its proposed X-ray laser, which was originally a centerpiece of the Strategic Defense Initiative (SDI) program, this would have been prohibited. However, nuclear components intended for use in space, such as the warhead for a nuclear-armed ABM interceptor or nuclear-armed surface-to-air (SAM) missile, can be tested underground and then deployed on a land-based interceptor missile.

The Outer Space Treaty prohibits nuclear weapons being placed in orbit, being installed on celestial bodies, and being stationed in outer space in any other manner. The Treaty also provides that the moon and other celestial bodies must be used "exclusively for peaceful purposes." The Outer Space Treaty does not prohibit flight testing in space of nuclear-capable missiles that make less than a full orbit. This loophole was closed, as between the United States and the Soviet Union, by the prohibition on fractional orbital bombardment systems (FOBS) in the SALT II Treaty of 1979, which never entered into effect. A similar provision will be included in the START Treaty, currently under negotiation. Neither the Outer Space Treaty, which has ninety-eight (98) parties including the United States and the Soviet Union, nor any other treaty defines the altitude at which space begins and the atmosphere ends, nor limits in any way orbiting or geo-stationary satellites that serve many militarily useful purposes, such as early warning, surveillance, monitoring, communications, and command and control. Historically, the Soviet Union has deployed more satellites at any one time than has the United States.

The ABM Treaty prohibits the development and testing, as well as the deployment, of space-based ABM systems and components. Space-based ABMs were not practical with the technologies of the 1960's and 1970's, but the miniaturization of electronics and computer parts has brought renewed interest in the feasibility of space-based ballistic missile defense. SDI, also known as Star Wars, was the best known example of the 1980's. The threat of proliferation in ballistic missiles has renewed interest in deploying defensive systems against short-range missiles to complement anti-aircraft defenses. The remarkable successes of the U.S. Patriot missiles in intercepting, but not necessarily destroying, Iraqi SCUDs in early 1991 is certain to create interest in some countries in missile defense for the 1990's. The Patriot and the Soviet SA-12 were originally designed as surface-to-air (SAM) anti-aircraft systems, but both have been modified to provide "point defense" anti-tactical missile (ATBM) capability. An ATBM system, whether mobile land-based, as is the Patriot, or sea-based, air-based or space-based, is largely exempt from the ABM Treaty, which is focused on defenses against *strategic* (that is, long-range) offensive ballistic missiles. The ABM Treaty limitations applicable to SAMs and ATBMs are that they not be given "capabilities to counter strategic ballistic missiles" and not be tested "in an ABM mode."

All three of the most prominent "gray areas" in the ABM Treaty—air-based and space-based sensors, anti-satellite systems (ASATs), and SAMs and ATBMs—are now the focus of programs in the United States and the Soviet Union. SAMs and ATBMs would raise particularly troublesome ABM Treaty issues if land-based components, such as the missile launchers and engagement radars, were netted with air-based and space-based sensors that provide target acquisition and detailed tracking information on strategic ballistic missiles.

Whether any of these three "gray areas" will be clarified by mutual agreement, and if so how, are leading issues in terms of the future viability of the ABM Treaty. The exploitation of rapid technological change is likely to erode the ABM Treaty unless new limitations and prohibitions that supplement or clarify the Treaty and reinforce its basic purposes are agreed upon.

B. The Unilateral Reinterpretation of the ABM Treaty

When the U.S. Executive determined in 1984-85 that the ABM Treaty, as traditionally interpreted, blocked the development and testing in space of programs important to the early deployment of certain aspects of a SDI program, the United States had two permissible legal options under the ABM Treaty. First, it could have withdrawn after giving six months notice under Article XV(2). The United States chose not to do so, probably because of the strong Congressional and international support for the ABM Treaty as the cornerstone of constraints on U.S. and Soviet strategic nuclear weapons programs and as a pre-condition to a START Treaty. Second, the United States could have sought the agreement of the Soviet Union to specific amendments, in accordance with Article XIV(1). The United States probably did not do so because the proposal of an amendment would have implicitly, if not explicitly, admitted to a present Soviet veto over the future course of SDI.

Instead, the U.S. Executive announced in October 1985 a unilateral reinterpretation that the development and testing of space-based ABM components, based on "other physical principles" (such as lasers or particle beams) that could substitute for traditional ABM components, were not covered at all by the ABM Treaty. Arguing that all such new devices were only subject to the deployment ban in Agreed Statement D, the U.S. Executive hoped to be able to conduct a vigorous testing program in space unconstrained by Treaty limitations.

The U.S. Congress rejected this reinterpretation because it was inconsistent with the text and purpose of the Treaty; controverted the 1972 Executive-Senate understanding at the time of ratification; was not supported by the negotiating history of the ABM Treaty, that had previously been classified; and was at odds with the subsequent practice of the United States and the Soviet Union. These avenues of inquiry as to the meaning of the ABM Treaty are those sanctioned by the Vienna Convention on the Law of Treaties.

Under the Constitution of the United States, a dispute of this type between the Executive and Congress would be judged a "political question," and the federal courts in the United States would not agree to decide the legal question. Further, there is no mandatory reference of legal disputes between the United States and the Soviet Union to international adjudication, such as the International Court of Justice, and no inclination in the United States to agree to do so on issues central to national security. However, the Congress must annually authorize and appropriate funds for defense programs, and starting in 1987 has mandated that SDI funds be spent consistent with the "traditional" interpretation of the ABM Treaty. The President has accepted and signed the legislation.

This Congressional action has preserved the ABM Treaty against its most serious legal challenge since entry into force in 1972. However, the U.S. Executive continues to base its international negotiating position with the Soviet Union in Geneva on the "reinterpretation," rejected by both the U.S. Congress and the Soviet Union. Because the Soviet Union has unequivocally stated that the "traditional" interpretation is correct, after incorrectly arguing in 1983 that even research (the purpose of which was to create systems that might eventually go beyond Treaty limits) was banned by the ABM Treaty, the two countries in their discussions of the ABM Treaty are far apart. Negotiations of agreed interpretations or amendments on many vitally important issues that have arisen under the ABM Treaty are stalemated.

C. The Krasnoyarsk Radar and Other LPARS

Prior to the "reinterpretation" dispute, the most serious disagreement that had arisen under the ABM Treaty involved the large-phased-array radar under construction at Krasnoyarsk in Kazakhstan SSR.

This was not the first issue involving a "large-phased-array radar" (LPAR) to arise under the ABM Treaty. The Soviet Union previously had challenged, as a prohibited ABM radar, but then accepted as a permissible radar for early warning and national technical means, an LPAR that the

United States constructed in the Aleutian Islands, Alaska; it is oriented toward the impact zone of the traditional Soviet ICBM test range in the Pacific Ocean. Later, the Soviet Union challenged the construction of early warning phased-array LPARs in Greenland and Fylindales Moor (UK) as not on the periphery of U.S. territory and, therefore, prohibited by Agreed Statement F. The United States contended they were both permitted modernizations of radars which had been based on older, mechanical-scan technology. These examples illustrate that neither the Treaty text nor its negotiating history sets forth clear criteria separating an early warning radar and LPARs for other permitted purposes from a prohibited ABM radar for battle management.

Notwithstanding the lack of precise guidance from the ABM Treaty text and the fact that phased-array technology can be used for many purposes, U.S. experts in and out of government unanimously agreed that the construction of the Krasnoyarsk radar violated the ABM Treaty and severely undercut support for arms control in the United States. This radar was neither on the periphery of the Soviet Union nor oriented outward, as required by the Treaty. The only disagreement among U.S. experts was whether that radar was simply for early warning, as most believed, or also for battle management. Finally in 1989, the Soviet Foreign Minister admitted that the Krasnoyarsk radar violated the ABM Treaty and would be dismantled. That is now underway, and this matter should soon be closed.

D. ASATs and Other Challenges for the Future

The "reinterpretation" dispute and the Krasnoyarsk radar are the clearest examples that the counter-intuitive premise of the ABM Treaty—severe restrictions on both ABM systems and gray-area technology are desirable, stabilizing, and necessary pre-conditions for limitations on strategic *offensive* systems—is not accepted by important elements of the national security bureaucracy in each country.

Unless and until broad and fundamental agreements in principle can be reached on the role of strategic defenses and the comprehensiveness of arms control in this area, it is unlikely that the intensive and detailed work on more precise agreements under the ABM Treaty with respect to ground-based systems, space-based weapons, and exotic sensors will be undertaken by the two governments. While the "devil is in the details," as more than one arms control expert has noted as negotiations reach the end game, no progress is even conceivable as long as there is fundamental disagreement on general principles. Finally, the ABM Treaty is clearly a field where international agreement should remain bilateral, at least for the foreseeable future, and not also become multilateral.

More broadly, there are no current negotiations underway limiting anti-satellite (ASAT) and defensive anti-satellite (DSAT) systems. There were bilateral negotiations on ASATs in 1978-79 that were recessed and not renewed. Subsequently, the Soviet Union submitted a draft treaty barring space weapons, including ASATs, to the United Nations, but the United States has had no interest in pursuing this subject. Satellites in orbit are similar in many respects to ballistic missiles in mid-flight. The United States not only has sought to avoid any treaty limits on SDI, but also has sought funds from Congress to perfect and deploy an ASAT system, particularly to reduce vulnerability of naval forces from surveillance in time of war. In 1989, the Secretary of Defense called the lack of an ASAT the "single most vulnerable point" in U.S. defenses.

The Soviet Union had begun testing in 1968 an ASAT launched by a modified SS-9 "heavy" ICBM, but it never proved reliable and testing was stopped in 1982. Starting in 1985, Congress prohibited testing of the more-sophisticated air-based U.S. ASAT and provided less research and development funds than requested.

An ASAT Treaty and the ABM Treaty would be inextricably woven together. Agreement within the U.S. government to pursue the former is not likely before the United States is ready to accept amendments and interpretations to clarify and increase the prohibitions of the ABM Treaty. An ASAT Treaty could either be comprehensive or limited to high-altitude satellites, but in either event the key issues will be prohibitions on testing. An ICBM, an ABM missile such as the type deployed with the Soviet Galosh system around Moscow, and even electronic counter measures have basic ASAT capabilities against low-orbit satellites. An ASAT Treaty presumably would not reach these types of residual ASAT capabilities.

If an ASAT Treaty were sought, it could well be accompanied by amendments to the ABM Treaty further restricting ABM activities, such as prohibiting any deployment, and at least exo-atmospheric testing, of fixed land-based ABM systems. Initially, the ASAT issues will have to be addressed by the United States and the Soviet Union alone, but eventually an ASAT Treaty could become multilateral.

Finally, additional or more specific limitations on space-based systems will present more vexing verification challenges than those dealt with in 1972 under the ABM Treaty, which set a precedent for acknowledging reliance on national technical means (NTM) of verification, as well as commitments to non-interference with and non-concealment from such means. Radically new arms control approaches, such as a ban on orbiting nuclear reactors in space, might require pre-flight inspection of payloads. However, there are other instances of newer technologies, such as passive space-based sensors, where agreement on any kind of pre-flight inspections is unlikely, but limitations on their capability would be effectively non-verifiable by NTM once deployed. In brief, verification will remain an important limitation on prospective agreements dealing with space-based systems and components. Because of costs and other factors, it is improbable that other countries individually or collectively will agree to fund and operate verification satellites approaching the NTM capabilities of the United States and the Soviet Union.

E.T. Agayev
Head of Branch, International Organizations Directorate,
USSR Ministry of Foreign Affairs

There presently exist a large number of international legal documents that regulate the regime of use of space. However, the provisions of these documents pertaining to prohibition of the use of space for military purposes and, in particular, the deployment and use of weapons in space, contain traditional wordings and formulas that fail to cover all current problems of military use of space and, consequently, cannot be effectively implemented to resolve the complex problems of preventing an arms race in space. Present-day trends in the development of space science and technology, in combination with continuing implementation of programs to develop space weaponry, illuminate the inadequacy of existing legal instruments for preventing the militarization of space. One can present in support of this statement a brief review of the principal international legal documents that directly regulate the regime of use of space for peaceful purposes. These documents can be divided into two principal categories: bilateral agreements, and multilateral international legal enactments.

Prevention of the militarization of space is a global problem that affects the interests of a great many states—large and small, developed and developing, a fact that dictates the urgent need for globalization of efforts to resolve this problem. One of the forms of globalization of the process of preventing the militarization of space is the signing and adequate implementation of multilateral agreements on the peaceful use of space. A number of such agreements have been signed and have entered into force to date.

The UN Charter is the first of a number of multilateral agreements in this area. In spite of the fact that the Charter was adopted long before the commencement of regular exploration of space, and consequently can only indirectly deal with the problem area of space, its fundamental principles and provisions extend to this area. Article 103 states that obligations under the Charter shall take precedence over all obligations of Organization member states under other international agreements. In addition, the 1967 Outer Space Treaty contains direct references to the Charter: In particular, Article III of the Treaty notes that the exploration and use of space shall be carried out in conformity with international law, including the UN Charter.

One can point to a number of provisions of the Charter that indirectly apply to the problem of peaceful use of space. In particular, they pertain to the obligations of states,

> To maintain international peace and security, and to that end: to take effective collective measures for the prevention and removal of threats to peace, and for the suppression of acts of aggression or other breaches of the peace, and to bring about by peaceful means, and in conformity with the principles of justice and international law, adjustment or settlement of international disputes or situations which might lead to a breach of the peace. (Paragraph 1(1)).

In addition,

> All Members shall refrain in their international relations from the threat or use of force against the territorial integrity or political independence of any state, or in any other manner inconsistent with the Purposes of the United Nations. (Paragraph 4(2)).

The signing on August 5, 1963, and the entry into force of the Treaty Banning Nuclear Weapon Tests in the Atmosphere, in Outer Space and Under Water constituted an important step along the way toward preventing the militarization of space. Conclusion of this agreement essentially constituted the first substantial arms control measure. At the same time it is one of the first treaties directly pertaining to a regime of use of space. Each of the Parties to the Treaty pledges to prohibit, prevent, and not conduct any test explosions of nuclear weapons or any other nuclear explosions at any place under its jurisdiction or control: in the atmosphere; beyond the atmosphere, including in space; and under water, including territorial waters and the high seas. In addition, each of the Treaty Parties pledges to refrain from inducing, encouraging, or participating in the conduct of any test explosions of nuclear weapons or any other nuclear explosions at any location that would be in any of the above-named environments.

The signing on January 27, 1967 and the entry into force of the Treaty on Principles Governing the Activities of States in the Exploration and Use of Outer Space, Including the Moon and Other Celestial Bodies was the next event in the process of efforts to ensure the use of space exclusively for peaceful purposes. This Treaty constitutes a basic international legal agreement that defines and regulates a regime of use of outer space. The preamble to the Treaty recognizes the "common interest of all mankind in the progress of the exploration and use of outer space for peaceful purposes." This Treaty contains specific provisions of a regime of use of space for peaceful purposes. In particular, Article III notes:

> States Parties to the Treaty shall carry on activities in the exploration and use of outer space, including the moon and other celestial bodies, in accordance with international law, including the Charter of the United Nations, in the interest of maintaining international peace and security and promoting international co-operation and understanding.

Article IV defines the basic restrictions on conduct of military activity in space:

> States Parties to the Treaty undertake not to place in orbit around the Earth any objects carrying nuclear weapons or any other kinds of weapons of mass destruction, install such weapons on celestial bodies, or station such weapons in outer space in any other manner.

The moon and other celestial bodies shall be used by all Treaty Parties exclusively for peaceful purposes. The establishment of military bases, installations, and fortifications, the testing of any type of weapons, and the conduct of military maneuvers on celestial bodies is forbidden. The use of military personnel for scientific research or for any other peaceful purposes is not prohibited. Finally, the "use of any equipment or facility necessary for peaceful exploration of the moon and other celestial bodies shall also not be prohibited." (Article IV).

The same wording is applied to the moon and other celestial bodies in the second paragraph of Article IV as is contained in the 1959 Antarctic Treaty, in which this wording signifies the complete demilitarization and neutralization of the Antarctic. One can therefore assume that a regime of total demilitarization and neutralization applies to the moon and other celestial bodies. One hindering element, however, is the fact that there are specific features to the potential uses of rockets and satellites in space, which affects the regimes governing the moon and other celestial bodies. Other restrictions have been established in regard to the rest of space: The only things prohibited are the placement into earth orbit of objects carrying nuclear weapons or any other kinds of weapon of mass destruction, as well as the deployment of such weapons in space in any manner whatsoever. The latter wording is quite vague. However, together with the preceding formula, it essentially means prohibition of the deployment in space of nuclear weapons and other kinds of weapons of mass destruction. There is a similar provision in the 1971 Treaty on the Prohibition of the Emplacement of Nuclear Weapons and Other Weapons of Mass Destruction on the Seabed and the Ocean Floor and in the

Subsoil Thereof. One should note thereby that, according to the definition contained in a 1948 UN General Assembly resolution, nuclear, radiological, chemical, and bacteriological weapons, as well as any other weapons with similar destructive characteristics that may be developed in the future, constitute weapons of mass destruction.

The 1967 Outer Space Treaty also provides for the possibility of inspections and observation of the activities of Parties in space:

> All stations, installations, equipment and space vehicles on the moon and other celestial bodies shall be open to representatives of other States Parties to the Treaty on a basis of reciprocity. Such representatives shall give reasonable advance notice of a projected visit, in order that appropriate consultations may be held and that maximum precautions may be taken to ensure safety and to avoid interference with normal operations in the facility to be visited. (Article XII).

Without going into a detailed analysis of this Treaty, one can make a number of comments pertaining to the limited possibilities of application of this Treaty for purposes of preventing the militarization of space. First of all, the idea of exploration and use of space for peaceful purposes is formulated too imprecisely, which has inevitably led to considerable differences in interpretation. In particular, in the opinion of some the term "peaceful" means "nonmilitary," while others consider this term synonymous with the term "non-offensive." Obviously a difference in practical approaches to implementing policy in the area of use of space lies behind these different linguistic interpretations. Furthermore, different rules and procedures have been established for the use of space proper on the one hand and the moon and other celestial bodies on the other.

Extremely narrow restrictions are prescribed in regard to space, which do not hinder, in particular, the orbital deployment of non-nuclear antisatellite weapons and antimissile systems.

The provisions of the Treaty that pertain to verification do not have any binding force, and their implementation depends to a considerable degree on the good will of the Parties.

The Treaty on the Non-Proliferation of Nuclear Weapons, which was signed on July 1, 1968, and which entered into force on March 5, 1970, occupies a special place among international legal enactments connected with the problem of preventing the militarization of space. By limiting the horizontal proliferation of nuclear weapons, this Treaty helps narrow the circle of states capable of deploying these weapons in space. The Treaty's role in preventing the militarization of space is limited, however, by the fact that not all nuclear states are parties to the Treaty and, in addition, there exist a good many so-called near-nuclear states.

The 1977 Convention on the Prohibition of Military or Any Other Hostile Use of Environmental Modification Techniques considers as an environmental modification technique "any technique for changing—through the deliberate manipulation of natural processes—the dynamics, composition or structure of the Earth, including its biota, lithosphere, hydrosphere and atmosphere, or of outer space." (Article II). The Convention Parties pledge "not to engage in military or any other hostile use of environmental modification techniques having widespread, long-lasting or severe effects as the means of destruction, damage or injury to any other State Party." (Article I, Paragraph 1).

The 1979 Agreement Governing the Activities of States on the Moon and Other Celestial Bodies reiterates and further develops the basic provisions of the 1967 Outer Space Treaty. Pursuant to this Agreement, the moon and other celestial bodies shall be used by states exclusively for peaceful purposes. It prohibits, in particular, the threat or use of force or any other hostile actions or threat of hostile actions. It also prohibits use of the moon and other celestial bodies for the conduct of any similar actions or the employment of any similar threats in regard to the earth, moon, spacecraft, and the personnel of spacecraft or man-made space objects. (Article III, Paragraph 2). Article III, Paragraph 3 of the Agreement, further developing the provisions of the 1967 Treaty, contains the obligation not to place into orbit "around or other trajectory to or around the moon objects carrying nuclear weapons or any other kinds of weapon of mass destruction or place or use such weapons on or in the moon." Pursuant to Article I of the Agreement, prohibitory provisions apply not only to the Moon but also to other celestial bodies in the solar system with the exception of the Earth. The principal space powers, however, are as yet not parties to this Agreement.

Finally, the International Telecommunications Convention was signed in 1982, governing the distribution of radio frequencies in space. Pursuant to the Convention, distribution should be accomplished in such a manner as to eliminate the possibility of troublesome interference. Article 38, Paragraph 1, however, states that: "Members retain their entire freedom with regard to military radio installations of their army, naval and air forces." This is a substantial reservation, which significantly diminishes the effectiveness of the Convention itself.

There are a number of bilateral Soviet-U.S. agreements which also establish a legal foundation for preventing the militarization of space.

On September 30, 1971, the Soviet Union and the United States signed two bilateral agreements—an Agreement on Measures to Reduce the Risk of Outbreak of Nuclear War Between the United States of America and the Union of Soviet Socialist Republics and an Agreement Between the United States of America and the Union of Soviet Socialist

Republics on Measures to Improve the USA-USSR Direct Communications Link.

The conclusion on May 26, 1972, of the Treaty Between the United States of America and the Union of Soviet Socialist Republics on the Limitation of Anti-Ballistic Missile Systems constituted a major step along the road toward averting an arms race in space. Of particular importance in this regard are the Treaty provisions pertaining to verification. Article XII, Paragraph 1, states, for example, that:

> For the purpose of providing assurance of compliance with the provisions of this Treaty, each Party shall use national technical means of verification at its disposal in a manner consistent with generally recognized principles of international law.

Paragraph 2 of that same Article guarantees the inviolability of these means of verification: "Each Party undertakes not to interfere with the national technical means of verification of the other Party operating in accordance with paragraph 1 of this Article." Thus prohibition against interfering with the functioning of reconnaissance satellites is given legal confirmation, which creates a basis for mutual restriction of use of antisatellite systems.

The 1972 ABM Treaty pledged the parties not to develop, test, or deploy not only sea-based, air-based, and mobile land-based ABM systems or components, but space-based ones as well. The Soviet-U.S. Treaty on Reduction and Limitation of Strategic Offensive Arms that is presently being drafted does not address space-based weapons. However, in a joint statement dealing with future negotiations on nuclear and space weapons and further strengthening of strategic stability, dated June 1, 1990, it was stated that following signing of a Treaty on Reduction and Limitation of Strategic Offensive Arms, the Parties will proceed without delay to hold consultations on future talks. Both Parties will be able to raise at these future talks any matters pertaining to any and all strategic offensive arms, and they are continuing without delay talks on ballistic missile defense and space within the framework of the existing structure of talks on nuclear and space weapons in Geneva. The effective application of existing international legal enactments in the domain of prevention of militarization of space is complicated, however, by the fact that the basic terms and concepts to be used in these agreements have not been sufficiently elaborated and defined. This applies in particular to such terms as space, peaceful purposes, and space weapons. First of all there exists space proper, which the 1967 Treaty does not sufficiently distinguish, on the one hand, from the earth's atmosphere and, on the other hand, from celestial bodies. As regards military use, for example, substantial differences between these three concepts are quite clearly evident, concepts which are of fundamental importance for interpreting existing agreements. The probability of militarization of space is greater than that of deployment of weapons on celestial bodies and is less than that of deployment of weapons in the atmosphere.

This approach to defining the term "outer space" was sufficient at the moment of signing of the 1967 Treaty. Nevertheless it is unclear as to whether at the present time it can be effectively used for the purpose of preventing military activities in space.

Of course, absolutely precise definitions and delimitations are not always necessary or possible. Space law depends to a considerable degree on the development of technology and at the present stage cannot be reduced to a standardized comprehensive compilation of rules, regulations, and definitions. In actuality space law has evolved gradually, in conformity with the requirements of the international community and assessments of these requirements, which change as technology advances.

In addition, there may be different opinions on the correctness of various definitions since, as we know, there exist two competing concepts in this area: a territorial concept, which prescribes establishment of firm delineations in conformity with physical criteria, and a functional concept, within the framework of which regulation of specific types of activity in space is of priority importance. The 1967 Treaty integrates elements of both concepts. There is a prevailing tendency, however, to view space as an integral whole, not to divide it into separate zones. Nevertheless this tendency can be undermined if proposals are adopted which call for the establishment of separate legal regimes for low-altitude and high-altitude satellites.

There exists an entire aggregate of problems in defining the term space objects and, in particular, space weapons. First of all, a special protection regime applies to a number of objects, certain satellites for example. Applying a protection regime to specific types of satellite involves a triple risk: Either they will be identified as possessing strategic importance and by virtue of this will become more vulnerable, or harm could be done to the status of satellites that are not covered by this regime. Finally, such a protection regime could legitimize certain types of military activity in space.

Defining the term space weapons is an extremely complicated matter, if only because many satellites are multi-purpose. Moreover, as regards antisatellite weapons, in addition to weapon systems specifically designed and built for this purpose, other weapons can be used as anti-satellite weapons on a temporary or permanent basis. In defining this term one must avoid two shortcomings: giving it too general and abstract a nature, eliminating the possibility of effective practical application, and, on the other hand, an excessively detailed definition, eliminating the possibility of taking the development of space technology into account.

One's attention is also drawn to the fact that as a rule missiles traveling in space are not viewed as a space weapon. In conformity with this position, prevention of an arms race in space does not lead to the necessity of limitation and prohibition of this type of weapon, in spite of the fact that their flight path passes through space.

Two principal categories of norms of customary law can be identified among the elements of the legal mechanism for the prevention of militarization of space. First of all, there are norms formed on the basis of existing treaties and the extension of their provisions beyond the framework of the circle of parties to these treaties. Second, there are general norms of customary law, constituting part of international law and pertaining to regulation of the regime of use of space.

The legal consequences of unilateral pledges by states are governed by customary law. As applied to the problem of preventing an arms race in space, one must consider not only the entire aggregate of international law norms but also the enactments of international organizations. Resolutions of the UN General Assembly take precedence among the latter. General Assembly resolutions pertaining to prevention of the militarization of space play an important role in accomplishing this task. They can serve as a foundation for drawing up international treaties in this area (the 1967 Treaty, for example) and can aid in interpretation of treaties and legal norms, as well as in formulation of norms of customary law.

One can note two types of resolutions directly connected with prevention of an arms race in space. First, there is Resolution S-10/2, the Final Document of the General Assembly's Tenth Special Session on Disarmament, which embodies a general agreement of states to take measures and to hold appropriate international talks. Second, there are the General Assembly resolutions directly pertaining to the problem of prevention of the militarization of space, in particular Resolution 40/87 of December 12, 1985, and Resolution 41/53 of December 3, 1986, as well as corresponding resolutions of subsequent General Assembly sessions, which contain proposals addressed to the States Parties to the Conference on Disarmament, pertaining to the adoption of specific measures in this area.

Discussion and debate on the linkage between peaceful purposes and the continuing militarization of space, as well as on the possibility of preventing military activities in space by proclaiming these peaceful purposes, will scarcely lead to any positive results in the near future. In this connection, it would seem, broad, constructive international cooperation is needed to achieve the stated goal, cooperation that meets the interests of all states, particularly of developing countries, and that reduces the possibility of militarization of space. In other words, efforts to prevent the militarization of space should include not only prohibition, limitation, and verification, but also comprehensive international cooperation in space, which as of yet has not reached an advanced stage.

In 1985, at the Fortieth Session of the UN General Assembly, the Soviet Union introduced a proposal entitled "On International Cooperation in the Peaceful Exploitation of Outer Space Under Conditions of Its Non-Militarization." This proposal contains main lines and principles of international cooperation in this area.

First, renunciation by states of the development (including R&D), testing, and deployment of space attack weapons would open up the way toward global peaceful cooperation. This cooperation would be organized and developed on an ascending line–from exchange of scientific and technical information and simple forms of cooperation to unification of states' capabilities for accomplishing the large-scale tasks of exploitation of space.

Second, such cooperation could develop in the following areas:

fundamental scientific space exploration and research, including the moon and other celestial bodies, and the launching of interplanetary space vehicles for these purposes;

utilization of the results of space research in biology, medicine, materials science, weather forecasting, and global satellite communications systems, resolution of problems of earth remote sensing, obtaining data for the benefit of geology and agriculture, exploitation of the world ocean, and assistance in the search for, detection, and rescue of survivors in the case of ships in distress and downed aircraft;

development and use of space hardware, including large international orbital scientific stations, as well as manned spacecraft of various types.

Third, peaceful exploitation of space should be carried out with steadfast observance of previously concluded treaties aimed at preventing an arms race in space, as well as the principles proceeding from the UN Charter.

Fourth, a world space organization for international cooperation in the peaceful exploration of space could be formed for the purpose of organization and implementation of coordination of states. The functions of such an organization would be as follows: to provide on a nondiscriminatory basis access by all states to the results of scientific and technological advances, to carry out international projects, to give comprehensive assistance to developing countries in getting involved in the exploration and utilization of space, to coordinate on an international scale the activities of other international organizations in this area, and to assist when necessary in monitoring compliance with agreements that already have been concluded or will be concluded in the future for the purpose of preventing an arms race.

Fifth, the Soviet Union proposed holding a representative international conference to consider the entire aggregate of above proposals.

At the Fifteenth Special Session of the UN General Assembly, the Soviet Union, Czechoslovakia, and Bulgaria presented a working document on the establishment of an international verification mechanism under UN auspices (Document A/S-15/AS.1/15). The co-authors proposed proceeding with discussion of the question of establishing under UN auspices a mechanism of extensive international verification of compliance with agreements on lessening international tension, arms limitation, and monitoring of the military situation in conflict areas. They proposed as one possible variation the idea of establishment in the future of an International Verification Agency (IVA) and a UN Data Bank, to which information pertaining to the problems of disarmament and verification would be sent.

Toward these ends the Conference on Disarmament has proposed the initiation of talks on the establishment of an international space surveillance agency, including software and logistic support of its activities.

The Soviet Union expressed its willingness to consider the matter of using Soviet launch vehicles to launch agency satellites, as well as of providing the UN data bank with specific information connected with monitoring and verification which would come from Soviet commercial satellites.

That same year, 1988, the Soviet Union presented at the Conference on Disarmament a document entitled "On Establishing an International Monitoring System to Prevent the Deployment of Weapons of Any Kind in Space" (Document SD/817). The Soviet Union proposed establishing an International Space Inspectorate. Its main function would be to perform monitoring activities to ensure that no objects launched into and deployed in space by the Parties were weapons or carry weapons of any kind. These measures would include the following: advance communication by the receiving state to inspectorate representatives of information on each forthcoming launch, including the date and time of launch, type of launch vehicle, orbital parameters, and general data on the space vehicle to be launched, with the permanent presence of teams of inspectors at all space launch facilities for purposes of verification; conduct of inspections at agreed-upon storage facilities, industrial plants, laboratories, and testing facilities; and verification of unannounced launches from undeclared launch sites by means of special on-site inspections.

As is indicated by UN discussion of the problems of limitation of the military use of space, positive resolution of the matter will depend on an entire aggregate of factors that determine the overall development of the international situation—confidence-building measures, the establishment of openness in military activities, and the success of Soviet-U.S. talks in this area.

8. Reduction in the Overall Level of Military Forces

John H. McNeill
Assistant General Counsel for International Affairs and Intelligence, U.S. Department of Defense, and Charles H. Stockton Professor of International Law, U.S. Naval War College

Almost exactly three hundred years ago, William Penn published one of his most visionary concepts, a plan for the future peace of Europe. Penn's plan, which called for a global parliament to sit in judgment on what we would now term disputes between sovereign states, later found resonance in many aspects of the Covenant of the League of Nations and the UN Charter. In addition, Penn's plan dealt implicitly with force reductions and arms control concerns. He pointed out that, if after establishment of his proposed global parliament (which would play the role of an "umpire"), a sovereign maintained an army large enough to endanger the rest,

> [T]he question may be asked by order of the sovereign states, why such a one either raises or keeps up a formidable body of troops, and to oblige him forthwith to reform or reduce them, lest anyone, by keeping up a great body of troops, should surprise a neighbor. But a small force in every other sovereignty, to what it is capable or accustomed to maintain, will certainly prevent that danger and vanquish any such fear.

Put succinctly, Penn made three points which have retained their force over the intervening three centuries, *i.e.*, assuming an effective "umpire" is in place, the status toward which the United Nations–with a viable political basis among the permanent members of the Security Council for dealing with threats to the peace–appears to be evolving today, then the armed forces of neighboring states should be reduced to levels that are inferior to those required for a successful surprise attack, yet still numerically sufficient to defend against such an attack. This goal remains as desirable now as when the Quaker sage wrote his famous essay; indeed, the goal may perhaps be more readily achievable–as well as more necessary—now than in any previous age.

What would be the strategic context of a reduction in the overall level of military forces? In the current world situation, nuclear weapons and other weapons of mass destruction are usually thought to represent a qualitatively different set of problems than is the case with so-called "conventional" forces. However, deterrence theory reflects the reality that the use of conventional arms in certain situations could lead to the use of nuclear weapons as well. Certainly, one could not intelligently address problems of conventional force operations without taking into account the strategic situation in which such operations would take place, and the existence of highly significant nuclear infrastructures complicates that situation considerably. Of course, this consideration is evident in the recent and historic London Declaration on a Transformed North Atlantic Alliance, issued by the heads of state and government participating in the meeting of the North Atlantic Council, July 5-6, 1990.

In Point 15 of that document, the NATO allies stated the following:

> To keep the peace, the Alliance must maintain for the foreseeable future an appropriate mix of nuclear and conventional forces, based in Europe, and kept up to date where necessary. But, as a defensive Alliance, NATO has always stressed that none of its weapons will ever be used except in self-defense and that we seek the lowest and most stable level of nuclear forces needed to secure the prevention of war.

The above should be read against the backdrop of Points 12 and 13, by which the same allies laid out in some detail their objectives for conventional arms reduction in Europe:

> [W]e put the highest priority on completing this year the first treaty to reduce and limit conventional armed forces in Europe (CFE) along with the completion of a meaningful CSBM package . . . We propose that, once a CFE Treaty is signed, follow-on talks should begin with the same membership and mandate, with the goal of building on the current agreement with additional measures, including measures to limit manpower in Europe . . . Our objective will be to conclude the negotiations on the follow-on to CFE and CSBMs as soon as possible . . . We seek through new conventional arms control negotiations, within the CSCE framework, further far-reaching measures in the 1990's to limit the offensive capability of conventional armed forces in Europe, so as to prevent any nation from maintaining disproportionate military power on the continent . . . We will make provisions as needed for different regions to redress disparities and to ensure that no one's security is harmed at any stage.

Interestingly, the twin goals of seeking "the lowest and most stable levels of nuclear forces needed" and preventing "any nation from maintaining disproportionate military power on the continent" echo Penn's plan. Indeed, the Preamble to the Treaty on Conventional Armed Forces in Europe (CFE Treaty), done at Paris, November 19, 1990, records that its twenty-two States Parties are:

> Committed to the objectives of establishing a secure and stable balance of conventional armed forces in Europe at lower levels than heretofore, of eliminating disparities prejudicial to stability and security and of eliminating, as a matter of high priority, the capability for launching surprise attack and for initiating large-scale offensive action in Europe.

There exist numerous methods for achieving reductions in the overall level of military forces. Should the strategy be to achieve this through an over-arching and global agreement on general and complete disarmament? Certainly, this has been tried before—for example, as reflected in the 1961 Soviet-U.S. Statement of Agreed Principles (known as the McCloy-Zorin Agreed Statement). This outline of an acceptable plan for general and complete disarmament marked the high-water mark in post-war Great Power interest in such an approach. The problem is, of course, whether to try to achieve the whole in one grand effort ("disarmament"), despite the inherent complexities of doing so. Would it not be more realistic to try first to achieve a more limited goal ("arms control")? Against this, proponents of disarmament—and indeed, more subtly, the opponents of arms control (as well as of disarmament conceptually)—maintain that it is not possible to "solve" part of the problem alone. The following objection to a partial approach employs reasoning along these familiar lines: It was put forward by the German delegate to the First Hague Peace Conference, in 1899.

> I think that the question of troops cannot be considered entirely alone, separated from the host of other questions to which it is almost subordinate. Such are, for example, the extent of public instruction, the length of active service, the number of established regiments, the troops in the army units, the number and duration of enrollments under the colour—that is to say, the military obligations of retired soldiers—the location of the army corps, the railway system, the number and situation of fortified places. In a modern army all such things are connected with each other . . . .

Indeed, it is just this difficulty, the requirement to identify and agree upon discrete and separable elements of the problems and to set aside those that are truly inextricable, that proved to be a major impediment to progress at the intractable MBFR Talks.

More pragmatically, it was the prior recognition by the post-World War I Powers that limitations on land-based forces at that time were politically impossible which ultimately yielded positive results in achieving a limited yet important goal. This success was realized at the Washington Naval Conference with the signature of the 1922 Naval Treaty. The same strategy has been employed recently in the CFE negotiation, which has been limited in scope to exclude subjects upon which agreement is highly unlikely; ironically, in the current era this approach resulted in the exclusion of naval forces and the inclusion of land forces, the reverse of 1922. But both negotiating efforts were ultimately successful in achieving realistic goals.

Another element that has proven crucial to successful arms control efforts of multilateral scope in the past has been the necessity to include political guarantees for the less powerful participants. For example, a Moscow Conference of Baltic States in the early 1920's broke down when no political guarantees were forthcoming to accompany the program of military reductions proposed by the host government. In more recent times, it is clear that important multilateral arms control arrangements such as the 1967 Treaty for the Prohibition of Nuclear Weapons in Latin America could not have succeeded without certain political guarantees and operational undertakings made legally binding upon the nuclear-weapon states in Protocols to that Treaty.

These then are some of the historic considerations and choices that must be faced when reduction in the overall level of military forces is contemplated. The just-concluded CFE Treaty offers the best example of the means available for the realization of the desired reductions within the categories of armaments to be addressed.

During the negotiation leading to the CFE Treaty–which commenced on March 9, 1989, following the adoption of a mandate agreed by both NATO and Warsaw Treaty Members–the participants considered the following types of weaponry, as well as personnel limitations, to fall within the ambit of their discussions:

–*Tanks*, the chief instrument of offensive attack on land;

–*Armored Combat Vehicles*, which provide infantry mobility and support during combat and can be a crucial factor in an offensive campaign;

–*Artillery*, which provides essential fire-power for the conduct of combat operations;

–*Combat Aircraft*, namely permanent land-based combat-capable (and non-naval) aircraft in the region, regardless of current role, mission, or assignment;

–*Attack Helicopters*, which provide fire support, flexibility and rapid mobility, giving them an important role in military operations.

Notably, the above elements of military forces do not include strategic ballistic or cruise missiles, strategic aircraft, or sea-based forces of any kind (although land-based naval aircraft in the area of control are subject to a separate political–but not legally binding–undertaking). Nor are limitations on weapons of mass destruction (atomic, biological, chemical), or military budgets included. Such forces and limitations were conceived of as other than "conventional." Also, there are no restrictions on the manufacture of treaty-limited armaments, since no individual weapons system is prohibited *per se* by the treaty.

How does the CFE Treaty deal with the critical categories of armaments it does regulate? And in what context can the twenty-two States Parties be assured that this Treaty can be implemented in a manner that enhances, rather than diminishes, their security?

The new Treaty reflects the momentous changes in regional and global security relationships that resulted from the political upheaval that occurred in Eastern Europe during 1989. Although this was not the only reason for the successful realization of the CFE Treaty–the transition from the MBFR talks had also indicated a trend toward a more comprehensive approach to conventional reductions, for example–it clearly provided both the political basis and negotiating momentum that crowned the effort with success. As a result, all member states of NATO and the Warsaw Pact participated actively in the negotiations (unlike the MBFR experience), and ultimately all became Parties to the new Treaty.

With regard to substantive issues in the negotiations, many of those which formerly had proven intractable in MBFR and other contexts were resolved early in the discussions. For example, the principle of asymmetrical reductions to reach symmetrical lower levels of capability was in essence accepted by the Soviet Union. Moreover, the Soviet approach to the need for verification procedures was much more open than had previously been the case. Both these positive developments were rooted in agreements achieved by the United States and the Soviet Union earlier in the decade, and reflected substantially in their bilateral 1987 Treaty Between the United States and the Union of Soviet Socialist Republics on the Elimination of Their Intermediate-Range and Shorter-Range Missiles (INF Treaty). That Treaty was also based on the requirement of asymmetrical reductions to symmetrical agreed levels–which resulted in the outright abolition of nuclear weapons systems falling within the constraints of the Treaty's provisions. Likewise, the INF Treaty for the first time recorded U.S. and Soviet agreement on procedures for on-site inspection of activities such as weapons destruction, as an agreed measure to promote confidence in verification of the treaty regime.

The dynamics of the CFE negotiations were such that these positive moves by the East were in effect matched by the West, which agreed to accept the inclusion of manpower, aircraft, and helicopters in the new agreement–an expansion of scope previously rejected by the NATO Allies.

These armaments are subject to numerical limitations per category; wisely, no attempt was made to assign relative weighted values to particular weapons systems within categories, *e.g.*, for the U.S. M1A1 tank as compared to the Soviet T-80, or even to compare, for example, certain tanks against highly capable armored combat vehicles.

Each of these categories is defined in several levels of detailed description in the text of the Treaty, after the fashion first elaborated in the bilateral Soviet-U.S. SALT I and, more especially, SALT II Agreements/Treaties. Indeed, the level of detail in the CFE Treaty marks a new plateau of achievement in supplying the specificity needed to implement such a complicated agreement among twenty-two different States Parties dealing with inherent problems of comparison among differing conventional armament systems. This approach yielded agreement on numerical levels for weaponry in the five categories, both on the basis of alliance levels and ceilings for individual State Parties. NATO reductions will be much less than those required for Warsaw Pact Members, since in all categories the latter group's holdings exceeded those of NATO Members.

The Treaty contains important definitions of the following sixteen categories and sub-categories of arms: battle tanks, armored combat vehicles, armored personnel carriers, armored infantry fighting vehicles, heavy armament combat vehicles, artillery, large caliber artillery systems, armored vehicle launched bridges, combat aircraft, combat helicopters, attack helicopters, specialized attack helicopters, multi-purpose attack helicopters, combat support helicopters, armored personnel carrier "look-alikes," and armored infantry fighting vehicle "look-alikes."

An example of the level of detail provided for in the definitions is found in the treatment of armored infantry fighting vehicles. First, we find that these are covered by the broader term, "armored combat vehicle," which is itself generically defined as a self-propelled vehicle with armored protection and cross-country capability. Since the armored infantry fighting vehicles are specifically included as armored combat vehicles, they are therefore covered by the numerical limitations of the treaty and subject to reduction in numbers if necessary, pursuant to the terms of the Treaty, *e.g.*, Article VI(B), which limits States Parties to 20,000 armored combat vehicles within the area of application (the Atlantic to the Urals) for that State Party. Regional sublimits within the area, carefully concentrated in Central Europe, but with levels of impact throughout the continent, and related "sufficiency" rules—*i.e.*, Treaty constraints related to the proportion of armaments that may be retained by any one State Party relative to those held by its alliance partners in the area of application—have been uniquely developed for this Treaty and address the need to reduce the risk of surprise attack through an equitable and rather elegant scheme.

The definition of an armored infantry fighting vehicle is itself detailed and complex. Under Article II.1(D) of the Treaty we find the following:

> The term 'armored infantry fighting vehicle' means an armored combat vehicle which is designed and equipped primarily to transport a combat infantry squad, which normally provides the capability for the troops to deliver fire from inside the vehicle under armored protection, and which is armed with an integral or organic cannon of at least 20 millimeters caliber and sometimes an antitank missile launcher. Armored infantry fighting vehicles serve as the principal weapon system of armored infantry or mechanized infantry or motorized infantry formations and units of ground forces.

This definition serves to make clear just what is included; associated, contrasting definitions of two other weapons systems included under the basic heading of "armored combat vehicle" are also provided, *i.e.*, for armored personnel carriers and heavy armament combat vehicles. This is of functional importance, since under Article IV(B), sub-limits are imposed on the numbers of armored combat vehicles (30,000), of which no more than 18,000 may be armored infantry fighting vehicles or heavy armament combat vehicles, and of these, no more than 1,500 may be heavy armament combat vehicles. Thus, the category of "armored combat vehicle" may be likened to that of a genus in biology; the armored infantry fighting vehicle is comparable to a species; and all are part of a family of like items undergoing regulation—conventional armaments.

But another, perhaps even more interesting, contrasting definition is provided and it is also highly relevant. In Article II.1(D), the Treaty provides a further set of definitions, including one for an "armored infantry fighting vehicle look-alike." Such vehicles are armored vehicles based on the same chassis as, and externally similar to, an armored infantry fighting vehicle that does not have a cannon or gun of 20 millimeters caliber or greater, and which has been constructed or modified in such a way as not to permit the transportation of a combat infantry squad. The framing of the definition in this way makes clear that, as a general rule, no modification of otherwise covered armor will be sufficient to exempt such arms from the regulatory provisions of the Treaty; providing for the exceptions explicitly in cases such as the armored infantry fighting vehicle look-alike suggests that the preferred way of dealing with an excess of arms within any category of limitations appears to be through destruction, rather than simple modification. Detailed procedures for the reduction of Treaty-limited armaments through destruction are provided in Section IV of the Protocol on Procedures Governing the Reduction of Conventional Armaments and Equipment, one of eight Protocols incorporated into the Treaty. Section IV contains special procedures to accomplish the destruction of armored infantry fighting vehicles.

Still another exception is provided for a certain number of armored infantry fighting vehicles held by organizations of a State Party that are designed and structured to perform internal security functions during peacetime and not structured and organized for ground combat against an external enemy. This is obviously a novel issue in the arms control context and a solution was agreed that, on the one hand, recognizes that such vehicles are not weapons of war but, conversely, takes into account the potential for circumvention represented by such vehicles and limits that risk accordingly in Article XII by including them under the relevant ceiling when their numbers become significant.

Finally, in order to provide clearly for the application of the definition to the stocks of armaments held by the States Parties, the necessity to establish an agreed data base was recognized. This device, modeled to a certain extent on the agreed data base first achieved in the (never ratified) SALT II Treaty and later successfully emulated in the INF Treaty, has the function of identifying the types and numbers of armaments controlled by the treaty. In the case of armored infantry fighting vehicles, sixteen existing types of such vehicles are set out in Section I.2(B) of the Protocol on Existing Types of Conventional Armaments and Equipment; similarly, five types and eighteen versions of armored infantry fighting vehicle look-alikes are identified in Section II.2 of the same Protocol. Interestingly, the Protocol language makes clear that all versions of the listed types are included as armored infantry fighting vehicles except those explicitly listed as look-alikes. The general rule of inclusivity again applies, reminiscent of the type of rules developed by the United States and the Soviet Union in SALT.

The actual numbers of each type of armament are to be provided pursuant to a common format for the exchange of such information. Although the format itself was agreed in advance and set out in an annex to the Treaty, no Party to the Treaty had available to it at the time of signature an agreed set of data from each side and each Party. Thus, in a real way, each Party's agreement nevertheless to sign the Treaty was an act of faith and represented an extension of good will toward every other Party. Yet, the void of agreed information created by this procedure was a major departure from the lessons of the past and the experience of both SALT II and INF: In both prior cases, the United States and the Soviet Union signed the Treaties only after agreement had been reached on data. The departure from this norm in the CFE context has led predictably to post-facto disputes over data (*e.g.*, with regard to both numbers of armaments and numbers of military sites) and has raised questions about the good faith of certain Party governments, despite the inclusion by the

Treaty drafters of a ninety-day post-signature period for revisions of initially provided data and a later 120-day residual level validation period after entry into force of the Treaty. However, it can be stated with confidence that the concept of agreed data is now recognized by all Parties as a crucially important one: The arguments pertain to implementation alone. It does appear, however, that, in this regard, the arguments between East and West over data and whether to verify before or after reductions have never really been resolved and may well continue in a new and potentially more destructive guise—that of a compliance issue.

From the above definitional examples, we have seen how the framers of the Treaty paid particular attention to the detailed categorization of armaments; how this level of detail permitted the imposition of limitations and reductions of the relevant categories and sub-categories; and how the rule of inclusion, supplemented by clearly and explicitly restricted exceptions, is applied throughout with logical and legal effect. The success of this elaborate scheme is heavily dependent on another important aspect of the CFE Treaty—its provisions concerning verification and compliance.

Again drawing upon, and implicitly endorsing, the Soviet-U.S. experience in SALT and INF, the Treaty contains now-familiar rules concerning the obligations and rights of the Parties in this sphere. Among the most significant of these are those set out in Article XV of the Treaty. Paragraph 1 of that Article states:

> For the purpose of ensuring verification of compliance with the provisions of this Treaty, a State Party shall have the right to use, in addition to the procedures referred to in Article XIV, national or multinational technical means of verification at its disposal in a manner consistent with generally recognized principles of international law.

Thus, the use of national or multinational technical means of verification, *e.g.*, the use of satellites in earth orbit to provide photographic imagery of relevant objects on another Party's territory, is endorsed as a basic right. As in the past, such use is to be "consistent with generally recognized principles of international law," language dating back to the 1972 ABM Treaty. This formulation is generally understood as a reminder that classical espionage remains inconsistent with those principles.

Similarly, the CFE Treaty repeats the provisions of the INF Treaty dealing with: (1) the principle of non-interference with national or multinational means of verification operating in accordance with Article XV.1; and (2) the principle that concealment measures impeding verification of compliance with the provisions of the Treaty shall not be employed. Both concepts are rooted in the Soviet-U.S. SALT experience, but the creation of a new and undefined additional possibility—that of "multinational" means of verification—may in time be a significant advance.

Another set of provisions that are of the greatest importance for maintaining the integrity of the CFE Treaty regime are those related to the actual conduct of inspections for the purpose of ensuring verification of compliance with the Treaty's provisions. Quite naturally, these provisions and the Protocol on Inspection are based in great measure on the largely unprecedented on-site inspection arrangements worked out for the 1987 INF Treaty, although some important aspects are based upon concepts first elaborated for the 1976 Treaty Between the United States of America and the Union of Soviet Socialist Republics on Underground Nuclear Explosions for Peaceful Purposes and its associated original Protocol. That Protocol addressed logistical and security questions arising from the admission of designated personnel of one of the Parties (along with their technical-data-recording equipment) to the nuclear test sites of the other Party.

As with INF, the CFE Treaty has been designed to address a somewhat limited set of verification requirements; however, to the extent they are applicable, the multi-tiered levels of responsibility to be exercised have resulted in well-conceived and uncompromising standards for inspection.

According to Article XIV.2, the immediate operational goals of the CFE Treaty inspection regime are three-fold:

(1) to verify compliance of the Parties with the numerical limitations established, on the basis of data provided under the Protocol on Information Exchange;

(2) to monitor the process of reduction of armaments in accordance with the Treaty; and

(3) to monitor the certification of multi-purpose attack helicopters and combat-capable trainer aircraft that have been recategorized/recertified pursuant to relevant Protocols permitting this result.

Moreover, the Protocol on Inspection—which comprises more text than the entire Treaty proper—provides a wealth of detail related to the actual conduct of inspections. As is the case under the INF Treaty, however, the inspectors enjoy the right of access to significantly less than all military-related areas. In the INF scheme, these areas are those directly implicated in the production, testing, or deployment of the armaments regulated by the Treaty. Very few INF-related areas were not made subject to some form of inspection, at least once, under that regime. Under the CFE Treaty, the inspection provisions—intensely detailed and painstakingly negotiated in advance to include the possibility of both ground and limited air inspection (via helicopter overflight)—may cover a larger number of declared sites than did INF, but a more rigorous quota system limits the effect of this broader scope, as does the forty-eight-hour limit on the duration of inspections of individual "objects of verification."

However, the CFE regime does provide something of an innovation–the possibility of challenge inspections. In what may prove to be a useful precedent, Section VIII of the Protocol on Inspection sets out a procedure for requesting challenge inspections on short notice. If the request is denied, the State Party to whom the request was directed is still obligated to provide all reasonable assurance that the area that was named in the request does not contain conventional armaments/equipment limited by the Treaty. Although the right to conduct–or more precisely, to request permission to conduct–challenge inspections is rather attenuated in the Treaty, since it will inevitably be restricted in practice to a limited number of areas, experience may prove the procedure to be not only worthwhile as a concept in itself, but also perhaps worth expanding in the future. On the other hand, CFE does not provide for the type of continuous monitoring over a period of years at critical defense installations of an industrial nature as does the INF Treaty, *e.g.*, the U.S. presence at the Votkinsk Machine Building Plant, which had been used by the Soviet Union for final assembly of SS-20 intermediate-range ballistic missiles.

How will disputes over data and other compliance matters be resolved after entry into force of the CFE Treaty? What remedies will be available to States Parties who remain dissatisfied or even feel threatened due to the failure of other States Parties to comply with the Treaty's provisions?

The CFE Treaty (Article XVI) establishes a body called the Joint Consultative Group (JCG) for the purposes of providing a forum within which States Parties are to address questions relating to compliance with, or possible circumvention of, the provisions of the Treaty. The JCG also is the forum for the Parties to seek to resolve ambiguities and differences of interpretation that arise from Treaty implementation, as well as the forum for consideration of matters of dispute arising therefrom.

It has become customary for bilateral Soviet-U.S. arms control agreements to establish bodies unique to each treaty to serve as fora for basically the same purposes as set out for the JCG in Article XVI. It is unusual, however, to attempt such a mechanism for dispute resolution in the context of a twenty-two-member body. In the accompanying Protocol on the Joint Consultative Group, it is specified that the proceedings of the JCG shall be confidential and that it shall meet twice per year; both provisions follow the model of the Soviet-U.S. Standing Consultative Commission established pursuant to the 1972 ABM Treaty. Cost shares are provided for expenses associated with operation of the JCG, and the forum is basically not constrained in the duration or scope of its work, except as provided in the treaty itself.

Should a State Party decide that extraordinary events related to the subject matter of the Treaty have jeopardized its supreme interests, it has the right to exercise its sovereignty and withdraw from the Treaty. Prior notification of 150 days must be provided, along with a statement of the extraordinary events cited for this purpose. This provision, of course, is modelled on that originally devised by the parties to the 1963 Treaty Banning Nuclear Weapon Tests in the Atmosphere, in Outer Space and Under Water; similar provisions are found in numerous bilateral and multilateral arms control agreements (*e.g.*, the 1972 ABM Treaty, and the 1972 Convention on the Prohibition of the Development, Production and Stockpiling of Bacteriological (Biological) and Toxin Weapons and on their Destruction). In an innovative supplement (Article XIX.3), the CFE Treaty also explicitly recognizes that there exists the right to withdraw if another State Party increases its holdings outside Europe in the types of armaments regulated inside Europe by the Treaty, when the increase is of such a proportion as to pose an obvious threat to the balance of forces within the area of application. This provision makes plain that the continued viability of the Treaty itself will be brought into question by the exercise of the right of withdrawal, since Article XXI.4 requires a conference of all parties no later than twenty-one days after notice of intent to withdraw is given by any State Party. Such a mechanism will undoubtedly have a salutary effect on compliance with the provisions of the Treaty and also on out-of-area deployments of Treaty-limited systems where the balance of forces may be influenced.

Certainly, the CFE Treaty is indeed the most far-reaching agreement to deal successfully with the problem of conventional armaments. It represents an historic breakthrough in terms of both scope and scale, and, as we have seen, is conceptually based upon a considerable number of crucially important arms-control building-blocks that were developed in the context of Cold-War-Era nuclear arms control agreements. And unlike some other important agreements in this century that contained provisions rather comparable in nature if not in scope, this Treaty is based on full respect for the equality and sovereignty of all States Parties.

Of no less importance in the overall European security picture is the Joint Declaration of Twenty-Two States, signed contemporaneously with the CFE Treaty, in which the same Parties reaffirmed their obligations under international law never to use their weapons except in self-defense or otherwise in accordance with the Charter of the United Nations. In addition, in Point 5 of NATO's 1990 London Declaration, quoted previously, the pledge is given that NATO Members will never in any circumstance be the first to use force. All other CSCE Members were invited to join in this commitment, and on November 19, 1990, all twenty-two Parties of the CFE Treaty issued a Joint Declaration recording, in essence, a mutual non-aggression pledge, albeit in terms not quite as forthcoming as the NATO Pledge. This was followed two days later by a renewed pledge by all thirty-four CSCE members—contained in the Charter of Paris for a New Europe—to refrain from the threat or use of force against the territorial integrity or political independence of any state (the Paris Charter language did not contain the additional, explicit commitments made in the other documents).

In sum, more work remains to be done, even taking into account the following: the political prerequisite by which both the United States and the Soviet Union had previously agreed to withdraw significant and substantial numbers of troops from Europe in the context of the CFE Treaty requirements (to the 195,000 level for each side); the provision for staged phases of reduction in the CFE Treaty; and the various non-aggression promises that have been made. More needs to be done, even assuming the success of the overall regime in enhancing security and stability—something no one can afford to take for granted. As reflected in NATO's London Declaration, the same negotiating partners, operating under the same mandate, are now expected to pursue substantial constraints on military personnel and the possibility of developing a robust aerial inspection regime. In conjunction with this effort, the thirty-four-nation Conference on Security and Cooperation in Europe (CSCE) is pursuing further and related measures to add to its recently adopted Vienna Document 1990, which incorporates a number of expanded notification measures and information exchange requirements designed to supplement the CSCE Stockholm Conference Document of 1986 in such areas as exchanges of information on military forces and military budgets, information on certain deployment plans, and expanded transparency measures, among others. It is hoped that the renewed effort by the CFE Treaty partners will be concluded before the next follow-up meeting of the CSCE takes place in Helsinki in 1992; similar hopes have been expressed for the CSCE's negotiations on Confidence- and Security-Building Measures. At that time it is possible an interlocking set of agreements will have crystallized, providing the foundation for a stabilizing and security-enhancing arms control regime predicated on genuine reductions in the overall levels of military forces. Based on transparency and elimination of the threat of surprise attack, as well as being applicable to all of Europe, such a regime could lead to the realization of William Penn's concept in a manner perhaps more breathtaking than even that great pragmatic visionary would have dared to dream.

S.V. Kortunov
Counselor, Arms Control and Disarmament Directorate, USSR Ministry of Foreign Affairs

A. Basic Principles of Reduction and Limitation of Conventional Forces

Until recently the principles of reduction and limitation of conventional forces could be discussed for the most part only at the theoretical level. In the past large reductions of conventional forces were of a unilateral nature and involved primarily wars coming to an end and transition by states to a peacetime period of development. Disarmament talks at various stages in history (including the seventeen-year talks on reduction of military forces and arms in Central Europe), however, boiled down merely to comparing various proposals by the parties to the talks.

The situation has now radically changed. A Treaty on Conventional Armed Forces in Europe has been concluded for the first time, prescribing radical force reductions within a broad geographic zone extending from the Atlantic to the Urals. Structural reorganization of the armed forces of the militarily largest states is taking place, in conformity with publicly declared military doctrines. Unilateral reductions of forces and arms are being carried out. Military forces are being withdrawn from foreign soil within a comparatively short historical time.

All these measures of genuine disarmament provide a wealth of material for analysis of their political, military, and legal aspects, which are in transition from the domain of theoretical discourse and assessment to the plane of historical reality. This provides a basis to discuss right now the fundamental principles of reduction and limitation of conventional forces, of course taking into consideration the fact that they are continuously being adjusted in the process of disarmament, as well as the fact that at the present time many of them are much more of a political than a legal nature.

These principles can conditionally be subdivided into three basic groups: first, those involving unilateral reductions of forces and arms; second, those proceeding from the results of international negotiations; and third, those pertaining to the problem of lowering the overall worldwide level of conventional forces.

Unilateral reduction of conventional forces involves a state reevaluating the level and nature of military threat, as well as economic and internal political pressure to reduce military spending. At the end of 1988, for example, Soviet leaders, having thoroughly analyzed the politico-military situation and the balance of military forces in Europe and Asia, came to the conclusion that the Soviet Union could take certain steps unilaterally, without waiting for specific agreements on mutual reductions at talks on this problem.

As subsequent events demonstrated, measures taken in this direction gave a strong impetus to the process of lessening military confrontation both in Europe and in Asia and, in particular, made it possible right in the first phase of the Vienna talks to reach a major agreement on radical reduction of military forces and arms, as well as to commence bilateral talks with the PRC on mutual reduction of forces and arms in areas adjoining the Soviet-Chinese border. They essentially built around the disarmament talks a totally new political context, narrowing the maneuvering room of those circles, both in West and East, that would have liked from the very outset to drown discussion of disarmament issues in fruitless confrontational debates, debate over numbers, and arguments over who has more arms and who should do more arms reduction.

Also of importance is the fact that principles of future multilateral reductions were contained in the unilateral arms reduction measures announced by M.S. Gorbachev before the United Nations on December 7, 1988: elimination of imbalances; reduction first and foremost of the most destabilizing arms; withdrawal of troops from the NATO-WTO line of direct contact; disbandment of withdrawn combined units; reorganization of the structure of divisions remaining in the Central European zone for the purpose of giving them unambiguously defensive functions, *etc.*

Unilateral steps in the area of disarmament are closely linked with the principle of reasonable sufficiency for defense. Enormous quantitative levels, the destructive power of conventional arms and military forces, and the fact that they are heavily armed with tactical nuclear munitions make extremely improbable a protracted conventional war in Europe or in the Far East without rapid escalation to a large-scale nuclear exchange. Taking this into consideration, the level of reasonable sufficiency applicable to conventional forces evidently should be determined not by the operational requirements of successful offensive operations but by ensuring sufficient defensive potential so that the aggressor cannot count on victory in a fast-moving high-intensity conventional war. Therefore requirements on quantitative levels of conventional forces in Europe can be substantially reduced. The emphasis is shifted thereby to quality of weapons, mobility and level of proficiency, logistic support, and combat readiness of units and subunits.

The same considerations are applicable to the situation on the Sino-Soviet border, especially considering the positive changes that have taken place in recent years in PRC policy and that country's measures pertaining to reduction of its military forces.

In the broad politico-military aspect, the implementation of the principle of reasonable sufficiency involves a restructuring of military forces which excludes the possibility of their employment in surprise large-scale offensive operations. The quantity, composition, disposition, and other parameters of arms in military arsenals as well as military organizational development should be in accordance solely with the purposes of defense, and should not be provocative or arouse fears or apprehensions on the part of the opposing side over its own security.

Experience indicates that large unilateral steps, especially in those areas in which considerable asymmetries in offensive arms have developed, can stimulate the entire negotiation process and make possible even more far-reaching agreements on a multilateral basis. At the same time one must also be clearly aware of the fact that there is an objective limit beyond which any actions in the direction of disarmament must be of a multilateral nature.

In addition, any unilateral steps have a serious shortcoming: That which has been withdrawn unilaterally can just as easily be returned as before, since there exist neither formal treaty obligations, nor an inspection regime, nor mutually agreed conditions, nor stipulated end results.

We should emphasize in this connection that in international disarmament practice preference is made to treaty measures. Within the group of principles involved in international disarmament negotiations, the principle of equality and equal security of the parties is fundamental.

This principle is formally articulated in a number of international documents. It signifies that in mutual reduction of arms and military forces, the parties should not seek unilateral advantages to the detriment of the security of the other party. This in turn signifies maintaining the existing balance of forces at minimum levels, while observing the requirements of mutual security. This principle was applied precisely in this manner in the Treaty on Conventional Armed Forces in Europe. Thus the principle of equality and equal security is a treaty principle, that is a principle that forms the basis for drawing up treaties on limitation of arms and military forces, and in this capacity it is operative only for the parties to specific treaties, bearing in mind that a single state or a group of states can be party to a treaty. Upon conclusion of a treaty, this principle is reflected in specific treaty provisions pertaining to limitation of arms and military forces. In the broad sense the principle of equality and equal security can be defined as equal provision of security to each state by all appropriate international legal means (the system of principles and treaty provisions).

Putting the formula of equality and equal security into quantitative and qualitative terms, one can conditionally state that equality, or parity, pertains to quantitative indicators of military means, while equal security pertains to the quality of security proper, its stability, and the inadmissibility and impossibility of aggression.

In the nuclear age, with the parties possessing the capability to destroy life on earth many times over, the quantitative indicator, or parity, loses its significance to a relative degree. The significance of the second part of the formula, however—equal security—increases to a great extent. A peculiarity of the present day, in contrast to past periods in history, consists namely in the fact that while in the past parity inalterably performed a stabilizing function and was virtually a synonym for equal security, that is, the two parts were in an inseparable organic linkage, today equal security has become a separate and independent category, which is no longer linked to maintaining quantitative equality.

Equality and equal security constitute a solid foundation for the establishment on an agreed-upon foundation of those parameters of arms and military forces whereby the possibility of mounting large-scale offensive operations will be excluded, but national security will be ensured. Closely linked with this is another principle of mutual reductions of conventional forces—the principle of ensuring military stability.

Stability in the domain of conventional military forces and arms signifies equalization of the historically developed imbalances and asymmetries on both sides, resulting in equal reduced levels of troop strength and principal types of arms on the part of the WTO and NATO states in Europe, in combination with adoption of specific limiting measures pertaining to disposition, aimed at preventing a threat of surprise attack.

In addition to troop strength, in main those types of arms that possess the greatest offensive potential and the capability to deliver strikes to considerable operational depth should be subject to reduction. At the Vienna talks the parties agreed to include within this category at the present stage tactical aircraft, combat helicopters, tanks, and large-caliber artillery, as well as armored personnel carriers and infantry fighting vehicles.

In the ideal case military activities should also be subordinated to accomplishing the task of military stability as well; military activity should not include actions arousing suspicions or misinterpretations. Neither the quantitative nor qualitative nature of the military power of states and alliances as well as military policy as a whole should per se impel the other side to build up its military power or create the impression of impending threat.

Reduction of military forces and arms should be accompanied by joint adoption of political measures to strengthen the confidence of the parties that there does not exist any threat of surprise attack. This requires further improvement of existing confidence-building measures and measures to strengthen security, prescribed by the document of the Stockholm Conference as well as the Paris Charter for a New Europe and their application to other types of military activity, including air force and naval activities. Establishment of an all-European conflict prevention center is also taking on considerable importance.

Within the context of international conventional forces reduction talks, the principle of reasonable sufficiency of conventional forces for defense is perceived in a new dimension; this principle evidently will boil down to the achievement of mutual agreements on reducing the military-strategic confrontation between the states taking part in the talks to interdependent (both in a quantitative and structural-qualitative respect), minimally low threshold levels of military forces and conventional arms. The remaining conventional forces and arms should possess the capability reliably to ensure stability of defense in any situation conditions, but at the same time should not possess the necessary potential to mount a surprise attack and large-scale offensive operations.

The idea is that reasonable sufficiency should be limited to the requisite level of conventional forces and arms required to defend the territory of the parties. Such sufficiency should reliably ensure equal both national and collective security of the states party to the talks as well as groups of states, while not creating thereby an actual or potential threat to the security of other countries.

From a practical aspect specific reasonable sufficiency for defense evidently should mean imparting to conventional military forces a predominantly defensive structure, maximum limitation of offensive strike systems within their units and combined units, changes in their disposition taking into account the new character of their assigned missions, and limitation of parameters of maintaining reserves and deployment mobilization, as well as the scope of development and production of new conventional weapon systems.

Limits of numerical strength and composition of military forces and conventional arms and of their structure and deployment evidently cannot be static, adjusted, coordinated, and agreed upon once and for all. On the contrary, as a rule these levels will be varying and dynamic, influenced not only by the disposition of forces in the world arena and the degree of political interrelations, by the existence of an actual or potential external military threat at the present time or for the foreseeable future, but also by the development of the internal political situation in the countries participating in negotiations and their economic and scientific-technical capabilities to produce and develop the requisite modern weapon systems and hardware to maintain their military potential at an adequate level for defense. In particular, this predetermines the concept of phased reduction of conventional forces.

In the case of the Vienna talks, for example, the Warsaw Pact states advanced the following concept of phased reduction of conventional forces. In the first phase—over the course of from two to three years—imbalances and asymmetries would be eliminated, and approximately equal ceilings would be achieved for the entire zone of reductions and for separate regions. Toward this end principal attention must be concentrated on reduction of the most destabilizing arms: strike aircraft, tanks, combat helicopters, and artillery, including multiple rocket launcher systems. As a result the military forces and arms of the parties would be reduced by ten to fifteen percent from the present lower levels of the military and political allies.

The parties would proceed even further in the second phase of reductions, cutting their remaining military forces and arms by one fourth.

Finally, in the third phase of reductions—by approximately one-half of that achieved in the second phase—military forces would finally be imparted a strictly defensive character. The quantitative parameters that will be the result of the third phase might look as follows for each of the parties:

armed forces—1 million men;
tanks—15,000;
strike aircraft—1,000 units or somewhat more;
combat helicopters—approximately 1,000 units;
artillery systems—approximately 20,000.

The principle of conformity between verification measures and the level and nature of reductions is also one of the most important principles of reduction of conventional forces. The main function of verification is to promote implementation of military forces and arms limitation and reduction measures and to increase the mutual trust that is embodied in the very fact of the entry into arms limitation agreements, and to provide objective information on the actual state of affairs regarding fulfillment. Therefore the principal demand made on verification is its effectiveness.

Each arms limitation agreement may have its own special verification measures and its own specific methods and means of implementation. In any such agreement, however, the main thing is material measures pertaining to arms limitation and reduction. It does not make sense, for example, to devise verification rules and procedures, and subsequently to make the scope and nature of obligations fit these procedures.

Verification should be used to ensure the viability of disarmament agreements. For this reason, in addition to effectiveness, adequacy is another principal requirement on verification. This means that verification measures should be fully in conformity with the scope and nature of the limitations being established. As experience in implementing international agreements in the area of disarmament has shown, the principle of commensurability of verification measures and arms limitation measures has proven to be fully valid. It is not mere happenstance that this is embodied in a number of universally recognized international documents, including the Final Document of the UN General Assembly's First Special Session on Disarmament.

National technical means of verification enjoy undisputed precedence among the great many methods of verification that can be used to ensure compliance with obligations by the parties to various agreements in the area of arms limitation and disarmament. This is confirmed by the experience of verification of compliance with strategic arms agreements and other previously concluded treaties and agreements. The capabilities of these means are being continuously improved. Consequently reliability of verification of compliance with agreements in this area with the aid of national technical means of verification is also improving.

However, in view of the fact that at the present time we are talking about the most far-reaching steps, leading to radical reduction of nations' military potential, additional measures are being drafted wherever necessary, measures based on cooperation, including on-site inspection. Intended to help increase the effectiveness of national technical means of verification, measures of this type should not, however, serve as an instrument of interference in the internal affairs of and do detriment to the interests of any of the parties, or be used for purposes having nothing to do with the tasks of verification.

An understanding of the fact that ensuring maximum openness of the military activities of states is an essential condition of disarmament has recently become more extensively affirmed throughout the world.

Openness of military activities has a direct relation to limitation of military potential to that which is reasonably sufficient for defense. For resolution of these issues depends first and foremost on the level and character of mutual military threat, assessment of which is extremely difficult and sometimes subjective precisely as a consequence of lack of objective information on the other side's military activity.

Without credible knowledge in this area, nations are essentially doomed to be hostage to erroneous notions about one another, and in their military organizational development to proceed from a "worst case," that is, in many instances going beyond that which is sufficient for defense, advancing to levels of offensive potential.

For a long time there was a widespread conviction in the Soviet Union that everything or almost everything pertaining to the military should be veiled in an impenetrable cloak of secrecy. It was determined, however, that excessive secrecy did not increase but rather weakened national security, generating suspicion and distrust on the part of other countries, including the United States, and therefore impelling these countries to build up their own military power.

Having analyzed this situation, the conclusion was reached in the Soviet Union that excessive secrecy in this area is at the present time becoming transformed from an element of ensuring the security of nations into a hindrance to strengthening security. When deep arms reduction is on the agenda, affecting the very heart of security of states and peoples, a requisite volume of credible information on the military potential of nations, the numerical parameters of these potentials, the structure and disposition of military forces, *etc.*, must be assured. In present-day conditions every state, especially a substantial military power, should essentially itself have an objective stake in presenting such information on its potential.

The fact is that steps to reduce arms and confidence-building measures are in a dialectical unity. This is manifested in the fact that, on the one hand, disarmament is attended by the establishment in politico-military relations between states of new standards of openness, trust, and mutual verification, which create a kind of "psychological comfort" in these relations and lead to greater predictability and stability; on the other hand, strengthening of mutual trust creates preconditions for further radical arms reductions.

The more far-reaching the confidence-building measures on which the parties reach agreement in the course of negotiations, the deeper the potential cuts in military forces and arms.

Feedback is also evident: The depth and nature of arms cuts predetermines the scale and nature of the confidence-building measures that are to attend these reductions.

At the present stage of disarmament, however, it is apparently time to proceed in this area from partial confidence-building measures and easing of mutual concerns on various particular issues to a broad-scale policy of openness. For this we must jointly establish standards and conditions as regards openness of military activity that would not hinder but rather help reach agreements on radical mutual reduction of military forces and arms.

And, finally, there is the third group of principles of military forces and arms reduction. They proceed from the objective need for globalization of the disarmament process in our interdependent world, but at the present stage they are only at the point of initial formation.

The primary issue is that, in conditions of large-scale cuts in conventional forces, the size of the share of other arms not covered by disarmament talks is growing in the military arsenals of nations. This development is fraught with the danger of undermining of military stability, which in conditions of radical disarmament measures inevitably takes on a comprehensive character. For example, exclusion of naval forces from the arms limitation and reduction process, in view of the substantial U.S.

military superiority, would contradict the principle of equal security and at a certain stage could have an impeding effect on progress in the area of conventional forces reduction. The same applies to tactical nuclear weapons. Military stability and sufficiency cannot be secured by reducing only conventional military forces. For this reason the application of limitations and reductions to all arms that influence military stability in one way or another should become one of the fundamental principles of disarmament.

The geographic extension of disarmament to all regions of the world is a no less important issue from the standpoint of military stability. Military stability will not be assured, for example, solely with regional measures of reduction of troops and arms in Europe if leading nations in a military respect continue delivering arms to "third world" countries. Attempts to establish in Europe what might be termed a "protected zone" or some kind of "security enclave" will be unsuccessful if it is surrounded by a raging ocean of wars and conflicts.

Finally, as is indicated by the practical experience of the disarmament process, purely quantitative reductions channel the arms race into the qualitative domain, which at present is in no way limited or restricted, including by the Paris Treaty on Conventional Armed Forces. And, considering the development of new precision, "smart" weapon systems, this process takes on a destabilizing character. For this reason there arises the task of holding the qualitative arms race in check. Two possible approaches here include adoption of objective limiting parameters and banning the deployment of systems that, in the subjective opinion of other states, present a threat to their security or to stability. The second procedure is probably more realistic. Presenting information on military programs by a specified amount of time prior to deployment of a given weapon system is a possible first step in this direction.

In one way or another, the principle of limiting the qualitative conventional arms race should become one of the fundamental principles in the process of reduction of conventional forces.

B. Regional Reduction of Conventional Forces (The Example of Europe)

Talks on reduction of forces and arms in Central Europe, held in 1973, were the first talks on regional reduction of conventional forces (CF), but these talks ended without result. New talks on conventional military forces in a broad geographic zone extending from the Atlantic to the Urals commenced in March 1989.

An agreement unprecedented in significance and scope was drafted within a comparatively short period of time, a mere year and a half–a

Treaty on Conventional Armed Forces in Europe, which one can venture to consider the most far-reaching and comprehensive agreement in history. Suffice it to say that reductions in Europe will amount to more than 120,000 units of various arms, that is, a dangerous military confrontation will be virtually eliminated.

In commencing the negotiations, which were conducted on a bloc alliance basis, the participating states agreed that the goal of this forum would be: establishment of a stable and secure balance of conventional forces in Europe at lower levels; elimination of imbalances and asymmetries in WTO and NATO arms which do detriment to stability and security; and priority elimination of the potential to mount a surprise attack and to launch large-scale offensive operations.

The fact that in the very first round of talks there was a fairly broad area of coinciding elements in the positions of the parties, which as an aggregate defined the configuration of the initial agreement, was a significant factor in achieving results in these negotiations. Briefly, these elements boiled down to the following:

> both the WTO and NATO gave precedence to initial reductions in those arms categories that comprise a potential for mounting a surprise attack and conducting large-scale offensive operations;
>
> they expressed willingness to reduce such arms to equal ceilings, which would be lower than the lowest levels currently possessed by the parties;
>
> both sides declared their intention to avoid fruitless debates over numbers and displayed willingness to examine the definitions of arms and to work out common criteria and methods of counting; and
>
> there was also manifested an agreement of views in regard to strict international verification, including on-site inspections.

The Treaty prescribes establishment of equal collective ceilings for each of the alliances in Europe, in five basic arms categories: tanks, armored fighting vehicles (AFV), artillery, combat fixed-wing aircraft, and attack helicopters (in line service and in storage). Pursuant to the Treaty, each of the military alliances shall retain 20,000 tanks, 30,000 armored fighting vehicles, 20,000 artillery pieces, 6,600 combat fixed-wing aircraft, and 2,000 combat helicopters. Limitations are also placed on assault bridge launchers in line-unit service.

Regional limitations are an important element of the Treaty: In addition to the entire zone to which the Treaty applies, extending from the Atlantic to the Urals, four regional zones are designated, the significance of which lies in achieving stabilization of the military situation on the continent and in eliminating the danger of unrestricted concentration of troops and arms in the zone of contact as well as a flow of arms to the flanks. There will be 7,500 tanks, 11,250 armored fighting vehicles, and 5,000 artillery systems, for example, in Central Europe, where both members of NATO—unified Germany and the Benelux countries (Belgium, Luxembourg, and the Netherlands)—as well as former members of the WTO (Poland, Czechoslovakia, and Hungary)—are situated.

The Treaty allows 10,300 tanks, 19,260 armored fighting vehicles, and 9,100 artillery systems in an expanded Central Europe which, in addition to the countries named above, includes Denmark, France, Italy, and Great Britain on the NATO side, and the Baltic, Belorussian, Carpathian, and Kiev military districts on the WTO side. These levels include the arms both of regular units and combat equipment located at storage depots.

One of the key provisions of the Treaty is the establishment of a national limit in the form of a level of sufficiency for a single country.

This level of sufficiency, at thirty-five plus or minus two percent, is calculated from the aggregate level of both alliances. Consequently, for the Soviet Union it comprises seventy plus or minus four percent of all arms possessed by the former members of the Warsaw Pact. The share of the other five former WTO countries will range from one-fourth to one-third of the alliance's arms respectively. Thus, taking into account the specific arms levels of the NATO countries, one can note that the Treaty allows the Soviet Union to possess the largest quantity of arms and equipment, beyond what any other country in Europe will possess—13,300 tanks, 20,000 armored fighting vehicles, 13,700 artillery systems, 5,150 combat fixed-wing aircraft, and 1,500 combat helicopters.

Although conceptually the Treaty is set up on a balance between military blocs, the mechanism of its implementation provides for a regular exchange of information and notification by each Party on quantity in arms categories limited by the Treaty, in that country's possession both prior to the Treaty's entry into force and at each phase of arms reduction, as well as notification of the maximum level of arms after reaching the final, Treaty-set arms ceilings for each alliance. Distribution of maximum end-levels for each country is done within the framework of alliances. Within the former WTO such end maximum national quotas are set forth in a special agreement (concluded in Budapest on November 3, 1990). In other words, the collective levels for each alliance will be comprised of the agreed levels of its members.

Arms levels for the Soviet Union, according to the agreement among the former WTO nations, are as follows:

Tanks—13,150 units, including 2,650 units at storage depots;

AFVs—20,000 units, including 2,080 units at storage depots;

Artillery—13,175 units, including 2,350 units at storage depots;

Combat fixed-wing aircraft—5,150 units;

Attack helicopters—1,500 units;

Assault bridge launchers in line-service units—462 units.

On the basis of politically binding declarations outside the framework of the Treaty, the number of land-based naval aircraft (not including patrol aircraft) is limited to 430 units for each group of states, including 400 units for a single country (for the Soviet Union). Permanently land-based naval attack helicopters are prohibited.

The Treaty prohibits a buildup of military potential by any state without an adequate reduction in the arms level of that alliance of which it is a member. Nor may an arms level buildup occur as a result of expanding the membership of an alliance. At the same time withdrawal of a state from an alliance shall not constitute a condition for that state to withdraw from the Treaty and, therefore, its arms level shall continue to be counted toward the collective level of the alliance of which this state was a member.

The Treaty shall be considered to have entered into force ten days after submission of the last instrument of ratification to the depositary—the Netherlands. The Treaty specifies that the period of reductions, which shall begin at the end of a 120-day initial data verification period, will last three years. Thus, pursuant to the Treaty, final arms levels will be reached forty months after the Treaty enters into force.

In order that no destabilizing distortions and asymmetries occur during treaty execution, phased reductions are prescribed: A twenty-five percent arms reduction is to be achieved in sixteen months, and sixty percent in twenty-eight months.

The purpose of approximately ten Protocols and Annexes to the Treaty is to ensure effective compliance and removal of concerns in connection with possible Treaty circumvention.

On-site inspections are the principal verification instrument. The number of inspections for each country is figured on the basis of number of verification sites—military units at the regiment, artillery battalion, and separate battalion levels possessing Treaty-limited military equipment (TLME).

Inspection activity is subdivided into four regimes according to intensity, in conformity with the phases of Treaty implementation. The heaviest schedule is specified for the period of verification of initial data and the period of verification of final levels—up to twenty percent of monitored sites. The annual quota of inspections for a single country after reaching final levels has been set at fifteen percent of monitored sites.

Reduction-targeted equipment will for the most part be eliminated, but a fairly large quantity may be converted to civilian use (750 tanks and 3,000 armored fighting vehicles). The process of elimination and conversion is also subject to verification.

A declaration by the government of the Federal Republic of Germany that it pledges to reduce the armed forces of unified Germany to a numerical strength of 370,000 men, including ground, air, and naval forces, is a component part of the Treaty. This reduction will commence from the moment the Paris Treaty enters into force. In conformity with these limitations, the military potential of the present Germany will be approximately half the aggregate military potential of the FRG and GDR before unification.

The adoption at the talks of a Document on Confidence- and Security-Building Measures constituted an event of great importance from the standpoint of the long-term interests of peace and security of the European peoples.

In comparison with the 1986 Stockholm Document on Confidence- and Security-Building Measures, the new Document goes considerably further in matters of transparency of the structure of military forces, their organizational development, and the conduct of military activity.

The new generation of confidence-building measures includes:

annual exchange of military information on military forces as regards military organization, from the regimental level on up, as well as personnel and principal weapon systems;

information on plans for deployment of principal weapon systems, with indication of type of weapons and weapon systems, as well as quantities;

information on military budgets on the basis of the UN Document for Standardized International Reporting on Military Expenditures.

Information on military forces can be evaluated by means of conduct of on-site inspections. The Treaty prescribes that within a year's time each state will be obligated to accept on its territory a specified number of inspections, which is figured on the basis of one visit for every sixty units, but not more than fifteen visits per year.

The adoption of pledges to develop contacts in the military domain by the participating states in the CSCE is a new element. They include visits to air bases, exchanges and visits between military leaders, commanders, and officers, between military establishments, and mutual visits to educational institutions, as well as contacts between scientists and experts in the field of military research and in related fields.

Measures directly aimed at reducing the threat of war and at preventing military conflicts impart a new quality to the Vienna Document. Of fundamental importance is the fact that these measures will be implemented not in the "traditional" bilateral manner but rather through a mechanism of new all-European security structures: a Conflict Prevention Center and a system of communications.

In utilizing the Conflict Prevention Center, Parties will consult and cooperate with one another in regard to any unusual and unscheduled activity by their military forces outside their normal peacetime stationing locations, and will also cooperate in the prevention and clarification of dangerous incidents of a military nature. It is provided in particular that in case of occurrence of such a dangerous incident, the Party whose military forces are involved in the incident shall promptly provide available information to the other Parties.

Success was not achieved in Vienna, however, in making progress toward resolving one of the central issues of the negotiations—the extension of confidence-building measures to naval activities.

Finally, the signing in Paris of the twenty-two-nation Joint Declaration was an important result of the disarmament process in Europe. A key point of this document is the solemn declaration by twenty-two nations that in the new era that is opening up in European relations they shall no longer be adversaries but shall build new partnership relations and extend the hand of friendship to one another. No less important is Article 4 of the Declaration, which sets forth the obligation of these states to maintain only that military potential that is necessary to prevent war and to ensure effective defense. It reflects the resolve of the European nations to ensure the continuity and sustained nature of disarmament and to build a common European home on the solid foundation of stability and mutual security.

This is particularly important since the political situation in Europe is developing so swiftly that it is already beginning to overtake the disarmament process.

The Treaty was conceived proceeding from what was in many respects a different political and military-strategic situation in Europe in comparison with the present situation, in a period when political and military confrontation had not yet been overcome.

The situation is different today. And what will it be by the moment Treaty implementation is concluded? By that time, that is, by the mid-1990's, a transition period from bloc to general European security structures should be concluded, structures which go far beyond the framework even of the full extent of the mandate of the Vienna talks; but the Treaty focuses primarily on eliminating imbalances and asymmetries in the conventional forces of the military alliances.

Gratifying in this regard is the desire and resolve on the part of all participants in the Vienna talks to continue them immediately following the Paris summit, on the basis of the previous mandate and with the same participatory structure. The all-European summit meeting to be held in Helsinki in 1992 will be the target point for completing these talks.

The purpose of the new talks—Vienna 1A—is to draft additional measures to strengthen military stability on the continent, including the establishment of limits on troop strength, leading to a further reduction of the threat of surprise attack and elimination of the possibility of the conduct of large-scale offensive operations in Europe. Possible topics include the further limitation and reduction of offensive components of military potentials, including altering the composition, structure, and disposition of military forces in such a manner that no doubts arise as to their purely defensive functions.

It will be necessary to accomplish a great deal within a short period of time, beginning with a search for a criterion for defining the term personnel, as well as for rules and procedures of counting. The structure of the Conventional Armed Forces Treaty could be adopted as a basis for a conceptual scheme for future agreements.

It will be necessary to determine approaches to resolving the question of "regulation and limitation" of mobilization measures, training of reservists, redeployments and concentrations of personnel, *etc.*, and to work out other measures of a stabilizing nature.

In armament categories, the first Conventional Armed Forces Treaty could be supplemented with provisions on limitation of engineer equipment and river-crossing equipment, with the aim of further reducing the threat of surprise attack.

It would also be useful to take a closer look at operation of the monitoring and verification mechanism from the standpoint of possibilities of improving it and making it less expensive. We feel that resolution of the question of aerial inspections could play an important role in this context.

As a parallel effort, it would make sense to commence in the very near future a multilateral search for an optimal mandate for new talks, which would commence following the Helsinki-92 Meeting.

Of course, efforts in the area of structural reorganization of military forces in Europe will require mating the approaches of the parties to formulation and implementation of their military doctrines. Incidentally, this linkage is reflected in the twenty-two-nation Joint Declaration. Practical discussion of doctrines, which was successfully begun in 1990, should be continued in this connection.

One could begin a discussion at a seminar, as is proposed by a number of neutral countries, of jointly understood criteria of the defensive nature of armed forces, proceeding from the declared principles of military doctrines. Subsequently such criteria could become practical recommendations to the thirty-four states in implementing military organizational development and would constitute an appreciable stabilization measure, which would "work" in the direction of further strengthening mutual security, trust and mutual understanding.

As regards the Vienna-2 talks, they would most likely be totally different—not on the basis of military blocs—talks with the participation of thirty-four nations. The purpose of a future forum for negotiations, all-European in nature, a forum to commence in the post-confrontation period, could be implementation in treaty form of the principle of reasonable sufficiency in its quantitative and qualitative dimension and in elimination of the material basis for conduct of war in Europe.

The new attribute of these talks should be expressed in their overall orientation toward forming on the continent a military configuration subordinated to the interests of collective security within the framework of a European commonality. In other words they should ensure the structural incapability of the military forces of all the parties to the CSCE to launch an attack as a material basis for a system of general European security.

In a more specific aspect, the basic parameters of Vienna-2 could be grounded on the following considerations:

Area of application. The French idea of an area extending "from San Francisco to Vladivostok" seems interesting, although, considering the specific features of the military balance in the Asia-Pacific region, simple decisions will scarcely be possible here.

Reductions. Arms levels remaining following implementation of Conventional Armed Forces Treaty I considerably exceed the corresponding stocks that existed at the beginning of World War II. Therefore the question of deeper cuts will continue to be relevant. Perhaps the most complex thing here will be the problem of selecting criteria in conformity with which end-levels will be established. It would be possible, for example, to effect reductions to an agreed percentage of the levels reached as a result of Conventional Armed Forces Treaty I (fifty percent reductions have been proposed); one could consider such factors as the area or length of borders of a given state (the first criterion would make it possible to avoid dangerous troop concentrations, while the second would make it possible to consider the quantity of forces essential to defend a country's borders). Probably there are also other potential approaches.

Changes in the structure of military forces and other parameters of the military technical aspect of military doctrines of states. The question of restructuring of the military forces of the Parties on a defensive basis will remain unresolved as a result of implementation of Conventional Armed Forces Treaty I. This will become one of the central tasks at a future stage of negotiations. Local approaches may also be employed—redeployment of unit elements of combined units, establishment of militarily thinned-down zones—as well as global approaches, such as disbandment of large force organizations possessing offensive potential, with reduction of their arms.

Dismantling of military infrastructure–munitions storage depots, POL storage depots, *etc.*–is also of considerable significance.

Confidence-building measures and stabilization measures. One can already note at the present time a considerable similarity between these two sets of measures. They will probably be integrated in the future. Evidently naval and air force activities will also have to be encompassed by measures of this kind, when such activities directly affect security in the area in which these measures are applied. As regards other naval activities, they could be discussed at naval talks.

Air forces. The experience of the CFE talks indicates that extremely broad scope with respect to air forces is the only way to resolve this problem. "Pulling" a given component (naval aviation, strike aviation, air defense aviation, *etc.*) from the general context only can lead to an impasse. For this reason thirty-four-nation talks on across-the-board limits on all their combat aircraft (including all naval, air defense, national guard, *etc.*, combat fixed-wing aircraft) would probably be the optimal approach.

Sufficiency. It would apparently make sense in this area to discuss both a universal approach and the principle of "regional sufficiency."

In conditions of transition to a new structure of political and politico-military relations in Europe, the conceptual approach to the task and substance of confidence-building measures should also apparently change. A concept of "a system of transparency and cooperation in the military domain" in place of "confidence-building and security measures" would be more in keeping with the new political and psychological climate.

For this purpose it would seem appropriate to be guided by the thesis that transformation of Europe into a "single integral security zone" constitutes the task of future thirty-four-nation talks.

Proceeding from the expanded interpretation of the concept of security that is forming in the world, as encompassing elimination of regional conflicts and focal points of tension, *etc.*, in addition to the elimination of the military threat, an effort should be made to interweave a system of stability of the politico-military situation on the continent into the fabric of negotiations, alongside a system of transparency of military forces and military policy.

The task of transforming Europe into a single integral security zone free of bloc alliances will require the creation of appropriate institutions in which all CSCE-participating states would play a role in determining policy on the politico-military aspects of European security. Evidently a permanent body should be established, invested with broad authorities, perhaps based on the Conflict Prevention Center. This body could, for example:

track and analyze development of the politico-military

situation in Europe within the context of the established system of collective security, and make appropriate conclusions or recommendations for their consideration at summit and high-level meetings of the CSCE-participating states;

serve as a "data bank" on military forces, military policy, and military programs of the CSCE-participating states, as well as an operational communications center;

organize consultations and clarification of unclear points at the request of individual members of a future system; and

play a certain role in verifying submitted information and in carrying out inspections on request (for example, maintaining its own staff of permanent or ad hoc inspectors with appropriate specialization-area training or its own fleet of aircraft to transport national inspectors, *etc.*).

In other words, the member states could delegate to an all-European agency a certain portion of their monitoring and verification authorities, the scope of which will increase substantially.

A collective assessment of the legitimate defensive requirements of each CSCE-participating state and analysis of the adequacy of its military budgets to these needs (with item-by-item consideration), programs in the area of development, procurement and deployment of arms and, possibly, research and development of military significance would constitute an important radical measure carried out either within the framework of a multilateral agency or by some other means.

On the whole it would seem that an effort should be made to shift the emphasis in a future system of transparency and cooperation in the military domain in Europe from military activity proper (in many respects this is yesterday's approach) to programs pertaining to the development, procurement, and deployment of principal types of arms and military equipment, including long-term programs, as well as budget appropriations for defense.

This would ensure transition to a new level of transparency and predictability, and consequently stability in the longer-term future.

B.R. Tuzmukhamedov
Docent, USSR Diplomatic Academy

C. Limitations on Naval Activity

The naval forces at the disposal of the major military powers possess considerable firepower, are highly mobile, and have traditionally played the role of a flexible military instrument for attaining foreign-policy objectives. The role of naval forces in the structure of military forces has increased as military hardware has become more sophisticated. As the process of genuine disarmament on land has progressed, with the physical destruction of arms (including weapons of mass destruction), and with unilateral reduction of the Armed Forces of the Soviet Union in progress and multilateral talks on this problem producing initial results, the importance of naval forces as an element of the military power of nations is growing substantially, just as is their potentially destabilizing role. Elimination of imbalances and asymmetries in the ratio of land forces is also aggravating these phenomena as regards naval forces.

In the period following World War II matters pertaining to limiting or reducing naval activity and naval arms were the subject of negotiations, but no agreements were reached on these questions. Soviet-American talks on limiting and subsequent reduction of military activities in the Indian Ocean, for example, were conducted from June 1977 to February 1978. These talks were broken off by the Americans.

Individual provisions of treaties aimed at arms limitation and narrowing the spatial scope of arms proliferation apply to naval activity and naval weapons. These measures are insignificant, however.

Some limitations applying to Soviet and U.S. sea-based strategic nuclear arms have been agreed upon. The 1972 ABM Treaty pledges the parties not to develop, test, or deploy sea-based ABM systems or components. The 1972 Interim Agreement Between the United States of America and the Union of Soviet Socialist Republics on Certain Measures in the Area of Limiting Strategic Offensive Arms stipulated, among other things, limits on submarine ballistic missile launchers and on ballistic missile submarines. The 1979 Treaty Between the United States of America and the Union of Soviet Socialist Republics on the Limitation of Strategic Offensive Arms, which has not legally entered into force but has been observed by the Parties, in addition to setting limits on submarine ballistic missile launchers and ballistic missile submarines, prohibited the development, testing and deployment of certain categories of ballistic missiles and launchers intended for deployment at sea. The Treaty on the Limitation and Reduction of Strategic Offensive Arms will set limits on sea-based strategic delivery systems and warheads, while a related separate document will specify the quantitative level of sea-launched cruise missiles permitted to be deployed on submarines and surface ships.

The 1971 Treaty on the Prohibition of the Emplacement of Nuclear Weapons and Other Weapons of Mass Destruction on the Seabed and the Ocean Floor and in the Subsoil Thereof prohibits the emplacement and deployment of nuclear weapons or other types of weapons of mass destruction on and under the seabed and ocean floor outside the boundaries of a specified zone, as well as structures, launchers, and any other devices specifically intended for the storage, testing, and employment of such weapons. Article V pledges the Parties "to continue negotiations in good faith concerning further measures in the field of disarmament for the prevention of an arms race on the seabed, the ocean floor and the subsoil thereof," but this Article has not been implemented to date.

The 1963 Treaty Banning Nuclear Weapon Tests in the Atmosphere, in Outer Space and Under Water prohibits the conduct of any nuclear explosions, among other environments, on the surface of the world ocean, in airspace above the world ocean, and under water, while the 1977 Convention on the Prohibition of Military or Any Other Hostile Use of Environmental Modification Techniques prohibits the use of methods of intentional manipulation of natural processes taking place in the hydrosphere that would have widespread, protracted-duration, or serious consequences, as means of destroying, damaging, or harming any Party.

Under certain conditions the provisions of the 1967 Treaty for the Prohibition of Nuclear Weapons in Latin America and the 1986 South Pacific Nuclear-Free Zone Treaty may apply to measures limiting naval activity.

In Antarctic waters limitation of naval activity boils down to prohibition of military maneuvers and testing of any and all kinds of weapons, pursuant to the 1959 Antarctic Treaty, as in areas of heavy maritime shipping traffic in conformity with the 1972 International Regulations for Preventing Collisions at Sea and a group of bilateral agreements on preventing incidents on the high seas and in airspace above the high seas.

Confidence-building measures in Europe apply to naval operations only when they are conducted in conjunction with ground forces exercises on the European continent. It was originally stated in this manner by the Document on Confidence-Building Measures and Certain Aspects of Security and Disarmament of the Final Act of the 1975 Conference on Security and Cooperation in Europe, and subsequently by the Document of the 1986 Stockholm Conference on Confidence- and Security-Building Measures and Disarmament in Europe, as modified by the Vienna Document of 1990. This Document, which made notification of military exercises mandatory, detailed to a greater extent information that is to be provided on naval components connected with ground forces conducting military exercises. The Concluding Document of the 1983 Madrid Meeting of the Conference on Security and Cooperation in Europe, which formulated the mandate of the Stockholm Conference and the Concluding Document of the Vienna Meeting of the Conference on Security and Cooperation in Europe, prescribed employment of confidence-building and security measures in regard to military activity taking place in waters adjacent to Europe, "whenever these activities affect security in Europe as well as constitute a part of activities taking place within the whole of Europe as referred to above, which they will agree to notify." Measures prescribed by the 1988 Agreement Between the United States of America and the Union of Soviet Socialist Republics on Notification of Launches of Intercontinental Ballistic Missiles and Submarine-launched Ballistic Missiles apply to this category.

The sole measure that specifically regulates activities of naval forces is a group of bilateral agreements to prevent incidents, but to date there are only ten participating states: the Soviet Union, on the one hand, and the United States, Great Britain, the FRG, France, Canada, Italy, the Netherlands, Spain, and Greece, on the other, while the number of such agreements is showing a tendency to increase. These agreements, which contain a number of standard wordings, prescribe measures seeking to ensure safety of navigation for naval ships on the high seas and flight safety for military aircraft above the high seas, and particularly to reduce the possibility of occurrence of hazardous situations when warships and aircraft are operating in direct proximity to one another. The parties pledge not to conduct maneuvers in areas of heavy shipping traffic, in which international rules of the road are in effect. Their warships and military aircraft shall not impede or present hazards to nonmilitary vessels nor to one another. These agreements have established regular channels of communication between the parties via the naval attaches in the corresponding capitals, which shall be used in the case of incidents, and also provide for regular, no less frequently than once each year, consultations between the parties.

The 1982 UN Convention on the Law of the Sea generally aims at preserving peace on the seas and oceans. This Convention is characterized in the preamble as an important contribution toward maintaining peace, justice and progress for all the peoples of the world. The Convention contains provisions for using various categories of waters for peaceful purposes. This term is laid forth in a general way in Article 301, "Peaceful Uses of the Seas," which states:

> In exercising their rights and performing their duties under this Convention, States Parties shall refrain from any threat or use of force against the territorial integrity or political independence of any State, or in any other manner inconsistent with the principles of international law embodied in the Charter of the United Nations.

This Article restates Article 2(4) of the UN Charter, which sets forth the principle of refraining from force in international relations. Consequently the essence of the term "peaceful uses" in this instance consists in observance of this principle when exercising various kinds of use of the sea. Inasmuch as Article 301 affirms that this principle extends to all spheres to which the Convention applies, it encompasses all categories of waters the regime of which it defines.

In other international treaties the term "peaceful uses" contains different and more specific content. Article 1, Paragraph 1, of the Antarctic Treaty, for example, reads:

> Antarctica shall be used for peaceful purposes only. There shall be prohibited, *inter alia*, any measures of a military nature, such as the establishment of military bases and fortifications, the carrying out of military maneuvers, as well as the testing of any type of weapons.

Article IV of the Treaty on Principles Governing the Activities of States in the Exploration and Use of Outer Space, Including the Moon and Other Celestial Bodies contains similar wording.

There is lacking in international law a general formula enabling one to give a uniform, universal interpretation of this term, which explains the existing differences in its official and doctrinal interpretation. The problem can be resolved by setting forth and specifying in each treaty what is understood by the Parties under the term "for peaceful purposes." Applied to the seas, this can be done apart from the UN Convention on the Law of the Sea, but coupled with it and in conformity with the norms and principles set forth in it.

The question of naval activity and naval armament was placed as a separate item on the agenda of the Thirty-eighth Session of the UN General Assembly, and resolutions have regularly been adopted on this question since that time. By decision of the General Assembly, a group of government experts worked from July 1984 through April 1985, drafting for the Fortieth Session a document titled "Study on the Naval Arms Race." This question was deliberated by the UN Commission on Disarmament from 1985 through 1990.

General Assembly resolutions on this question were for the most part of a procedural nature, renewing the placement of a corresponding item on the agenda of the Commission on Disarmament. At sessions of this body principal attention was devoted to confidence-building measures in the world ocean, particularly such measures as concluding a multilateral agreement on preventing incidents on the high seas, ensuring greater openness, and exchange of information on naval matters.

Meaningful discussion of these and other confidence-building measures, as well as of measures to limit naval activities and arms, lacks the support of a number of major Western naval powers, and the United States, which initially attempted to keep this item off the Commission's agenda, has since 1987 refused to discuss this issue. In the opinion of the United States, naval forces have traditionally played an important role in the system of ensuring national security. The United States explains the need for large navies by the necessity of ensuring the security of extended sea lines of communication, on which it is dependent by virtue of geographic factors. In contrast to the counterpart strategic forces covered by agreements or negotiations, a large part of U.S. naval forces is not involved in confrontation with the Soviet Navy but performs other missions, primarily in Third World areas, and for that reason it is inappropriate to raise at talks with the Soviet Union the question of reducing these forces and limiting their activities. In addition, naval forces are capable of playing a stabilizing and even peacemaking role which, in the opinion of the United States, has been demonstrated by recent experience in the Persian Gulf. Finally, official U.S. spokesmen equate any step to limit the daily activities of naval forces with infringement of freedom of the seas.

Certain NATO countries (Italy, Norway, Iceland, and Canada at various times) and other states bound to the United States by alliance relations, while not accepting the idea of naval activities and naval arms reduction talks, do not reject certain variations of confidence-building measures and restraint in the naval domain, such as measures pertaining to preventing incidents, notification of ships in distress and emergency situations, *etc.* Norway, for example, at one time advanced the idea of establishing on Norwegian soil an international center for prevention of incidents at sea with informational and consultative functions.

Some states (India) reject the idea of special talks on naval issues, since they feel that the question of reducing naval forces should be decided exclusively within the context of the overall process of nuclear and nonnuclear disarmament, which is beginning with the Soviet Union and the United States. China, which until lately held a similar position, has recently acknowledged in principle the expediency of multilateral limitation of naval forces, but it continues to insist that these measures should be applied primarily to the Soviet Union and the United States.

Some neutral and nonaligned countries, in particular Sweden, Finland, and Indonesia, take a very firm position on this issue. Sweden, for example, among other things proposes conclusion of a multilateral convention on prevention of incidents, including all naval arms in the reduction process, prohibiting long-range sea-launched cruise missiles and sea-based tactical nuclear weapons, renewing a number of agreements on the laws and customs of naval warfare, such as the Hague Convention on Emplacement of Automatic Subsurface Contact Mines, *etc.*

Proceeding from the position that limitation and reduction of naval activity and naval arms and confidence-building in the world ocean will make a substantial contribution toward assuring international security, the Soviet Union has authored or co-authored specific initiatives in this area, takes active part in discussing this issue in the United Nations, and supports the proposals of other countries. The Soviet Union has proposed a number of ideas to the UN Commission on Disarmament and the UN Ad Hoc Committee on the Indian Ocean. These and other proposals were set forth in synthesized form in the working document entitled "Limitation and Reduction of Arms on the High Seas," presented by the Soviet delegation jointly with Bulgaria and East Germany at the Third Special UN General Assembly Session on Disarmament.

The authors of the document proceed from the position that limitation and reduction of naval activity and arms can be accomplished in a phased manner, beginning with relatively simple measures, on which there already exist elements of mutual understanding. Both global and regional approaches are possible in implementing these measures, including the establishment in areas of heavy shipping traffic zones of reduced concentration of arms and heightened confidence, and even including demilitarization of agreed-upon waters. As a result of limitation measures, the effective strength, armament and organizational structure of naval forces should be limited to maximum requirements for defense but should be insufficient for the conduct of offensive operations. Establishment of a reliable system of verification and openness in the naval domain, including employment of national technical means of verification, measures based on cooperation, on-site inspection, and an international mechanism within the framework of or under the auspices of the UN Organization, is a component part of these proposals. Agreement on measures to achieve a total ban on sea-based tactical nuclear weapons should be a priority.

The Soviet Union has recently been actively advancing the idea of talks on the entire issue of naval nuclear arms, in addition to strategic arms, with the goal of radical reduction and subsequent total elimination of such arms.

It is obvious, however, that meaningful talks on this topic are impossible without the participation of the large naval powers. The United States and a number of other Western countries reject such an opportunity, and there is little probability that the situation will change radically in the immediate future.

It would seem that an increase in the number of bilateral agreements on preventing incidents—standard agreements in their basic provisions but differing in details connected with strength and composition of naval forces, region of probable coordination, and other factors—is at the present time a fairly promising direction to take in this area. At a later date they could be integrated into a system by linking the channels of communication they have established and consolidating the regular consultations by the parties which are conducted in connection with these agreements. Presumably in the future it would be possible on this basis to establish either an independent structure or to include a naval element in an organization with a broader scope of activities aimed at reducing the military threat. It would make sense to extend measures to prevent incidents to cover submarines and to draft special measures to apply to warships and other ships with nuclear propulsion plants.

In this connection one could recommend a number of modest but feasible confidence-building measures, in particular: when warships flying the flags of parties to such agreements are sailing in immediate proximity to one another, training exercises should be conducted for the purpose of practicing rules and procedures of preventing incidents (the first agreement in this regard was reached between the Soviet Union and France in June 1990; in the future it makes sense to address this matter on a multilateral basis); joint training should be conducted for navigation officers of countries party to agreements; commentaries to agreements should be jointly drawn up, with a uniform interpretation of the provisions contained in said agreements.

As regards actual limitation and reduction of naval activity and arms, it would seem that substantial preconditions for this could emerge in the course of successful development of the Vienna talks on Conventional Armed Forces in Europe. If a further agreement is reached on deep cuts, with elimination of asymmetries and the capability of military forces to launch a surprise attack and conduct large-scale offensive operations, one of the West's main arguments in support of maintaining a high level of naval presence in the North Atlantic and the regular conduct of large-scale exercises to rehearse airlifting and sealifting of troops and arms from the United States to Western Europe will disappear once and for all. This argument, which has already been significantly weakened by changes in Eastern Europe and by the shift by the Soviet Union and the United States from confrontation to coordination in their relations with elements of partnership, consisted in the claim that the allegedly existing substantial superiority of Warsaw Pact forces over NATO could require, in case of an armed conflict in Europe, urgent and immediate movement of reinforcements from the United States.

Preconditions for the limitations and reductions being considered would be created as a result of the achievement and implementation of agreements on reduction of strategic offensive arms in particular, since elimination of sea-based weapons, including both delivery systems and platforms, would lead to depreciation of related other assets, such, for example, escorts. It would be essential thereby to find a solution to the problem of limiting antisubmarine warfare assets and their activities, such as, for example, by establishing zones free of such assets and activities, simultaneously restricting ballistic-missile submarine combat patrol areas to within the boundaries of these zones.

As an aggregate, however, radical reductions of conventional forces and strategic arms may in the future cause a tipping of the balance in structures of military forces in favor of naval forces, which will make it necessary to limit them in an agreed-upon manner, or unilaterally.

A.L. Semeyko
Head of Branch, Political Department,
RSFSR Ministry of Foreign Affairs

D. Overall Reduction of Military Expenditures

Reduction of military expenditures is one of the most important aspects of disarmament. It creates additional guarantees of the irreversibility of lessened military confrontation. At the same time a decrease in military appropriations is closely linked to the process of economic development, since the released funds are for the most part transferred over to peaceful purposes.

The question of linkage between military expenditures and pace of economic growth (in present-day conditions) has been examined in great detail in studies by various authors beginning in the latter half of the 1940's. It would seem that many if not the majority of scholars are in agreement that in the long run a high level of military spending has a negative effect on the functioning of the economy of individual countries. At the same time everybody is familiar with examples of "economic miracles" in states in which the level of military spending was low or minimal in the postwar period.

One can state with assurance that high military expenditures over the course of decades have served as one of the key reasons for the increase in crisis phenomena in the economy of the Soviet Union. The actual size of the share of military expenditures was so high that what we had was more a war economy in peacetime. Soviet President M.S. Gorbachev, disputing those who show skepticism toward already achieved disarmament agreements, noted that until quite recently military expenditures comprised eighteen percent of national income in the Soviet Union. If the confrontation of the first half of the 1980's had continued, in the period 1986-1990 Soviet military expenditures could have increased by an additional forty-five percent, with an overall national income growth of only twenty-one percent.

In some respects a similar picture is observed in the United States, where high military expenditures are leading to a growing federal budget deficit, to an increase in the national debt, and are heating up inflationary trends. It is not mere happenstance that it is military budget items that are presently becoming the object of the sharpest debate over what budget items should suffer in order to comply with the Gramm-Rudman-Hollings Amendment, which is aimed at reducing the U.S. federal budget deficit.

The linkage between reducing military expenditures, global economic processes, and solving the problems facing mankind as a whole, which are becoming increasingly critical, is becoming increasingly important today. The "third world's" foreign debt, population growth, deterioration of the environment, hunger, AIDS, illiteracy, *etc.*—enormous resources must be made available in order to attain reliable general security in the twenty-first century. For this reason the community of interests of East and West, North and South find expression in this interpretation of constructive linkage between rolling back military expenditures and ensuring stable development.

Should reduction of military expenditures be an independent measure, to be achieved through international talks, or should it be attendant to disarmament, assuming the form of "peace dividend" from the curtailment of various national defense programs? The debate on this score is once again heating up.

In 1973 the Soviet Union and its allies submitted before the United Nations a proposal to reduce by ten percent the military budgets of the Permanent Members of the Security Council and to use part of the funds saved by these cutbacks for aid to developing countries. The motives for this proposal were as follows: Cutting military expenditures, particularly by states possessing nuclear weapons as well as substantial military potential, would effectively help curb the arms race and help move toward disarmament. And although this initiative was not implemented, it did provide impetus for initiation of a purposeful effort within the United Nations to compare the military expenditures of various countries and to draw up principles for possible negotiations in this domain. Outside the United Nations, at the European level, throughout the 1980's the Soviet Union and its allies repeatedly proposed to the NATO states that direct talks be held on holding the line on and reducing military expenditures. To date, however, the first "peace dividend" has been obtained by states unilaterally, as a consequence of limitation or reduction of various categories of their weapons and armed forces.

The situation today has changed radically as regards the question of reducing defense appropriations, due to improvement in the world situation and new approaches by East and West to assessing today's military-strategic realities. An exceptionally favorable political environment has been established for addressing in a practical manner the issues of comparison and reduction of military expenditures.

First of all, savings have been experienced since initiation of the process of genuine nuclear disarmament, namely the implementation of the INF Treaty. According to published figures, total budget savings from this treaty will run about 300 million rubles for the Soviet Union and 1.7 billion dollars for the United States in the period up to 1996.

Second, an agreement on radical measures to reduce conventional arms and military forces in Europe has been reached at the twenty-three-nation Vienna talks. Considering the fact that even in the case of nuclear states the bulk of military budgets goes for maintaining and upgrading conventional arms (and of course 100 percent of military budgets in the case of non-nuclear states), the slated large-scale measures to reduce military confrontation in Europe would mean a large reduction of defense expenditures. Implementation by the Soviet Union and the United States of the agreement to reduce their strategic nuclear arms will also obviously produce considerable effect.

Third, considerable reductions in defense expenditures are already being carried out unilaterally by both East and West. Soviet military expenditures in 1990 have been reduced by 8.2 percent in comparison with the preceding year: from 77.3 to 70.9 billion rubles. Volume of military production in the Soviet Union will decrease by 19.5 percent over a two-year period (1989-1990). It was also announced that, taking into account reduction of expenditures in 1988-1990, overall savings in defense expenditures will run almost 30 million rubles in comparison with the ratified five-year plan. In addition, the Soviet Government intends, if the international situation permits, to reduce the percentage share of defense expenditures in national income by a factor of 1.5-2 by the year 1995. Substantial measures are being carried out by the East European countries, as well as by the NATO members. The latter have rescinded the decision, which has been in effect up to the present time, to increase their defense budgets by three percent annually, and have proceeded to cut back military expenditures for a number of military programs. The U.S. Secretary of Defense submitted to Congress proposals for a possible twenty-five percent reduction in U.S. military forces over the next five years, including deactivation of a number of divisions, reduction of the number of aircraft carriers and the total number of warships, and deactivation of a number of tactical and strategic air wings. It is appropriate to note here that such a development of events has in fact proven to be consonant with proposals by the East European countries. Suffice it to mention Warsaw Pact initiatives calling for a mutual pledge not to increase military budgets by the Soviet Union and the United States, the Warsaw Pact and NATO, calling for a one-time or sequential reduction of defense appropriations as specific disarmament measures are carried out, and calling for freed-up funds to be used for economic and social needs.

Fourth, the Soviet Union has recently undertaken a number of important steps aimed at increasing openness and giving impetus to realistic comparison of military budgets. In 1987 the Soviet Union announced that its military budget figures published up to that time had reflected only expenditures of the USSR Ministry of Defense on maintenance of armed forces personnel. Financing of research and development (R&D), however, as well as arms and military hardware procurements, had been carried in other Soviet State Budget items. Effective in 1989, the Soviet Union proceeded to publish overall data on its military expenditures. In 1990, for example, the overall total of 70.9 billion rubles in military expenditures breaks down as follows: 31.0 billion rubles for procurement of arms and equipment; 13.2 billion rubles on research and development; 19.3 billion rubles on maintaining army and navy; 3.7 billion rubles on military construction; 2.4 billion rubles on pension payments to military personnel; 1.3 billion rubles for other expenditures. By publishing expanded military expenditure figures and making public future reductions to be made in coming years, the Soviet Union reaffirmed its policy of building greater trust and confidence and ensuring *glasnost'* and openness in military matters.

Fifth, considerable progress in this area has been achieved in the United Nations. The UN General Assembly has passed a number of resolutions calling for the conduct of detailed studies of comparability in military expenditures for purposes of comparison of official figures. Several such studies were conducted by the United Nations between 1976 and 1985. An international standardized system of UN reporting on military expenditures has been drawn up and has gone into effect. In accordance with this system, which is based on the U.S. military budget structure, it has been recommended that states submit to the UN figures on their military expenditures in their national currency, broken down by budget items (maintenance of personnel; maintenance and upkeep of military equipment; arms procurements; construction; and research and development) and by force categories (strategic forces; ground forces; naval forces; air forces; and logistics and control).

Almost all NATO countries, Australia, New Zealand, Sweden, Finland, Austria, Ireland, and some nonaligned states are taking part in the UN reporting system. Romania began submitting figures on its military expenditures from 1985. It is anticipated that in 1990 counterpart figures will also be submitted to the United Nations by the Soviet Union and a number of other East European countries.

Also of importance is the fact that a fairly detailed list of principles for military budget talks has been drawn up and adopted at the United Nations, with Soviet and U.S. participation. This set of principles prescribes the following: accession by the leading states to the UN system of reporting on military expenditures; formulation and use of a method of comparing military expenditures between countries with different budget systems and covering different periods of time; discussion of possible ways to reduce military expenditures, as well as appropriate verification measures. Agreement has also been reached in the United Nations on general political approaches to possible talks in this regard.

Obviously all these steps will facilitate the initiation of a meaningful dialogue between the major military powers, particularly the Soviet Union and United States, on the matter of comparability of military budgets, and they could promote future transition to independent talks on reducing military expenditures. Of course one should welcome and encourage the present trend–parallel reduction of military expenditures of East and West as a consequence of improvement of relations between them and as a result of disarmament. Both possibilities are highly promising. And surely in any case the main thing is an end result in the form of a genuine "peace dividend."

Thus obtaining savings in military expenditures is an entirely attainable goal. The next and even more important question is the question of what absolute and relative savings can be achieved.

First of all, we should note that there exist a number of limitations (and the deeper the process of disarmament becomes, the more clearly evident becomes the substantial nature of these limitations) to potential benefits from reduction of military programs. They include the following: the need to find jobs for and retrain military personnel discharged as a result of implementation of disarmament measures; logistical costs for the processes of eliminating arms, military equipment, and ammunition and preventing adverse effect on the environment, *etc.*; and conduct of conversion at defense enterprises, their reconfiguration to the manufacture of civilian goods. Since these elements are common both to East and West, it is becoming increasingly important to take them into consideration. As we know, for example, as a result of protests by local environmental groups in the Soviet Union, it was decided not to use for destroying chemical weapons an enterprise in the town of Chapayevsk that had been built specifically for this purpose. And plans to transport U.S. chemical weapons to Johnston Atoll for elimination have evoked protests in countries in the South Pacific. One sees that increase in the volume of weapons reduction initially results frequently not only in no savings but even causes additional expenditures.

Also needed is the organization of reliable, comprehensive verification of compliance with disarmament agreements. Existing experience in the elimination of intermediate-range and shorter-range missiles and discussion of verification issues at the NST talks, "open skies" talks, and at the

Conventional Armed Forces in Europe talks indicate establishment in the near future of an extensive, costly international monitoring and verification system, employing the entire conceivable aggregate of means—from the traditional inspector's binoculars to orbital surveillance and global computer networks.

A new factor in this matter for the Soviet Union will be the planned military reform, which includes a gradual transition to a combined method of manpower acquisition (with an increase in the percentage share of persons recruited on a volunteer, contract basis). A more professional army will be more costly; at the present time, for example, the cost of maintaining primary-rank enlisted personnel in the Soviet Union and the United States differs by a factor of more than 100.

Finally, some portion of the savings obtained by reducing military expenditures may not be directly "transfused" from the military into the civilian sector, but may go toward reducing the budget deficit. Legislative authorities in the Soviet Union and the United States—the Supreme Soviet and Congress respectively—have already given appropriate instructions to their respective governments. Although, of course, improvement in the government finances of any country will have a favorable indirect effect in the long run.

We should make particular mention of conversion. In the Soviet Union a State Program for Conversion of the Defense Industry for the Period up to the Year 1995 has been drawn up and submitted for consideration by the country's leaders. Transition to the manufacture of civilian goods will be carried out at more than 400 enterprises. Supporting this complex process will cost the state 10-11 billion rubles in the period up to 1995.

Thus a number of economic and technical factors are adjusting the initial estimates of the potential freeing of funds from the reduction of military budgets. It is true that the elimination of arms unquestionably produces an economic effect. In order for this effect to become really appreciable, it is important to consider the political aspects of the matter as well, for development of the process of disarmament is inseparably linked with the future of relations between the Soviet Union and the United States, relations in Europe, in the "third world," and with the bringing of stability to the world system as a whole. The level of trust between superpowers has grown to an unprecedented degree; they are essentially shifting from rivalry to interaction. At the same time, while agreeing to mutual quantitative reductions in their arsenals, they are carefully watching to ensure that the qualitative indices of their combat potential do not worsen, in order to continue maintaining a military-strategic balance. And, as a consequence, East and West are continuing their modernization programs.

It would seen that the main possibilities for reducing defense expenditures today lie precisely with modernization and mutual limitation of modernization, for immense amounts are spent on military research and development and on arms procurement: more than sixty percent of the Soviet and more than forty percent of the U.S. military budget. It is necessary to pay and train military personnel, and existing military equipment must be serviced and maintained. The question of the appropriateness of continuing modernization of nuclear and conventional weapons, at least at current levels, is increasingly being brought to the forefront in discussions.

It is indicative that the ideological element, such as accusations of "militarism" or "aggressiveness" directed against the other side, has now practically disappeared. The Soviet Union and the United States have acknowledged the impossibility of victory in nuclear war and the need to prevent such a war, and they have declared that they will not seek military superiority. The principle of reasonable sufficiency for defense is being incorporated into military organization development. An exchange of views has commenced on how to eliminate mutual concern regarding the military doctrines of East and West and to give them an unambiguously defensive thrust. In these conditions essentially two arguments are raised across the board for consideration by the countries' legislative bodies and public opinion: We must keep an eye on the other side and on overall development of the world situation. The fact that international debates about military budgets are thus being reduced to a common denominator is an extremely important factor. One can probably conclude that a presumption is forming that with an increase in trust, mutual openness, and strengthening of the underpinnings of the global security, it will be possible radically to reduce national and worldwide military expenditures. The "peace dividend" which is already being reaped today may tomorrow become a powerful source of prosperity.

P.G. Litavrin
First Secretary, Arms Control and Disarmament Directorate, USSR Ministry of Foreign Affairs

E. Limitations on Arms Sales and Arms Transfers

The problem of limiting the global trade in arms has to date not been given adequate attention by the world community. And yet, against the background of progress being made in the process of disarmament, the lag in this area is looking increasingly more abnormal, for in the final analysis settlement of regional conflicts, increase in confidence between states, and a radical reduction of conventional arms can scarcely occur if the problem of limiting worldwide trade in arms is not resolved.

Attempts at legal regulation of international arms trade were undertaken following World War I, when the League of Nations was formed. Point 4 of Woodrow Wilson's "Fourteen Points" called for limiting national armed forces to a minimal level, and also presumed limiting the transfer of arms. Efforts to implement these proposals were unsuccessful, however. Attempts by the Western states to embargo arms deliveries to the belligerents during the Spanish Civil War also proved ineffective. Germany and Italy continued arms transfers to the putschists, and the embargo became transformed into a discriminatory measure against the legally constituted Republican Government.

Establishment of the United Nations and adoption of the Charter and the first documents of this organization fostered the formulation of criteria of legal and illegal arms transfers. The UN Charter, confirming the right of states to collective and individual self-defense, also held as legitimate arms transfers to a state acting in conformity with the UN Charter. At the same time the idea was that arms transfers to an aggressor should not be permitted. A differing interpretation of aggression, however, has frequently complicated the adoption of a corresponding resolution. In 1959 the Warsaw Pact member states proposed to the NATO member states that they enter into an agreement pledging not to aid an aggressor, which would have introduced considerable clarity into the question of limiting arms transfers and would have established mutually agreed-upon criteria and definitions. Finally, in 1974, a definition of aggression was hammered out at the United Nations (Resolution 29/3314), from which follows the inadmissibility of transferring any arms to an aggressor, although in actual practice the definition of aggression continues to be given different interpretations. For many years, for example, the UN General Assembly has been passing resolutions which recommend to the Security Council that it prohibit the transfer of arms to Israel, but in the Security Council the United States has impeded implementation of these resolutions. Attempts to build a foundation of international law for limiting arms transfers have not always ended in failure. In particular, Security Council Resolution S.418 was adopted in 1977, establishing a mandatory embargo on the transfer of arms to the Republic of South Africa.

The Soviet Union and the United States held bilateral talks in 1977-1978 on limiting arms transfers, which attested to the fundamental possibility of this problem being placed on the agenda and discussed by the world's two leading military powers, although ultimately these discussions did not come to a successful conclusion.

The Soviet Union has repeatedly proposed discussion of the problem of arms transfers and that restrictions be imposed on arms transfers: at the First Special UN General Assembly Session on Disarmament in 1978; in the January 5, 1983, Prague Declaration by the Warsaw Pact member states; and in M.S. Gorbachev's reply to the leaders of the Club of Rome on October 27, 1985. Our proposals have not, however, met with positive response or broad international support. The main reason for this is apparently the fact that the Soviet proposals were made in conditions of continuing acute international confrontation and distrust, and in conditions where regional conflicts were not being settled but, on the contrary, were continuing to escalate. We should note that our country as well was not prepared for constructive actions. It is difficult to imagine that a serious international dialogue on limiting arms transfers could have gotten started during the war in Afghanistan, during a time of Soviet arms deliveries to Central America and a lack of any information on supplying of Soviet "special equipment" to friendly countries.

Today the situation is changing: Cessation of some regional conflicts and diminished intensity of others, a general improvement in the international atmosphere, a radical improvement in Soviet-U.S. relations, and major breakthroughs in a number of areas of disarmament are objectively creating the preconditions for commencing discussion of this problem both on a bilateral and multilateral level.

We must, however, speak out on what is hindering this process. Both the political and economic interests of various countries continue to differ in approach to the problem of restricting arms transfers. They are manufacturers and purchasers, countries occupying foreign soil and countries fighting to liberate their lands, developed and developing nations, dictator regimes and countries in which democracy has been around for several hundred years. Obviously their interests do not coincide. We must state that the weapons manufacturers also hold very strong views. For them the export of weapons is a means of reducing costs, keeping production running at full capacity, and a source of enormous profits, especially in conditions where in Europe major reductions in conventional arms are being placed on the agenda.

In this same connection there arises the question of what is to be done with the enormous quantity of arms in Europe targeted for reduction, particularly Soviet armaments. Although a small part of this could be sold or transferred out of Europe prior to signing of an agreement in Vienna, this is clearly not the way arms should be eliminated. A good deal of justifiable concern is being expressed to the effect that disarmament in Europe could lead to further militarization of the "third world," which is continuing at a rapid pace.

Finally, insufficient *glasnost'* and openness in matters pertaining to global trade in arms are impeding the organization of multilateral negotiations and consultations. One can scarcely hope for a constructive and substantive dialogue on this topic if the flow of weapons to various regions continues and there is growth in the re-export of and the "black market" in arms.

A transition from a state of being armed far beyond reasonable sufficiency to a level of reasonable sufficiency for defense, and limiting of the proliferation primarily of the most destructive and destabilizing systems, *e.g.*, ballistic missiles and their technologies, should form the basis of an approach to this problem. It would be desirable for arms suppliers and purchasers to adhere to a policy of mutual restraint and self-limitation in areas of armed conflicts in the context of their political settlement. A formal understanding among the countries of Latin America, which have agreed not to acquire additional quantities of heavy weapons, provides an example in this area.

Of course, at the present time we are not advocating unilateral termination of Soviet arms transfers and military assistance. Such a step could cause negative political and economic consequences, and the main thing is that it would not lead to a positive result, because the ensuing vacuum would be filled by other suppliers. It would seem that coordinated steps are needed here. For example, reaching some more general international formal understanding, such as a suitable convention that could be opened for signing. A regional agreement could form a beginning. Gradually expanding, with the passage of time it would include new parties. But preliminary steps are also necessary to proceed to such an agreement.

In our opinion solving the problem of limiting arms transfers could begin with affirmation of *glasnost'* and openness in this domain, in order to calm concerns, to eliminate suspicion, and to build confidence between peoples. In 1988, at the UN General Assembly, it was decided to conduct a special study to determine ways and means of ensuring openness in the area of international arms transfers and to submit it in the form of a report to the UN Secretary General. At the same time a UN resolution would call upon the international community to display restraint in the area of arms transfers and to step up national monitoring of arms manufacture and transport. Such measures could be a first step toward confidence-building and in combating the black market in arms.

The Soviet Union affirmed its willingness to participate in such a study as well as to take part in establishing at the United Nations a register of arms sales and transfers, including the drafting of its parameters. The question of publishing information on such transactions will arise in this connection.

A letter dated August 15, 1990, from USSR Foreign Minister Eduard Shevardnadze to the UN General Secretary, on the matter of limiting international arms transfers, defines our country's approach to this problem and specifies those principles by which one should be guided in this matter, including the questions of *glasnost'* and openness. There have been major changes in the Soviet Union's approach to the problem of international arms transfers. There must be a shift in the position of other countries as well in order for these changes to be translated into results. In the meantime the importance of limiting trade in arms and the need to take coordinated steps on the part of the world community are increasing in connection with events in the Persian Gulf.

B.R. Tuzmukhamedov
Docent, USSR Diplomatic Academy

In recent years missiles and missile technologies have become available to an increasing number of countries. They import them, manufacture them under license or jointly with the traditional manufacturers, and also develop their own designs. India, Israel, Saudi Arabia, Iraq, Iran, Syria, Libya, the Republic of South Africa, South Korea, Taiwan, and other countries possess missiles, as a rule with a range of 300 kilometers or less. A number of countries have tested medium-range systems (Israel, the Republic of South Africa, and India). As we know, some of these countries are involved in unsettled crises (the Near and Middle East, Persian Gulf, Southern Africa, *etc.*); these weapons could be used if these crises become further aggravated, such as occurred during the war between Iran and Iraq and the 1991 war in the Persian Gulf. Some of these countries are suspected of intentions to obtain access to weapons of mass destruction and even to obtain possession of such weapons, while Iraq is suspected of intentions actually to employ such weapons. There is a lack of coordinated and effective multilateral measures to deter and limit proliferation in this area.

At the present time certain measures are prescribed by the Soviet-U.S. ABM and INF Treaties. In 1987 seven developed capitalist countries—the United States, Great Britain, France, the FRG, Italy, Canada, and Japan (later joined by Spain)—adopted a "regime of unilateral restraint" in regard to the export of missiles with a range in excess of 300 kilometers and a throw-weight of greater than 500 kg as well as the attendant technology. This regime is weakened by the merely recommendatory nature of its component guideline principles, which may allow private-sector manufacturers to circumvent its provisions. It could serve as a basis for dialogue, however, if it were improved by development of cooperation and mutual information exchange among the principal technology developers and manufacturers, as well as by spelling out restrictions on arms transfers, with an eye to a future formulation of a fully effective legal regime.

The Soviet Union supports the formulation of practical measures in this area. In particular, it has proposed as a possible way to resolve the problem the establishment of an international mechanism on analogy with the IAEA that, while prohibiting proliferation, at the same time would not close off access by interested countries to rockets and rocket technology for their utilization for peaceful purposes. Since 1987 the Soviet Union has been discussing this problem with a number of exporter nations (*e.g.*, the United States, Great Britain, and France). The degree of agreement reached in the course of these consultations, which has enabled the Soviet Union to accede to the above-mentioned regime, is reflected in the appropriate section of the Joint Declaration on Non-Proliferation, signed in the course of the Soviet-U.S. Washington summit in 1990. In particular, this Declaration voices support of the aims of the missile technology monitoring regime, which applies to missiles and certain missile-related equipment and technologies, with all countries called upon to observe the spirit and guiding principles of this regime. The Declaration also notes that the Soviet Union and the United States are prepared to engage in bilateral and multilateral dialogue on this problem and to continue efforts aimed at strengthening international restrictions to impede the proliferation of missiles and missile technologies.

9. Verification of Arms Control Agreements and the Rights of Domestic Sovereignty

John B. Rhinelander
Partner, Shaw, Pittman, Potts & Trowbridge

Verification is an all encompassing process that includes not only the monitoring and evaluation necessary for present treaties, but also the design of new verification regimes. The Office of Technology Assessment of the U.S. Congress has written that, "Arms control monitoring may be thought of as the continuous assembling of many pieces of a puzzle to form a coherent picture."

A. NTM and OSI

The Treaty Between the United States of America and the Union of Soviet Socialist Republics on the Limitation of Anti-Ballistic Missile Systems (ABM Treaty) and the companion Interim Agreement on Certain Measures With Respect to the Limitation of Strategic Offensive Arms (Interim Agreement) were landmarks in terms of verification when agreed to by the United States and the Soviet Union in 1972. These SALT I agreements explicitly provided that "each Party shall use national technical means of verification at its disposal in a manner consistent with generally recognized principles of international law." They also contained the corollary provisions prohibiting both interference with national technical means of verification (NTM) and deliberate concealment measures impeding verification by NTM. No prior agreement had referred to NTM. The published texts provided no information on what NTM entailed, but the United States and the Soviet Union understood that NTM included:

(1) satellites, both orbiting and geo-stationary, equipped with photographic cameras and other sensors, that operate in outer space, that is, above the atmosphere and therefore outside the sovereign territory of any state; and

(2) radars and other types of sensors operating on the

ground, at sea or in the air, but located outside the national territory of the other party.

The availability of sophisticated NTM, and the decision within the U.S. government that it could rely on NTM to monitor certain types of provisions in arms control agreements, was the first verification breakthrough and it made SALT I possible. Prior to 1968, the United States had insisted that on-site inspection (OSI) was necessary for SALT-type agreements. Because the Soviet Union had then categorically refused any type of OSI, limitations on and reductions of strategic nuclear weapons systems remained non-negotiable. However, the type of limitations acceptable to the United States starting in 1968 were only those that could be monitored by NTM.

Thus, for instance, the SALT I agreements, as well as the subsequent Treaty Between the United States of America and the Union of Soviet Socialist Republics on the Limitation of Strategic Offensive Arms (SALT II Treaty) of 1979, focus on fixed land-based launchers, which are large and visible from space, and do not rely on limits on missiles, which can be hidden from space sensors by moving them inside buildings.

Soviet agreement to accept intrusive OSI, reflected for the first time in the Treaty Between the United States of America and the Union of Soviet Socialist Republics on the Elimination of Their Intermediate-Range and Shorter-Range Missiles (INF Treaty) of 1987, marked a major change in what was within the scope of agreement previously acceptable to the United States. While President Reagan coined the phrase, "trust but verify," which he repeated at every opportunity, the thought behind it represented consistent U.S. policy since the beginning of the nuclear age. U.S. society was open and a great deal of information on U.S. military programs was publicly available. The Soviet Union was a closed, secretive society, and the United States needed to monitor, by its own capabilities, Soviet activities of concern.

Information from satellites and other technical sources removed much of the uncertainties, and wide margins of errors, reflected in prior U.S. estimates. A classic example is President Kennedy's understanding, after his election and access to satellite information in 1961, that there was no "missile gap" favoring the Soviet Union. The reverse was in fact true.

B. Effective Verification

Verification raises the fundamental issue, whether the sources are NTM or OSI, what constitutes "effective" verification for purposes of U.S. policy. The definitions given over time have differed somewhat, but Ambassador Paul Nitze's is generally accepted–if the other side moves beyond the limits of the Treaty in any militarily significant way, we would be able to detect such a violation in time to respond effectively and thereby to deny the other side the benefit of the violation. Former Secretary of Defense Harold Brown stated his approach a little more succinctly and pointedly—"any Soviet cheating which would pose a significant military risk or affect the Strategic Balance would be detected by our intelligence in time to respond effectively."

Military significance, under these views, is an acceptable criterion, particularly if NTM is supplemented by various "cooperative measures." The Soviet Union had refused to proffer any information on its systems at SALT I, and insisted that the United States knew what it needed from NTM. During SALT II, at the insistence of Senator Mathias, an arms control supporter who bluntly stated that the Senate would not ratify the SALT II Treaty unless the Soviets provided specific information on its systems subject to limitations, the Soviet attitude changed. Data was provided for and exchanged, and the SALT II Treaty contained numerous "counting rules," or conclusive presumptions, designed to take the guess work out of certain activities monitored by NTM, at least for purposes of Treaty compliance, such as the number of warheads on a deployed ICBM.

The second verification breakthrough came with the INF Treaty. The Soviet Union agreed to OSI. When it did, the United States then had to scale back some of its OSI demands which, in the posture of anticipated Soviet refusal, had reached rhetorical positions unacceptable to the United States itself when the Soviets actually accepted them.

The Krasnoyarsk radar is a good example of both the capabilities and limits of NTM, and the additional assurances brought by OSI. The United States, based on NTM, concluded that that radar was at least an unlawful early warning radar, but perhaps a more destabilizing ABM radar. Informal OSI to the radar site in 1987 by a Congressional delegation confirmed the former, but rejected the latter. Therefore, while the radar, standing alone, was never militarily significant from the perspective of many U.S. experts, all agreed that it was a major political and legal issue representing the exact type of prohibited long lead-time item (requiring many years to construct) that the United States had focused on during the SALT I negotiations. Further, the construction of that unlawful radar raised basic questions of Soviet intent. NTM was adequate, but OSI dispositive, to confirm the unlawfulness of the radar at that location, but also to resolve its purpose. The Soviet decision to dismantle the Krasnoyarsk radar reflects successful completion of a difficult compliance matter.

By contrast to the ABM Treaty, a chemical weapons agreement prohibiting manufacturing and possession of chemical weapons can never be "effectively" verified. The problem is not the inherent limitations in NTM or OSI, but the fact that some chemical factories can be converted in a matter of days from lawful to unlawful production. There is no long lead time, or buffer, from any particular moment in time. Accepting a treaty that is not effectively verifiable may be acceptable to the United States with respect to chemical and biological weapons, which do not affect the strategic balance. It is not acceptable with respect to nuclear weapon systems.

C. Cooperative Measures

The INF Treaty of 1987 established a stringent new type of verification regime between the United States and the Soviet Union, including OSI as part of a series of cooperative measures. The INF Treaty approach was followed in part in the multilateral Treaty on Conventional Armed Forces in Europe (CFE Treaty) of 1989, and will be expanded upon in the START Treaty. These new types of measures include:

1. a data base and data exchanges, periodically updated, on locations, numbers and technical parameters;
2. advance notification of certain movements;
3. baseline inspections to verify initial data;
4. elimination inspections as equipment is destroyed;
5. close-out inspections of facilities that have stopped production;
6. short notice inspections at declared facilities and at "suspect sites";
7. monitoring shipments from certain production facilities;
8. the opening of the roofs of certain buildings to show to satellites specific weapons are not concealed inside, and the display or parking of certain equipment in the open; and
9. procedures to monitor the number of warheads on deployed missiles.

These provisions are over and above the explicit reference to, and continued reliance on, NTM and the corollary non-interference and non-concealment measures, carried over from SALT I and SALT II.

START will also contain a requirement that certain types of flight test data not be encrypted (that is, coded) and that radio signals transmit certain types of data during test flights. This addresses a contentious issue which has existed under SALT II.

D. Continuing Privacy and Secrecy

Under the Constitution of the United States, there are certain rights that cannot be modified by treaty or statute, including those in the Fourth Amendment which prohibits "unreasonable searches and seizures" without a prior court-ordered search warrant. Accordingly, the United States cannot grant by treaty automatic, self-executing OSI rights to enter and inspect all types of private property. This may not be a major treaty concern since the Fourth Amendment protections do not apply to U.S. government property and could by contract be waived in advance by all government contractors. However, as an example on the other extreme, OSI rights could not be granted by treaty to inspections of ordinary residential homes in the United States and at least certain categories of privately owned factories with no government contracts.

Notwithstanding the radical changes toward transparency and openness reflected in the most recent arms control treaties, there are certain types of facilities and equipment that will undoubtedly remain off limits to full OSI. One example is the payload of certain types of satellites, particularly those with NTM sensors. Another is certain defense, intelligence, and production facilities. Various OSI and cooperative measures can, however, be designed to prove that certain activities are not being done (such as a limited inspection to determine prior to launch that a nuclear power generator is not part of a satellite's payload, and a limited inspection to determine the amounts of weapon-grade materials being converted to peaceful purposes without disclosing design features of warheads).

E. Adaptation

Agreements in force, such as the ABM Treaty, must be the subject of compliance, interpretation, and particularly adaptation since technological change cannot be stopped. This will consequently require new verification packages. OSI and cooperative measures, for instance, will be necessary if important new interpretations and amendments are agreed upon to supplement the ABM Treaty.

New types of measures may also be the preconditions of new agreements. An example would be the verification protocols agreed upon by the United States and the Soviet Union in 1990 for the Treaty Between the United States of America and the Union of Soviet Socialist Republics on the Limitation of Underground Nuclear Weapon Tests (TTBT) and the Treaty Between the United States of America and the Union of Soviet Socialist Republics on Underground Nuclear Explosions for Peaceful Purposes (PNET). The protocols could be the basis of verification provisions for a multilateral, comprehensive test ban treaty (CTBT). There are, however, no current negotiations on a CTBT.

Verification cannot compel compliance. It can in the appropriate context provide timely information so that states, individually or collectively, can decide on appropriate counter-measures in the case of non-compliance by another state. Modern technology, particularly that used for NTM, provides a sound basis for entering into international security agreements that was not available before the missile age. The ballistic missile—the technology that has greatly enhanced the threat of total destruction when coupled with a nuclear warhead—provides an important tool for managing stable relations through the transparency and instant information it can assure by placing satellites in orbit in space. With information from satellites and other forms of NTM, particularly if supplemented by cooperative measures including OSI, states may be more willing to forego certain activities than they were when compliance rested largely on trust.

B.R. Tuzmukhamedov
Docent, USSR Diplomatic Academy

In its most general form, verification can be defined as a group of methods of observation of performance of treaty obligations and analysis of obtained data. Verification is carried out by presenting to each party information on fulfillment of obligations by the other parties. Thus verification helps achieve the goals of a treaty, helps to prevent and to detect violations of treaty provisions, and provides assurance of compliance with treaty provisions.

Absence within the domain of intergovernmental relations of agencies ensuring compliance with the norms of international law that are equivalent in powers and authority to those that supervise (verify and ensure, by compulsion when necessary) compliance with the provisions of internal laws endows verification with certain functions of ensuring performance of international obligations. The process of verification includes the collection, processing, and synthesis of data and, as a result, the reaching of a decision on the state of affairs regarding the performance of obligations. Selection of variations of response actions in case of violation, however, is not a prerogative of verification.

Sovereignty is generally defined as independence and supremacy of authority by the state on its territory. The concept of sovereignty forms the basis of a number of generally recognized principles of international law, and its content is set forth in fundamental sources: the UN Charter, the 1970 Declaration of Principles of International Law, and the 1975 Declaration of Principles of the Final Act of the Conference on Security and Cooperation in Europe.

A state, in exercising its sovereignty, has the right to be a participant in international treaties, corresponding to which is the obligation to carry out its international obligations fully and in good faith. In exercising this right, a state seeks to be informed on performance by a "partner" state of its obligations, at the same time being an object of similar endeavor on the part of the "partner" state. Verification is an instrument that, on the one hand, conduces exercise of this right and, on the other hand, creates guarantees of observance of obligations that correspond to this right. Performance of these two principal legal functions of verification should meet the criterion of noninterference since, both in unrestricted and in qualified form, it does detriment to the rights inherent in sovereignty: In the former case the state whose actions are the object of verification may form the impression that its territorial supremacy is being infringed upon, and in the latter case that it is limited in its capability to obtain assurances of complete performance by other states of their international obligations.

However, no matter how rigorous the requirements of the criterion of noninterference on verification may be, exercise of verification obviously presupposes a certain degree of intrusion into the area of sovereign rights. Verification is not an exception in this regard; analogies can be found, for example, in maritime law. In exercising the right of innocent passage of a territorial sea, a vessel under the flag of one state may find itself within the boundaries of a substantial portion of the territorial waters of another state without requesting the latter's permission, but this will not constitute an infringement of sovereignty. Both the agencies of authority of the littoral state and the foreign vessel crossing its territorial sea possess mutual rights and obligations in connection with innocent passage, which in combination ensure the interests of the littoral state and the flag state. Accordingly, the right of innocent passage is a result of coordination of the sovereign rights of the corresponding states, which makes possible regulated exercise of these rights in their common interest. Achievement of this right was preceded by a long period of evolution, in the course of which a balance was struck between the interests of the littoral state—initially military, and subsequently economic and environmental—and international navigation.

Verification is also a result of similar coordination of sovereign rights. In contrast to the right of innocent passage, however, its exercise presumes deeper penetration into the domain of a state's territorial supremacy. And the object of verification in the area of arms control involves material means and actions that were traditionally viewed as a fundamental attribute of the sovereignty of a state, the means of its protection and support. This circumstance, as well as the confrontational and ideologized approaches that were long dominant in international relations, greatly complicated the search for and limited the choice of possible solution to the problems of disarmament, including verification, causing a lag in this area of intercourse between states.

In the meantime development of the world community led to a situation where many problems—economic, food supply, energy, environmental, informational, and demographic—which had in the past been viewed as national or regional problems, became transformed into global problems, requiring global solutions; international intercourse has become simplified thanks to modern means of communication, mass information, and transportation. Transformation of the content of sovereignty in the direction of its de-absolutization was taking place under the effect of these factors. For example, the concept of internal jurisdiction was changing along with increase in the interdependence of states; this term could no longer signify total and unrestricted freedom of action on the part of the territorial sovereign within the boundaries of its territory, whether it pertained to environmental standards or human rights norms. While exercising self-limitation and imposing certain rules on their conduct, at the same time states have begun more extensively exercising their sovereign rights not individually but collectively. To quote former USSR Minister of Foreign Affairs Eduard Shevardnadze,

> Today the question is voluntary transfer of a portion of one's rights in the common interest and, as paradoxical as it might seem, to strengthen national security while simultaneously strengthening the general security. The interdependence of events in an interlinked world is increasingly dictating to us the need to delegate a portion of national prerogatives to an international organization.

And the sovereignty of the state does not suffer but even gains thereby. For example, an environmental crisis, a nuclear incident, or the production and export of narcotics in one state are outside the jurisdiction of its neighbor, but they directly affect that neighbor's exercise of its sovereign rights and may place in question its ability to function as a sovereign. By transferring certain authority over to international institutions, states broaden by means of these institutions the extent of their exercise of authority, and affirm their sovereignty, while avoiding interference in the internal affairs of other states.

Only in the last several years have these tendencies begun to extend increasingly more broadly to the military domain of interaction between states, one result of which was the signing of the Stockholm Document, the INF Treaty, the Vienna Document, and the CFE Treaty, as well as progress at the NST talks in Geneva. The most notable feature of reached agreements and agreements that are currently being negotiated is the provisions for verification, which in large measure were the reason for reaching these agreements.

Verification provisions, which have existed in international treaty practice in one form or another for quite some time, became the rule for arms limitation and reduction agreements from the end of the 1950's, when the Antarctic Treaty was concluded and nuclear test ban talks were being held.

Some experience was also obtained in earlier years. For example, pursuant to the 1940 Soviet-Finnish Agreement on the Aaland Islands, which called for their demilitarization, the duties of the Soviet consulate established on these islands, in addition to those functions which are customary for such an establishment, included verification of compliance with the Agreement and, when necessary, raising the question of conducting a joint inquiry. This experience was of limited application, however, due to its local nature and taking into account both the circumstances under which the agreement was concluded and the international situation as a whole. Significant agreements concluded in the period between the two world wars, on prohibiting the use of chemical and bacteriological weapons and on limitation and reduction of naval armaments, did not prescribe verification measures. Proposals for such measures, including the establishment of a verification commission and organization of international on-site inspections on suspicion, presented by the Soviet Union to the League of Nations Preparatory Commission for Organization of a Conference on Arms Reduction and Limitation in 1928, did not receive the support of other states. The main argument presented by the opponents of verification measures was that arms reduction should be grounded on mutual trust and good faith between governments. Arguments also included the assertion that the proposed measures could constitute interference in the sovereign rights of states.

In the postwar period questions of verification were an obstacle to genuine disarmament for a long period of time, and were also used as a pretext not to adopt significant measures in this area. The West's principal argument was the thesis that the Soviet Union was a "closed society," that the Soviet Union was unwilling to agree to comprehensive verification, and that it was an unreliable partner. This explained the overstated verification standards contained in Western proposals, which their authors themselves had no intention of following and in other cases were unwilling to follow. The Soviet Union in turn was concerned by the U.S. nuclear monopoly and, after this monopoly came to an end, by U.S. superiority in nuclear weapons and delivery systems, as well as by control over the voting mechanism in the United Nations by U.S. diplomats, which affected the content of its initiatives. One cannot deny the existence of internal factors that influenced an attitude toward verification which Eduard Shevardnadze called "an allergy," acknowledging that "for a long time our attitude toward any kind of verification, especially on-site inspection, was reserved." In relations between the Soviet Union and the United States there existed no trust, on which at the intergovernmental level rests confidence in the absence of a threat to the rights inherent in sovereignty and the possibilities of exercising these rights; in addition, mutual distrust was encouraged. The situation which prevailed is illustrated by an incident that took place on May 1, 1960, when a U.S. reconnaissance aircraft was shot down over the territory of the Soviet Union, which complicated relations between the two states and, in particular, served as grounds for canceling a scheduled summit meeting.

Partial resolution of the conflict between the need for agreed-upon control of nuclear potential and the difficulty of reaching agreement on verification measures became reality with the development of technical means of collecting data on installations located outside the boundaries of a state's territorial sovereignty. These means, which were designated "national technical means of verification" (NTMs), the characteristics of which in large measure determined the content of agreed-upon arms limitation measures, for a long time were the principal method of verification of compliance with arms limitation agreements. Additional measures based on cooperation were worked out for the purpose of increasing the effectiveness of NTMs. On-site inspections, carried out by teams of inspectors, both national and international in makeup, began to be practiced increasingly more extensively, as the content of limitations further developed and confidence grew.

Matters of verification, particularly from the mid-1980's on, became a subject of detailed deliberation within UN bodies, particularly in the General Assembly's First Committee and the Disarmament Commission. The General Assembly noted at its Forty-third Session that the United Nations, pursuant to its Charter, could broaden its functions in the area of verification of compliance with multilateral agreements, and requested that the Secretary General conduct, with the assistance of a group of government experts, a detailed study of the role of the United Nations in this area, and to submit a report to the Forty-fifth Session.

UN documents and materials also contain general approaches to this problem, in particular validation of the principles of verification. The Final Document of the UN General Assembly's First Special Session on Disarmament in 1978 is an authoritative source of these principles. Paragraphs 31, 91, and 92 of this Document were adopted as the basis for a proposed list. We should note that the UN Disarmament Commission's special report at the Third Special Session of the UN General Assembly on Disarmament lists sixteen principles in Section 12, "Verification in All its Aspects," and this list is called "not exhaustive."

First of all it is essential that any verification system, its establishment, structure, and functioning conform to the generally recognized principles of international law set forth in the UN Charter and other primary sources of these principles. While all these principles as an aggregate form a common indivisible legal foundation of contemporary international relations, some of them take on pre-eminent significance in the area in question. These include first and foremost the principles of noninterference in internal affairs, sovereign equality, good-faith performance of obligations under international law, cooperation between states, and peaceful settlement of disputes. Verification measures should not do detriment to the security of any of the parties, threaten their socioeconomic development, or be of a discriminatory nature. The legitimacy of verification is embodied in its support of treaty provisions, as well as in an equality of rights and obligations of parties to an agreement. The interests of all parties should be secured in the conduct of verification measures—both the interests of those who are performing the verification and those whose activities are being verified. All this creates the conditions for legitimacy of verification.

Since we are talking about arms limitation and disarmament measures, that is, measures pertaining to the most sensitive area of national security of states, an agreed-upon system of verification should ensure prompt and timely detection of violations that threaten the higher state interests of the parties to an agreement as well as the fate of the agreement proper. Therefore prompt and truthful information on the state of affairs is essential. For this reason, in order to carry out its functions, verification should meet the principle of effectiveness. Effectiveness of verification is a guarantee of stability of any agreement: There will be assurance that the obligations assumed by the parties are being carried out, and the agreement proper will be firm.

Of fundamental importance in reaching agreement on verification measures is the question of commensurability of scope of verification and scale of practical disarmament measures. Depending on the specific features of the agreement, determined by the characteristics of the weapons in question and the nature of measures (freeze, limitation, reduction, elimination), makeup of participants, *etc.*, employment of various verification measures is possible, measures that should be in conformity with these specific features. Herein lies the essence of the principle of commensurability, which was formally articulated in the Final Document, which states: "The form and conditions of verification prescribed in any specific agreement shall depend on the purposes, scope and nature of the given agreement."

The importance of rigorous compliance with agreements on disarmament measures, both for the security of individual states and for international peace and security, determines the equal right of each party to an agreement to verification of compliance with the agreement. Herein lies the content of the principle of universality of verification. Different states possess different capabilities to carry out verification measures, which determines their capability to take part in such activities. As is noted in the Final Document, however, arms limitation and disarmament agreements should provide for participation in the verification process by the parties directly or through the UN system. The principle of universality may be variously implemented. In some cases, such as in the Soviet-U.S. SALT I talks, universality of verification is achieved by implementation of verification measures based on national means, performed by the parties independently from one another. In other cases, when it is necessary to verify compliance with multilateral agreements, such as the Seabed Treaty, the significance of joint measures increases—consultations by the parties, as well as performance of international procedures within the framework of the United Nations. Meriting attention in this connection is one of the conclusions of the working group formed on the UN Disarmament Commission to study the problem of verification in all its aspects:

> Direct participation by all states in each of the aspects of verification activities could lead to the development of complex and unwieldy procedures which could not be employed in actual practice. In addition, duplication of capabilities which certain states already possess could be unwarrantedly costly.

On this basis a conclusion was reached on the desirability, on the one hand, of assigning responsibility for verification to a group of countries possessing the requisite national means and, on the other hand, of stepping up international efforts in this area. The experience with operation of the Nuclear Non-Proliferation Treaty, verification of compliance with which is handled by the International Atomic Energy Agency (IAEA), is promising as regards achieving universality of verification. All Parties to the Treaty can take part in the verification process by means of this agency. This experience demonstrates the possibility that, as we move toward a nuclear-free world, universality of verification could be ensured by use of comprehensive international procedures and mechanisms, and there would be an increase in the democratic spirit of verification.

The Final Document of the UN General Assembly's First Special Session on Disarmament states that: "Where appropriate, a combination of several methods of verification as well as other compliance procedures should be employed." This provision embodies the principle of mutual supplementation of various means and methods of verification, which is achieved by means of their concurrent or phased implementation. Such a combination is prescribed, for example, by the INF Treaty, the Document of the Stockholm Conference on Confidence- and Security-Building Measures and Disarmament in Europe, and the CFE Treaty, pursuant to which verification may be carried out both using national means and by conduct of on-site inspections. Implementation of the principle of mutual supplementation leads to an aggregate effect whereby parallel or sequential conduct of two forms of verification—national means and on-site inspections including variations—makes it as difficult as possible to circumvent treaty provisions, which not only makes it possible promptly to detect violations but also effectively to deter such violations. Experience has been amassed to date in devising, reaching agreement on, embodying into treaty provisions, and the operation of mechanisms for verifying fulfillment of obligations under arms limitation and reduction agreements. Agreements currently in effect and presently being negotiated prescribe various verification measures and specific methods and means of performing verification. Experience to date attests both to the effectiveness of existing methods, which are chiefly based on national technical means of verification, and to their capability in the future reliably to serve the purposes of verification. The reliability of NTMs increases as they become technically more sophisticated, as well as when special provisions are incorporated into agreements that prohibit interfering with the operation of or jamming NTMs, and prohibiting the employment of intentional masking or concealment measures that hinder verification of compliance with treaty obligations. Although the term national technical means of verification has not been comprehensively defined by treaty texts, provisions which prohibit active and passive countermeasures against NTMs, as well as the requirement that employment of NTMs be in conformity with generally recognized principles of international law, fill in to a significant degree the legal vacuum that existed prior to signing of the first strategic arms limitation agreements. Counterpart articles of like content are to be found in the ABM Treaty, in the SALT I Interim Agreement, and in the SALT II Treaty.

Other additional measures based on cooperation have been incorporated into a number of treaties for the purpose of further developing these limitations—for example, provision of weapons subject to regulation with special identifying markings, and active assistance by the verified party to the NTMs of the other party in situations prescribed by a treaty.

The successful functioning of NTMs is also fostered by other additional measures, such as agreed-upon rules of counting systems covered by an agreement, exchange of quantitative data on arms, their locations and technical characteristics, notification of forthcoming activities such as test missile launches or missile elimination, *etc.*

Employment of NTMs in pure form, when neither the verifying nor the verified party take any additional active measures in connection with verification, minimizes conflicts with the traditional interpretation of the term territorial sovereignty, if we leave aside debate over its upper limit, since there is no physical penetration of the territorial boundaries of the state being verified. Even in this case, however, neither party possesses unlimited freedom of action, since the operator of national technical means must make his actions conform to certain legal criteria, and the party being subjected to verification must not impede the operation of these means. These limitations increase to the extent that the need to encompass weapon systems with treaty measures comes into conflict with the technical capabilities of NTMs. The parties voluntarily and on a mutual basis limit their freedom of action, believing that in this way they will best serve their own higher national interests.

The examples of the Antarctic Treaty, the Document of the Stockholm Conference on Confidence- and Security-Building Measures and Disarmament in Europe, the INF Treaty, and a number of other agreements demonstrate the possibility of devising and employing such verification measures as on-site inspection, that is, visits by teams of inspectors of one party to the territory of the other party or installations belonging to it on other territory, for the purpose of verifying compliance with agreed-upon obligations. The degree of intrusiveness of inspections into the domain of rights inherent in sovereignty can vary. The Antarctic Treaty, for example, provides for inspections that are unlimited in time and space (within the bounds prescribed by the Treaty), which is due to the specifics of the territory in question, not one part of which is under anybody's sovereignty. Extensive rights regarding verification inspections are granted to the Parties to the Stockholm Document, but they are limited in time of conduct and number, as well as in space within the bounds of the zone of employment of confidence-building and security measures. On-site inspections under the INF Treaty, unprecedented in depth and number, encompass all phases of treaty implementation. These include verification of initial data on arms inventory, observation of the elimination process and monitoring of remaining, as yet undismantled weapons, and monitoring to ensure that manufacture of arms covered by the Treaty does not occur. Still these inspections contain limitations in the form of specified quotas and their restriction to prior-declared sites (operational bases, production facilities, elimination sites, *etc.*). As the process of disarmament advances, as it encompasses new systems, as adopted measures become increasingly detailed, with a simultaneous increase in trust between the parties and in their confidence that arms limitation is both feasible and workable, states are showing growing willingness to accept increasingly more intrusive inspections. It is assumed that the Convention banning chemical weapons, the drafting of which is close to completion, will prescribe, among other types of inspections, inspection on request of any site or installation, without right of refusal.

There is some experience in employment of multilateral forms of verification of compliance with treaty obligations. In some instances we are dealing with already existing mechanisms that perform corresponding measures in connection with a given treaty. Pursuant to the Nuclear Non-Proliferation Treaty, for example, verification of compliance by Parties that do not possess nuclear weapons is entrusted to the IAEA, which provides safeguards and which performs international inspections. In other cases the parties to a treaty form a special agency to which they assign verification functions. For example, in addition to the IAEA's verification of compliance with obligations under the Treaty for the Prohibition of Nuclear Weapons in Latin America, corresponding functions, including on-site inspections, are performed by the Agency for the Prohibition of Nuclear Weapons in Latin America, established under this Treaty. In such cases it would seem that one can expect an even more tolerant attitude on the part of the inspected party toward inspection, since inspection is performed by agents of a derivative subject of international law (an international organization), which enables one reasonably to count on their impartiality and good faith.

A number of treaties prescribe a combination of national and international means of verification. Provisions of this type are to be found, for example, in the Seabed Treaty, pursuant to which the verification system consists of several stages and can be carried out unilaterally, collectively by several Parties, or by means of international procedures within the framework of the United Nations and in conformity with the UN Charter. This same Treaty, as does the Convention on the Prohibition of Military or Any Other Hostile Use of Environmental Modification Techniques, prescribes turning to consultative mechanisms for purposes of verification, in which mechanisms experts function on a national basis. Such bodies, which supplement NTMs and inspections and which help achieve the goals and implement the provisions of the corresponding agreements, have been established on the basis of Soviet-U.S. nuclear arms limitation and reduction agreements.

Thanks to major breakthroughs in recent years in the area of disarmament, verification is no longer an insuperable obstacle to adoption of arms limitation and reduction measures. Complications involving verification at negotiations in progress are due more to either technical difficulties in devising adequate and effective means of verification or to a lack of agreement on the scope of items to be limited or reduced, depending on the specifics of the subject of negotiation.

Practical difficulties of a legal nature are also determined in large measure by the specific features of specific talks, although some generalizations are possible. As disarmament measures become broader and deeper, accompanied by more comprehensive and penetrating verification measures, the problem of assured access by international and national inspectors to installations subject to regular or unscheduled verification advances to the forefront. Closely linked to this is the problem of protecting confidential information constituting a military, trade, or industrial secret to which inspectors may gain access. And this information may relate to nonmilitary or military production at a monitored installation that does not come under the agreement. For example, military toxic chemical agents and products not for military use but employing a manufacturing technology that constitutes an industrial secret may be produced at the same chemical industry facility. Or, for example, both elimination-targeted weapons and those that are not yet covered by agreements may be manufactured at the same missile production facility.

In this situation there arises the problem of the relationship between treaty-mandated verification and provisions of national law concerning protection of classified information, as well as, in certain cases, protection of private property against unwarranted or court-unauthorized searches (such as the Fourth Amendment of the U.S. Constitution), which on-site inspection may encroach under certain circumstances. There is also the continuing problem of verification of compliance in regard to weapons subject to reduction that are located on the territory of third countries.

Possible solutions to the problem of potential conflict between the provisions of national laws and the inspection mandated by international treaties include writing clauses into contracts between business owners and the government that impose an obligation not to hinder inspection. In the case of enterprises not in a contractual relationship with the government, one can utilize on the basis of analogy provisions of national law that provide for mandatory government inspections, such as inspections to determine compliance by a given enterprise with labor or environmental protection standards, extending these provisions to inspections prescribed by treaty. Certain measures pertaining to technical means of verification are also possible, such as more extensive use of automatic devices installed on the periphery, around the perimeter, or on the territory of inspection-targeted installations, or at transportation hubs. In principle they could serve as an alternative to on-site inspections in those cases where a government or company object to the presence of inspectors at production facilities. With the use of such devices it would be possible to consider the possibility of removing sensor readings by both the inspecting and inspected parties to an equal extent, which would increase the latter's assurance that the scope of information required by an agreement is not exceeded.

It is hardly likely, however, that such measures will provide a long-term solution to the problem. The optimal solution would seem to be either to amend national legislative enactments that potentially hinder verification, or to pass a special law governing foreign or national inspections on national territory. Assuring protection of confidential information can be achieved not only by means of careful regulation of the rights and obligations of inspectors, with precise specification of the limits of permitted activity, but also by taking into account the experience of protecting trade and industrial secrets from disclosure by civil servants who have access to them. Several organizations have such experience, such as the INMARSAT International Maritime Satellite Communications Organization. As regards verification on the territory of third countries, in addition to further developing the experience in resolving this problem acquired during the drafting and implementation of the INF Treaty, one might study the question of involving corresponding countries in negotiations at the stage where provisions dealing with inspections are being considered.

Part II. International Legal Principles and Rules in the Political Sphere

1. The Principles of Sovereignty, Sovereign Equality, and National Self-Determination

Harold G. Maier
David Daniels Allen Professor of Law, Vanderbilt University

Traditionally lawyers, scholars, judges, and statespersons describe the international community as a community of independent sovereign states. The term "sovereign" echoes a time when dealing with a sovereign state meant dealing with a specific individual whose word was recognized as authoritative by his or her people. The modern use of that term continues to encourage an unfortunate tendency to treat nation states as if they were independent sentient entities, capable of feeling, thinking, and acting independently of human agency or intervention. In fact the term "sovereign state" describes nothing more–and nothing less–than a group of people located in an artificially bounded geographic area whose general commonality of interests is largely defined by that common territorial bond and by their acceptance of the proposition that some few of their number may legitimately make and enforce rules about relationships between the group and individuals and between the group and other such groups.

Put in less functional but more traditional terms, a sovereign state has a fixed population living in a defined territory and having a central government. Whatever the formalities, sovereign status for international purposes arises with the combination of local and international recognition of the legitimacy of the exercise of authority by centralized institutions within territorial boundaries on behalf of the people that make up a state's population.

The characterization "sovereignty" describes jurisdictional competencies, both internal and external. Two of sovereignty's principal elements–territory and population–indicate where and upon whom the third required element–a government–may exercise authority. Taken together, the three elements establish the necessary collective identity to permit the members of the population to interact as a single entity with other groups similarly situated in the world community. The exercise of governmental authority is the exercise of legitimate power, not merely coercive power. The people living within a given territory legitimate the exercise of power by a central government by recognizing that a few members may act on behalf of the population group both internally and externally.

Sovereignty is a metaphor for a conduit for communication. Without group acceptance of the legitimacy of a centralized communication process, there can be no sovereignty, either for internal or for external purposes. Externally, lacking a reliable communication conduit, no other state could even begin to engage in relations with the people in the territory in question. There would be no one to talk to whose listening or response could make any difference in the way in which the population group would conduct itself with respect to other members of the international community, including the communicator.

The recognition of a state by other members of the world community is, in fact, merely an acknowledgement that the internal recognition of the central institution's governmental legitimacy has occurred. Absent this condition, there could be no international intercourse. The legitimacy of the state as an international community member is pre-conditioned on the explicit or implied internal acceptance by its population that some central institution may act in a governing capacity.

This internal acceptance of the authoritative nature of central institutional acts does not necessarily include acceptance of the correctness of all those acts, of the personnel that operate these institutions, or of a particular form of government. A population may object almost unanimously to the *manner* in which its government conducts itself or to the personnel who operate it. It is only when the population objects to the *institution* of government per se that it rejects status as a sovereign state. Internal recognition of legitimacy amounts merely to acceptance that acts of the institution will be treated as governmental in character.

Therefore, changes in internal patterns of participation, in patterns of group myth, *i.e.*, political philosophy, changes in boundaries or modification of internal institutions, *e.g.*, markets, political parties, *etc.*, changes in internal distributions of power, wealth, skill, *etc.*, changes in the use of strategy, *e.g.*, from coercion to persuasion, *etc.*, or changes in outcomes of the group process will not change the status of the nation as a sovereign state unless these changes also reflect lack of acknowledgement by the populace of the legitimacy of central representation of group interests. Thus, acceptance that the acts of a central institution have governing authority does not necessarily imply that the populace has participated in selecting the members of the acting institutions, that it has any influence on the acts that they carry out, or that the acts are acceptable to the population. A population's recognition of the legitimacy of some central governing power is not the same as an acceptance of the moral or legal validity of the acts carried out by the central authority.

Internal recognition of the legitimacy of centralized governmental institutions does not imply either legal or moral approval of the acts of those institutions. Internal recognition implies only that the territorially bound population group can be represented by centralized communicators. There can, of course, be disputes about whether the individuals that exercise ruling power are the proper persons to perform those functions. There can be disputes about whether the acts of the government are really beneficial to the population as a whole. The central government may be viewed as oppressive. The population's recognition that *some* central authority may legitimately act for the group is not thereby diminished. Thus, totalitarian regimes are no less sovereign than democratic ones; but they too depend on the psychological acceptance by their populations of the legitimacy of central government as a precondition for their sovereign status. All attributes of statehood flow from this single recognition of legitimacy. Once it has occurred, other nation states cannot ignore it if they wish to maintain intercourse with the group of human beings who inhabit the territory of the sovereign state involved.

This internal recognition of the legitimacy of guidance and control by a centralized institution is a necessity if a nation is to interact with other nations. Therefore, it is also a *sine qua non* of sovereignty. This is so because the demand-response-accommodation process that characterizes international law formation and international relations generally can only operate when a central institution can speak with legitimacy in the international community for the human beings whose welfare and authority it represents.

Internal acceptance of the legitimacy of acts by a few on behalf of the many is a prerequisite for participation in a consensual international legal system. A state's functional capacity to act as a community member is conditioned on the explicit or implicit acceptance by its own population that some central institution may act in a governmental capacity over and on behalf of that population. If a population group does not recognize the legitimacy of some centralized authority to communicate on its behalf, then indicia of consent to be legally bound to other nations by persons purportedly exercising such authority could never create those reliable expectations of generally conforming conduct that are a prerequisite to any system of law, consensual or otherwise. Recognition of a state by other members of the international community is nothing more than the acknowledgement that this centralized conduit for communication exists and that acceptance of obligation through that conduit is an act recognized as legitimate by the population group on behalf of whom the central communicators speak. Thus, recognition of one state by another is both a pragmatic acknowledgement of a set of real world facts and an agreement that the newly recognized entity will be the beneficiary of legal rights in return for being the obligee of legal duties.

International recognition of sovereign status is a legal prerequisite to interaction with other world community members because without the functional capacity to communicate that it identifies, no amount of rhetoric could make such interaction possible. The absence of international recognition of sovereign status does not necessarily negate an inference that the populace of a given territory has opted to act as a group *vis-à-vis* other groups in the international community. On occasion, refusal to recognize a new state may amount to a refusal to accord legal rights to that state, even though the state has otherwise attained all the functional prerequisites of sovereignty. In those instances, refusal to recognize is a political act, not a determination that the facts required to permit effective interaction with the state do not exist.

In such circumstances refusal of recognition amounts to notice that the refusers will not interact with the object state in terms of the requirements of international law. Put another way, refusal of recognition serves notice of instability in the relationships between the non-recognizers and the non-recognized. In this sense, non-recognition of a state is different from the refusal to recognize a government. The latter refusal does not deny the legal rights of the state whose government is denied recognition but merely refuses to communicate with the state through a specific group of people who purport to represent it in a governmental capacity.

It is not uncommon for some states to recognize the existence of another and, by doing so, acquiesce that relationships between them should be governed by legal principles, while other states refuse such recognition and thereby give notice that they will not be bound by international legal norms in their dealings with the unrecognized state. The pattern of recognition and non-recognition of the state of Israel is illustrative. Refusal to recognize the existence of the sovereign state when the prerequisite conditions otherwise exist does not necessarily deny the existence of those conditions. But such refusal at least asserts that the state refusing recognition will not treat that other population group as if it had collective rights under international community law. Conversely, a state unrecognized by its neighbors need not accept toward the non-recognizers any obligations arising from international consent under the law of nations, at least in so far as those obligations are interstate obligations, rather than universal ones. This principle of reciprocal obligation is the fundamental consideration that informs the principle of equality of sovereign states.

The principle of sovereign equality does not suggest that all sovereign states are equal in wealth, power, or size, any more than the statement in the U.S. Declaration of Independence that "all men are created equal" argues that all human beings are of equal ability. The sovereign equality principle does teach that once community recognition of sovereignty identifies a population group as having collective legal rights and duties with respect to other such groups, those rights and duties will be viewed as being reciprocal by other community members who granted such recognition. No consensual legal system could exist without such a principle of reciprocity and equality. Without it, the weaker community members, the very ones who need the greatest legal protection, would have to consent to participate in a system in which they would be eternally legally subservient.

The concept of sovereignty, in the international sphere, is derived from geographical and social relationships that define the social and geographic spheres of mutual interests of the people governed. Some states, however, are pieced together from formerly separate political, ethnic or cultural entities, sometimes by force, sometimes by political arrangement. Some states exercise hegemony over other territories without actually incorporating these territories into the "parent" sovereign state. In both situations, either formally or informally, the "parent" state controls any communication conduit established in the subgroup and therefore controls both its intragroup relationships and those with the world community. In either instance, sometimes from the outset, sometimes over time, the population of such subgroups may conclude that the existing centralized institutions of the "parent" state are not appropriate institutional mechanisms either to represent the subgroup *vis-à-vis* its own individual members or to speak for it internationally.

Assertions of the right of self-determination are really assertions that a central governmental structure does not have legitimate authority to control and speak for the ethnic, geographic, cultural, or economic unit that claims the self-determination right. The continuing problem involved in attempting to ascribe a right of self-determination to such a unit is determining the nature and status of "the self" that is to do the determining.

When recognition of the legitimacy of the central mechanisms of government as applied to the subgroup breaks down, an issue of the right of self-determination arises. The "parent" central government may respond in several ways. It may release the subgroup to become a new and separate sovereign state with its own central government. It may continue to impose hegemony by force of arms. It may attempt to modify its central governmental form and policies to attempt to make itself a more politically acceptable representative of the subgroup's needs. Only the first and the third alternative provide a basis for stable future relationships between the subgroup and the "parent" state. Even under the third alternative, if the requisite perception of a commonality of interest cannot be created, eventually the subgroup is likely to create or retain a sufficiently strong separate self-awareness to emerge as an independent sovereign state. It is only in the second instance that the issue of self-determination is truly of any significance. And in that circumstance alone is the issue of whether an international legal right to self-determination exists functionally irrelevant. The inherent instability of the second instance will in time necessarily convert it into instance one or three. In the meantime, as to those subgroups subjected to the "parent's" central government by force of arms, international legal claims of a self-determination right are in effect meaningless in the absence of an objective functional context in which to define the "self" that has that determination right.

The principle of sovereignty is essential to the continued growth and increasing sophistication of an international legal system. Far from being divisive, that principle represents perhaps the best hope for peace and the ultimate effective protection of international human rights. The corollary of sovereign power is sovereign responsibility. The more exclusive the power over nationals and territory, the more responsibility the international community can reasonably require from the governments that exercise that power. Weakening sovereign rights necessarily weakens the sources of responsibility in the international community and thus weakens the community itself since reliable community expectations can only develop in circumstances that permit fixing responsibility for meeting them. Thus, there is a very real and direct connection between the principle of sovereignty and the future success of an international legal community striving for the development of a truly reliable system of community law.

V.I. Kuznetsov
Professor and Head of Department,
USSR Diplomatic Academy

Modern sovereign equality of states is grounded on the idea of sovereignty of the participants of international intercourse, which was born in the era of feudalism and has been preserved up to the present day, changing its content over the course of centuries. The overwhelming majority of constitutions of present-day states specify that sovereignty belongs to the people. The people are sovereign and the source of the sovereign power of the state, although in the literature one can frequently encounter the assertion that it is the state that is sovereign, inasmuch as it functions as an intermediary entity between the various social groups of the population, thus expressing their common national interests. But the state is a sovereign entity only as a special organization of rule responsible for expressing (representing in the international arena) the sovereignty of the people resident in it.

Numerous internal and external actions that states undertake can be viewed as manifestations of state sovereignty only to the extent that the will of the people is expressed in them. Therefore, in upholding the sovereignty of the state we are upholding the right of peoples to their own national territory, to free determination of their own political, economic, and social system, and a right to cooperation with other peoples on the basis of full equality.

Sovereignty of the state is a reality of the present stage of development of human society. In analyzing the legal content of state sovereignty (or, more precisely, the sovereignty of the people, objectified in the state), however, one should not forget for a single moment that the relationship between state sovereignty and popular sovereignty is that of form and content.

In the Declaration of Principles of the Final Act of the Conference on Security and Cooperation in Europe, states assumed the obligations to respect the rights inherent in sovereignty. The latter signifies that in their mutual relations states shall respect one another's historical and sociopolitical uniqueness, the diversity of their positions and views, domestic laws, and administrative regulations, the right to determine and carry out their relations with other states as they see fit and in accordance with international law, *etc.*

In recent years it has frequently been stated that international law constitutes a higher legal order than the domestic laws of a state. The conclusion is sometimes drawn from this that normal international relations are impossible without limiting sovereignty. And yet sovereignty is a fact of international relations, not a product of international law. The norms of international law are created by states by means of agreements concluded on a basis of equality. Hence it follows that no state, group of states, or international organization can impose on other states international legal norms that they have created. The inclusion of a state or other party to international law in any other legal system may be accomplished only on a voluntary basis.

Today states are with increasing frequency handing over a portion of their powers, which previously had been considered to be inalienable attributes of state sovereignty, to international organizations they have created. This occurs for various reasons, including an increase in the number of global problems, broadening of the domains of international cooperation, and, correspondingly, an increase in the number of parties to regulation under international law.

There is every reason to assume that the vitally important need to maintain peace, the logic of integrative processes, and other such circumstances of contemporary international affairs will impel states to create legal structures that would adequately reflect these realities. As we know, with strict observance of the voluntary principle, states may proceed further in development of the principles of international law.

The above-noted new trends in development of the institution of international organizations by no means signify a decrease in significance of the principle of sovereignty in relations between states. It is important to note that states hand over a portion of their powers voluntarily to international organizations, and in so doing are not limiting their sovereignty but on the contrary are exercising one of their sovereign rights—the right to enter into agreements. In addition, states as a rule retain the right of supreme oversight over the activities of international organizations (the principle of unanimity in the Security Council, the principle of vital interests in the EC, *etc.*).

Inasmuch as we are living in an era of sovereign states, the principle of respect for sovereignty will continue to remain an important element of the system of principles of contemporary international law. Strict observance of sovereignty guarantees the free development of each state and people.

It is especially important to emphasize the close linkage existing between the principle of sovereignty of states and their obligation not to interfere in matters that essentially come under their internal jurisdiction. International law in principle does not regulate matters pertaining to the internal political situation of states, and therefore any measures by states or international organizations by means of which they attempt to hinder a subject of international law from settling its internal problems independently should be considered interference. In practice determination of the question of matters pertaining to the domestic jurisdiction of states frequently gives rise to disputes.

The concept of domestic jurisdiction of a state changes with the development of international relations and the increase in the interdependence of states. In particular, the modern concept of noninterference does not mean that states may arbitrarily declare any and all matters to fall within their internal jurisdiction. The international obligations of states, including their obligations under the UN Charter, constitute a criterion that enables one correctly to approach resolution of this complex issue.

There is no doubt that the concept "matters essentially coming under the domestic jurisdiction of the state" is not a purely terminological concept. Certain events, although taking place within the territorial boundaries of a specific state, may be considered as not pertaining exclusively to the domestic jurisdiction of that state. For example, if the UN Security Council establishes that events taking place within the territorial boundaries of a state constitute a threat to international peace and security, such events cease to be the internal affair of the state in question, and actions by the United Nations in connection with the events shall not constitute interference in the internal affairs of said state.

The obligation of states strictly to observe human rights both domestically and in the international arena becomes particularly significant in this connection. In the Document of the Copenhagen Meeting of the Conference on the Human Dimension of the Conference on Security and Cooperation in Europe, the participants affirmed that:

> [T]hey will respect each other's right freely to choose and develop, in accordance with international human rights standards, their political, social, economic and cultural systems. In exercising this right, they will ensure that their laws, regulations, practices and policies conform with their obligations under international law and are brought into harmony with the provisions of the Declaration of Principles and other CSCE commitments.

The above wording gives reason to conclude that interest on the part of any state in strict observance of human rights in other states should not automatically be viewed as interference in the internal affairs of these states or as violation of their sovereignty.

Sovereignty does not signify the complete independence of states or, even more so, their isolation, inasmuch as they are living and coexisting in an interlinked world. On the other hand, an increase in the number of matters that states voluntarily subject to international regulation does not signify automatic removal of such matters from the sphere of domestic jurisdiction of states.

Since all states are sovereign, all states are equal under the law. The principle of sovereign equality signifies that all parties to international relations are equal and that each is obligated strictly to respect the sovereignty of other participants in the international system, that is, their right within the boundaries of their own territory, in the case of states, to exercise legislative, executive, administrative, and judicial authority without any interference whatsoever on the part of other states, and independently to carry out their own foreign policy. The sovereign equality of states forms the basis of modern international relations, which is reflected in the most generalized form in Article 2(1) of the UN Charter, which states: "The Organization is based on the principle of the sovereign equality of all its Members."

This principle is embodied in the statutes of the international organizations of the UN system, in the statutes of the overwhelming majority of regional international organizations, in multilateral and bilateral agreements of states and international organizations, and in the legal enactments of the agencies of international organizations. The objective patterns and mechanisms of development of international relations and their gradual democratization have led to a substantial broadening of the content of this principle. In contemporary international law the content of the principle of sovereign equality of states is reflected most fully in the Declaration on the Principles of International Law Concerning Friendly Relations and Co-operation Among States in Accordance with the Charter of the United Nations, adopted by the UN General Assembly at its Twenty-fifth Session on October 24, 1970. Later the principle of sovereign equality of states was further developed in the Declaration of Principles of the Final Act of the 1975 Conference on Security and Cooperation in Europe and in the Concluding Document of the Vienna Meeting of the Conference on Security and Cooperation in Europe.

The principal function of the principle of sovereign equality is to ensure legally equal participation in international relations by all states, regardless of differences of an economic, social, political, or other nature. Since states are equal participants in international intercourse, they all possess legally identical rights and obligations. According to the Declaration of 1970, the content of sovereign equality contains the following elements:

a) states are legally equal;
b) every state enjoys the rights inherent in full sovereignty;
c) every state is obligated to respect the fact of the legal entity of other states;
d) the territorial integrity and political independence of a state are inviolable;
e) each state has the right freely to choose and develop its own political, social, economic, and cultural systems;
f) each state is obligated to carry out its international obligations fully and conscientiously and to live in peace with other states.

Other elements of the principle of sovereign equality include the right of the state to membership in international organizations, to be or not to be party to bilateral and multilateral treaties, including the right to be or not to be party to treaties of alliance, and the right to neutrality. One should note that in view of the dynamics of international relations, attempts to draw up a complete list of elements of the principle in question would be fruitless.

Pointing to the linkage between the principle of sovereign equality and respect for the rights inherent in sovereignty at the same time makes concrete and broadens the framework (content) of the principle of sovereign equality, which forms the basis of international cooperation. The noted linkage is particularly clearly manifested in the area of international economic relations, where the problem of protecting the sovereign rights of developing states stands out most acutely. In recent years the need for respecting the rights inherent in sovereignty has been pointed out particularly frequently in connection with the achievements of the scientific and technological revolution, which must not be utilized to the detriment of other states. The problem of direct beaming of television broadcasts, military or other hostile use of environmental modification techniques, the problem of protecting the environment, which is being manifested increasingly more critically, *etc.*, are most frequently mentioned in this connection.

The legal equality of states does not signify their actual equality, and this circumstance is frequently taken into consideration in practical international relations. One example of this is the special legal status of the permanent members of the UN Security Council, on the unanimous agreement of which the resolution of issues depends in many instances.

In a number of other contemporary international organizations, the founding states have departed from formal equality in voting (one country-one vote) and have adopted the method of so-called weighted voting, whereby the number of votes possessed by a country depends on the magnitude of its contribution to the organization's budget as well as other such factors. In voting by the Council of Ministers of the European Community, for example, on a number of matters states possess an unequal number of votes; the small member countries have repeatedly noted at a highly official level that this provision helps strengthen their national sovereignty. The principle of weighted voting has been adopted in a number of UN international financial organizations. Special circumstances connected with the administrative activities of certain recently formed international organizations have resulted in the Soviet Union consenting to the procedure of weighted voting on the INMARSAT Council.

* * *

The principle of self-determination of peoples and nations is one of the fundamental principles of contemporary international law, which was formally embodied in the UN Charter and has been further developed in a number of subsequent documents. One of the most important UN goals is "[t]o develop friendly relations among nations based on respect for the principle of equal rights and self-determination of peoples." (Article 1(2) of the Charter). This goal is made concrete in many provisions of the Charter. In Article 55, for example, it is closely linked with the task of raising living standards and resolving international problems in the economic and social domains, in the areas of health care, education, culture, human rights observance, *etc.*

Following adoption of the UN Charter, the principle of self-determination has repeatedly been affirmed in UN documents, beginning with General Assembly Resolution 6/545. Such documents include the 1960 Declaration on Granting of Independence to Colonial Countries and Peoples, the 1966 Covenants on Human Rights, the 1970 Declaration on the Principles of International Law, and the 1975 Declaration of Principles of the Final Act of the Conference on Security and Cooperation in Europe, in which the right of peoples to determine their own fate is particularly emphasized.

Emergence of the principle of self-determination of peoples was preceded by declaration of the principle of nationality, under the banner of which an economically and politically strengthened bourgeoisie combated outdated feudalism. The principle of nationality, however, did not become dominant even in the international law of the era of bourgeois revolutions, since it presumed the self-determination of nations based only on the attribute of nationality.

The content of self-determination varies, depending on the historical circumstances. There was a time when self-determination reduced to the problem of forming independent national states, since nations historically formed after states. The aspiration of a nation to form its own state consequently is connected with a specific stage of societal development.

The historical situation today is different from what it was in the period of bourgeois-democratic revolutions at the end of the eighteenth and nineteenth centuries, with which the era of national movements and the creation of national states coincided. The normative content of self-determination to date cannot help but be influenced by the circumstance that following the collapse of colonial empires human society entered a period in its development in which the question of self-determination of nations, in the sense of formation of independent national states, had been basically settled. At the same time even today the principle of self-determination is an active principle of contemporary international law.

The main element in the normative content of the principle of self-determination is expressed in UN documents. The 1970 Declaration on Principles of International Law, for example, stresses:

> The establishment of a sovereign and independent State, the free association or integration with an independent State or the emergence into any other political status freely determined by a

> people constitute modes of implementing the right of self-determination by that people.

The right of national self-determination does not disappear, however, if a nation has formed an independent state or has joined a federation of states. Not only dependent but also sovereign nations and peoples are parties to the right of self-determination. With the attainment of national independence the right of self-determination merely changes its content, which finds expression in a norm of international law.

Under present conditions, when the overwhelming majority of peoples have gained political independence and have formed independent states, emphasis is increasingly placed on economic aspects in the content of the right of self-determination: for example, the right of each people freely to dispose of its natural wealth and resources. One should also view as elements of the struggle for self-determination the struggle by developing countries against "cultural imperialism," "informational imperialism," *etc.*

The contemporary normative content of self-determination includes both the rights of peoples and the obligations of states that correspond to these rights. For example, corresponding to the right of peoples freely, without any outside interference whatsoever, to determine their political status and to carry out economic, social, and cultural development is the obligation of states not only to respect this right but also to foster this right by means of joint and individual actions.

Without strict respect for and observance of the principle of self-determination of peoples, it is impossible to perform many vitally important tasks facing the UN, such as the task of promoting universal respect for and observance of human rights and basic freedoms for all, regardless of race, sex, language, or religion. It is also impossible to maintain relations of peaceful coexistence between states without strict observance of this principle. Every state, in accordance with the 1970 Declaration, is pledged to refrain from any and all coercive actions which could hinder peoples from exercising their right of self-determination. An important element of this principle is the right of peoples to request and receive support in accordance with the goals and principles of the UN Charter if they are deprived of the right of self-determination by means of violence or coercion.

The principle of self-determination of peoples and nations is a right of peoples and nations, but not an obligation, and exercise of this right may be manifested in various ways. Self-determination should not be carried out from a separatist position, to the detriment of the territorial integrity and political unity of sovereign states. On the other hand, if a people has a government that has been formed by legal means and that represents its interests, any coercive actions from without that obstruct the process of self-determination may be viewed as violating the principles of noninterference and the sovereign equality of states.

The right of peoples and nations to self-determination is closely linked to freedom of political choice—an important element of the new political thinking in international relations. Peoples which have exercised self-determination freely choose not only their internal political status but also their external political orientation. Connected with this, in particular, is the right of liberated states to denounce unequal treaties, to implement a policy of nonalignment, and to take part in resolving both world and regional problems that particularly acutely affect the interests of developing countries.

Thus self-determination means the right of peoples to choose that path of development that to the greatest degree is in accordance with their historical, geographic, cultural, religious, and other traditions and conceptions. Respect for the freedom of political choice is becoming the foundation for cooperation rather than rivalry and antagonism.

2. Prevention and Peaceful Resolution of International Conflicts, Crises, and Disputes

Louis B. Sohn
Woodruff Professor of International Law,
University of Georgia School of Law;
Bemis Professor of International Law,
Emeritus, Harvard Law School

A. Relevant Principles of International Law

The basic duty of all states is to live together in peace with one another as good neighbors and to avoid creating any situation that may lead to a dispute, conflict or crisis. If nevertheless a dispute, conflict, or crisis arises, two other interrelated duties come into effect—to refrain from using or threatening force to impose a solution on an adversary, and to try instead to find a settlement by peaceful means. There is also a subsidiary duty not to aggravate or extend the dispute. In resolving the dispute, conflict, or crisis, states have the duty to ensure that the settlement does not endanger peace, security, and justice.

As a first step in resolving a dispute or preventing its aggravation, a state has the duty to notify the other state concerned that it believes that a situation has arisen that is likely to impair friendly relations between them, and to invite that state to exchange views on the subject. The other state has then the duty to proceed expeditiously to an exchange of views regarding the clarification of the situation, and the best method for its prompt resolution.

Unless the parties agree otherwise, they have an obligation to seek a resolution of the dispute by direct negotiations through diplomatic or other channels. Once negotiations have started, the parties are under an obligation to negotiate meaningfully and to seek in good faith and in a spirit of cooperation an early and equitable settlement of the dispute, acceptable to all parties.

If it has not been possible to settle the dispute by direct negotiations, the parties have the duty to proceed to an exchange of views with respect to the next steps to be taken. If no agreement on any further procedure can be reached, either party to the dispute has the right to submit it unilaterally to any settlement procedure provided for in a previous agreement between the parties. Should no such agreement be available, and the dispute is likely to endanger the maintenance of international peace and security, the parties to the dispute have the duty to refer it to the Security Council of the United Nations. The Council has the authority to recommend to them appropriate procedures or methods of adjustment or to recommend such terms of settlement as it may consider appropriate.

The existence of an obligation to resort to any other methods of settlement of disputes depends on the acceptance by the parties to the dispute of additional agreements, general, regional, or bipartite, and to resort to joint consultation arrangements, good offices, mediation, conciliation, arbitration, or judicial settlement.

If any such procedure or method has been initiated, either unilaterally or by agreement, there is another basic obligation that no party unilaterally may commence another procedure or method until the previous procedure or method has been concluded. Nevertheless, the parties to a dispute may at any stage of the proceedings settle the dispute by negotiations or decide together to refer the dispute or some aspects of it to another procedure.

B. Relevant Treaty Norms

Obligation to Settle a Dispute by Peaceful Means

These basic principles are spelled out in the Charter of the United Nations and other documents supplementing and interpreting the Charter provisions, which are discussed in later sections of this chapter.

In its preamble the Charter makes clear that the peoples of the United Nations are determined to "live together in peace with one another as good neighbors." Article 2(3) of the Charter enunciates the principle that "All Members shall settle their international disputes by peaceful means in such a manner that international peace and security, and justice, are not endangered." More specifically, Article 33(1) of the Charter provides that

> The parties to any dispute, the continuance of which is likely to endanger the maintenance of international peace and security, shall, first of all, seek a solution by negotiation, enquiry, mediation, conciliation, arbitration, judicial settlement, resort to regional agencies or arrangements, or other peaceful means of their own choice.

An additional obligation is imposed on the parties to a dispute by Article 37(1) of the Charter, which provides: "Should the parties to a dispute of the nature referred to in Article 33 fail to settle it by the means indicated in that Article, they shall refer it to the Security Council."

The Charter also contains the parallel principle that "All Members shall refrain in their international relations from the threat or use of force . . . in any . . . manner inconsistent with the Purposes of the United Nations." One of these Purposes is "to bring about by peaceful means, and in conformity with the principles of justice and international law, adjustment of international disputes and situations which might lead to a breach of peace."

In the case of *Nicaragua v. United States*, the International Court of Justice decided that this principle concerning non-use of force is binding not only on Members of the United Nations but must be regarded as a principle of customary international law binding on all states. Similarly, the principles of the Charter relating to the settlement of disputes by peaceful means have by now become a part of customary international law, binding on all states, whether or not they are Members of the United Nations.

Obligation Not to Aggravate the Dispute

Several general and regional international agreements contain the obligation not to aggravate or extend a dispute. For instance, the Geneva General Act of 1928, revised in 1949, provides in Article 33(3) as follows: "The parties undertake. . . to abstain from any sort of action whatsoever which may aggravate or extend the dispute." Similar provisions may be found in the 1957 European Convention for the Peaceful Settlement of Disputes (Article 31(3)), and in the 1964 Protocol of the Organization of African Unity relating to the Establishment of the Commission of Mediation, Conciliation and Arbitration, Article 15 ("Member States shall refrain from any act or omission that is likely to aggravate a situation which has been referred to the Commission.").

Obligation to Negotiate

The duty to negotiate appears not only in Article 33 of the UN Charter, but is also a preliminary condition for submitting a dispute to other methods of dispute resolution. For instance, the 1928/1949 Geneva General Act for the Pacific Settlement of International Disputes can be resorted to only in a dispute "which it has not been possible to settle by diplomacy" (Article 1). Similarly, the American Treaty for Pacific Settlement (Pact of Bogotá) applies only to a controversy which "cannot be settled by direct negotiations through the usual diplomatic channels" (Article 2(2)); the 1932 conciliation convention between France and the Soviet Union is restricted to disputes "which it may not have been possible to settle through the diplomatic channel" (Article 1); and the 1928 arbitration treaty between France and the United States applies only "when ordinary diplomatic proceedings have failed" (Article 1).

THE DUTY TO EXCHANGE VIEWS REGARDING SETTLEMENT PROCEDURES

This duty is most clearly stated in Article 283 of the 1982 UN Convention on the Law of the Sea, which reads as follows:

> 1. When a dispute arises between States Parties concerning the interpretation or application of this Convention, the parties to the dispute shall proceed expeditiously to an exchange of views regarding its settlement by negotiation or other peaceful means.
>
> 2. The parties shall also proceed expeditiously to an exchange of views where a procedure for the settlement of such a dispute has been terminated without a settlement or where a settlement has been reached and the circumstances require consultation regarding the manner of implementing the settlement.

OBLIGATION NOT TO START CONCURRENT PROCEEDINGS

Article 4 of the 1948 American Treaty for Pacific Settlement (Pact of Bogotá) provides explicitly that:

> Once any pacific procedure has been initiated, whether by agreement of the parties or in fulfillment of the present Treaty or a previous pact, no other procedure may be commenced until that procedure is concluded.

On the other hand, the 1982 UN Convention on the Law of the Sea safeguards the right of the parties to settle the dispute even when some other procedure is in full swing, or to agree together to submit it to another procedure which may be more appropriate for the settlement of the dispute. Its Article 280 provides that:

> Nothing in this Part impairs the right of any States Parties to agree at any time to settle a dispute between them concerning the interpretation or application of this Convention by any peaceful means of their own choice.

Obligation to Notify and Consult

This obligation is most common in agreements on economic matters. For instance, the 1977 General Agreement on Tariffs and Trade (GATT) provides in Article 22(1) that:

> Each contracting party shall accord sympathetic consideration to, and shall afford adequate opportunity for consultation regarding such representations as may be made by another contracting party with respect to any matter affecting the operation of this Agreement.

Elaborate procedures were developed later to implement this provision, and special panels are often established to facilitate the consultations.

Similarly, the 1988 Free Trade Agreement between the United States and Canada provides for a joint commission to resolve disputes that may arise over the agreement's interpretation or application, and "to consider any other matter that may affect its operations." To facilitate this task, the agreement establishes a system of notification by each party of any proposed or actual measure that might materially affect the operation of the agreement, and for a system of consultations for arriving at a mutually satisfactory solution.

A 1989 agreement between the European Community and the Soviet Union relating to trade and commercial and economic cooperation established a joint committee empowered to "seek appropriate means of avoiding possible difficulties in the fields of trade and cooperation," and to "formulate and submit to the authorities of the Contracting Parties recommendations for solving any problems that arise."

A survey of other recent agreements on a variety of subjects would disclose many versions, less or more elaborate, of such provisions for structured consultations within the framework of a joint commission. This has become a favored method for preventing the escalation of a dispute, conflict or crisis.

C. Positions of States at International Negotiations Dealing with the Drafting of New International Treaties

Many bilateral treaties on the settlement of international disputes, providing usually for conciliation, arbitration, and reference to the Permanent Court of International Justice, were concluded between 1928 and 1948. After the Second World War, however, this trend diminished and only a few such treaties were concluded. Instead, a variety of dispute resolution clauses was included in agreements dealing with many subjects, but each such "compromisory" clause was limited to the interpretation or application of a particular treaty. Multipartite treaties often allow reservations to such clauses; in later years these clauses became optional, requiring a separate acceptance declaration.

A breakthrough came in the 1982 UN Convention on the Law of the Sea, which provides obligatory jurisdiction over most disputes under that convention. The only concession was to allow a state to select the tribunal it prefers, subject to being obliged in any case to go to arbitration if it had not made a choice, or if the choices of the two parties should differ.

In recent years, while some new states have accepted the obligatory jurisdiction of the International Court of Justice, others have terminated their acceptance. Some new attempts are being made at present to remedy this situation.

D. Declarations and Statements by States

Some joint Soviet and United States statements have been made expressing willingness to accept the jurisdiction of the International Court of Justice with respect to the interpretation or application of certain treaties. The Soviet Union has actually notified the United Nations that it withdraws reservations to the Court's jurisdiction to interpret several treaties. The Soviet Union has also presented to the United Nations a proposal to prepare a general treaty containing eight basic obligations for the settlement of disputes, some of which parallel the principles stated in Section (A) of this chapter.

E. Resolutions of the UN General Assembly

The General Assembly has adopted by consensus several important declarations relating to the settlement of disputes of which the most important is the section on the settlement of international disputes of the 1970 Declaration on Principles of International Law Concerning Friendly Relations and Co-operation Among States in Accordance with the Charter of the United Nations. The importance of that Declaration was emphasized by the Court in the *Nicaragua v. United States* case.

This declaration was followed in 1982 by the Manila Declaration on the Peaceful Settlement of International Disputes (General Assembly Resolution 37/10), which contained, *inter alia*, thirteen basic state obligations in that area; and in 1988 by the Declaration on the Prevention and Removal of Disputes and Situations Which May Threaten International Peace and Security, which, in addition to stating several principles, contained recommendations for enhancing the role of the Security Council and the General Assembly in the resolution of disputes.

All three instruments restate, with some variations, the principles outlined in section (A) of this chapter.

F. Conclusions

The principles listed in Section (A) above and the treaties and official statements supporting them, listed in Sections (B) to (E) of this chapter, cover most basic issues and the only thing that is needed is to codify them in one comprehensive convention on the subject.

In view of space limitations, this chapter has not dealt with the problems of enhancing the role of various international institutions and the problems of their jurisdiction. It deals only incidentally with the issue of preventing disputes and their escalation, as this is also an area where institutional arrangements rather than principles are needed. Nevertheless, as such arrangements are very important in the international economic area, it might be useful to call attention to proposals to establish joint committees of government experts, with strong binational secretariats, that would for each pair of states:

(a) monitor on a continuing basis the trade relations between the two states;

(b) bring to the attention of their Governments as early as possible any emergent disputes;

(c) suggest to them the steps that may be taken to prevent the further deterioration of the situation;

(d) recommend the best means for dealing with a particular dispute;

(e) maintain rosters of experts acceptable to both Governments from which members of fact-finding groups, mediators or conciliators may be chosen, and to assist the two Governments in selecting from these rosters the most appropriate persons for the settlement of a particular dispute or group of disputes;

(f) to assist the two Governments in reviewing the recommendations of the group of experts to which a particular dispute or group of disputes was referred;

(g) to prepare proposals for long-range solutions that would diminish the chances of a recurrence of particular categories of disputes; and

(h) to make recommendations for improving the means for settling future disputes.

S.A. Yegorov
Docent and Deputy Head of Department,
USSR Diplomatic Academy

The terms "international conflict" and "international crisis" are generally used to designate differences between states that present a threat to international peace and security. To date neither international law doctrine nor treaty law practice have elaborated a generally recognized uniform definition of the above terms. This is a fairly complicated task, inasmuch as an actual international conflict possesses an extremely broad spectrum of attributes and properties of an economic, social, political, ideological, diplomatic, military, and international legal nature.

From the standpoint of international law, an international conflict can be viewed as a special political-legal relationship between two or more parties to international law (for the most part states), which reproduces in a concentrated and acute form the social conflicts and legal relations underlying this relationship.

International political crisis should be defined as a special phase in the development of a current international conflict, attended by the threat of escalation into armed struggle by the parties in conflict. This is essentially that same political-legal relationship as other conflicts, but it has reached the highest political level in its development as a consequence of a sharp aggravation of the struggle between the parties to the conflict. A crisis may encompass the relations of the immediate parties to the conflict, states of a specific region, states of different regions, and major world powers. It can become worldwide in scale and consequences. A state of crisis signifies a turning point in the course of a conflict. In certain circumstances it may be followed by a phase of conscious shift by one of the parties to practical use of military force for the purpose of satisfying its interests.

Every conflict can lead to a crisis. A crisis may pass, however, but an international conflict may remain, in an open or latent state, and may repeatedly give rise to similar crises. In practice the relationship between an international conflict and an international crisis is a relationship between the whole and a part. For this reason one cannot equate an international conflict with an international crisis and view them as phenomena of the same scale. In our view both too broad and too narrow approaches to interpretation of this sociopolitical phenomenon are impermissible in defining the term "international conflict."

While the terms "international conflict" and "crisis" are used most frequently within the context of political science studies of disagreements between states, utilization of such categories as situation and dispute is typical primarily of international law analysis of such differences.

The concept of an international situation that can lead to friction or cause a dispute, as well as that of a situation that can threaten the maintenance of international peace and security, first appeared in the UN Charter. At the UN Conference in San Francisco, the words "or situations" were appended to the word "disputes" in amendments by the Big Four powers to proposals pertaining to establishment of a general international security organization, proposals drawn up at the Dumbarton Oaks Conference. The report of the First Committee of the First Commission stated that if the word "adjustment" were to be retained in the draft UN Charter in addition to the word "settlement" (of disputes), the word "situation," as a broader term, should be added to the word "disputes."

The word "situation" is contained in a number of Articles of the UN Charter (Articles 11(3), 14, and 40). A number of Articles contain the words "dispute and situation" (Articles 1(1), 12, 34, 35(1), and 36(1)). At the same time there is no definition of the terms "dispute" and "situation" in the UN Charter. This does not provide sufficient basis for the clear-cut delineation and analysis of those Articles of the Charter in which these terms appear.

According to international law doctrine, a dispute occurs when states mutually present claims against one another pertaining to one and the same object of dispute. In a situation there occurs a clash of interests of states, but it is not accompanied by mutually declared claims, although it does evoke friction between them. "Situation" is a broader term than "dispute." Any dispute between states can create a situation, but not every situation constitutes a dispute. A situation may give rise to a dispute, but it may also not lead to a dispute. A common attribute that characterizes both a dispute and a situation is a clash of interests of states that engenders international friction.

Two kinds of disputes and situations are differentiated: disputes and situations the continuation of which threatens international peace and security, and disputes and situations the continuation of which does not involve such a threat. In light of UN goals it is more important to settle disputes and resolve situations of the former type, while at the same time within the context of these same goals any and all disputes and situations should be resolved, for disputes and situations that do not threaten international peace and security nevertheless engender international friction. The existence of such friction impedes the development of friendly relations and mutually beneficial cooperation between states and complicates the process of establishment of comprehensive international security.

The UN Charter does not establish criteria for dividing disputes and situations into the two categories stated above. Determination of this matter comes under the jurisdiction of the Security Council. According to Article 34 of the Charter,

> The Security Council may investigate any dispute, or any situation which might lead to international friction or give rise to a dispute, in order to determine whether the continuance of the dispute or situation is likely to endanger the maintenance of peace and security.

Nor has UN practice worked out general criteria for dividing disputes and situations into the above categories. This complex problem has not been satisfactorily resolved primarily because the question of whether or not a dispute or situation constitutes a threat to international peace and security is determined by the specific circumstances of each specific dispute, and also depends to a considerable degree on the character of the foreign policy of the disputing parties or parties drawn into the situation.

In any case it would seem indisputable that the principle of peaceful resolution of international disputes applies to all international disputes and situations, regardless of whether or not they threaten international peace and security. At the same time one must bear in mind the following legal consequences proceeding from the difference between the terms "dispute" and "situation."

First, removal of permanent members of the Security Council from participation in voting on the basis of Article 27(3) of the UN Charter, which prescribes that "in decisions under Chapter VI, and under paragraph 3 of Article 52, a party to a dispute shall abstain from voting," applies only to disputes and not to situations.

Second, while according to Article 36(1) of the UN Charter the Security Council may recommend a procedure or methods of settling both a dispute and a situation, in accordance with the precise meaning of Articles 37 and 38 the Security Council may recommend the conditions or terms for settlement only of a dispute, and not a situation.

Third, a matter can be turned over to the UN International Court of Justice on the basis of Article 36(3) also only in the case of disputes, and not in the case of situations.

International disputes are extremely diversified and can be classified according to various criteria: by the object or subject of the dispute, by the degree of threat to international peace, and by whether they are regional or global, bilateral or multilateral. International dispute as a category under international law has been formally articulated in numerous multilateral and bilateral agreements. The UN Charter prescribes certain procedures for settling certain types of dispute, including "any dispute, the continuance of which is likely to endanger the maintenance of international peace and security" (Article 33); "international disputes" (Article 2(3)); "any disputes," that is, according to the meaning of Chapter VI of the UN Charter, disputes which do not constitute a direct threat to international peace (Article 38); "local disputes" (Article 52); "legal disputes" (Article 36); and "legal disputes" (Article 36 of the Statute of the International Court of Justice).

The UN Charter does not contain an expanded definition of the term "international dispute," a statement of the content of the above-mentioned categories of disputes, or a clear delineation between legal and political disputes. At the same time, Article 36(2) of the Statute of the International Court of Justice contains a list of criteria that give an idea of how one should define disputes of a legal nature. According to this provision of the Statute, disputes pertaining to the following constitute legal disputes coming under the jurisdiction of the UN International Court of Justice:

a. the interpretation of a treaty;
b. any question of international law;
c. the existence of any fact which, if established, would constitute a breach of an international obligation;
d. the nature or extent of the reparation to be made for the breach of an international obligation.

A special place among the great diversity of international disputes is occupied by territorial disputes (that is, disputes over the location of a boundary line and ownership of a specific piece of territory), which are often attended by dangerous political crises and armed conflicts.

The principle of peaceful resolution of international disputes has been established in modern international law and is generally recognized. According to this principle all international disputes should be resolved solely and exclusively by peaceful means. In other words states are not entitled to resort to any other means and methods of resolving disputes which arise between them than peaceful means.

The emergence of this principle and its acquisition of specific legal content has gone through several stages.

The first steps in the direction of limiting the right of states to war were undertaken in the course of the 1899 and 1907 Hague Peace Conferences, at which a Convention for the Pacific Settlement of International Disputes was adopted. The General Protocol on the Pacific Resolution of International Disputes, drawn up by the League of Nations in 1924, stated that war of aggression constitutes an international crime and that:

> If it has refused to submit the dispute to the procedure of pacific settlement provided by articles 13 and 15 of the Covenant as amplified by the present Protocol, or to comply with a judicial sentence or an arbitral award or with a unanimous recommendation of the Council,

any State shall be presumed to be an aggressor. (Article 10). A resolution of the Sixth Inter-American Conference of 1928 stated that: "War of aggression constitutes an international crime against the human species" and that "the American States will employ all pacific means to settle conflicts which may arise between them." From the mid-1920's the Soviet Union began concluding treaties of nonaggression and conciliation procedure with states of West and East, treaties which prescribed mandatory peaceful resolution of disputes. A Treaty of Nonaggression and Neutrality with Germany was concluded in 1926, for example, and a Treaty of Guarantee and Neutrality with Persia in 1927.

The next step toward recognition of the principle of peaceful resolution of international disputes as a generally recognized principle was adoption in 1928 of the Paris Treaty Providing for the Renunciation of War as an Instrument of National Policy. Article 2 of this Treaty clearly stated:

> The High Contracting Parties agree that the settlement or solution of all disputes or conflicts of whatever nature or of whatever origin they may be, which may arise among them, shall never be sought except by pacific means.

We should note that this Treaty is one of the few international legal documents in which dispute and conflict are used, in our opinion, as synonymous terms. It would seem that conflict thereby also encompasses the phase of armed struggle.

In the UN Charter the principle of peaceful settlement of international disputes was raised to a new and higher level as one of the fundamental principles of modern international law. Subsequently the content of this principle was set forth in detail in the 1970 Declaration of Principles of International Law and the 1975 Final Act of the Conference on Security and Cooperation in Europe.

The adoption by the UN General Assembly in 1982 of the Manila Declaration on Peaceful Settlement of International Disputes and in 1988 the Declaration on Prevention and Removal of Disputes and Situations Which May Threaten International Peace and Security and on the Role of the United Nations in this Field were of considerable significance for affirmation of the principle of peaceful resolution of international disputes in the practice of international relations.

Both documents, recognizing the fundamental responsibility of states for preventing and settling disputes and situations, at the same time emphasize the important role that the UN and its agencies can play in this regard. It is noted that strengthening of this role of the UN will increase its effectiveness in resolving matters of maintaining international peace and security. An important feature of the 1988 Declaration is the fact that it contains provisions dealing not only with settlement but also prevention of disputes continuation of which may threaten the maintenance of international peace and security, as well as provisions that define the corresponding mechanism of cooperation of states at the regional and universal levels.

According to Soviet international law doctrine, the following body of rights and obligations of states party to a dispute constitutes the legal basis of the principle of peaceful resolution of international disputes.

States are obligated to resolve their disputes exclusively by peaceful means. The 1970 Declaration of Principles of International Law states: "Every State has the duty to refrain from the threat or use of force . . . as a means of solving international disputes, including territorial disputes and problems concerning frontiers of States." The 1975 Final Act of the Conference on Security and Cooperation in Europe states: "No . . . threat or use of force will be employed as a means of settling disputes, or questions likely to give rise to disputes, between them." A demand that exclusively peaceful means be used is contained in a number of other documents of recent years, both of a legally binding and moral-political nature.

States shall not leave their international disputes unresolved. This provision signifies the obligation, first of all, to resolve an international dispute at the earliest possible time and, second, to continue searching for ways to reach a settlement if a method of settlement of a dispute that was mutually agreed upon by the parties to the dispute has failed to produce the desired result. Resolution of an international dispute at the earliest possible time (the Final Act of the Conference on Security and Cooperation in Europe, in particular, speaks of "rapid" settlement of a dispute) should be understood to mean strict observance of a mutually agreed time frame for settlement. In connection with this, a time frame for submitting disputes for settlement prescribed by some multilateral and bilateral agreements places on the parties to the dispute the obligation not to limit themselves to any one means or procedure of peaceful settlement of the dispute, but also to use other means as well if the dispute has not been resolved by the originally selected method.

States are obligated to refrain from actions that would aggravate a dispute between them. In this case it is primarily a question of the need to refrain from actions that could impede settlement of a dispute, create a threat to maintenance of international peace and security, or alter the present situation in favor of one of the parties to the dispute and thus do detriment to the interests of the other party.

States are obligated to settle their disputes on the basis of international law and justice. This demand presumes application of the fundamental principles of international law as well as corresponding norms of contract law and customary law in the process of resolving disputes. According to

Article 38 of the Statute of the International Court of Justice, settlement of disputes on the basis of international law involves application of: a) international conventions, whether general or particular, establishing rules expressly recognized by the contesting states; b) international custom, as evidence of a general practice accepted as law; c) the general principles of law recognized by civilized nations; and d) judicial decisions and the teachings of the most highly qualified publicists of the various nations, as subsidiary means for the determination of rules of law. Article 38 of the Statute also prescribes that the obligation of the Court to settle disputes on the basis of international law shall not prejudice its power to decide a case *ex aequo et bono* if the parties agree thereto.

States have a right freely to choose a specific means of peaceful settlement. This right proceeds from the principles of sovereign equality and noninterference in the internal and external affairs of independent states. At the same time, however, this right does not exclude the possibility of states to express agreement in advance to mandatory application of specific settlement procedures.

A listing of generally recognized means of peaceful settlement of international disputes is to be found in Article 33 of the UN Charter, according to which states are obligated to endeavor to resolve their disputes by means of "negotiation, enquiry, mediation, conciliation, arbitration, judicial settlement, resort to regional agencies or arrangements, or other peaceful means of their own choice." Thus this is not an exhaustive list.

Soviet international law doctrine and diplomatic practice give precedence to negotiations, viewing them as the simplest, most flexible, and most effective means of peaceful settlement of disputes and conflicts. This is due, in particular, to the fact that the specific goals, makeup of participants, level, forms, and other procedural matters pertaining to the conduct of negotiations are determined by the parties to the dispute themselves. The results of negotiations can be either resolution of the dispute on its substance, or reaching of a formal understanding on employment of another peaceful means of resolving the dispute.

Consultations as a means of peaceful resolution of disputes began to be particularly actively utilized by states in the period following World War II. This institution found embodiment in numerous bilateral and multilateral agreements. Parties resorting to consultations can determine in advance the frequency of meetings and can establish consultative commissions. Consultations can ensure a search for compromise solutions by the parties to a dispute and stable contacts between them, as well as the implementation of agreements reached on preventing the occurrence of future disputes and crisis situations.

Good offices constitute actions by a party not involved in the dispute (for example, states or international organizations), for the purpose of establishing direct contacts between the disputants. Good offices may be rendered both in response to a corresponding request on the part of direct parties to a dispute and at the initiative of the third party. The offer of good offices should not be viewed by the parties to a dispute as an unfriendly act. The party offering the good offices does not take direct part in negotiations to settle a dispute. Good offices frequently develop into mediation. In contrast to good offices, mediation presumes more active participation by the third party in resolving the dispute. Taking part in bringing the disputants to an agreement through the negotiations in which they are taking part, the mediator's job is to help work out a resolution to the dispute that is acceptable to the parties. He is entitled to propose possible solutions. The mediator's proposals, however, are not obligatory on the disputing parties. Detailed regulation of the procedure of rendering good offices and performing mediation is contained in the 1899 and 1907 Hague Conventions for the Pacific Settlement of International Disputes.

Commissions of inquiry and conciliation commissions are a variation of international conciliation procedure. Such commissions may be established by the disputing parties both with and without enlisting representatives of a third party. The job of commissions of inquiry is to investigate and determine the actual facts of a dispute. The activities of conciliation commissions are directed toward working out an acceptable solution on the substance of a dispute. The final documents of both commissions are of a recommendatory nature for the parties to a dispute. The establishment and activities of such commissions are regulated by a number of multilateral and bilateral agreements.

International arbitration is one of the oldest means of peaceful resolution of international disputes, consisting of submitting a dispute, by the agreement of the parties, for adjudication by a third party, whose decision is final and binding on the parties to the dispute. The legally binding force of the decision is the main element that distinguishes arbitration from all the above-mentioned means of peaceful settlement of disputes and conflicts. An individual arbitrator, a group of arbitrators from third countries, or a group of arbitrators on a parity basis from the states parties to the dispute or conflict, with a neutral chairman (the chief arbitrator)—may function as third party. The parties to the dispute themselves determine the jurisdiction of arbitration, limiting it to the object of their dispute. Legal enactments regulating the conditions and procedure of international arbitration include, in particular, the above-mentioned Hague Conventions of 1899 and 1907, the 1928 General Act for the Pacific Settlement of International Disputes, revised by the UN General Assembly in 1949, the draft regulations on the arbitration process adopted by the Commission on International Law in 1958, the 1948 Bogotá Pact, *etc.*

Court adjudication is basically similar to arbitration proceedings. The difference between arbitration and an international court consists mainly in the procedure of its establishment and pertains chiefly to the method of formation, numerical makeup of the court, *etc.* The main similarity between a court and arbitration is the finality of the decision and its binding force on the parties to the dispute. The International Court of Justice is the principal judicial body of the international community today. Its activities are carried out on the basis of its Statute, which is an integral component part of the UN Charter, as well as in conformity with the rules of the International Court of Justice. The existence of the International Court of Justice, however, does not exclude the possibility of establishment of special international courts on the basis of appropriate agreements. In recent years the Soviet Union has advocated more effective utilization of the possibilities of the International Court of Justice and acknowledgment by all of its mandatory jurisdiction on mutually agreed-upon conditions. The Soviet Union recently recognized the Court's binding jurisdiction regarding the interpretation and application of a number of agreements in the area of human rights. Previously the Soviet Union had recognized the binding jurisdiction of an arbitral tribunal or a court with respect to a number of specific international treaties. In the opinion of the Soviet Union, the General Assembly and Security Council could have turned more frequently to the International Court of Justice for advisory opinions on debatable international legal issues. In September 1989 the USSR Minister of Foreign Affairs and the U.S. Secretary of State approved a working document entitled "Mutually Acceptable Conditions Pertaining to Recognition of the Jurisdiction of the United Nations International Court of Justice" and agreed to propose to the three other permanent members of the UN Security Council that this issue be discussed.

Regional bodies and agreements are also important instruments of settlement of international disputes and conflicts. Resolution of international disputes by regional international organizations such as, for example, the Organization of African Unity (OAU), the Arab League (AL), and the Organization of American States (OAS), is done in conformity with the normative documents on which the activities of these organizations are grounded. As regards the United Nations, within this organization, in addition to the International Court of Justice, the General Assembly and Security Council also have jurisdiction in the area of peaceful settlement of international disputes.

As already noted, adoption of the Final Act of the 1975 Conference on Security and Cooperation in Europe, the 1970 Declaration of Principles of International Law, the 1982 Manila Declaration, as well as the 1988

Declaration on Prevention and Removal of Disputes and Situations Which May Threaten International Peace and Security and on the Role of the United Nations in This Field contributed to further development of the content (that is, the aggregate of rights and obligations of parties to international law) of the principle of peaceful resolution of international disputes, set forth in the most general form in Article 2(3) of the UN Charter.

Of all the documents enumerated above, however, only the 1975 Final Act, in the portion pertaining to principles, can be viewed as a source of international law. One should bear in mind thereby that this document is not equivalent to an international treaty, has a limited sphere of application as regards number of parties, and is valid only for the European states that signed it, plus the United States and Canada. As for the other documents, in spite of all their great moral and political significance for the international community, constituting declarations of the UN General Assembly, they are only of a recommendatory nature and are not legally binding on states.

In light of the new political thinking, the concept of the principle of peaceful resolution of international disputes requires further development by means of drafting and adoption, both at the universal and at the regional level, of legal provisions articulating more specifically the corresponding aggregate of rights and obligations of states that define the linkage between the principle in question and other generally recognized principles of international law. The Soviet Memorandum on Enhancement of the Role of International Law, dated September 29, 1989, notes the need for formulation and adoption of a universal and comprehensive international legal enactment in which the principle of peaceful resolution of disputes would be further developed and made more specific.

The mechanism of implementation of this principle also requires further improvement. Such a mechanism presently exists in the form of a system of international legal means of peaceful settlement of disputes, prescribed in particular in the UN Charter.

A leading role within the system of means of peaceful settlement of disputes should obviously continue to be played by negotiations, since the realities of today's world demand that one should count on the internationalization of dialogue and the negotiating process. Such a variation of negotiations as consultations should take on particular significance thereby (primarily at the regional level). A proposal calling for adoption of a procedure of mandatory consultations by the European states, as well as by the United States and Canada, presented in the 1970's by a number of East European countries, would appear to be fruitful in this regard. This procedure would make it possible to use the dual function of consultations: as an independent means and, at the same time, depending on circumstances, as a means of promoting agreement by parties to a dispute to use other means of settlement.

In view of the fact that over the course of many years inadequate attention was devoted in the Soviet Union, in contrast to a number of capitalist countries, to problems of settlement of conflict situations at the theoretical and practical level, it is valid to raise the question of formulation of an orderly theory of international negotiations. Of practical and theoretical interest is the conclusion reached by Soviet scholars that the effectiveness of negotiation as a means of settling international disputes and conflicts will become considerably greater if negotiation is grounded on the principle of problem resolution, not on the principle of maximizing gain.

Also meriting attention is the idea of establishing an all-European agency for settling international disputes, such as a commission of inquiry, mediation, and conciliation, to which all disputes would be mandatorily given over at the unilateral request of a party to the dispute in question if that party, once again unilaterally, considers that all means of settlement have been exhausted. As for the decisions of such a body, it would be best to make them of a recommendatory nature.

The idea of establishing regional judicial procedures for considering and resolving disputes could be implemented in a similar manner. The states of a region could, on mutually agreed-upon terms and conditions, recognize the jurisdiction of such courts as mandatory. This also applies to the arbitration procedure of considering disputes.

The accomplishment of the task of preventing the occurrence of conflicts depends to a significant degree on the development of cooperation between states. Various confidence-building measures adopted on a bilateral and on a regional level, such as demilitarized zones and international monitoring and verification, serve this same goal. This would make it possible to possess an objective picture of events that are occurring, to detect preparations for military operations in a prompt and timely manner, to hinder surprise attack, to take measures to prevent a military conflict, and to prevent its spread and aggravation. The institution of UN military observers and UN peacekeeping forces should be more extensively utilized for the purpose of separating the troops of quarreling parties and maintaining observation of cease-fires and truce agreements.

Nongovernmental commissions and groups should be more extensively enlisted to analyze the causes, circumstances, and methods of settling various specific conflicts.

Sending of special UN Security Council missions to areas of current and potential conflicts would help strengthen the authority of the Security Council and increase the effectiveness of its decisions.

It is essential to make every effort to encourage and assist the UN

Secretary General in his performance of missions pertaining to good offices, mediation, or conciliation.

UN cooperation with regional organizations should be substantially expanded in order to seek ways of political settlement of crisis situations and regional conflicts.

Soviet legal scholars note that various legal-procedural consequences for parties to a dispute or conflict, beginning with the reaching of agreement on specific means of peaceful settlement, correspond to general substantive-legal obligations pertaining to peaceful resolution of international disputes and conflicts. Further improvement of procedural regulation of the application of peaceful settlement mechanisms is one of the most important ways to heighten its effectiveness. This is particularly important in connection with the task of settling so-called internationalized internal conflicts.

Thus the contemporary system of peaceful settlement of international disputes and conflicts constitutes an aggregate of substantive and procedural norms of international law. Effective operation of this system can be ensured only as a result of proper application of the law and progressive development of the above-stated norms, taking into account the specific features of the present stage of development of international relations, which requires a new political and legal approach to resolving the problem of maintaining international peace and security.

3. THE PRINCIPLES OF COOPERATION AND GOOD FAITH FULFILLMENT OF INTERNATIONAL OBLIGATIONS

William D. Jackson
Professor of Political Science, Miami University

The obligation that states have to obey established rules of international law is the most basic obligation of states under international law. This fundamental norm constitutes the *sine qua non* for effective international law. It reflects and gives legal expression to the common interest shared by all states in an effective international law system. The duty of states to fulfill in good faith international obligations has been extensively affirmed in the practice of states and in a large number of multilateral treaties, as well as in resolutions and declarations of the UN General Assembly. As the Declaration of Principles of International Law, adopted by consensus by the UN General Assembly in 1970, affirms, "Every State has the duty to fulfill in good faith its obligations under the generally recognized principles and rules of international law."

The duty to fulfill obligations that derive from treaties in force and generally recognized principles of international law is limited only insofar as it binds states to fulfill an existing body of law. In the latter half of this century evidence has accumulated to support the view that the general obligation of a state under international law extends beyond good faith observance of existing norms to include an obligation to cooperate with other states and international institutions with respect to the achievement of certain purposes, goals, and conditions, which include, but are not limited to, the further development of international law. On the basis of the present evidence, however, one cannot claim that states have a general and non-specific duty to cooperate, although a basis for such a contention could be found in earlier natural law approaches to deriving the duties of states. But even within the confines of modern positive law, evidence of more specific duties to cooperate can be found. The scope and extent of a state's duty to cooperate is likely to be further clarified as a result of the future practice of states, the evolution of *opinio juris*, and changes in both objective global conditions and the subjective recognition of areas of human activity that involve the principle of "common heritage," or forms of interdependence among states that require cooperative approaches.

At the present stage of the development of international law, however, one may suggest that states have implicitly, as well as explicitly in specific treaty commitments, acknowledged duties to cooperate with respect to realms of international activity of considerable scope. Members of the United Nations have accepted such obligations by virtue of their consent to membership in an organization with the declared purpose (in Article 1 of the Charter) "[t]o develop friendly relations among nations" and:

> [t]o achieve international co-operation in solving international problems of an economic, social, cultural or humanitarian character, and in promoting and encouraging respect for human rights and fundamental freedoms for all . . . .

A more specific obligation to cooperate is entailed in a member's commitment under Article 2(3) to "settle their international disputes by peaceful means in such a manner that international peace and security, and justice, are not endangered." Members also consent to act cooperatively insofar as they agree to give the organization "every assistance" in carrying out actions taken by the United Nations in accordance with its Charter (Article 2(5)), and in implementing decisions of the Security Council (Article 25). A further broad obligation is present in Article 56, by which members pledge to take "joint and separate action in cooperation with the Organization" with respect to the activities set out in Article 55. The latter include the promotion of:

> a. higher standards of living,
>
> b. solutions of international economic, social, health, and related problems; and international cultural and educational cooperation; and
>
> c. universal respect for, and observance of, human rights and fundamental freedoms for all . . . .

The view that these provisions of the Charter are only declarative and do not entail the acceptance of obligations to cooperate is all the more difficult to sustain in view of the fact that promoting cooperation with respect to the settlement of disputes, economic, social, and cultural subjects, and advancing universal respect for human rights constitute the declared fundamental purposes of the United Nations. Further affirmation that acceptance of the UN Charter involves acceptance of duties to cooperate can be found in the 1970 UN Declaration on Principles of International Law. According to that instrument,

> States have the duty to cooperate with one another, irrespective of the differences in their political, economic and social systems . . . in order to maintain international peace and security and

to promote international economic stability and progress, the general welfare of nations . . . .

In terms of the contribution that the development of contemporary international law can make to the strengthening of international security, the general acknowledgment by states of a duty to cooperate in the maintenance of international peace and security represents the emergence of an important new standard. The further affirmation and elaboration of this principle in instruments such as the 1975 Helsinki Accords, for example, reflects and encourages the growing expectations on the part of governments and the international community in general both that states involved in international conflicts or in situations that pose a threat to international peace and security have an obligation to undertake active diplomatic and political efforts to cooperate to strengthen international security, and that a general obligation exists to undertake cooperative approaches in the fields of economics and human rights.

Although cooperation with other states was once wholly discretionary, such is no longer the case. But if the principle of cooperation is to attain a more than general and largely symbolic significance in international relations, its further clarification and elaboration will have to be achieved. Clearer delineation of the types of actions and policies that violate the duty to cooperate with respect to the maintenance of international peace and security would be desirable. In particular, it would constitute a positive evolution in community standards to develop a norm that a state's persistent refusal to participate in negotiations endorsed by appropriate bodies of the United Nations for the strengthening of international security is a violation of that state's duty to cooperate in the maintenance of international peace. Similarly, it would represent a valuable achievement to develop a norm that refusal by a state to take part in diplomatic negotiations with respect to arms control and disarmament objectives endorsed by the United Nations constitutes a failure to meet a duty to cooperate. Beyond such potentially constructive elaborations on the meaning of the duty of a state to cooperate with the United Nations and other states in the maintenance of international peace and security, it also may be desirable to encourage the emergence in contemporary international law of other standards of cooperative behavior with respect to the maintenance of international peace. These would include, *inter alia*:

1) an obligation, under a state's general duty to cooperate and apart from specific treaty requirements, to give advance notification of missile test launches;

2) an obligation under general international law applicable to all states to give advance notification of military maneuvers, movements, or exercises of a significant scale;

3) an obligation to act with due regard for the encourage-

ment of compliance by all states with the Charter's prohibition of the aggressive use or threat of the use of military force when transferring weapons or weapons technology to other states; and

4) an obligation on the part of all states to cooperate in the maintenance of international peace and security through the rejection of offensive military doctrines and force structures.

Although the evolution in such directions of international legal norms and community expectations regarding the appropriate behavior of states would represent a desirable advance, only the enlightened legal practice of states in developing and affirming the meaning of the principle of cooperation with respect to the strengthening of international peace and security can effect the progress of international law in this direction.

John Norton Moore
Walter L. Brown Professor of Law, University of Virginia

Robert F. Turner
Associate Director, University of Virginia Center for National Security Law

A. Introduction

At the root of many of the difficulties hindering Soviet-U.S. relations in past years have been fundamentally conflicting perspectives on issues of world order, the rule of law, and the nature and role of the State–including respect for the rights of individuals. While some differences will inevitably remain, recent developments in Soviet-U.S. relations resulting from new trends in Soviet political thinking hold great promise for promoting a further relaxation of tensions, improved understanding, cooperation, and, ultimately, a revitalized relationship based upon mutual respect, reciprocity, and the rule of law. It is still too early to project the detailed outcome of the revolutionary struggle now underway in the Soviet Union, which is itself fundamentally premised on the centrality of democratic institutions and the rule of law; but it is not premature to examine the great benefits which the rule of law offers to both sides in their future relations.

B. Bases of Obligations of International Law

Relations between and among States are governed, in general, by rules and principles established by treaty and by customary international law. Arguably the most fundamental of all such principles is the maxim *pacta sunt servanda* ("agreements are to be obeyed"), which reflects the obligatory nature of the modern international system.

Treaties and other international agreements provide a major source of international obligation. Thus, such landmark instruments as the 1928 Kellogg-Briand "Pact of Paris" and the 1945 UN Charter established clearly and unequivocally the cardinal legal principle that aggressive uses of force are unlawful. Since 1945 more than 30,000 treaties—more than 2,000 of which involved more than two State parties—have been registered with the United Nations. These agreements regulate virtually every facet of international behavior: providing rules for governing treaty relations and "rules of the road" for aircraft and ships engaged in international commerce, allocating oceans jurisdiction, assigning frequencies and establishing standards for international telecommunications, clarifying the rights of diplomats, providing regimes for the control of armaments, establishing critically important human rights standards, and much more.

International conventions, of course, are not the only basis of international legal obligation. State practice, for example—when accompanied by broad community acceptance that such practice constitutes legal obligation (*opinio juris*)—will also create binding rights and duties. Such rules of "customary international law" are as basic to the international legal system as treaty obligations themselves. Moreover, they may also be heavily influenced by broadly accepted treaty obligations, such as the UN Charter or the Vienna Convention on the Law of Treaties.

Thus, a norm may exist in both treaty and custom. Today, for example, it is widely recognized that the prohibition against the use of aggressive force is legally binding even upon countries which have failed to ratify the UN Charter or other treaties expressly prohibiting such conduct.

Certain legal norms are of such fundamental importance that they are held by the world community to be binding upon all States and permit of no derogation. In addition to the prohibition against the aggressive use of force, embodied in Article 2(4) of the UN Charter, examples include the prohibitions against genocide, slavery, torture, and certain other fundamental standards of international human rights. Often referred to by the Latin term *jus cogens*, these "peremptory norms" of international law are binding upon all States; and their violation is viewed as an offense against all nations.

While international conventions and custom are the most important sources of legal obligation, they are not the only sources. The Statute of the International Court of Justice, for example, provides that its judges may also consider "the general principles of law recognized by civilized nations" and, as a subsidiary means, "judicial decisions and the teachings of the most highly qualified publicists of the various nations . . . ."

Quite apart from the sources of law, several bodies of law seem particularly important for the future of Soviet-U.S. relations and, indeed, for world order generally. Most central of these is the UN Charter and its aforementioned prohibition against aggressive attack. If these two great nations can join in standing firmly against aggression—as is illustrated by the position of the Soviet Union and the United States in the recent Gulf crisis—their efforts will provide a unique opportunity for enhancing world order. Mankind must no longer accept war as an inevitable part of the human condition. War—like slavery before it—can and must be ended. At no time in human history has there been greater opportunity to realize this hope than at present—if a joint Soviet-U.S. commitment can be achieved to prevent aggression in the international system.

A second body of law of great importance in Soviet-U.S. relations is that encompassing international human rights standards binding on all nations. Such standards are a core underpinning of democratic institutions and of Soviet new thinking. Nothing is more important to the health of the continuing relationship between our two countries than a continuation of recent trends in implementation of these human rights. Of particular importance to these trends, the recent Copenhagen round of the CSCE process has broadened the international human rights commitment to the realization of the rule of law internally as an essential element in permanent and effective realization of human rights. This development, also reflected in the Soviet new thinking, is of momentous importance in international law generally and in Soviet-U.S. relations particularly. Yet another body of rules of great importance in the future of Soviet-U.S. relations are those embodied in the Vienna Convention on the Law of Treaties intended to ensure full compliance with treaty obligations.

C. National Self-Interest and the Rule of Law

All too often, non-lawyers (and even some lawyers) assume that there is a conflict between "national self-interest" and the constraints provided by a "rule of law." While it is true that rules of law sometimes prevent a State from pursuing a course of action that it might otherwise believe to be to its advantage; from a long-term perspective every State should recognize that clear and just normative standards, combined with established mechanisms for peacefully resolving disputes, are in everyone's self-interest. Rules of law provide stable expectations, protect the rights of minorities and individuals, and promote international peace and cooperation. As Thomas Jefferson argued in a 1790 letter to the Marquis de Lafayette only days after accepting office as the first American Secretary of State:

> I think with others, that nations are to be governed with regard to their own interest, but I am convinced that it is their interest, in the long run, to be . . . faithful to their engagements, even in the worst of circumstances, and honorable and generous always.

D. Municipal Legal Systems and the Prospects for Peace

The democratic–and rule of law–revolution now sweeping Eastern Europe and the Soviet Union may well produce benefits far beyond regional borders. From the days of Immanuel Kant and Thomas Paine it has been argued that republican or democratic States are by their nature more inclined to be peaceful and law abiding. Municipal tyranny, by this theory, breeds a general contempt for legal norms. A dictator who routinely ignores the most fundamental interests of his own subjects is unlikely to be sensitive to the rights of aliens or of foreign States; while a democratically elected leader who is accustomed to respecting the sanctity of the individual citizen is more likely to respect the rights and interests of foreigners.

That there is a correlation between democratic decision-making and a propensity to behave peacefully and in accord with the rules of law would seem self-evident. Unconstrained power breeds unconstrained conduct. In 1770, William Pitt argued in the *Case of Wilkes*: "Unlimited power is apt to corrupt the minds of those who possess it, and this I know, my Lords, that where laws end, tyranny begins." Lord Acton echoed this theme in 1887 with his famous dictum: "Power tends to corrupt, and absolute power corrupts absolutely."

Nearly two centuries ago, Immanuel Kant argued that republican government was a precursor to a peaceful international environment. Writing in *Perpetual Peace*, he reasoned:

> The republican constitution . . . also gives a favorable prospect for the desired consequence, *i.e.*, perpetual peace. The reason is this: if the consent of the citizens is required in order to decide that war should be declared . . . , nothing is more natural than that they would be very cautious in commencing such a poor game, decreeing for themselves all the calamities of war. Among the latter would be: having to fight, having to pay the costs of war from their own resources, having painfully to repair the devastation war leaves behind, and, to fill up the measure of evils, load themselves with a heavy national debt that would embitter peace itself and that can never be liquidated on account of constant wars in the future. But, on the other hand, in a constitution which is

> not republican, and under which the subjects are not citizens, a declaration of war is the easiest thing in the world to decide upon, because war does not require of the ruler, who is the proprietor and not a member of the state, the least sacrifice of the pleasures of his table, the chase, his country houses, his court functions, and the like. He may, therefore, resolve on war as on a pleasure party for the most trivial reasons, and with perfect indifference leave the justification which decency requires to the diplomatic corps who are ever ready to provide it.

It has been observed by more than one commentator that democratic governments are far less likely to engage in armed aggression than authoritarian or totalitarian regimes. Indeed, no modern democracy has launched an aggressive attack against another democracy.

E. Strengthening the "Rule of Law" in Soviet-U.S. Relations–Some Fundamental Principles

Soviet-American relations have improved dramatically in recent months–with potential for further improvements still. Whether these improvements will continue will be determined in large part by the success or failure of the ongoing democratic revolution in the Soviet Union; but, at the moment, the potential for further improvement seems substantial.

Progress is being made. Under the rubric of the Conference on Security and Cooperation in Europe (the "Helsinki process"), dramatic accord has been achieved on such fundamental areas of long-standing discord as the protection of individual human rights. The logical next step in that process is an increased emphasis upon the "rule of law" in both international and internal affairs. The first important step in this direction has been taken at the recent Copenhagen round of the CSCE process, which extended agreement to the internal requirements of the rule of law as a fundamental element in the realization of agreed human rights.

Most critical, in the international arena, is the question of world order. The initial cooperation of the two governments in the Security Council's effort to deter Iraqi aggression stands as a shining beacon to a possible new era of cooperation and shared interests in this area. Whether overt or covert, aggressive force ought not be a permissible means of effecting foreign policy. This rule applies irrespective of the relative political or military power of antagonists, and prohibits support for paramilitary and terrorist groups and other aggressive "secret warfare" as well as more direct armed aggression.

Recent statements made by Soviet leaders in connection with the repudiation of the so-called "Brezhnev Doctrine" and in support of international cooperation against the Iraqi attack on Kuwait have provided great encouragement to advocates of the rule of law in international affairs in both the United States and the Soviet Union. Surely no American Secretary of State could quarrel with former Foreign Minister Shevardnadze's October 23, 1989, assertion to the Supreme Soviet that "national strength" lies "most of all in a renewed, democratic, rule-of-law society, in a free people, in the free man." America's first Secretary of State, Thomas Jefferson, could not have said it better.

More recently, in addressing the General Assembly of the United Nations, former Foreign Minister Shevardnadze emphasized:

> It is good that we have adopted a universal human yardstick of good and evil, that we are calling aggression by its proper name and consider it necessary to condemn and punish its perpetrator and to help the victim of injustice. . . .
>
> What we need . . . is to create as soon as possible a moral and legal environment in which anyone guilty of grave crimes against humanity, of participating in atrocities, in taking hostages, acts of terrorism or torture, and those guilty of particular ruthlessness in the use of force, could not escape punishment and would not be absolved from personal responsibility even if they acted under orders.

Enhanced Soviet-U.S. cooperation in other areas of international law, such as the Law of the Sea, have also been welcomed. Only time will tell whether the vision of Eduard Shevardnadze will survive under his successors; but there is great hope in the United States that this will be so.

Beyond such cooperative efforts in international affairs, however, the Soviet-U.S. relationship can be strengthened and advanced by attention to internal legal institutions as well. Today the United States recognizes that the historic disenfranchisement of Black Americans was a great moral wrong; and it continues to seek ways to guarantee fundamental civil and political rights for all of its people. At the same time, the people of the Soviet Union are seeking to come to terms with specific past wrongs–such as the excesses of the Stalinist period–and, perhaps more importantly, with some fundamental questions about the nature and role of the State. The core of this new thinking in the Soviet Union seems to be a welcome focus on the importance of democratic institutions and a civil society based on the rule of law. Thus, free and democratic elections have been held at the municipal level to promote genuine self-determination; and, there is an ongoing and vital consideration of new constitutions, democratic institutions, and legal structures.

Among the fundamental principles of the rule of law that have proven their value for the United States are several previously identified by one of the present authors when serving as co-chairman of the American delegation to a Seminar on the Rule of Law in Moscow and Leningrad in March 1990:

> *Government of the people, by the people, and for the people*—This statement, made famous by President Abraham Lincoln's 1863 Gettysburg Address and embodied in the French Constitution, captures political principles traceable from Aristotle through Locke. For the United States, this principle means that government ought to be carried out under a written and reasonably permanent "higher law" or constitution, drafted by the people or their elected representatives and conveying to the central government certain limited rights and powers. Government derives its power *solely* from the people.
>
> *Separation of Powers and Checks and Balances*—James Madison wrote in essay forty-seven of the *Federalist Papers*:
>
> > The accumulation of all powers legislative, executive and judiciary in the same hands, whether of one, a few or many, and whether hereditary, self appointed, or elective, may justly be pronounced the very definition of tyranny.
>
> The American Founding Fathers were greatly influenced by Montesquieu's *The Spirit of the Laws* and the principles drawn therefrom and embodied in the American Constitution have proven their value during two centuries of practice.
>
> *Representative Democracy and Protection of Individual Rights*—By definition, all truly "democratic" governments place policy decisions ultimately either directly in the people (rare), or through a "republican" system in the hands of men and women who are freely chosen by the people. Every democracy faces the problem of how to protect fundamental human freedom and dignity against government action—whether arbitrary or mandated by a majority. The most important and recurrent answer to this issue has been the provision of constitutional guarantees of basic human freedoms—frequently denominated as a "bill of rights." Other partial answers, however, involve building in checks against factionalism and hasty laws through representative democracy, bicameralism and cautious modes of legislative deliberation and action, as well as endowing government only with limited authority not extending to compromising such basic freedoms.
>
> *Limited Government and Federalism*—Yet another key underpinning of the rule of law is found in the related principles of limited government and federalism. Alexander Hamilton argued in the *Federalist Papers* that a specific bill of rights was unnecessary, since the proposed Constitution only empowered the new government

to exercise carefully limited powers; but the widespread desire to incorporate specific prohibitions on certain types of government conduct wisely prevailed. Limited central government serves an important function in the rule of law by maximizing regional and local control of governmental functions principally affecting peoples at a local level. This principle simultaneously makes government more responsive to and controllable by the people and encourages a diversity in public policies adopted within different regions according to local conditions, needs, traditions and desires. It directly incorporates an insight of participatory democracy that groups affected by decisions should have a voice in those decisions.

Judicial Review By an Independent Judiciary–An independent judiciary is a critical component of the principle of separation of powers, as well as of an effective principle of constitutionalism in embodying and realizing the major conditions of the consent of the governed. Because of the great importance of judicial review as a central mechanism for constitutional enforcement and for maintenance of the rule of law, it should be considered a fundamental principle in its own right. Time and again, dating back to the landmark 1803 case of *Marbury v. Madison*, the U.S. Supreme Court has affirmed its authority to strike down legislative acts that conflict with the higher law of the Constitution. The very existence of such a safeguard exerts a positive influence on government officials who might feel tempted to disregard the rights of the people.

These fundamental principles, and more, are also reflected in the important new Document which emerged from the recent Copenhagen Meeting of the Conference on the Human Dimension of the CSCE. In a revolutionary leap in the development of the rule of law, the thirty-four nations engaged in the CSCE process have understood that meaningful protection of fundamental human rights requires democratic institutions and the rule of law. This understanding of the next stage in international human rights is of momentous importance for the future of human rights, the rule of law, world peace, and Soviet-U.S. relations.

Specifically, some of the fundamental rule of law principles embodied in the landmark Copenhagen Document are reflected in the following excerpts:

> The participating States . . . recognize that pluralistic democracy and the rule of law are essential for ensuring respect for all human rights and fundamental freedoms, the development of human contacts and the resolution of other issues of a related humanitarian character. They therefore welcome the commitment

expressed by all participating States to the ideals of democracy and political pluralism as well as their common determination to build democratic societies based on free elections and the rule of law.

* * *

The participating States express their conviction that full respect for human rights and fundamental freedoms and the development of societies based on pluralistic democracy and the rule of law are prerequisites for progress in setting up the lasting order of peace, security, justice and co-operation that they seek to establish in Europe.

* * *

They solemnly declare that among those elements of justice which are essential to the full expression of the inherent dignity and of the equal and inalienable rights of all human beings are the following:

> free elections that will be held at reasonable intervals by secret ballot or by equivalent free voting procedures, under conditions which ensure in practice the free expression of the opinion of the electors in the choice of their representatives;
>
> a form of government that is representative in character, in which the executive is accountable to the elected legislature or the electorate;
>
> the duty of the government and public authorities to comply with the constitution and to act in a manner consistent with law;
>
> a clear separation between the State and political parties; in particular, political parties will not be merged with the State; . . .
>
> military forces and the police will be under the control of, and accountable to, the civil authorities;
>
> human rights and fundamental freedoms will be guaranteed by law and in accordance with their obligations under international law . . .

The participating States declare that the will of the people, freely and fairly expressed through periodic and genuine elections, is the basis of the authority and legitimacy of all government. . . .

F. Conclusion

As the Cold War comes to an end, the Soviet Union and the United States face a critical period in their relationship. People of good will on both sides wish to see a continued warming and a long-standing cooperative relationship. Undoubtedly, conflicting perceptions of self-interest will promote discord over some matters of importance; but, if both sides begin from a shared commitment to the "rule of law"–in both external and internal affairs–the likelihood of building a true and lasting friendship will be dramatically enhanced.

These are the years of freedom, and men and women around the globe are demanding a role in choosing responsive and representative governments. The Soviet Union is today playing a critical role in this world revolution, and the United States must remain committed to assisting this process.

A new era of international cooperation founded upon such fundamental shared goals as non-aggression, the binding nature of international obligations, the sanctity of the individual, and the rule of law could pave the way for a broad range of cooperative endeavors: improved trade, scientific, educational, and technical exchanges, and the like. Few, if any, developments in Soviet-U.S. relations would do more to promote genuine international security and peace than the continued development of respect for the "rule of law" in the coming years.

V.I. Kuznetsov

Professor and Head of Department, USSR Diplomatic Academy

The principle according to which states are obliged to cooperate with one another occupies an important place within the system of legal norms that seek to ensure international security. The norms of international law and the provisions of the UN Charter comprise the legal foundation of cooperation. Extensive, mutually beneficial international trade, with maximum utilization of the international division of labor and the absence of any and all discrimination, constitutes the economic foundation of cooperation. The principal goal of cooperation is the development of international exchange and creation of a community of states governed by rule of law.

The idea of international cooperation among states, regardless of their political, economic, and social system, in various domains of international relations for the purpose of maintaining international peace and security, constitutes the principal idea in the system of norms contained in the UN Charter.

The preamble to the Charter, Articles 1, 2, 11, 13, and 62, and Chapter X clearly attest to the presence in contemporary international law of the obligation of states to cooperate with one another. Following adoption of the UN Charter the principle of cooperation was formally embodied in the bylaws of many international organizations, in international treaties and conventions, and in numerous resolutions and declarations.

The 1970 Declaration of Principles of International Law and the Declaration of Principles of the Final Act of the Conference on Security and Cooperation in Europe occupy an important place in development of the principle of cooperation and in defining its content under international law.

Adherents of some schools of international law assert that the obligation of states to cooperate is not of a legal but of a declarative nature. Such claims are no longer true. Of course there was a time when cooperation was a voluntary act on the part of government, but subsequently the demands of developing international relations led to a voluntary act becoming a legal obligation.

Upon adoption of the Charter, the principle of cooperation took its place among other principles subject to mandatory observance in accordance with international law. Pursuant to the Charter, for example, states are obligated "[t]o achieve international co-operation in solving international problems of an economic, social, cultural, or humanitarian character," and are also obligated "to maintain international peace and security and, to that end: to take effective collective measures for the prevention and removal of threats to the peace."

The principle of cooperation as a legal category also proceeds from other provisions of the Charter, in particular from the provisions of Articles 55 and 56. The content of Article 55, for example, attests to two kinds of UN member obligations: the obligation of states to cooperate with one another in attaining the goals specified by the Charter, and their obligation to cooperate with the UN in order to attain these goals.

The most recent treaty practice indicates that states formally embody the principle of cooperation as a legal regulator of their relations on various matters. The Treaty on Principles Governing the Activities of States in the Exploration and Use of Outer Space, Including the Moon and Other Celestial Bodies, for example, emphasizes that "[i]n the exploration and use of outer space, including the moon and other celestial bodies, States Parties to the Treaty shall be guided by the principle of cooperation and mutual assistance." The 1979 Agreement Governing the Activities of States on the Moon and Other Celestial Bodies contains a similar obligation of the States Parties.

More and more new areas of intergovernmental relations are becoming areas of cooperation. A major step forward in this regard was taken by the participants in the 1989 Vienna Meeting within the framework of the Conference on Security and Cooperation in Europe. For example, they accepted, "in principle, the mandatory involvement of a third party when a dispute cannot be settled by other peaceful means." This provision is one of the manifestations of the principle of cooperation among states.

The Concluding Document devotes considerable attention to measures aimed at eradicating terrorism. The participating nations agreed:

> to reinforce and develop bilateral and multilateral co-operation among themselves in order to prevent and combat terrorism as well as to increase efficiency in existing co-operation at the bilateral level or in the framework of groups of States.

Protection and fostering of human rights and basic freedoms is becoming a new and promising area of intergovernmental cooperation. The states taking part in the Copenhagen Meeting of the Conference on the Human Dimension of the Conference on Security and Cooperation in Europe acknowledged that "the recognition of these rights and freedoms constitutes the foundation of freedom, justice, and peace" and that the activities of states in defense of human rights, grounded on principles of justice, which are set forth in detail in the Conference Document, comprises the basis of a state governed by rule of law.

The contemporary lawmaking process shows that states are increasingly more frequently assuming obligations (as is the case within the context of the Helsinki Process) to refrain from any actions which would do detriment to relations between states and would impede development of their cooperation. Of course the specific forms and scope of cooperation depend on the states themselves, on their needs and material resources, on their domestic legislation and on the international obligations they have assumed. An analysis of international legal documents reflecting the intentions of states (such as the 1970 Declaration of Principles), however, attests to an endeavor by states to impart a universal character to the principle of cooperation.

Claims that the obligation to cooperate applies only to UN member states are at variance with the actual state of affairs and with the norms of international law. There are numerous statements in the UN Charter proper that indicate that the UN member nations, in creating this organization, did not intend to wall themselves off from the rest of the world. Their commitment to universal international cooperation was manifested first and foremost in the well-known provision embodied in Article 2(6) of the Charter.

As for the scope of this principle, its imperative nature emerges most clearly from the obligation of modern states to cooperate in the area of maintaining international peace and security, disarmament, outlawing weapons of mass destruction, *etc.*

Other areas, in addition to those mentioned above, include cooperation in eliminating all forms of racial discrimination and all forms of religious intolerance, cooperation in the economic, social, cultural, technical, and commercial domains in conformity with the principles of sovereign equality and noninterference, and cooperation in the area of promoting economic growth throughout the world, especially in developing countries.

The effectiveness of international cooperation is directly linked with the absence in international relations of discrimination based on political, economic, and social differences of modern states. Every state, regardless of its socioeconomic characteristics or level of development, can and should make a contribution toward the development of international cooperation.

The obligation of states to cooperate with one another naturally presupposes their good faith observance of the norms of international law and the UN Charter. It is impossible to develop friendly relations and cooperation with states if a state is waging an aggressive war, if it interferes in the affairs of other sovereign states and breaches its assumed obligations.

The principle of good faith fulfillment of international obligations arose in the form of international legal custom at early stages in the development of statehood, while today it is formally embodied in numerous bilateral and multilateral international agreements.

This principle is formally embodied as a generally accepted standard of conduct in the UN Charter, the preamble of which stresses the resolve of UN members "to create conditions whereby justice and respect for obligations proceeding from treaties and other sources of international law can be observed." Pursuant to Article 2(2) of the Charter, "All Members, in order to ensure to all of them the rights and benefits resulting from membership, shall fulfil in good faith the obligations assumed by them in accordance with the present Charter."

In connection with the above wording, there sometimes arise differences in views as regards the sphere of application of the principle of good faith fulfillment of obligations: Does this principle apply only to obligations proceeding from the UN Charter, or does it apply in equal measure to all obligations assumed by legal parties on the basis of international treaties?

The development of international law since the UN Charter clearly confirms the universal nature of the principle in question. According to the Vienna Convention on the Law of Treaties, "[e]very treaty in force is binding upon the parties to it and must be performed by them in good faith." In addition, a "party may not invoke provisions of its internal law as justification for its failure to perform a treaty."

The sphere of application of this principle has expanded appreciably in recent years, a fact which is reflected in the wording of various documents of international law. According to the 1970 Declaration of Principles of International Law, every state is obligated to carry out in good faith the commitments it has assumed pursuant to the UN Charter, namely those proceeding from generally recognized principles and rules of international law, as well as obligations proceeding from international treaties that are valid in accordance with generally accepted principles and rules of international law.

One readily notes that the authors of the Declaration were seeking to emphasize the need for good faith observance first and foremost of those obligations that are encompassed by the concept of "generally recognized principles and rules of international law" or that proceed from them.

Five years later, in the 1975 Declaration of Principles of the Final Act, the signatory states agreed to:

> fulfil in good faith their obligations under international law, both those obligations arising from the generally recognized principles and rules of international law and those obligations arising from treaties or other agreements, in conformity with international law, to which they are party.

Obligations "under international law" are without question broader than obligations "arising from the generally recognized principles and rules of international law." In addition, in recent years states have been adopting, at a regional level in particular, important instruments that, strictly speaking, do not constitute obligations "under international law" but that they nevertheless intend strictly to fulfill.

For Europe these are the documents adopted in the context of the Helsinki process. The Concluding Document of the Vienna Meeting of representatives of the participating nations of the Conference on Security and Cooperation in Europe stated that they "reaffirmed their resolve to implement fully, unilaterally, bilaterally and multilaterally, all the provisions of the Final Act and of the other CSCE documents."

The concept of good faith exists in various legal and sociocultural systems, a fact that is directly reflected in observance by states of their assumed obligations. The concept of good faith has been formally articulated in a large number of international treaties, in many UN General Assembly resolutions, in declarations of states, *etc.* One should recognize, however, that definition of the precise legal content of the term good faith may cause difficulties in real-world situations.

It would seem that the legal concept of good faith should be drawn from the text of the Vienna Convention on the Law of Treaties, chiefly from the parts "Application of Treaties" (Articles 28-30) and "Interpretation of Treaties" (Articles 31-33). Application of the provisions of a treaty is determined in large measure by its interpretation. From this point of view it is logical to assume that application of a treaty will be in good faith if the treaty has been interpreted in good faith, "in accordance with the ordinary meaning to be given to the terms of the treaty in their context and in light of its object and purpose."

As regards the moral content of good faith, this term is defined in the V.I. Dal explanatory dictionary of the Russian language as honesty, truthfulness, and a strict God-fearing attitude in one's actions. One should stress that content common to mankind as a whole, not national, religious, or class content, should be invested in the term honesty and decency.

The principle of good faith fulfillment of international obligations extends only to valid agreements. This means that the principle in question is applied only to international treaties entered into voluntarily and on a basis of equality.

Any unequal international treaty first and foremost violates the principle of sovereign equality of states and as such violates the UN Charter, since the UN Organization "is based on the principle of sovereign equality of all its Members," which in turn have assumed the obligation "to develop friendly relations among nations based on respect for the principle of equal rights and self-determination of peoples."

In contemporary international law it should be considered as generally recognized that any treaty which is in conflict with the UN Charter is invalid and that no state may cite such a treaty or make use of its benefits. This position is precisely in conformity with Article 103 of the Charter. In addition, no treaty shall conflict with an imperative norm of international law as it is defined in Article 53 of the Vienna Convention on the Law of Treaties.

The binding force of an international treaty and, consequently, the mandatory nature of its observance is grounded on the voluntary consent of the parties to the treaty. As we know, any coercion of a state, its agencies or authorized representatives conducting negotiations leads to distortion of the will of the participants in the negotiations. Such a distortion of will ultimately leads to invalidity of the treaty being concluded.

One more exception to the general rule of good faith observance of international obligations is widely recognized in modern international law, an exception connected with so-called immutability of circumstances (*clausula rebus sic stantibus*). According to this rule, a contract may be terminated if the actual status of the parties to the contract has changed radically and had led to the creation of a situation that is incompatible with the goals and principles of the previously signed treaty. In the postwar period the question of application of this *clausula* arose most frequently in connection with the attainment of independent statehood by former colonies. It would be erroneous, however, to assert that all treaty obligations that extended to colonial territory are no longer valid with the gaining of independence.

In this instance the point is that liberated countries, by virtue of the principle of self-determination, have the right not only to repudiate treaties but also have the right to accede to or reconclude treaties that do not infringe upon their sovereignty.

Recent legal and political-legal documents have with increasing frequency pointed to the linkage between the obligation of good faith observance of international treaties and the domestic lawmaking process of states. In particular, the participants in the Vienna meeting agreed in the 1989 Concluding Document to:

> ensure that their laws, regulations, practices and policies conform with their obligations under international law and are brought into harmony with the provisions of the Declaration of Principles and other CSCE commitments.

Formulas of this kind attest to expansion of the sphere of application of the principle of good faith observance of international obligations by all parties to international law.

4. Measures for Strengthening Mutual Guarantees of Non-Aggression Among States

John H. McNeill
Assistant General Counsel for International Affairs and Intelligence, U.S. Department of Defense, and Charles H. Stockton Professor of International Law, U.S. Naval War College

Thucydides, the ancient Greek historian and father of political science, records that at the end of the first ten years of the Peloponnesian War, a treaty of peace was agreed between Athens and Lacedaemon, as well as among many allies of each—the Peace of Nicias in 421 B.C. Among the principal articles of the treaty was the following:

> It shall not be lawful to take up arms, with intent to do hurt, either for the Lacedaemonians and their allies against the Athenians and their allies, or for the Athenians and their allies against the Lacedaemonians and their allies, in any way or means whatsoever. But should any difference arise between them they are to have recourse to law and oaths, according as may be agreed between the parties.

Followed by an alliance between the two principal powers themselves, this pact endured for some six years and ten months, after which hostilities resumed, continuing for another twenty years. One critical reason for the failure of the peace to last for the fifty years its drafters intended appears to be that not all of the important members of the concerned alliances became parties to it. Ultimately, the pressures on the Treaty partners generated by the hostilities that continued among these non-parties became too severe for the Treaty to continue.

This early example of a non-aggression pact dating back two-and-a-half millennia illustrates some of the problems that have continued to be associated with such agreements down to the modern era. In addition to the difficulties arising from the lack of participation by all significant members of the opposed alliances, it appears that the provisions of the Peace of Nicias were critically deficient insofar as they lacked verification/dispute resolution procedures necessary to support the credibility of the non-aggression arrangement. For example, Thucydides notes that unallayed Athenian suspicions of Lacedaemonian non-compliance contributed substantially to a climate of growing distrust, reinforcing those pressures that resulted in the collapse of the peace.

The best known examples of the non-aggression pact in the modern era are of course those entered into by the German Reich in 1939 with the Soviet Union, Estonia, Latvia, and Denmark. It was the German-Soviet Non-Aggression Treaty of August 23, 1939, with its secret supplementary Protocol delimiting the mutual spheres of interest of the two Parties in Eastern Europe, that created the preconditions for the subsequent German attack on Poland–which in turn led shortly thereafter to the formal beginning of World War II.

In addition to these arrangements, Germany had in effect also entered into a non-aggression agreement pursuant to its Joint Declaration concerning peaceful relations with Poland on January 26, 1934, which Hitler canceled on April 28, 1939, following the unilateral statement of guarantee given by Great Britain regarding Polish independence. During 1938, Great Britain had of course joined with Germany in a joint declaration stating their mutual desire never to go to war again and their resolve to deal peacefully with any questions that might arise between them. This declaration was issued on the very day after signature of the infamous Munich Agreement concerning cession of the Sudetenland by Czechoslovakia.

It is the 1939 German-Soviet Treaty of Non-Aggression that provides the most familiar example of this diplomatic-legal genre. In its first Article, the Parties obligated themselves "to desist from any act of violence, any aggressive action, and any attack on each other, either individually or jointly with other powers." The Treaty provisions also included undertakings by each Party not to lend support to any third country engaging in belligerent acts toward the other, and not to participate in any grouping of powers whatsoever that was directly or indirectly aimed at the other. Disputes and conflicts were to be settled exclusively through friendly exchanges of opinion or via arbitration. The Treaty by its terms was to terminate after ten years, but was extendable. These provisions were quite similar in form and content to the German Non-Aggression treaties with Denmark, Estonia, and Latvia.

Interestingly, the 1934 German-Polish Joint Declaration made explicit reference to the 1928 Pact of Paris, the so-called Kellogg-Briand Pact. This important Treaty was adhered to by a great many member states of the international community, and made clear that recourse to war for the solution of international controversies was condemned and renounced as an instrument of national policy. All disputes were henceforth to be settled through pacific means alone. The Pact was entered into outside the League of Nations framework, and thus survived the demise of the League. It is completely congruent with the obligations of Member States of the United Nations and, accordingly, is regarded as retaining legal vitality today.

The Pact of Paris, entered into against the background of the League Covenant, represented a fulfillment of the philosophy on which the Covenant was based. That document, of course, was the first to succeed in having most of the world's nations agree not to engage in hostilities except in certain strictly defined circumstances, *e.g.*, cases involving self-defense, enforcement of sanctions, or failure of the League's peace-keeping machinery. Remaining gaps in the League security architecture regarding the use of force were effectively closed by the 1928 Pact. After its enactment, international law can be said to have completed its evolution from a system under which nations were free to choose to go to war with one another—as was the case as recently as 1914—to a system under which the initiation of aggressive war was forbidden. This conclusion was reflected in both the Charter for the Nuremberg War Crimes Tribunal and in the Charter of the United Nations.

Under the UN Charter, Articles 2(3), 2(4), and 51 make clear that all parties are obligated to resolve their disputes peacefully and that the use of force in international relations—specifically, against the territorial integrity or political independence of any other state—is forbidden; unlike the Covenant and the Pact, the Charter also contains an explicit recognition of the inherent right of its members to engage in self-defense. In addition, the use of force is permitted pursuant to resolutions of appropriate UN organs, *e.g.*, UN Security Council Resolution S.678 of November 29, 1990, enacted under Chapter VII of the Charter and authorizing member states to use all necessary means to uphold and implement previous Security Council resolutions calling for Iraqi withdrawal from the territory of Kuwait, and to restore international peace and security in the area.

The limitations on the use of force were reconfirmed in the well-known Declaration on Principles of International Law Concerning Friendly Relations and Co-operation Among States in Accordance with the Charter of the United Nations, UN General Assembly Resolution 25/2625. This Declaration, adopted unanimously, is considered by many to have legal content and significance far beyond that of typical resolutions adopted by that body; indeed, it was drafted and adopted with the explicit intent that it would be binding.

Subsequently, the United Nations continued its work to clarify further international legal standards in this area, for example through a successful, multi-year effort to elaborate an agreed Definition of Aggression, approved

December 14, 1974, by UN General Assembly Resolution 39/3314. In 1987, the General Assembly adopted the Declaration on the Enhancement of the Effectiveness of the Principle of Refraining from the Threat or Use of Force in International Relations (UN General Assembly Resolution 42/22). Among the principles stated in the Declaration, which itself represented ten years of work in relevant organs of the United Nations, are the following:

> The principle of refraining from the threat or use of force in international relations is universal in character and is binding regardless of each State's political, economic, social or cultural system or relations of alliance.
>
> No consideration of whatever nature may be invoked to warrant resorting to the threat or use of force in violation of the Charter of the United Nations.

Against this background, one may well ask, what is the purpose of a non-aggression pledge by one country to another? What does it add? In legal terms, it is readily apparent that the UN Charter and the rules of customary international law at the current stage of development already prohibit aggression by one state against another. Accordingly, would it not be a mistake to encourage non-aggression pacts in the modern era? It is after all a basic tenet of legal interpretation that treaties cannot be assumed to contain absurdities or redundancies. It might therefore be concluded that, by the mere negotiation of a non-aggression pact, the states involved may be implying both to each other and to third states that they do not believe themselves to be already prohibited from engaging in acts of aggression. Were such negotiations to be undertaken on a broader basis, it might lead some states to the conclusion that the international prohibition against aggression was itself no longer operable. This might be followed in turn by a destabilizing breakdown in the credibility of the international legal foundation upon which the authority of the United Nations to maintain international peace and security rests.

On the other hand, can it be said that as a political matter such undertakings could never have value? Surely, it is now well recognized that non-aggression pacts of the type entered into during the 1930's by Germany were in actuality harbingers not of peace, but of war. Indeed, they were integral elements in a strategy of criminal aggression. But it would not be correct to conclude that all such pacts will automatically prove to be invitations to conflict.

When can a non-aggression treaty have genuine value? The answer must be that this result will be obtained whenever the acceptance of such explicit undertakings serves to strengthen the stability of the relationship between the parties, and if it is entered into in a political and strategic context that benefits from the existence of the agreement.

One example of an incremental approach to negotiating a non-aggression pact is illustrated by a recent agreement entered into by India and Pakistan. Signed on December 31, 1988, each party pledged in this agreement not to attack nuclear facilities of the other. Meanwhile, negotiations on a mutual non-aggression pact of general applicability were to continue between the rival states. This step-by-step strategy has therefore led to a limited goal, but has also succeeded in raising important questions about whether the parties feel free to attack other, non-nuclear targets. The dilemma is whether a partial solution such as this might result in making war more, rather than less, likely. Perhaps for this reason, the agreement has not yet entered into force. Indeed, it appears that reticence by at least one party to provide a list of facilities to be covered by the agreement raised concerns on the part of the other and has contributed substantially to the delay in implementation, which in any case would have to be carried out during an ongoing and active territorial dispute between the two signatories.

Another and more attractive approach to non-aggression guarantees is illustrated by NATO's London Declaration on a Transformed North Atlantic Alliance of July 6, 1990. In Point 5 of that document, issued by the heads of state and government participating at the meeting of NATO's North Atlantic Council, it was stated:

> We will remain a defensive alliance and will continue to defend all the territory of all of our members. We have no aggressive intentions and we commit ourselves to the peaceful resolution of all disputes. We will never in any circumstance be the first to use force.

This pledge was not made dependent upon a similar statement by member states of the Warsaw Treaty Organization; rather, it was freely given as a statement of alliance plans and policy.

In the London Declaration, the NATO Members went on to propose to Warsaw Treaty members that a joint declaration be undertaken in which all would solemnly state that they were no longer adversaries and all would reaffirm their intentions to refrain from the threat or use of force against the territorial integrity or political independence of any state, or from acting in any other manner inconsistent with the purposes and principles of the UN Charter or the Final Act of the Conference on Security and Cooperation in Europe (*e.g.*, the ten principles contained in the 1975 Helsinki Final Act).

Perhaps of more critical importance, the pledge contained in the London Declaration was put forward in the context of exceptional political change in Europe and against the backdrop of the negotiation of the Treaty on the Reduction of Conventional Armed Forces in Europe, subsequently signed at Paris, November 19, 1990. It was the anticipated signature of this Treaty, and the occurrence of widespread political realignment in Eastern Europe on a scale that made it possible, which provided the essential prerequisites for the London pledge.

The London Declaration also contained a further important element—the announcement that NATO will prepare a new Allied military strategy moving away from "forward" defense, where appropriate, and towards a reduced forward presence. Equally important, "flexible response" is to be modified to reflect a reduced reliance on nuclear weapons. Thus, historic political developments in the East have been met with revolutionary changes in Western strategy.

What other elements have contributed to the new strategic situation in Europe? Adoption of the Vienna Document 1990 by the CSCE States reaffirms their mutual commitment in tangible terms to take effective and concrete action designed to make progress in strengthening confidence and security and in achieving disarmament, "so as to give effect and expression to the duty of states to refrain from the threat or use of force in their mutual relations as well as in their international relations in general." This statement was issued jointly by the thirty-four participating states—comprising in addition to NATO and Warsaw Treaty Members twelve other European states, several of whom are neutrals.

Thus, we see that NATO's pledge was made not in a political and strategic vacuum, but in circumstances encompassing the signature of a broadly inclusive conventional arms reduction treaty and a continually strengthened CSCE regime. These permitted changes in NATO military strategy, to which was added an undertaking that the Federal Republic of Germany would reduce the personnel strength of its armed forces to a significantly lower level judged acceptable by all CFE Treaty signatories. Moreover, Germany and the Soviet Union concluded a treaty on November 9, 1990, in which each pledged it would refrain from the threat or use of force directed against the territorial integrity or political independence of the other side. The historical ironies abound, of course, with regard to this agreement, and it must surely represent a unique example of a non-aggression arrangement entered into while one party tolerates the presence on its soil of over 300,000 armed troops of the other. To the evolving political and strategic situation in Europe, however, this particular pledge has added little, in view of what was consummated ten days later.

On November 19, 1990, NATO's suggestion to the Warsaw Treaty Parties that the pledge of non-use of force be made mutual was accepted. In conjunction with the signature at Paris of the CFE Treaty, the twenty-two Parties thereto issued a Joint Declaration in which the following was stated:

> They recall their obligations under the Charter of the United Nations and reaffirm all of their commitments under the Helsinki

> Final Act. They stress that all of the ten Helsinki Principles are of primary significance and that, accordingly, they will be equally and unreservedly applied, each of them being interpreted taking into account the others. In that context, they affirm their obligation and commitment to refrain from the threat or use of force against the territorial integrity or the political independence of any State, from seeking to change existing borders by threat or use of force, and from acting in any other manner inconsistent with the principles and purposes of those documents. None of their weapons will ever be used except in self-defense or otherwise in accordance with the Charter of the United Nations.

This formulation makes very clear that the Helsinki Final Act, even though a politically but not legally binding document, is regarded for this purpose to be of the same political and moral weight as the UN Charter itself. It is the sum of the provisions of the two documents taken together which, reaffirmed, form the necessary preconditions for the pledge regarding the non-use of force. Thus, the pledge, in the new European context, is not a mere instrumentality but actually represents the logical consequence of the mutually reinforcing body of agreements that led to its acceptance. This result suggests a sea-change in the manner in which non-aggression pledges may be viewed in the future. No longer are they necessarily the opening bids in a cynical game of winner-take-all *realpolitik*. Instead, in the right circumstances, they can be viewed as the desirable outcome of prudent policies designed to enhance collective security and strategic stability.

At this point, the precise question of identifying measures for strengthening guarantees of mutual non-aggression may be considered. Answers to this question require certain assumptions to be made. First, it is plain that the UN Charter represents a mutual non-aggression guarantee which, if anything, has been demonstrated to possess even greater relevance at the dawn of the post-Cold-War era. How can this guarantee be strengthened? Clearly, one method has recently been implemented–the demonstration of unprecedentedly strong resolve on the part of the international community to oppose and redress the aggressive war of conquest waged upon Kuwait by Iraq. This experience provides enormous credibility to the rules of international law restricting the use of force in the modern age.

What else can be done? Certainly, the path chosen by the CFE Treaty Parties is one calculated to further strengthen the Charter guarantees, and has resulted in making those guarantees as specific and credible as possible by creating the conditions where risks, *e.g.*, of surprise attack, have been reduced to an acceptable level.

But there are other possibilities. The development in recent years of a network of interlocking agreements between the United States and the Soviet Union provides a useful precedent, which may prove worthy of emulation by other states.

This Soviet-American process has led to the establishment of an operational environment for the armed forces of the two parties in which tensions have been reduced and mutual confidence enhanced through the identification and application of procedures designed to ensure that the international legal rights of each are respected by the other when military, naval and air operations are underway. The 1972 Agreement Between the United States of America and the Union of Soviet Socialist Republics on the Prevention of Incidents On and Over the High Seas (Incidents at Sea Agreement) represents the first step taken in this direction. This Agreement, which was designed to address the immediate issue of navigational safety, also had the effect of causing the naval forces of both sides—undersea, surface, and air—to operate in a manner that was not only inherently safer than was the case in the unmanaged situation which preceded it, but also permitted the respective forces of each side to recognize that the resultant operational environment was less suited to, and therefore less attractive for employment in, a surprise attack by the other. This agreement has worked remarkably well since its inception, and its success has formed the basis of other efforts; among the most significant of these is the 1989 Agreement Between the United States of America and the Union of Soviet Socialist Republics on the Prevention of Dangerous Military Activities.

This Agreement, now in force for more than a year, was the product of a mutual effort by both sides to identify policies and actions that would assist their armed forces in avoiding involvement in certain dangerous military activities that were not already subject to existing arrangements, such as the Incidents at Sea Agreement. In effect, the 1989 Agreement supplements the 1972 Agreement, and regulates the armed forces of a Party when operations in proximity to the armed forces of the other are undertaken near the national territory of that other Party. In such situations, it also regulates the use of lasers, as well as interference with command and control networks, and provides for the establishment of "special caution areas" within which each Party's armed forces are to establish and maintain communications with the other, in order to prevent the occurrence of any dangerous military activities. One of the provisions of this Agreement that is most relevant to the use of force is Paragraph 2 of Article II, which specifies that:

> The Parties shall take measures to ensure expeditious termination and resolution by peaceful means, without resort to the threat or use of force, of any incident which may arise as a result of dangerous military activities.

Thus, the Parties recognize that the perceived threshold of threat may be low when armed forces are operating in a state of high readiness and in proximity to each other. Accordingly, this Agreement deals explicitly with the obligation of each Party to avoid the use of force, especially in circumstances where such acts might be viewed by the other as aggressive, thus possibly triggering a response in self-defense. In so doing, this Agreement provides an excellent example of how to strengthen the guarantee of the UN Charter against aggression.

In conclusion, it can be stated with confidence that guarantees of mutual non-aggression among states today enjoy wide-spread applicability, both in terms of the global reach of the UN Charter provisions, as well as those undertaken in regional and bilateral contexts. These guarantees are strengthened primarily by the existence of a vigorous UN commitment to maintaining international peace and security. The UN machinery, crucially important to the rule of law in international affairs, can be usefully supplemented by appropriate pledges of non-aggression, such as in the Joint Declaration by the twenty-two signatories of the CFE Treaty, *i.e.*, by all the states who are members either of NATO or the Warsaw Treaty—thus avoiding the error made so long ago in the Peace of Nicias. Although in legal terms these pledges could not add to the all-encompassing norm of international law that already prohibits the use of aggressive force in international affairs, such pledges can perform the useful function of making more explicit and specific the precise content and scope that the relevant parties envisage for their mutual application of the normative rule. Although a non-aggression pact entered into in circumstances devoid of strategic stability and transparency might result in an increase in the risk of outbreak of hostilities by heightening the prospects for success of a surprise attack, it is also the case that in other circumstances—such as those currently prevailing in Europe, where a sufficient political and military infrastructure exists—that non-aggression pledges can be entered into as the logical consequence of other measures already adopted to effect stability and transparency, such as reductions in numbers of weaponry and in levels of military personnel, and the establishment of on-site monitoring procedures.

Guarantees of mutual non-aggression, then, can have value in the modern era. Several methods to strengthen them have already been identified, as have the political and strategic processes within which the pledges themselves are best integrated. It may be, as a result, that such pledges will enjoy a renaissance and become familiar once again; we can but hope that such familiarity will become welcome and that such pledges will lead to the future strengthening, rather than the subversion, of international peace and security.

B.M. Klimenko
Professor, USSR Diplomatic Academy

A. Principles of the Inviolability and Integrity of State Territory and of the Inviolability of State Borders

The principle of inviolability and integrity of state territory is one of the fundamental principles of international law. This is a relatively new principle of international law, which became finally and firmly established with adoption of the UN Charter in 1945, but the process of development of its content is continuing, and the various elements of this principle have been variously articulated in international law. Nor has the very name of the principle been finally and ultimately established.

The UN Charter prohibited the threat or use of force against the territorial integrity and political independence of any state as well as in any other manner incompatible with the goals of the UN. (Article 2(4)). Thus the UN Charter finally and irrevocably prohibited the use of force against territorial integrity, in contrast to the Covenant of the League of Nations, which did not contain such a total prohibition. In addition, the UN Charter was then and continues to be the international agreement with the greatest multilateral participation, and correspondingly the principle of territorial integrity incorporated in the Charter has become for all states a common principle of international law. This has exerted considerable influence on many other instruments of international law.

The 1970 Declaration of Principles of International Law Concerning Friendly Relations and Co-operation Among States in Accordance with the Charter of the United Nations reflected a number of the points of this principle, although it did not mention its name and did not separately set forth its content. All provisions pertaining to the inviolability and integrity of state territory are set forth in articulating the content of the first principle of the Declaration, which states verbatim the formula contained in Article 2(4) of the UN Charter, and thus combines two principles—the prohibition of the threat or use of force, and the territorial integrity of a state.

Adoption in 1975 of the Final Act of the Conference on Security and Cooperation in Europe, the final article of which set forth the content of the principle of "Territorial integrity of States," constituted a further stage in development of the principle of inviolability and integrity of state territory. Article IV of the Declaration of Principles of the Final Act reads:

> The participating States will respect the territorial integrity of each of the participating States.

> Accordingly, they will refrain from any action inconsistent with the purposes and principles of the Charter of the United Nations against the territorial integrity, political independence or the unity of any participating State, and in particular from any such action constituting a threat or use of force.

This part of Article IV is somewhat broader than the wording in the UN Charter, since it places primary emphasis on refraining from any actions against territorial integrity, while the UN Charter speaks of refraining from the threat or use of force. It follows from this that the wording of Article IV has in mind a much broader list of prohibited actions than just the threat or use of force. In addition, Article IV makes direct mention of the indivisibility of any signatory state, which is lacking in the UN Charter.

The last part of Article IV goes even further and states:

> The participating States will likewise refrain from making each other's territory the object of military occupation or other direct or indirect measures of force in contravention of international law, or the object of acquisition by means of such measures or the threat of them. No such occupation or acquisition will be recognized as legal.

All this synthesizes and further develops the three basic points contained in a number of other instruments of international law: prohibition of armed invasion of foreign soil, other than in strictly specified instances; prohibition of acquisition of territory by means of the threat or use of force; and prohibition of military occupation of foreign soil, except for strictly specified instances.

Trends in the development of this principle are leading to the prohibition of other actions than the threat or use of force. It has already been noted in Soviet international law literature that the principle of inviolability and integrity of a state's territory may include prohibition of the use of a state's territory, including its resources, without the consent of the territorial sovereign, and that a state shall not alter the natural conditions of its territory in such a manner as to do detriment to the natural conditions of the territory of another state. All this finds confirmation in the theory and practice of international law. These new elements have not yet been codified, although they are contained in many instruments of international law.

From the legal point of view different elements of the principle of inviolability and integrity of state territory possess different legal force, since some are mentioned in treaties while others are mentioned in resolutions, and they also are of differing effect and force for different states, since the UN Charter is binding on all states, while the 1975 Final Act is binding only on its signatories. This prescribes ways for further strengthening this principle.

The inviolability of state borders is one of the new principles of international law and constitutes one of the most important foundations of security of European states. The idea of assuring the borders of European states began to gather momentum from the end of the 1950's, in response to territorial claims by revanchist forces in postwar Europe, which were seeking to redraw the borders established pursuant to the Potsdam Agreement. This idea had its first legal embodiment as the principle of inviolability of borders in the 1970 Treaty Between the Soviet Union and the FRG, and subsequently in treaties between the PPR, GDR, CSSR, and the FRG.

The Final Act of the Conference on Security and Cooperation in Europe, to which there are a great many signatories, formally articulates the principle of inviolability of the borders of the European states. Article III of this Act's Declaration of Principles reads:

> The participating States regard as inviolable all one another's frontiers as well as the frontiers of all States in Europe and therefore they will refrain now and in the future from assaulting these frontiers.
>
> Accordingly, they will also refrain from any demand for, or act of, seizure and usurpation of part or all of the territory of any participating State.

The wording of the principle of inviolability of borders allows for a fairly broad interpretation, but the basic content of this principle can be reduced to three elements: 1) recognition of existing borders as legally established in conformity with international law; 2) renunciation of any and all territorial claims at the present time and in the future; and 3) refraining from any other actions against or encroachments of these borders, including the threat or use of force. This content of the principle of inviolability of borders substantially distinguishes it from the principle of inviolability and integrity of state territory and the traditional principle of inviolability of state borders, which also provides a basis for considering the European principle of inviolability of borders to be a new principle of international law. Of course the new principle of inviolability of borders is binding only on signatories to the Helsinki Final Act. Extension of this principle to other states requires appropriate instruments of international law, either bilateral or multilateral. In actuality there exist a great many disagreements and territorial disputes, while in some places boundary lines have not been established at all or have been established incorrectly. All these factors constitute an impediment to expanding the sphere of application of this principle, but it is not an insuperable obstacle.

The traditional principle of inviolability of state borders is a principle of general international law and involves the obligation of states not to commit arbitrary shifting of the boundary line on the ground and not to cause or allow it to be crossed without due permission or other than by established procedures. This latter also constitutes the right of every sovereign state: the right to control the crossing of its border by persons and vehicles. All agreements between the Soviet Union and adjacent states pertaining to border regulations also proceed from the principle of the inviolability of state borders.

Treaties of contiguous states on the establishment of a border between them contain a general description of the location of borders, as well as general obligations of the parties pertaining to determination of the boundary line on the ground and to marking the border. A treaty description of the location of the border, joint determination on the ground of the boundary line by the parties concerned, and marking of the border essentially expresses the parties' consent to the given location and position of the boundary line. The principle of inviolability of the border, which finds expression in demarcation, delimitation, and other documents that pledge the parties strictly to observe the location of a boundary line on the ground, also constitutes an expression of this consent. General and continuing observance of these rules as legally binding has also made them customary law norms of general international law.

The crossing of a state border should take place in accordance with the rules and regulations established by the state onto the territory of which persons or vehicles are passing. Each sovereign state establishes a certain procedure of arrival of foreigners onto its territory. The most general expression of this is the generally recognized regulation prescribing that it is necessary to obtain an entry or transit visa issued by the state of arrival or transit. In principle, foreign vehicles also enter the territory of a territorial sovereign only with the permission of that sovereign. In the case of regular transport communications, such transportation movements are determined as a rule by international treaties. There also exist customary law norms of general international law in this domain, but custom also presumes a state's consent. States may establish a simplified border crossing procedure, such as without an entry, exit, or transit visa, by agreement with other states or by unilateral enactment. The territorial sovereign also establishes the rules and procedures of the direct physical crossing of its border. These include regulations and procedures pertaining to border crossing locations and times, as well as rules and regulations pertaining to health inspection, customs inspection, and other types of inspection.

The flow of persons and vehicles across borders has increased sharply in recent decades, and this phenomenon reflects the natural process of development of international intercourse and humanitarian cooperation, including the development of interpersonal contacts on the basis of family ties, professional interests, tourist travel and sport, and broadening of contacts in the domain of culture and education, science and technology, and environmental protection. Thus there is taking place change in the relationship of legal norms pertaining to the location of a boundary line on the ground and the rules and procedures of border crossing. Principles and rules pertaining to inviolability of a boundary line on the ground are becoming more stringent, while at the same time provisions concerning crossing of the border are becoming more relaxed.

The traditional principle of inviolability of borders in general is recognized by the overwhelming majority of states. But the content and legal force of this principle vary from case to case, which in the final analysis is due to the fact that this principle is grounded on international legal custom and is not formally embodied in any multilateral international treaty. These uncertainties frequently lead to deviations from this principle, and sometimes to direct violations of the principle as well, all of which could be eliminated by formulating a more explicit content of this principle and its formal articulation in some universal international document.

B.R. Tuzmukhamedov
Docent, USSR Diplomatic Academy

B. Confidence-Building Measures

In general terms confidence-building measures (CBMs) can be defined as special measures, prescribed by treaty or determined by some other manner, undertaken for the purpose of generating confidence that the actions of one party do not have the purpose of harming the security of another party, in particular if these actions could be interpreted and assessed as preparations for a surprise attack, and yet in fact they are harmless. In the Comprehensive Study of Confidence Building Measures conducted by a group of government experts in 1981 on the instructions of the UN Secretary General, it was noted that the ultimate objective of confidence-building measures "consists in strengthening international peace and security and in helping build confidence and mutual understanding between countries, which will create and improve conditions for fruitful international cooperation."

Confidence forms the basis of any activities in the domain of intercourse between states and for that reason is a determining factor in ensuring international security in any area. Parties taking part in the formation and maintenance of international security are entitled to count on assurance that they can trust one another to the extent of not relying on the threat or use of force in their relations. New approaches in ensuring international security in conditions of changing relations between alliances and states that were previously in confrontation are constructed on the basis of existing security institutions; for this reason observance of the principles of the UN Charter and other norms of international law and a conscientious attitude toward international treaties is an important confidence-building measure. Confidence in international relations can exist only with rigorous and uniform observance of the legal, moral, and political obligations assumed by states.

Confidence is composed of many factors. Confidence-building measures that have been adopted and that presently are being formulated pertain primarily to the military domain. Confidence-building measures in the military domain do not constitute measures of actual disarmament and do not assume the functions of the latter; however, adopted separately or as attendant measures, they create favorable conditions for initiation of talks or promote progress at talks already under way.

An analysis of these measures reveals trends both toward a broadening of the aggregate of measures and of the scope of covered military activities, and also, as applied to Europe, toward an increase in the binding force of measures on which agreement is being reached. This latter trend is manifested in the fact that, while measures prescribed by the Final Act of the 1975 Conference on Security and Cooperation in Europe were carried out on a voluntary basis, measures specified by the Document of the 1986 Stockholm Conference on Confidence- and Security-Building Measures and Disarmament in Europe and the 1990 Vienna Document are politically binding.

Confidence-building measures, which originally boiled down to improving communications between parties (a group of agreements on establishing direct communication links) and ensuring safety of maritime navigation (a group of agreements on preventing incidents on the high seas), in time began to include notifications and other information on military activities (with an increase in the period of submitting notifications and scope of submitted information), exchange of observers and inspections at the sites of conduct of military activity. Agencies established pursuant to treaties on arms limitation and reduction measures began to be assigned confidence-building functions. While confidence-building measures agreed upon in the 1960's-1970's were for the most part aimed at reducing the danger of armed conflict using nuclear weapons, subsequent measures were intended to reduce the risk of conflict by conventional forces. Recently, particularly since the signing of the Stockholm and Vienna Documents, confidence-building measures have been transformed from military-technical measures limited to the providing of information on absence of preparations for a surprise attack into comprehensive measures characterized by a degree of confidence that enables the negotiating partners to formulate and apply not only notificational but also restraining measures, and in the future limiting measures as well.

The term "confidence-building measures" proper was given legal substance by the Final Act of the 1975 Conference on Security and Cooperation in Europe, where it was used in Section 2 of the Document on Confidence-Building Measures and Certain Aspects of Security and Disarmament. This Document prescribed certain measures pertaining to notification and observation of military activities, the purpose of which was to help lessen the danger of an armed conflict, misunderstanding or misassessment of military activities, which could cause fears and apprehensions, especially in conditions where Parties lack clear, prompt, and timely information on the nature of such activities. Agreed-upon measures include the following: a) advance notification of large (involving more than 25,000 men) ground forces exercises, to be communicated not less than twenty-one days prior to commencement of such exercises; b) voluntary notification of smaller exercises; c) voluntary invitation for foreign observers to attend military exercises; d) voluntary notification of large troop movements; e) fostering of exchanges of military personnel by invitation, including visits by military delegations.

The above measures were of limited, symbolic nature from the military standpoint, although they did foster confidence-building, lessening of military tension and stabilization of the situation in Europe, as well as the drafting of and reaching agreement on more far-reaching measures embodied in the Document of the 1986 Stockholm Conference. These measures include the following: a) notification forty-two days in advance of military activities in which at least 13,000 men and 300 or more tanks are to take part; b) if more than 17,000 men are to take part in a military activity, two observers from each participating state in the Conference on Security and Cooperation in Europe shall be invited to observe the activity; c) the participating states shall submit to one another lists of all notification-requiring activities by November 15 of the year preceding the year in which these activities are to be conducted; d) measures involving the participation of more than 40,000 men shall be included on a list two years in advance and may not be conducted without prior notification one year in advance; notification shall be given two years in advance for activities involving the participation of more than 75,000 men; e) a state receiving a request to perform an inspection may not turn down such a request; inspection on the ground, from the air, or by both means shall be permitted and shall be carried out within thirty-six hours from the moment the corresponding request is received.

The agreements reached at the Stockholm Conference prescribe not only notification of exercises, large troop movements, and other military activities, but also certain measures pertaining to restraining such activities. These measures pursue the goal of effecting a transition to an integral system that would encompass the aggregate of confidence-building, security, and disarmament measures. Such an integral system is being formed in the course of the talks being held in Vienna on confidence-building and security measures by the thirty-four states participating in the Conference on Security and Cooperation in Europe and the twenty-two-nation talks on conventional forces in Europe. Both sets of talks are being conducted pursuant to decisions articulated in the Concluding Document of the 1989 Vienna Meeting of Representatives of the States Participants in the Conference on Security and Cooperation in Europe. The document stresses the "complementary nature of the efforts within the framework of the CSCE process aimed at building confidence and security and establishing stability and achieving progress in disarmament, in order to lessen military confrontation and to enhance security for all."

A number of bilateral agreements that specifically prescribe confidence-building measures are currently in effect; some confidence-building measures are prescribed as attendant measures in arms limitation or reduction agreements. Measures of this kind that have been agreed upon and are being implemented can conditionally be subdivided into several types.

1. *Measures that ensure predictability in the conduct of certain types of military activities.* The 1971 Agreement on Measures to Reduce the Risk of Outbreak of Nuclear War Between the United States of America and the Union of Soviet Socialist Republics, among other notification measures, prescribes mutual notification of scheduled missile launchings if the flight of a launched missile is to extend beyond the national territory of the launching party in the direction of the other party. This obligation was made more specific in the 1988 Agreement Between the United States of America and the Union of Soviet Socialist Republics on Notifications of Launches of Intercontinental Ballistic Missiles and Submarine-launched Ballistic Missiles, by introducing the requirement that the area of missile launch and the impact area be indicated, by broadening the overall parameters of notification, and by extending the provisions to cover all strategic ballistic missile launches.

The 1972 Agreement Between the United States of America and the Union of Soviet Socialist Republics on the Prevention of Incidents On and Over the High Seas (supplemented by the 1973 Protocol), as well as similar agreements between the Soviet Union, on the one hand, and the UK, FRG, France, Italy, Canada, the Netherlands, Spain, and Greece on the other, prescribe measures aimed at reducing the possibility of occurrence of hazardous or dangerous situations when warships and military aircraft are operating in proximity to one another. In particular, the Parties pledge strictly to observe international regulations for preventing collisions at sea; warships are prohibited from simulating attacks by training their weapons in the direction of another nation's warships and nonmilitary vessels; and aircraft are prohibited from simulating attacks, executing aerobatic maneuvers above warships and civilian vessels, and releasing objects in the vicinity of such vessels in such a manner as to present a danger to or impede navigation.

The 1989 Agreement Between the United States of America and the Union of Soviet Socialist Republics on the Prevention of Dangerous Military Activities aims at preventing such types of activity by the military forces of the parties as: entering the other party's national territory; dangerous use of lasers; impeding one another's actions in special caution areas, to be designated in each specific instance; generating interference with or jamming the other party's command and control networks. The agreement and its annexes specify the procedure for establishing and maintaining communication between military forces personnel down to and including the level of warship, aircraft, ground asset and ground forces subunit commander, and procedures for handling incidents involving entry into national territory.

2. *Communications links and consultation mechanisms.* The 1963 Memorandum of Understanding Between the United States of America and the Union of Soviet Socialist Republics Regarding the Establishment of a Direct Communications Link (Hot-line modernization agreements were signed in 1971 and 1984) called for the establishment of a continuously operating, reliably functioning communications link for use in emergency situations, in particular for immediate notification when there is danger of outbreak of nuclear war. Similar direct communications links were established between Moscow and London and between Moscow and Paris. In 1987 a Agreement Between the United States of America and the Union of Soviet Socialist Republics on the Establishment of Nuclear Risk Reduction Centers was signed, with two Protocols, calling for the establishment of such centers in the capitals of both countries, connected by fax links. Notifications of ballistic missile launches and notifications prescribed by the INF Treaty, in particular notification of scheduled missile elimination and the intention to conduct an on-site inspection, are communicated via these centers. The possibility of changing the list of notifications is prescribed, as well as transmission of other messages by the parties at their own discretion, as a gesture of good will and for the purpose of confidence-building.

Some agreements have established consultation mechanisms fostering confidence-building between the parties. These include the Standing Consultative Commission established pursuant to the ABM Treaty to assist in implementation of the goals and provisions of this Treaty and a number of other agreements, a Special Consultative Commission prescribed by the INF Treaty, a Joint Military Commission established to consider matters pertaining to the Agreement on Prevention on Dangerous Military Activities, as well as annual consultations and regular communications via naval attaches pursuant to the agreements on prevention of incidents. A similar mechanism–a joint commission on observation and inspections–is to be established for the purpose of helping implement the goals of a future strategic offensive arms treaty.

The Center for the Prevention of Conflicts, established in accordance with the 1990 Paris Charter for a New Europe, should become a qualitatively new mechanism. The Center promotes confidence- and security-building measures by combining the functions of collection and dissemination of information on the military activities of states, helping to increase the transparency of such activities, and clarifying unclear and disputable situations.

3. *Attendant measures.* These measures might include various measures fostering the fulfillment of obligations under disarmament agreements and facilitating verification of compliance. These, for example, would include such measures as exchange of quantitative and other data on arms subject to limitation, reduction or elimination pursuant to the SALT II Treaty, the INF Treaty, the CFE Treaty, and a future treaty on strategic offensive arms, as well as obligations, prescribed by a number of agreements, not to impede national technical means of verification and not to use intentional masking or concealment measures impeding verification with the aid of such means.

4. *Openness and glasnost' in military matters.* These measures, in contrast to such above-listed attendant measures as exchange of data, are carried out by states on a unilateral basis, in particular in conformity with domestic laws. Such measures could include open parliamentary discussion and resolution of matters pertaining to military doctrine, military budget, armed forces manpower acquisition and equipment, employment of military forces beyond national boundaries, arms transfers abroad, *etc.*, as well as voluntary invitation of foreign observers to military installations and activities and public disclosure of information on military matters such as by turning it over to the United Nations.

5. *Military contacts.* Confidence-building measures of this type have recently been placed into a separate group, which is connected with a general improvement in relations between states of opposing military-political alliances, as well as the transformation of these alliances, plus positive experience in employing confidence-building measures in Europe. They consist in development of personal relations between military personnel of all ranks, which constitutes an important supplement to

military-technical confidence-building measures. The USSR Ministry of Defense has twelve interministerial agreements with the counterpart establishments in other countries, for the most part NATO member countries, on the basis of which get-togethers of military personnel and mutual visits of military units, military educational institutions, and other facilities are carried out.

The matter of confidence-building measures has been deliberated by the United Nations since 1978. Paragraph 93 of the Final Document of the UN General Assembly's First Special Session on Disarmament stressed the need to create an atmosphere of trust between states in order to further the disarmament process. A group of government experts appointed by the UN Secretary General, working from April 1980 through August 1981, prepared a study, which was mentioned above. The question of confidence-building measures was considered by the UN Commission on Disarmament, which submitted to the UN General Assembly's Third Session on Disarmament "Draft Guiding Principles for Appropriate Confidence-Building Measures and for Implementation of Such Measures on a Global or Regional Level." The document stated that confidence-building measures should not take the place of disarmament measures nor serve as a preliminary condition for their implementation. Effective disarmament measures, first and foremost nuclear disarmament, are of particular importance as regards confidence-building. In spite of the importance of confidence-building measures, however, the principal role is played by disarmament measures, and only disarmament can make a decisive contribution toward preventing war.

Also on the UN agenda is an item entitled "Objective Information on Military Matters," which is directly related to confidence-building measures. Resolution 44/116E, adopted on this agenda item at the Forty-fourth Session of the General Assembly with 132 members voting in favor, including the Soviet Union and the United States, notes that adoption of confidence-building measures which:

> promote openness and transparency would reduce the risk of misperceptions of military capabilities and intentions . . . . [B]alanced and objective information on all military matters . . . would contribute to the building of confidence among States and to the conclusion of concrete disarmament agreements . . . . [G]reater openness and transparency would contribute to enhancing security.

As noted above, talks on confidence-building measures and strengthening security are being held in Vienna, convened on the basis of the Concluding Document of the Vienna Meeting of Representatives of the States Participants in the CSCE. Their purpose is:

> to build upon and expand the results already achieved at the

> Stockholm Conference with the aim of elaborating and adopting a new set of mutually complementary confidence- and security-building measures designed to reduce the risk of military confrontation in Europe.

The talks are being conducted on the basis of a mandate agreed upon at the Madrid CSCE Meeting in 1983.

In the course of the talks the WTO countries proposed reaching agreement on a new generation of confidence-building measures, which would not only increase the predictability and transparency of military activities but would also limit them, encompassing both the activities of ground forces and naval and air-force activities. The NATO countries placed emphasis on expanding exchange of information, observations, and inspections, limiting them to ground forces activities, while refusing to discuss the possibility of covering the independent activities of air and naval forces by future measures. Their position was limited to certain refinement of the provisions of the Stockholm Document.

Bringing positions on a number of measures regarding ground-forces activities closer together and into agreement was accomplished in the process of talks, although this did not extend to such broad measures as were proposed by the WTO countries; agreement was also reached on matters connected with provision of information on military budgets, establishing a system of communications among the CSCE participating countries, and expanding of military contacts. A seminar on military doctrines was held within the context of these talks. At the same time some agreement was reached regarding covering independent air force activities by future measures; however, the NATO countries considered as a possibility the exchange only of static information, on air force basing, for example, while excluding dynamic information due to difficulties of verification: information on force redeployments, for example, including troop maneuvers—while the WTO countries insisted on the exchange of information of both categories, proposing various verification alternatives.

As regards naval activities, in conformity with the NATO countries' interpretation of the Madrid mandate, these activities are covered by the agreed-upon measures only if they are conducted as an integrated activity jointly with ground forces and under unified operational command. In the opinion of the WTO member states expressed during negotiations, naval forces activities should have been covered by confidence-building measures whenever they affect security in Europe. A possible alternative for bringing positions on naval forces closer together can be found in a proposal by neutral and nonaligned countries on monitoring and observation of amphibious operations, which prescribes that confidence-building measures shall include naval ships conducting and supporting the amphibious landing of troops.

A new direction in talks on problems of confidence-building measures is connected with the "open skies" concept advanced by the U.S. President in May 1989. The "open skies" policy calls for overflights by unarmed aircraft above the territories of the countries party to such an agreement, for the purpose of monitoring military activities. The first two rounds of a conference on this problem were held in Ottawa and Budapest in the first half of 1990, identifying areas for future joint search for solutions.

At the present time Europe is the only region in which militarily significant confidence-building measures are being applied and developed. It would make sense for similar measures, taking the European experience and regional specifics into account, to be formulated for regions other than Europe.

Utilization of current and past experience also makes sense as regards such special measures as measures to prevent incidents and dangerous military activity (increasing the number of bilateral agreements and linking them into an integrated system), establishment of direct communications links, and improvement of military contacts (joint practicing of skills in applying procedures to prevent incidents and dangerous military activity, including the training of personnel and conduct of field exercises, and joint training of nuclear risk reduction center personnel).

Meriting attention are unilateral confidence-building measures of a limited nature, containing elements of arms control, such as reduction of troops, arms and military infrastructure and their withdrawal from foreign soil, as well as, within the framework of the development of measures to prevent surprise attack, the reduction of military activities in border areas adjacent to the territorial waters of other states and in the vicinity of transportation hubs that are potential embarkation points for troops and arms, and the removal of certain strategic forces elements from alert status or relaxation of their operational readiness level.

Future evolution of confidence-building measures could consist in broadening the area of application of existing confidence-building measures and, wherever advisable and feasible, in integrating them into a system, and in strengthening the deterrent and limiting nature of confidence-building measures, whereby they will proceed to move in the direction of disarmament measures.

B.M. Klimenko
Professor, USSR Diplomatic Academy

C. Establishment of Nonmilitarized Zones

Limitation of military forces and arms in border areas constitutes an important measure for preventing a surprise attack. Plans calling for the establishment of zones of limited arms and military forces have been contained in a number of initiatives, especially in the last ten years. Corresponding precedents also exist in international law. Prevention of a surprise attack has always been the purpose for establishing demilitarized zones along national borders. In 1923, when the British representative at the League of Nations proposed the establishment of border demilitarized zones under League auspices, the purpose of this was to prevent a sneak attack and to facilitate the determination of aggressors. A U.S. draft treaty on disarmament and security also recommended the establishment of demilitarized zones, because such zones "would more easily provide that security which is essential for sequential disarmament." A draft treaty of mutual assistance drawn up within the framework of the League of Nations in 1923 and the 1924 Protocol for the Pacific Settlement of International Disputes recommended the establishment of demilitarized zones as zones capable of preventing surprise attacks and facilitating the unequivocal determination of such attacks. Neither of these documents entered into force, however.

The Soviet State has long been familiar with the practice of establishing demilitarized zones. Pursuant to the February 2, 1920, Peace Treaty between Soviet Russia and Estonia, temporary demilitarized zones were established along the borders of both states. A number of similar zones were established by the October 14, 1920, Peace Treaty with Finland as well as the June 1, 1922, Agreement with Finland. Pursuant to the 1921 Treaty between the RSFSR and Turkey, a demilitarized zone was established along the border, on Turkish territory. The Soviet Government in principle viewed favorably an increase in the number of demilitarized zones. In the response by People's Commissar for Foreign Affairs G.V. Chicherin, dated March 12, 1924, to a draft multilateral treaty of mutual assistance proposed by the League of Nations, several provisions of this treaty were supported. In particular, the provisions calling for the establishment of border demilitarized zones were supported, with minor changes. This reply contained a recommendation that there be extensive establishment of partially demilitarized zones on both sides of national borders, in which only limited regular forces could be deployed, monitored by mixed commissions of the parties.

Nevertheless the idea of establishing border demilitarized zones did not enjoy widespread acceptance during the period between the two world wars. This issue was discussed too long and fruitlessly in the League of Nations in the 1920's, while in the 1930's preparations for World War II were in full swing. This opportunity was passed up at that time. And in place of demilitarized zones, so-called "fortified areas" were constructed along the borders. Today the existence of nuclear weapons has radically altered the situation. In these new conditions it would be highly imprudent to let a similar opportunity slip by.

A system for preventing surprise attack that was proposed by the Soviet Government at the end of the 1950's included reducing military forces at the boundary between the two military blocs–the Warsaw Pact and NATO–and establishment of extensive ground and air surveillance in order to prevent a dangerous concentration of military forces in that area. A proposal by the Warsaw Pact member nations for a program of reduction of military forces and arms, dated June 11, 1986, called for reducing the concentration of troops along the line of contact between Warsaw Pact and NATO countries precisely with the aim of lessening the danger of attack. Prevention of the possibility of surprise attack was also one of the purposes of a Polish Government memorandum dated July 22, 1987. Finally, the July 16, 1988, Declaration by Warsaw Pact Member Nations directly noted that reduction and elimination of the danger of surprise attack was the purpose of establishing zones of reduced level of arms along the line of contact between the two military-political alliances.

If plans of this kind were to be implemented, the experience in the conduct of monitoring and verification in zones of limitation of conventional arms and military forces would be of considerable importance for expanding such zones and establishment of totally demilitarized zones, also with subsequent expansion of such zones. The June 11, 1986, proposal by the Warsaw Pact member nations noted that reduction of military forces and conventional arms would be carried out under the monitoring and oversight of national means and international procedures, including on-site inspections. An international consultative commission would also be established, containing representatives of the nations of the Warsaw Pact, NATO, and other European countries. The document noted that on-site verification of the reduction of military forces and the destruction or storage of arms could be performed with the participation of representatives from this commission; monitoring posts could also be established at major rail centers, airports, and seaports. The Polish Government memorandum also called for the establishment of a system of national and international monitoring and verification, including on-site observation and inspection and the establishment of checkpoints.

Zones of limitation of conventional arms and military forces could be established not only along the line of demarcation of military alliances but along national borders in general. These could be completely or partially demilitarized zones. Extensive implementation of this measure would promote limitation of conventional arms and adoption of a doctrine of minimum military sufficiency for defense, and would also promote the security of nations, since it would create substantial obstacles against the mounting of surprise offensive operations. It is precisely in this connection that M.S. Gorbachev notes the advisability of monitored withdrawal from borders of "nuclear and other offensive weapons, with subsequent establishment of zones with reduced density of arms as well as demilitarized zones along borders . . . ."

With favorable conditions, an entire system of demilitarized zones could be established along the borders of many states. Such a system would constitute a substantial contribution toward the establishment of comprehensive international security. First of all, a fully demilitarized zone approximately 100 kilometers deep would be established along any border; only a minimum essential number of border guards could be deployed in this zone. Secondly, another, partially demilitarized zone would be established behind this border zone, of approximately the same depth, with deployment of the minimum quantity of military forces essential for defense. Thirdly, the two above zones, plus a third zone, also 100 kilometers deep, let us say, behind the first two zones would comprise a nuclear-free corridor between adjacent countries.

International monitoring and verification is of considerable importance for implementation of these measures. One should note in this connection M.S. Gorbachev's proposal for establishment under UN auspices of a mechanism of "extensive international verification of compliance with agreements pertaining to lessening international tension, arms reduction, as well as monitoring of the military situation in conflict areas." One of the tasks of this mechanism would be to gather appropriate information that "would make it possible to possess an objective picture of events taking place, promptly to detect preparations for military operations, and to make it difficult to carry out a surprise attack . . . ." All these things happen to be highly applicable to border areas.

Performance of international monitoring in the first zone would be facilitated by virtue of its total demilitarization. The methods and forms of monitoring mentioned in the July 11, 1986, declaration of the Warsaw Pact member nations and in the July 22, 1987, Polish memorandum, in particular the exchange of requisite information, performance of on-site observations and inspections, establishment of checkpoints on zone boundaries, establishment of mixed commissions of the interested parties to conduct monitoring and verification, *etc.*, could be employed in the second, partially demilitarized zone. Finally, monitoring and verification measures to ensure a nuclear-free status could be employed throughout the entire nuclear-free corridor along both sides of the border, in particular national and international monitoring measures, including the establishment of a permanent international commission, which would conduct on-site inspection when necessary. All these methods and forms of monitoring and verification could be linked to the activities of the above-mentioned international monitoring and verification mechanism under UN auspices.

The effectiveness of the above-mentioned demilitarized zones could be increased by, in addition, carrying out specific confidence-building measures in these zones. The immediate aim of all confidence-building measures is to promote mutual understanding and confidence-building in regard to the military activities of the parties, as well as the strengthening of the factor of stability and security in relations between states. And the creation of confidence on the part of countries that a surprise attack will not be launched against them is, in the final analysis, the common objective.

5. PREVENTION AND CONTROL OF INTERNATIONAL TERRORISM

Paul B. Stephan III
Percy Brown, Jr. Professor of Law, University of Virginia

A. GENERAL PRINCIPLES AND RULES

The most fundamental problem facing that part of international law that governs terrorism is definitional. There are two aspects to the controversy: identifying what distinguishes international terrorism from other kinds of armed conflict, and determining what forms of terrorism transgress international norms.

Everyone would agree that, at a minimum, terrorism consists of the use of force against noncombatants, but something more is necessary to distinguish it from other kinds of organized violence. Some scholars have suggested that its definitive aspect is the use of violence for psychological rather than for classically military ends—the terrorist does not seek to attain concrete military objectives, or even to use the mission's success as a basis for building a military organization, but rather attempts to demoralize a target society by undermining its self-confidence and stability. Terrorist actions often seek to provoke disproportionate retaliation, as classical military activity does not, in order to aggravate popular dissatisfaction with the status quo.

Of course, this definition presents debatable issues. Some would argue, for example, that saturation bombing of civilian targets and the mining of harbors qualify as terrorism, because such attacks are meant to unnerve the general civilian population. The rejoinder, however, is that attacks on legitimate economic targets can be justified under the law of armed conflict, assuming the use of force otherwise is appropriate. As long as economic damage rather than psychological terror is the principal purpose for a mission, the action should not be termed "terrorism."

The U.S. Congress has followed the purpose-based definition of terrorism in at least two instances. The Foreign Intelligence Surveillance Act, which specifies those areas in which the intelligence agencies of the

United States can conduct investigations, includes "international terrorism" among the subjects of legitimate intelligence activity. The Act describes terrorism as conduct that (1) would violate the criminal laws of the United States were it to occur within U.S. jurisdiction; (2) occurs totally outside the United States or otherwise transcends national boundaries; and (3) has one of three purposes: (a) intimidation or coercion of a civilian population; (b) intimidation or coercion of a government's policy; or (c) attempting to affect the conduct of government by kidnapping or assassination. Second, the Omnibus Diplomatic Security and Antiterrorism Act of 1986 asserts U.S. criminal jurisdiction over homicides and assaults performed against citizens of the United States, or conspiracies to carry out such acts, anywhere in the world, if the Attorney General certifies that the offense was "intended to coerce, intimidate, or retaliate against a government or a civilian population."

Other jurists are dissatisfied with a definition that depends on the subjective intent of the actors, arguing that in practice no one can apply such a standard in a way that others will accept as neutral and law-based. A few publicists have tried to escape this trap by referring to terrorism as "internationally proscribed violence." Unfortunately, this ultimately circular definition causes more problems than it solves, as there exists no consensus about what the international community proscribes. The difficulty lies in the existence of international law of a principle recognizing the legitimacy of struggles for national self-determination, and the willingness of many members of the international community to use this principle to justify particular instances of international terrorism.

This deep problem has its roots in a paradox. Although some forms of violence seem antithetical to the maintenance of civilized existence, most members of the international community have revolutionary antecedents and therefore accept the principle that under specified circumstances an all-out attack on an established order can be justified. During the nineteenth century the United States and France were leaders in developing a "political offense" concept that allowed a nation to shelter persons who had committed acts of terror against other regimes. During the twentieth century, with the ascendance of the principles of national self-determination and decolonization, the number of struggles that arguably qualify as "political" have grown. The United Nations in particular has consistently applied political qualifications to all of its condemnations of terrorism. The most sweeping declaration, General Assembly Resolution 40/61, still has been interpreted by member states as containing exceptions for persons exercising their right of national self-determination and struggling against racist or colonial regimes. Even cases of purely domestic terrorism, directed by citizens against their own state (one might count Germany's Red Army Faction and the Italian Red

Brigade as examples) have been defended as attacks on regimes that engage in oppression and alien domination outside their national borders.

The conflict between the principles of non-use of force, on the one hand, and of legitimate struggle for self-determination, on the other hand, might not be as troubling if the international community had adapted the law governing armed conflict to apply some restraints on politically based terrorism. Unfortunately, the movement in recent years has been in the opposite direction. Protocol I to the Geneva Conventions, produced by the Geneva Diplomatic Conference on the Reaffirmation of International Humanitarian Law Applicable in Armed Conflict, contains several articles that in effect impose less rigorous limitations on terrorists and terrorist organizations than those governing conventional armed combat. Among other matters, the Conference came to the conclusion that terrorists could mask themselves by blending into the civilian population both immediately before and after engaging in acts of terror. The United States ultimately rejected Protocol I (although initially it had signed the Protocol) because of the failure to devise acceptable rules for limiting the freedom of scope for political terrorism.

Given the lack of agreement about what constitutes internationally proscribed terrorism, it should surprise no one that the international community also is divided about the appropriate responses a target nation can undertake. In the aftermath of the Entebbe affair, some publicists condemned the Israeli raid by asserting that the principle of national sovereignty precluded any attempt to combat an ongoing terrorist action on the soil of another nation. Although the United Nations has not explicitly repudiated this extreme position, the experience of the 1980's suggests that states may take appropriate and proportionate measures to rescue those of its citizens held hostage by another state, or by organizations protected by another state.

Some publicists have argued in particular that the right of self-defense, memorialized in Article 51 of the UN Charter but previously recognized as an inherent aspect of national sovereignty, includes the right to take proportionate measures to defends a state's nationals from attack. The United States has asserted this principle, *inter alia*, as justification for the abortive attempt to rescue the Tehran embassy hostages. Other states and scholars dispute whether a terrorist action, if tolerated by a state but not implemented through its uniformed armed forces, can constitute an "armed attack" against which self-defense is justified. Proponents of the first position argue that the "narrow" approach is overly formalistic and out of touch with modern realities and contemporary state practice; proponents of the "narrow" position claim too elastic a concept of self-defense would provide too many pretexts for aggression. The question remains unresolved.

Much more controversial is the use of reprisals to punish and deter international terrorism. The UN Security Council has condemned several reprisal actions by Israel, but a motion to condemn the United States for its April 15, 1986, attack on Libya did not pass. Some UN resolutions, as well as the commentary of some jurists, suggests that a nation may never engage in reprisals once a particular terrorist operation has ended. Other jurists have argued that proportionate measures taken to deter an imminent and specific threat of violence fall within the legitimate scope of self-defense. The United States justified its attack on Libya by reference to this principle. Furthermore, it has sought to demonstrate the operational validity of the concept by condemning various actions by Israel that, in the judgment of the U.S. government, constituted excessive responses to threats that were not imminent or specific.

Another controversial form of self-help is the apprehension of terrorists outside the territorial jurisdiction of the target state. Ideally the issue should never arise. If all nations were to recognize a common concept of international terrorism and to agree either to extradite or to prosecute terrorists found within their borders, self-help would never be necessary. But the lack of agreement about the scope of internationally proscribed terrorism means that many nations are faced with the choice of pursuing self-help or allowing what can be regarded as dangerous criminal activity to go unpunished. The kidnapping of Nazi war criminal Adolf Eichman is only the most prominent example of a nation placing its right to capture an international terrorist above the respect normally due to another nation's sovereignty.

In some instances, the dilemma is mostly symbolic, as the nation harboring the fugitive tacitly welcomes the opportunity to rid itself of an unwelcome guest. In others, the prosecuting state may not regard its interest in punishing terrorism as sufficiently great to outweigh its desire to maintain good relations with the harboring state. But in many cases a sharp conflict can arise between the principle of national sovereignty and the obligation to prosecute or extradite international criminals. Ideally states should rely on consultations and cooperation to reconcile such conflicts, but the absence of a widely accepted mechanism for balancing national sovereignty and the obligation to punish has created serious, and on occasion dangerous, tensions. Self-help is disfavored in international law, as a state is not likely to be the most objective judge of the merits of its own claims. Yet unless the international law system can come up with effective measures that address the legitimate interests of states that frequently find themselves the targets of international terrorism, self-help, and the concomitant erosion of important norms of international law, is likely to occur more often.

Although no one can ignore these serious shortcomings in the international law governing terrorism, the international community has not completely failed to develop legal means for combatting international terrorism. Successes have come in two general areas: the development of multilateral and bilateral agreements that clarify and narrow the principle of legitimate insurrection as a limitation on proscribed terrorism, and the identification of particular forms of terrorism that cannot be justified regardless of their political context.

In spite (or perhaps because) of the failure of the United Nations to develop a workable concept of internationally outlawed terrorism, several nations have reached important multilateral and bilateral agreements about the definition of terrorism and the obligation to prosecute or extradite. Prominent examples include the European Convention on Extradition and the U.S.-U.K. Supplemental Extradition Treaty. What these agreements reflect is a shared belief among the parties that the covered nations have sufficiently free and open political systems to strip all moral authority from armed attacks on the established order. They distinguish, in other words, between radical politics, which the member states at least tolerate and sometimes encourage, and violent politics, which the parties find intolerable.

The agreements implement this belief by narrowing considerably the political offense exception to the duty to extradite. The European Convention, for example, enumerates offenses that cannot be characterized as political, including violations of the Hague and Montreal Conventions on civil aviation and of the New York Convention on internationally protected persons, in addition to hostage taking and offenses involving bombs, automatic firearms, and other weapons of mass terror. Although the European Convention does allow the parties to state reservations to the obligation to prosecute or extradite, it restricts this discretion in cases involving collective danger, the targeting of victims with no connection to the alleged grievance, or the use of cruel or vicious methods.

To be sure, some might see a tension between agreements such as the European Convention, which imply a distinction between nations with open and closed political systems, and principles of equality and nondiscrimination in international law. But unless the political offense exception itself constitutes a norm of international law, the decision of states selectively to restrict the concept does not violate any international duty. Rather than criticize the process, publicists might do better to identify and to formalize the criteria that states should use when deciding which nations ought to have a broader right to receive jurisdiction over international terrorists.

Without intending to demean the principle of national self-determination, one can perceive great pressure building in the international system for more limitations on political justifications for terrorism. There are few great nations in the world today that do not face within their borders some form of separatist struggle based on claims of decolonization and national self-determination. To take only a few prominent examples, Native American, Puerto Rican, and Black independence movements in the United States have justified acts of violence on these grounds; Native Americans and Francophones in Canada have made similar claims; the United Kingdom continues to wrestle with the Irish question; and the Soviet Union has faced armed disorders in the Caucasian and Central Asian republics. Without attempting to assess the merits of these disputes, it seems unlikely that any of these states will be content to see perpetrators of acts of mass violence escape to other nations and then claim the protection of the political offense principle.

The other achievement of international law involves the specification of particular acts of terrorism that, for the most part, the international community accepts as intolerable regardless of the political context. The challenge for the future will involve using those Conventions that have been widely accepted as models for the identification of other areas of protected activity. These conventions, and the areas where further development is possible, are best discussed in terms of the broad categories of the terrorist acts they involve.

B. Measures Against Terrorism on Land

Some international consensus has been achieved in two areas: the protection of internationally significant persons, and a prohibition of hostage-taking. Both of these obligations reflect widely (although, regrettably, not universally) observed norms that in recent years have been codified in various conventions. As recent experience in Iraq demonstrates, more work is needed to develop internationally acceptable sanctions to be applied to states that violate these norms.

Throughout history nations have accorded special status to diplomats and heads of state. Norms such as immunity from judicial process as well as a heightened obligation to protect their persons from physical danger reflect a simple insight about international discourse: Unless nations respect the representatives of other states, relations among states will be even more unreliable and dangerous than the normal exigencies of the world require. Although instances of international assassination of heads of state and of abuse of diplomats have occurred, they are remarkably rare. During the unprecedented conflagration of the 1939-1945 war, for example, heads of state and diplomats received relatively cordial treatment.

In the aftermath of the war, an effort was made to elaborate on the scope of this norm. An important early achievement was the Vienna

Convention on Diplomatic Relations, which defines the category of protected persons and specifies a duty to protect them. By the beginning of the 1970's, however, it had become clear that several international terrorist organizations had begun to choose diplomats as targets of choice. Prompted by several fatal attacks, including the murder of the American ambassador to Sudan, the United Nations again took up the matter. The result was the Convention on the Prevention and Punishment of Crimes Against Internationally Protected Persons, Including Diplomatic Agents.

The Convention identifies as protected persons heads of states, heads of government, foreign ministers, diplomats, and consuls, as well as members of their households, during the time they are in a foreign state and engaged in the conduct of international relations. The status of diplomats and consuls in particular is determined by reference to other international conventions, particularly the Vienna Conventions on Diplomatic Relations and on Consular Relations. All parties must establish jurisdiction over the murder, kidnapping, or similar assaults against protected persons, and must adhere to the duty to prosecute or extradite persons that commit these crimes. The Convention also contains a less specific obligation to cooperate in the prevention of such attacks.

The Convention itself contains no language qualifying this duty by excepting attacks that occur as part of a struggle for national self-determination. During the debates before and after its adoption, however, a number of states asserted the self-determination principle as a limitation on the duty to protect. The General Assembly enacted a non-binding resolution to this effect before adopting the Convention. The fact that some states remain willing to assert this ground as a basis for refusing to act in conformity with the Convention remains a cause for deep concern. Although proponents of national liberation struggles can argue that differences in the conditions of combat justify the application of norms that differ from those governing conventional armed conflict, it is difficult to understand why a departure from this particular norm is necessary.

The actions of self-described national liberation groups aside, the conduct of states under the Convention has been for the most part acceptable. Until recently the major departure has been Iran's seizure of the American embassy staff in December 1979. This action, which involved torture and other assaults as well as an illegal detention, was condemned by the International Court of Justice but has not resulted in either compensation or an apology by the Iranian government. Even those events, which took part in the context of revolutionary upheaval, pales beside the government of Iraq's seizure of diplomats in transit from Kuwait pursuant to a promise of safe conduct. One can hope that this blatant violation of international law will result in the adoption of stronger measures to protect against future transgressions.

Another convention that has attempted to limit the scope of permissible terrorist activity is the International Convention Against the Taking of Hostages. The use of hostages is a particularly despicable tactic in any armed struggle. The UN Security Council has unequivocally condemned hostage taking, both in general (as in its resolution of December 18, 1985) and in the context of the Iraqi invasion of Kuwait. The Convention is the United Nations' most concrete step to implement this judgment.

The Hostage Convention defines the offense as seizing and threatening to injure or to continue to hold hostages with the goal of compelling another party to undertake or to refrain from undertaking some action. Parties are obligated to treat such conduct as a serious crime, to take measures to secure the release of the hostages, and to cooperate in the prevention of hostage taking. Although the Convention does not apply to some struggles for national self-determination, it was drafted in such a way to make its prosecute-or-extradite obligation inoperative only when a comparable obligation exists under the Geneva Conventions of 1949 and their Additional Protocols. It is the position of many publicists, as well as that of the U.S. government, that a Party to the Hostage Convention must regard itself as always bound by a duty to prosecute or extradite under one of the two sets of Conventions. It is conceivable, however, that other states might reject this interpretation and regard some hostage taking as justifiable.

Two other problematic aspects of the Hostage Convention are its limitation on the duty to extradite and its posture toward self-help. Under the Convention a state may not extradite a hostage-taker if it has substantial grounds for believing the state requesting jurisdiction has as its intent persecution of a person "on account of his race, religion, nationality, ethnic origin or political opinion." In the view of the U.S. government, this limitation does not apply to the duty to prosecute. In other words, a state that will not extradite must prosecute a hostage-taker.

Finally, the Convention contains language stating that none of the duties it imposes justifies "the violation of the territorial integrity or political independence of a State in contravention of the Charter of the United Nations." This provision, although formally innocuous, leaves unresolved the question of whether intervention to rescue hostages held by a state violates the Charter or other norms of international law. As mentioned previously, a number of states have interpreted international law as condoning proportionate measures used to terminate ongoing terrorist hostage seizures. Perhaps the aftermath of the Iraqi crisis, involving as it did the grossest violation of the hostage-taking norm in modern history, will contribute to a wider international understanding of the appropriate measures a state may undertake to rescue victims of this form of international terrorism.

C. Measures Against Terrorism Affecting Aviation

Until the beginning of the 1970's many nations, including the United States, condoned some forms of terrorist attacks on civil aviation if they accepted the underlying political ends of the persons taking the action. During the 1950's, for example, many Western countries refused to return to Czechoslovakia, Poland, the Soviet Union, and Yugoslavia persons who had hijacked airplanes in order to flee those countries. But after a series of terrorist events in the late 1960's, the UN General Assembly in December 1969 adopted a resolution calling on nations to take effective measures to prevent and punish unlawful diversions of civil aircraft and other attacks on civil aviation. The ensuing treaties on aircraft hijacking and sabotage, and in particular the manner in which states have implemented them, represent the high water mark of international cooperation in the struggle against terrorism.

The Convention on the Suppression of Unlawful Seizure of Aircraft (the Hague Convention), adopted in December 1970, provides important tools for combatting attacks on civil aircraft. Parties are obligated to prosecute or extradite persons who seize aircraft and attempt to divert them. The Convention on the Suppression of Unlawful Acts Against the Safety of Civil Aviation (the Montreal Convention), adopted the following year, extended this obligation to sabotage, bombing, and similar acts that endanger aviation. A 1988 Protocol further strengthened protection of civil aviation by outlawing acts of violence against persons and property at international airports.

Over the United States' objection, the Hague and Montreal Conventions did not include language that, in the view of the United States, would forbid an exception for political offenses. A concern exists that states might treat particular attacks on civil aviation as arising out of a struggle for national self-determination, and as a result might refuse either to extradite or to prosecute. So far, however, state practice has seemed to recognize that such struggles cannot justify attacks on civil aircraft, which by their nature involve innocent victims and the risk of mass murder. Extradition has been the norm rather than the exception, and in almost all cases where a state has retained jurisdiction over hijackers a prosecution has ensued. An important event in this new era of international cooperation was the joint actions of the Soviet Union and Israel in apprehending airline hijackers in December 1988. In spite of the lack of normal diplomatic relations between those two countries, their governments worked together to free the hostages, to capture the criminals, and to return the terrorists to the jurisdiction of the Soviet Union, the target of the attack.

Some breakdowns in cooperation have occurred. In 1978, when

persons seized a Polish jetliner and diverted it from East to West Berlin, the subsequent criminal prosecution was tried by a special court established in Berlin under the four powers agreement rather than under FRG, DDR, or Polish jurisdiction. The U.S. judge, through several debatable rulings involving trial procedure, may have undermined confidence in the seriousness of the prosecution, and the defendants were acquitted. The destruction of Pan American Flight 103 over Lockerbie, Scotland, was a cruel reminder that terrorism, possibly with the covert support of particular governments, remains an ongoing threat. But on balance the Hague and Montreal Conventions have contributed to international security by promoting cooperative efforts to prosecute terrorists, thereby deterring assaults on civil aviation.

D. Measures Against Terrorism on the Seas

International law is not as developed with respect to terrorist attacks on civil navigation, possibly because seagoing vessels have not been common targets. Terrorists seem to prefer to go after international flights, perhaps because it is easy to focus the media's attention on a large plane stranded on a runway, or perhaps because terrorists believe that the popular masses will associate flights with economic élites. It is harder to bring a hijacked ship within range of television cameras, and the popular image of the common seaman may undercut whatever political point the terrorist hopes to make. But terrorist attacks on navigation have occurred, demonstrating some of the inadequacies of the current state of the law.

The traditional law of piracy might cover terrorist attacks on ships and persons in cases where the victims are not subjects of the country with which the attacker is engaged in conflict. In the *Achille Lauro* affair, for example, the professed political end of the terrorists who seized the ship and murdered one of its passengers was to further a national liberation struggle in Israel, but neither the ship nor its passengers were Israeli. Unfortunately, the 1958 Geneva Convention on the High Seas and the 1982 UN Convention on the Law of the Sea propose to exclude from the definition of piracy any action that does not have a private end, which in the view of the United States means that political acts do not constitute piracy. If this distinction reflects an international consensus, then all of the difficulties inherent in the political offense exception to international crimes would apply to piracy.

Because of these inadequacies in traditional international law, the widespread adoption of the Convention for the Suppression of Unlawful Acts Against the Safety of Maritime Navigation (along with the Fixed Platform Additional Protocol) becomes all the more important. This measure covers both hijacking and sabotage directed against ships, and applies obligations on its parties similar to those found in the Hague and Montreal Conventions. If the international community demonstrates the same willingness to treat attacks on civil navigation as unjustifiable even in the context of struggles for self-determination, and cooperate as closely in the extradition and prosecution of persons that carry out such attacks, then it may be possible to enhance the security of seagoing vessels from the depredations of terrorists.

A.V. Zmeyevskii
First Secretary, International Law Directorate, USSR Ministry of Foreign Relations

A. General Principles and Rules

Terrorism is one of the most troubling global problems, and it is directly linked to problems of ensuring international security. Today terrorism has reached such a scale that it has become transformed into a factor destabilizing the normal development of international relations. Terrorist actions have an explosive potential capable of paralyzing the political will of governments and of creating crisis situations fraught with the peril of sharp aggravation of the international situation. The potential threat of use by terrorists of nuclear, chemical, biological and other materials to achieve their objectives arouses particular concern on the part of the world community.

Efforts to combat terrorism constitute a struggle to normalize the overall international situation. There also exists an inverse linkage: Implementation of a policy directed toward eliminating tension in the world, toward ending regional crises and conflicts works steadfastly toward diminishing the level of terrorism both in individual countries and regions and in the world as a whole.

The process of development of international cooperation to counter terrorism and the forming of its fundamental principles and rules has passed through specific historical stages. Initial multilateral efforts by states in this area date from the end of the 1920's to the latter half of the 1930's. In the course of international conferences on standardization of criminal laws, in spite of certain costs connected with the political tendency of the resolutions drawn up at these conferences, some experience was amassed in multilateral efforts to search for ways to accomplish joint measures to combat terrorism. In the Madrid Conference in 1934 the participants succeeded in formulating and adopting a definition of terrorism, which was defined as the employment of any means capable of terrorizing the population, for the purpose of destroying any social organization. Due attention was devoted in Madrid to the creation of mechanisms that would make it possible to carry out the criminal prosecution of terrorists beyond national boundaries. The "standardizers" came very close to recognition of the objective need for bolstering measures undertaken at the national level with the drafting of corresponding international legal norms and agreements.

The drafting of a Convention for the Prevention and Punishment of Terrorism, completed in 1937 under the auspices of the League of Nations, as well as a Convention on the Establishment of an International Court of Criminal Justice, constituted a new phase of international cooperation of states in this area. Although neither of these Conventions entered into force, many of their provisions formed the basis for the development of such current principles and rules of international coordination in the fight against terrorism as inescapable punishment of criminals, universal jurisdiction, the obligation of Parties either to extradite or to prosecute a criminal, mutual exchange of pertinent information, *etc.*

The present-day parameters of international cooperation in this field essentially emerged in the postwar period. At the present stage they form a system of international measures to combat terrorism, which includes cooperation at global and regional levels as well as on a bilateral basis.

At the global level such coordination is concentrated in the UN and its specialized agencies, particularly the International Civil Aviation Organization (ICAO), the International Maritime Organization (IMO), and the International Atomic Energy Agency (IAEA). An international legal basis for such cooperation has been established and is operating under their auspices. There are seven universal agreements: the 1963 Tokyo Convention on Crimes and Certain Other Acts Committed Aboard Aircraft; the 1970 Hague Convention for the Suppression of Unlawful Seizure of Aircraft; the 1971 Montreal Convention for the Suppression of Unlawful Acts Against the Safety of Civil Aviation; the 1973 New York Convention on the Prevention and Punishment of Crimes Against Internationally Protected Persons, Including Diplomatic Agents; the 1979 International Convention Against the Taking of Hostages; the 1979 Convention on the Physical Protection of Nuclear Material; and the 1988 Protocol on the Suppression of Unlawful Acts of Violence at Airports Serving International Civil Aviation, supplementing the Montreal Convention. The following were adopted in 1988 but have not yet entered into force: the Rome Convention on the Suppression of Unlawful Acts Against the Safety of Maritime Navigation, and the Protocol on the Suppression of Unlawful Acts Against the Safety of Fixed Platforms Located on the Continental Shelf.

At the regional level matters of cooperation in the campaign against terrorism are deliberated within the framework of such forums as the Conference on Security and Cooperation in Europe, the EC, the Council of Europe, the Organization of American States (OAS), the South Asian Association for Regional Cooperation (SAARC), *etc.* A number of international instruments governing cooperation at this level have been drawn up and are in operation: the Final Act of the Helsinki Conference and the Concluding Documents of the Madrid and Vienna meetings of the Conference on Security and Cooperation in Europe; the resolutions and decisions adopted by EC bodies; the 1971 Convention to Prevent and Punish Acts of Terrorism Taking the Form of Crimes Against Persons and Related Extortion That Are of International Significance, drafted by the OAS; the 1977 European Convention on the Suppression of Terrorism, drafted by the Council of Europe; and the 1987 SAARC Regional Convention on the Suppression of Terrorism.

Cooperation on a bilateral basis takes place in the form of dialogue at various levels, as well as on the basis of bilateral agreements. In the 1970's for example, the Soviet Union entered into bilateral agreements with Afghanistan, Iran, Finland, and Turkey (the latter did not enter into force, as it was not ratified by the Turkish Government) on cooperation in preventing the hijacking of civil aircraft. Bilateral agreements on suppressing terrorism, including at an intergovernmental level, have been concluded, for example, between Italy and Turkey, France and Spain, France and Venezuela, and the United States and Italy.

Discussion of the specific features of coordination among states in the campaign against terrorism on the regional level and on a bilateral level perhaps should be the subject of a separate study. This article, however, deals with the fundamental principles and rules governing at the world level cooperation between states in combating acts of international terrorism committed during peacetime. A prohibition of acts of a terrorist nature during armed conflicts is prescribed by rules of international humanitarian law, in particular the provisions of the 1977 Additional Protocols to the 1949 Geneva Conventions for the Protection of War Victims.

Among the basic principles governing the conduct of parties to international law in combating terrorism, a key position is occupied by the principle of universal condemnation and acknowledgment of the unlawfulness of terrorism in all its manifestations, regardless of where terrorist acts are committed. From the standpoint of legislative form and content, this principle, and particularly its first part, is at the development stage. At the present time the forming of universal condemnation of terrorism is essentially implemented in the form of political declarations of a unilateral, bilateral, and multilateral nature, as well as in the resolutions of international organizations.

Universal condemnation of terrorism on a consensual basis can most probably be considered one of the historic services of the UN to mankind. On December 9, 1985, the UN General Assembly adopted without a vote Resolution 40/61, in the very first point of the statement of provisions in which it "[u]nequivocally condemns, as criminal, all acts, methods and practices of terrorism wherever and by whomever committed, including those which jeopardize friendly relations among States and their security."

Condemnation of terrorism also finds expression in universal treaty documents. In particular, the above-cited point of UN General Assembly Resolution 40/61 is reproduced word for word in the preamble to the 1988 Convention on the Suppression of Unlawful Acts Against the Safety of Maritime Navigation.

As for the acknowledgment of the unlawfulness of terrorism in all its manifestations, regardless of where terrorist acts are committed and by whom, this part of the principle in question, in addition to the above, is also grounded on corresponding provisions of virtually all current universal international agreements in this area, which designate as crimes the list of unlawful intentional actions that it contains. Condemnation of terrorism as an unlawful act is beginning to move increasingly from the political and diplomatic domain to the international legal level, thus opening up additional possibilities for expanding the political and legal foundation for coordinated actions by the international community to suppress terrorism.

Also of importance is the fact that the unlawful nature of acts of terrorism is recognized by the international community, regardless of who commits such acts and where they are committed. The fight against terrorism tolerates no exemptions. It is apparently not mere happenstance that a new determination of acts of terrorism as "not justifiable" appeared in UN General Assembly Resolution 44/29, adopted by consensus in December 1989. No references to any motives, including motives that would extenuate or justify such acts, are contained in any of the current universal agreements in this area.

We feel that the next logical step to be taken by the international community toward eliminating any exceptions in the fight against terrorism could be condemnation of this phenomenon and acknowledgment of its illegality regardless of the motives for committing terrorist acts. Ideas proceeding in this direction are contained in letters by the representatives of the Soviet Union and other East European countries distributed at the Forty-second and Forty-fourth UN General Assembly Sessions (Document A/42/416 of June 24, 1987 and Document A/S.6/44/4 of October 17, 1989).

A paradoxical situation has developed today: Efforts have been unsuccessful to find a generally acceptable definition of terrorism, although everybody understands what this phenomenon means. Elements present include unlawful force, as a rule with the use of weapons, plus the attempt to intimidate large segments of the population and innocent victims, as well as an international element in the case of terrorist acts extending beyond national borders. Of course terrorism is an objectively complex, extremely dynamic phenomenon, in which sometimes even its fundamental components undergo changes. For example, at the end of the last and beginning of the present century, as well as somewhat later, political motivation was viewed as a component element of terrorist actions, at least at the international level. "Yet it is now found," reads a study on this issue, prepared in 1972 by the UN Secretariat (Document A/C.6/418),

> that quite similar acts, spreading similar terror or alarm among a given population are done for ordinary criminal motives, such as extortion of large sums. . . . From the standpoint of the innocent there is no reason to limit international discussion to terrorist acts with political aims, while leaving very similar acts with ordinary criminal aims. (Page 6).

In addition to legal problems, terrorism has a number of other aspects: historical, philosophical, psychological, technical, *etc.* We feel, however, that in the final analysis it is not these objective difficulties that have prevented reaching a common understanding of this problem.

The impasse in which efforts to reach a generally acceptable definition of terrorism, including international terrorism, found itself, was not created today or yesterday, and in large measure was created artificially. The ideological weighing down of this problem was clearly manifested in the course of the work of the Special Committee on International Terrorism established by the UN General Assembly at the beginning of the 1970's. The majority of those on the committee rejected determinations, interpretation of which could place national liberation and revolutionary movements in the same category with terrorism. The concept of state terrorism (as the most dangerous variation of international terrorism), that is, actions undertaken at the governmental level for the purpose of undermining the sovereignty and independence of other states, for the purpose of impeding exercise of the right of peoples to self-determination, a concept which was advanced by the nonaligned countries, proved unacceptable to the Western states.

On December 17, 1984, the UN General Assembly adopted, at the initiative of the Soviet Union, Resolution 39/159, entitled "The Inadmissibility of the Policy of State Terrorism and Any Actions by States Aimed at Undermining the Socio-political System in Other Sovereign States." In particular, this resolution condemned the policy and practice of terrorism in intergovernmental relations as a method of conduct of affairs with other states and peoples. One hundred and seventeen members voted for the resolution, nobody voted against it, while thirty states abstained, including the United States. The concept of state terrorism did not undergo further development in the United Nations.

Various propaganda campaigns (which became particularly intensified at the beginning of the 1980's), with accusations of involvement in terrorism or of support of terrorism by certain states, also had an extremely destructive effect on the search for mutually acceptable solutions in the matter of defining international terrorism.

The elimination of artificially created barriers and obstacles presents states with new possibilities as regards development of the principle of cooperation in the campaign against terrorism, consistent embodiment of which opens up wide the way toward effectively combating this phenomenon.

Fundamental parameters of intergovernmental coordination in this area include consistent adherence to international law in the campaign against terrorism. This most important point has been reflected not only in corresponding General Assembly resolutions. The preamble to the 1988 Rome Convention acknowledges, in particular, recognizes "the need for all States, in combating unlawful acts against the safety of maritime navigation, strictly to comply with rules and principles of general international law."

The fight against terrorism can be waged only with "clean hands," with reliance on values common to all mankind. Protection of the life, liberty and dignity of each individual and of entire peoples should constitute the point of departure for consolidation of international efforts in this area.

Deideologization of cooperation in these matters is essential, as is, in particular, a move away from equating with international terrorism, for political or ideological reasons, the national liberation struggles of peoples, conducted on the basis of and in conformity with the UN Charter, to exercise their right to self-determination.

The basic foundation of any cooperation, and particularly in such a delicate area as combating terrorism, is confidence-building. Without this it is impossible to raise the common denominator of willingness of states to interact and to form a common front in the fight against this phenomenon.

The principle of cooperation of states in the struggle against terrorism has found expression in many resolutions of bodies of the UN, ICAO, IMO, and other international organizations and has been formally articulated in all current universal as well as regional and bilateral agreements governing the interaction of states against various manifestations of terrorism.

The Declaration on the Enhancement of the Effectiveness of the

Principle of Refraining from the Threat or Use of Force in International Relations, adopted by the UN General Assembly in 1987, specifies two principal areas in which cooperation of states should be carried out in this area "at the bilateral, regional and international levels."

1. *Active assistance in eliminating the causes of international terrorism.* Coordinated efforts of states to eliminate focal points of international tension and regional crises and conflicts that constitute fertile soil for terrorist acts and other manifestations of violence, take on particular significance in this connection. It is the duty of every state to make a contribution toward international efforts to eliminate the root causes of this phenomenon. The UN Special Committee on International Terrorism has listed among such causes, in particular, the use of force contrary to the UN Charter, aggression, infringement of the political independence, sovereignty and territorial integrity of states, racism, a policy of apartheid and genocide, fascism and neofascism, maintenance of an unjust and unequal international economic order, political, social, and economic injustice and exploitation, violation of human rights, hunger, want, poverty, suffering, *etc.* Drawing attention to the study conducted by the Special Committee on this subject, the UN General Assembly repeatedly appealed to states and UN Agencies to help accomplish the gradual elimination of the root causes of international terrorism, devoting thereby special attention to all situations, including colonialism and racism, and situations connected with mass and gross violations of human rights and basic freedoms, as well as situations resulting from foreign domination and occupation, which can give rise to international terrorism and place international peace and security in jeopardy (*e.g.*, UN General Assembly Resolutions 42/159 of December 7, 1987, and 44/29 of December 4, 1989).

2. *Prevention and suppression of international terrorism.* An analysis of treaty provisions currently in force in this area enables one to identify a number of components of this area of cooperation. First of all, there is cooperation by states within the framework of international agreements on these matters to which they are party, including bringing their domestic legislation into conformity with these agreements. Such interaction proceeds from an imperative principle of international law: good-faith fulfillment of international obligations, which in international practice has found expression in a number of international legal documents, including the 1969 Vienna Convention on the Law of Treaties: "Every treaty in force is binding upon the parties to it and must be performed by them in good faith." (Article 26).

Joint efforts by states for the purpose of drawing up new agreements in this area are a logical continuation of this cooperation. In particular, at the present time work is in progress within the framework of the ICAO on a convention to govern an international regime of tagging explosives for the purpose of ensuring their detection.

Preventive measures undertaken by states constitute a most important area of cooperation, in particular measures to prevent preparation and organizational activities on their respective territories aimed at carrying out on or outside their territories terrorist acts directed against other states and their citizens. The norms prescribing such measures were set forth in the 1937 Convention for Prevention and Punishment of Terrorism, drawn up under League of Nations auspices, and they also are embodied in agreements currently in force. For example, Article 4 of the 1979 International Convention Against the Taking of Hostages specifies the obligation of Parties to cooperate in preventing crimes involving seizing hostages, in particular by:

> taking all practicable measures to prevent preparations in their respective territories for the commission of those offenses within or outside their territories, including measures to prohibit in their territories illegal activities of persons, groups and organizations that encourage, instigate, organize or engage in the perpetration of acts of taking of hostages.

Provisions pertaining to the inadmissibility of and prevention of such activities are also contained in UN General Assembly resolutions, including the 1970 Declaration on Principles of International Law Concerning Friendly Relations and Co-operation Among States in Accordance with the Charter of the United Nations and the 1987 Declaration on the Enhancement of the Effectiveness of the Principle of Refraining from the Threat or Use of Force in International Relations, as well as in other international legal documents.

Cooperation of states in the exchange of appropriate information and coordination of necessary measures is an important element in preventing and combating terrorist acts. In view of the delicate nature of such coordination, current universal agreements in this area do not provide for extensive regulation of this area of cooperation. For example, Article 4 of the 1973 Convention on the Prevention and Punishment of Crimes Against Internationally Protected Persons, Including Diplomatic Agents, is limited to an obligation of Parties to cooperate in the area of preventing such crimes, in particular by "exchanging information and co-ordinating the taking of administrative and other appropriate measures as appropriate to prevent the commission of those crimes."

International agreements currently in force contain provisions that impose on the States Parties obligations pertaining to effective suppression of terrorist acts. This is expressed in particular in legally binding requirements to neutralize and to take into custody persons committing such acts who are on the territory of the corresponding State Party.

The effectiveness of cooperation to combat terrorism is inseparably linked with ensuring the inescapable punishment of persons who have committed crimes. Established in all multilateral agreements currently in force in this area (with the exception of the 1963 Tokyo Convention) is a principle which makes it possible to establish jurisdiction over a crime and consequently creates the possibility of ensuring the inescapable punishment of a criminal, regardless of where he may be located and where the crime was committed (the principle of universal jurisdiction). This principle is grounded on operation of the mechanism of "either extradite or prosecute," when a state, if it has not initiated criminal prosecution of a criminal located on its territory, is obliged to hand him over to another Party (of course if the latter makes a corresponding request) for criminal prosecution. The effective functioning of this principle depends in large measure on the degree of trust between states and on their political will and willingness to cooperate in order to ensure that terrorists receive deserved punishment.

An essential element of interaction by states in combating terrorism is the mutual rendering of assistance in criminal procedure. For example, Article 13 of the 1979 Convention on Physical Protection of Nuclear Material specifies, in particular, that:

> States Parties shall afford one another the greatest measure of assistance in connection with criminal proceedings brought in respect of offenses set forth in Article 7, including the supply of evidence at their disposal necessary for the proceedings.

The principle of peaceful settlement of disputes arising between contracting parties and pertaining to interpretation or application of corresponding conventions is an important component of cooperation in combating international terrorism. Universal agreements currently in force provide the possibility of settlement of such disputes by means of negotiation, via arbitration, or before the International Court of Justice. In practice the majority of states have stipulated reservations to the effect that they do not consider themselves bound by procedure of mandatory adjudication by court or arbitration. The importance of this principle could increase considerably if the interested states reach agreement, on mutually acceptable conditions, on extension of mandatory jurisdiction of the UN International Court of Justice or an arbitral tribunal to disputes that may arise pertaining to interpretation or application of universal agreements currently in force pertaining to the suppression of terrorism.

Interaction of states on these matters is increasing within the framework of international organizations both of a universal and regional nature. The UN General Assembly has repeatedly appealed to its specialized organizations (the ICAO, IMO, World Tourist Organization, as well as the IAEA) to increase their contribution toward development of such cooperation. Pursuant to the most recent UN General Assembly Resolution (44/29), the UN Secretary General was instructed to poll the opinion of member states regarding ways and means of strengthening the role of the UN and counterpart specialized organizations in combating international terrorism. This matter is to be discussed at the Forty-sixth Session of the General Assembly in 1991.

These are the basic principles and parameters that determine the development of cooperation by states in combating international terrorism.

The lack of a generally recognized definition of international terrorism, which has made it impossible to draft a uniform universal convention to combat international terrorism, has placed its imprint on the forming of interaction by states in this area, which has been concentrated on manifestations of terrorism which present the greatest threat to the interests of international intercourse. Among special protective measures that have been devised, one can conditionally specify measures against terrorism on land and on air and sea lines of communication.

B. Measures Against Terrorism on Land

In 1973 a Convention on the Prevention and Punishment of Crimes Against Internationally Protected Persons, Including Diplomatic Agents, was drafted and adopted under UN auspices. This document, just as all other universal agreements on these matters, specifies as criminal offenses not only an extensive list of terrorist acts proper but also other unlawful acts of violence associated with or in large measure analogous to terrorist acts, occurring in a specific area. This approach, one factor of which is the absence of a generally recognized definition of international terrorism, is reflected even in the names of these agreements that direct states to combat a broad range of criminal offenses.

Article 2 of the Convention includes among such crimes deliberate murder, kidnapping, or other attack against the person or freedom of an individual enjoying international protection (heads of state and government and other persons listed in Article 1), violent attack on the offices, residence, or vehicles of a person enjoying international protection, which can threaten the person or freedom of said individual; threats of any such attack; attempts at any such attack; and actions as an accomplice to any such attack. This list of criminal acts is influenced in large measure by the corresponding provisions of the 1937 Convention, which was drawn up under League of Nations auspices; this list, as prescribed by this Convention, in no way frees a Party from the obligation in conformity with international law to take all necessary measures to "prevent other attacks on the person, freedom or dignity of an internationally protected person."

This same article places on signatory states the obligation to establish "appropriate penalties which take into account their grave nature."

The principle of universal jurisdiction, the purpose of which is to ensure inescapable punishment, regardless of who has committed a crime and where it was committed, is formally articulated. The mechanism for the operation of universal jurisdiction comprises the combination of a number of elements, including the obligation of a Party to establish its authority over a crime ("compulsory jurisdiction"):

(a) when the crime is committed on the territory of that State or on board a ship or aircraft registered in that State;

(b) when the alleged offender is a national of that State;

(c) when the crime is committed against an internationally protected person as defined in article 1 who enjoys his status as such by virtue of functions which he exercises on behalf of that State. (Article 3(1)).

The principle according to which a Party is obligated either to surrender a presumed criminal who is on the territory of that state to another Party that has made such a request on the basis of the above-stated principles of compulsory jurisdiction, or to hand him over to local agencies of competent jurisdiction for the purpose of criminal prosecution, constitutes a central element of universal jurisdiction. (Article 7).

The universal nature of the jurisdictional mechanism described above is also confirmed by the fact that the convention does not exclude any criminal jurisdiction exercised in regard to this category of crimes in conformity with national law. (Article 3(3)).

The Convention defines the principal areas of cooperation by its Parties. They include, in particular:

cooperation in the prevention of crimes, including taking measures to prevent preparations within their respective territories for the commission of those crimes within or without their territories; exchanging information; and coordinating measures taken to prevent crimes. (Article 4);

cooperation for the purpose of the criminal prosecution of offenders within the framework of the above-described Convention mechanism "either extradite or prosecute" (providing to interested Parties information on the whereabouts of a presumed criminal, on the circumstances of commission of a crime, and on the victims of a crime; taking, in accordance with internal law, measures to ensure the presence of a criminal on the territory of a Party for the purpose of criminal prosecution or extradition; and transferring of a case to proper authorities for the purpose of criminal prosecution). (Articles 5, 6, 7);

cooperation on matters of criminal procedure, including states providing one another "the greatest measure of assistance in connexion with criminal proceedings brought in respect of the crimes . . . including the supply of all evidence at their disposal necessary for the proceedings" (Article 10), with information on the final results of criminal proceedings undertaken to be communicated to other Parties through the UN Secretary General;

cooperation on settling disputes, involving the settlement of disputes concerning the interpretation or application of the Convention by means of negotiations or submission of the dispute to arbitration or the International Court of Justice. (Article 13).

The obligations of host countries to protect foreign diplomatic agents from terrorist acts are set forth in general form in the 1961 Vienna Convention on Diplomatic Relations. In particular, it specifies the obligation to take all appropriate measures to prevent any offenses against the person, freedom, or dignity of a diplomatic agent. (Article 29). The host state bears the special obligation to take all appropriate measures to protect the premises of a diplomatic mission "against any intrusion or damage and to prevent any disturbance of the peace of the mission or impairment of its dignity". (Article 22(2)).

The 1975 Vienna Convention on the Representation of States and Their Relations with International Organizations (which did not enter into force) also prescribes measures to protect the heads of missions, a mission's diplomatic personnel, and heads of delegations in international bodies and at international conferences from illegal acts. In particular, the host country has the obligation to take all appropriate measures to prevent any offenses against the person, freedom, or dignity of such persons, and also to prosecute and punish persons who have committed such offenses. (Articles 28, 58).

The question of "effective measures to increase the protection, safety and security of diplomatic and consular missions and representatives" is regularly considered by the UN General Assembly on the basis of reports on this problem, specially prepared by this organization's Secretary General, reports which present an alarming picture of illegal acts against the lives and dignity of diplomatic agents and the members of their families.

The 1979 International Convention Against the Taking of Hostages is directed against one of the most widespread terrorist actions. The provisions of this Convention can only conditionally be called measures to combat terrorism on land, since the norms contained in this Convention also apply to cases of hostage-taking committed on air and sea lines of communication.

According to the Convention, the crime of taking hostages is committed by any person who seizes or detains another person and threatens to kill, harm or continues to hold another person (hostage) for the purpose of compelling a third party, namely–a state, an international intergovernmental organization, any natural person, a legal entity, or a group of persons–to carry out or to refrain from carrying out any act as a direct or indirect condition for freeing a hostage. (Article 1(1)). The definition of such crimes also includes an attempt to take a person hostage as well as participation as an accomplice to any person who commits or attempts to commit such an act. (Article 1(2)).

The Convention's basic provisions are in large measure analogous to the provisions of other universal agreements on suppressing various manifestations of terrorism. In particular, its operation is grounded on the principle of universal jurisdiction based on the mechanism "either extradite or prosecute"; it also contains similar provisions on cooperation in the areas of preventing acts of hostage-taking, exchanging appropriate information, rendering of criminal procedural assistance, settling disputes, *etc.*

At the same time the Convention also contains certain differences. For example, alongside criteria of jurisdiction mandatorily established by a signatory state regarding a crime (the place where a crime was committed, nationality of the presumed perpetrator, purpose of the crime–to compel a state to perform or refrain from performing some act), optional (modal) jurisdiction is introduced, when a crime has been committed against a hostage who is a citizen of the given state. (Article 5).

The provisions in Article 9(1), which specify in particular the possibility of refusing to surrender a presumed criminal if the Party to which the surrender request is addressed has substantial grounds to believe that such a request "has been made for the purpose of prosecuting or punishing a person on account of his race, religion, nationality or ethnic origin or political opinion," constitute a serious flaw of this Convention.

We feel that such a formula leaves open possibilities for various abuses and undermines the very idea of cooperation in combating terrorism without any exceptions, regardless of the motives for committing terrorist acts. It became a stumbling block for many states in defining their position regarding participation in the Convention. The Soviet Union, which voted against including these provisions, did not accede to the Convention until 1987. In connection with this it released a statement. This statement reads:

> The Union of Soviet Socialist Republics condemns international terrorism, which takes the lives of innocent people, threatens their freedom and the inviolability of their person, and destabilizes the international situation, regardless of the motives given for terrorist actions. Proceeding from this position, the Union of Soviet

> Socialist Republics holds that Paragraph 1, Article 9 of this Convention should be applied in such a manner that it is in conformity with the proclaimed goals of the Convention, including development of international cooperation in taking effective measures to prevent, prosecute, and punish for the commission of all acts of taking hostages as acts of international terrorism, including by surrendering presumed criminals.

The provisions contained in this point of Article 9 predetermined in large measure the reserved attitude toward the Convention on the part of other states as well. The United States, for example, did not ratify it until the end of 1984, Canada and Switzerland finally ratified it in 1985, while France has not yet become a party to the Convention.

The provisions of the 1979 Convention on the Physical Protection of Nuclear Material are directed against one of the most dangerous varieties of terrorism–nuclear terrorism. It is employed chiefly against nuclear material dedicated to peaceful purposes and in the process of international transportation. The importance of this problem becomes obvious if one considers that every year there are more than 1 million transportation movements involving radioactive materials worldwide. In many instances the Convention is applied to nuclear material used for peaceful purposes during domestic use, storage, and transportation. (Article 2). Transportation of nuclear material is not permitted if protective safeguards fail to meet the levels specified in the annex to the Convention. (Article 4).

The heightened danger presented by nuclear material predetermined appearance in the Convention of a provision obligating States Parties to specify their central authority and point of contact having responsibility for the physical protection of nuclear material and for coordinated measures to counter illegal acts in regard to such material. Parties to the Convention are also obligated to cooperate, including by exchange of information, and to assist one another in obtaining the return and safeguarding of nuclear material in case of such request on the part of any state, in the case of theft, robbery, or any other illegal seizure of such material or genuine threat of such actions. The Convention leaves determination of methods of implementation of such cooperation to the discretion of the interested states. (Article 5). States Parties are obligated to take appropriate measures:

> to protect the confidentiality of any information which they receive in confidence by virtue of the provisions of this Convention from another Party or through participation in an activity carried out for the implementation of this Convention. (Article 6).

Article 7 of the Convention considers the following categories of intentional actions to be law violations punishable by each State Party:

(a) an act without lawful authority which constitutes the receipt, possession, use, transfer, alteration, disposal or dispersal of nuclear material and which causes or is likely to cause death or serious injury to any person, or substantial damage to property;

(b) a theft or robbery of nuclear material;

(c) an embezzlement or fraudulent obtaining of nuclear material;

(d) an act constituting a demand for nuclear material by threat or use of force or by any other means of intimidation;

(e) a threat:

(i) to use nuclear material to cause death or serious injury to any person or substantial property damage, or

(ii) to commit an offense described in sub-paragraph (b) in order to compel a natural or legal person, international organization or State to do or to refrain from doing any act;

(f) an attempt to commit any offense described in paragraphs (a), (b) or (c); and;

(g) an act which constitutes participation in any offense in paragraphs (a) to (f)

shall be made a punishable offense by each State Party under its national law.

The Convention is based on the principle of universal jurisdiction, reinforced by the obligation of States Parties either to extradite or to prosecute a presumed perpetrator. Two criteria of mandatory determination of national jurisdiction have been established: when the crime has been committed on the territory of a signatory state or on board a ship or aircraft registered in that state, as well as when the presumed perpetrator is a citizen of that state. The possibility is also provided for determining national jurisdiction (modal or optional) in the case of criminal offenses when a State Party "is involved in international nuclear transport as the exporting or importing state." (Article 8(4)).

Other Articles of the Convention are essentially analogous to the provisions of international universal agreements aimed at combating various acts of international terrorism.

By an edict of the Presidium of the USSR Supreme Soviet entitled "On Criminal Penalties for Unlawful Actions Involving Radioactive Materials," dated March 3, 1988, Soviet laws were brought into conformity with the provisions of the Convention. The provisions of this edict go even further: In addition to nuclear materials, they also apply to sources of ionizing radiation and radioactive substances; in addition, the term "radioactive materials" used in the edict applies not only to materials used for peaceful purposes.

In addition to nuclear terrorism, there exists a realistic threat of terrorist acts involving use of other means capable of bringing about mass casualties: chemical and bacteriological material. In view of this fact, at the Forty-fourth Session of the UN General Assembly the Soviet Union and a number of other East European states submitted a proposal "to proceed with study of the possibility of drafting a document which would govern measures pertaining to physical protection of chemical and biological materials, including against terrorist acts" (Report A/S.6/44/4, dated October 17, 1989). In Resolution 44/29, dated December 4, 1989, the UN General Assembly requested that the UN Secretary General poll the opinion of UN Member States and special agencies, *inter alia*, in regard to this proposal.

C. Measures Against Terrorism Affecting Aviation

Although terrorist activities involving aircraft peaked in the 1970's, even today air transportation remains that mode of international transportation that is the most frequent target of criminal acts.

The Convention on Offences and Certain Other Acts Committed on Board Aircraft, which was drawn up under the auspices of the ICAO and adopted in Tokyo in 1963, was the first practical step toward the formation of a universal legal foundation for suppressing illegal acts of violence involving air transportation. Although a number of the provisions of this Convention leave something to be desired and constitute halfway measures, on the whole adoption of the Convention signaled the beginning of a new phase of universal cooperation among states.

The Convention is directed against a broad range of unlawful acts involving air transportation, both of a criminal and other nature (including endangering an aircraft, disorderly conduct, and refusal to obey lawful orders aboard an aircraft), the consequences of which go beyond national boundaries. The excessively broad sphere of application of the Convention clearly predetermines the absence of such key elements of an effective campaign against terrorism as ensuring inescapable punishment of criminals, specifically articulated in an obligation either to extradite such persons or to prosecute them. The universality of the Convention is seriously undermined by the fact that its provisions cannot be viewed as a legal basis for extradition. This is a serious drawback, since far from all states are bound to one another by international legal obligations in matters of extradition of criminals.

At the same time, the Convention contains a number of specific provisions that laid down the foundation for establishing an international legislative basis for organized efforts to combat illegal acts committed against air transport.

In particular, it defines the authority of an aircraft commander "when he has reasonable grounds to believe that a person has committed, or is about to commit, on board the aircraft, an offence or act contemplated in Article 1." In such situations an aircraft commander is authorized to use against a presumed lawbreaker "reasonable measures including restraint," that are needed to protect the safety of an aircraft or persons and property aboard an aircraft; to maintain order and discipline on board; and to enable the aircraft commander to hand over such a person to the proper authorities or to expel him from the aircraft on the territory of any State Party. The commander of an aircraft "may require or authorize assistance of other crew members and may request or permit, but not require, the assistance of passengers to restrain any person whom he is entitled to apprehend." (Article 6). And no aircraft commander nor any crew member, nor any passenger, nor aircraft agent or administrative officer, nor any person on behalf of whom a flight is being made shall be liable in any court action "on account of the treatment undergone by the person against whom the actions were taken" (Article 10) for actions undertaken pursuant to the Convention.

The obligation of states to "take all appropriate measures to restore control of an aircraft to its lawful commander or to preserve his control of the aircraft" in a case "[w]hen a person on board has unlawfully committed by force or the threat thereof an act of interference, seizure, or other wrongful exercise of control of an aircraft in flight or when such an act is about to be committed" is articulated for the first time in this Convention. (Article 11).

The Convention prescribes that State Parties shall permit on their territory the forced deplaning of any person who is suspected of committing or has committed crimes and other acts specified in the Convention. In connection with turning such persons over to the authorities of the country in which an aircraft lands, that country is obliged to conduct without delay a preliminary investigation of the circumstances of the case, to inform other interested states of the results of such investigation, and also to inform them of its intention to exercise jurisdiction. (Articles 12 and 13). When a state refuses to accept a person who has been put off a plane on its territory and handed over by the aircraft commander, it may return said person to the territory of the state of which he is a citizen or of which said person is a permanent resident. (Article 14).

The deficiency of a number of provisions of this Convention resulted in a reserved attitude toward it by a number of states. The Soviet Union, for example, did not accede to the Convention until 1987, with the statement that such a step "shall not affect its rights and obligations proceeding from bilateral and multilateral agreements currently in force pertaining to combating acts of unlawful interference in civil aviation activities of which it is a Party." (Edict of the Presidium of the USSR

Supreme Soviet dated December 4, 1987).

The drafting under ICAO auspices and adoption in 1970 of the Hague Convention for the Suppression of Unlawful Seizure of Aircraft was the next step taken by the international community in the direction of increasing cooperation to combat unlawful acts threatening the safety of civil aviation.

The Convention obligates States Parties to take harsh measures of punishment against unlawful actions specified by the Convention to be an offense, when any person on board an aircraft in flight (that is, from the moment all its outer doors are closed after loading to the moment any of these doors is opened for deplaning):

> unlawfully, by the threat or use of force, or by means of any other form of intimidation, seizes that aircraft or exercises control of it, or attempts to carry out such an action, or
>
> is an accomplice of a person who carries out or attempts to carry out any such action. (Article 1).

The Convention does not apply if the point of departure and point of actual landing of an aircraft on board where an offense has been committed are on the territory of one and the same state. Cases when the criminal is on the territory of a state other than the state of aircraft registration constitute an exception. (Article 3).

The provisions of the Convention aim to ensure inescapable punishment of the criminals. Operation of the Convention is grounded on the principle of universal jurisdiction. It specifies the obligation of States Parties either to extradite or to prosecute presumed criminals. The Convention specifies explicit criteria on when a signatory state is obligated to establish its jurisdiction over an offense, if:

> an offense is committed on board an aircraft registered in the state in question;
>
> an aircraft on board which an offense is committed lands on its territory and the presumed criminal is still on board;
>
> an offense has been committed on board an aircraft that has been leased without crew to a lessee the principal place of business or, if he has no place of business, the permanent domicile of whom is in this state. (Article 4).

The provisions of the Convention dealing with preventing criminal actions, exchanging information, mutual rendering of criminal procedural assistance, and settling disputes concerning the application and interpretation of its provisions, subsequently formed the basis of wordings embodied in other international agreements on the suppression of terrorism, including the above-described conventions on the suppression of the seizing of hostages and on protection of diplomatic agents.

The next logical step in strengthening international cooperation in the area of aviation safety was adoption in 1971 of the Montreal Convention for the Suppression of Unlawful Acts Against the Safety of Civil Aviation, which was drawn up under the ICAO.

The Convention lists the following unlawful and intentional actions as offenses:

> an act of violence against a person on board an aircraft in flight (this concept coincides with the corresponding wording of the Hague Convention), if such act may threaten the safety of that aircraft;
>
> destruction of an aircraft in operation (from the commencement of aircraft preflight preparation by ground crew or flight crew for a specific flight until the passage of twenty-four hours after any landing), or the causing of damage to such an aircraft that disables it and may threaten its safety during flight;
>
> placing, or actions leading to placing on board an aircraft in service, by any means whatsoever, a device or substance that is likely to destroy that aircraft, or to cause damage to it that renders it incapable of flight, or to cause damage to it that is likely to endanger its safety in flight;
>
> destruction of or damage to air navigation equipment or interference with its operation, if such act can threaten the safety of aircraft in flight;
>
> communication of deliberately false information, threatening the safety of an aircraft during flight.

An attempt to commit any of the above-listed offenses, as well as complicity in the commission of or in an attempt to commit any such offense, shall be considered an equivalent offense. (Article 1). The States Parties to the Convention shall have the obligation to apply severe punishment for such offenses. (Article 3).

The geographic scope of the Convention is quite broad: The Convention shall not apply if the specified aircraft's points of takeoff or landing are located on the territory of a single State Party, with the exception of cases when "the offence is committed or the offender or alleged offender is found in the territory of a State other than that State." (Article 4).

The Convention proceeds from the necessity of ensuring inescapable punishment of the perpetrators. For this purpose it establishes universal jurisdiction. It specifies an obligation pursuant to which a State Party shall either extradite a perpetrator or shall turn the perpetrator over to its own proper authorities for the purpose of criminal prosecution.

The Convention sets forth the following criteria for mandatory establishment by the States Parties of their jurisdiction:

> an offense has been committed on the territory of the state in

question, on board or involving an aircraft registered in that state;

an aircraft on board which an offense has been committed lands on its territory, and the presumed perpetrator is still on board;

an offense has been committed on board or involves an aircraft that has been leased without crew to a lessee the principal place of business of which or, if the lessee does not have a principal place of business, the permanent domicile of whom is located in that state. (Article 5).

Other provisions of the Convention are analogous to articles in other international agreements on suppressing various manifestations of international terrorism, which are grounded on the principle of inescapable punishment of the perpetrators.

In 1988 the Montreal Convention was supplemented by a Protocol on Combating Unlawful Acts of Violence at Airports Serving International Civil Aviation. This provided underpinnings of international law to protection against terrorist and other criminal offenses of such an important international air transportation hub as airports. The Protocol added to Article 1 of the Montreal Convention new Subparagraph 1 *bis*:

Any person commits an offense if he unlawfully and intentionally using any device, substance, or weapon:

a) performs an act of violence against a person at an airport serving international civil aviation which causes or is likely to cause serious injury or death; or

b) destroys or seriously damages the facilities of an airport serving international civil aviation, or aircraft, not in service located thereon, or disrupts the services of the airport,

if such an act endangers or is likely to endanger safety at that airport.

States Parties to the Montreal Convention also have the obligation to establish their jurisdiction over the above-listed offenses when the perpetrator is located on their territory and they do not extradite said perpetrator.

As regards the drafting of new universal instruments in the area of aviation safety, work is being completed under the ICAO on drafting a convention that will establish an international legal regime for tagging explosives for the purpose of their detection, particularly on board aircraft.

Drafting of standards and recommended practices in the area of ensuring safety of civil aviation against terrorist and other unlawful acts is of considerable practical importance in the activities of the ICAO. As a rule, this area of cooperation encompasses those issues on which normative agreement appears difficult for all states (response measures to acts of unlawful interference, exchange of information, and security instruction and training, ground security measures and security measures on board aircraft, drafting and implementation of national programs in this area, *etc.*). Standards have been drafted and recommendations synthesized in the ICAO-published "Security Guide for Protecting Civil Aviation Against Acts of Unlawful Interference."

One deficiency of the international law basis in the area of aviation safety is the fact that it does not apply to "aircraft in military, customs, and police service."

The parameters of coordination among countries' law enforcement agencies in the area of detecting and neutralizing terrorists and other criminals have not yet been articulated as formal procedures, rules and regulations, in the beginning at least in general form.

We feel that as progress is made in confidence-building, deideologization of cooperation, and removal of various obstacles and stereotypes that still exist in this area, those matters that still remain outside the regulatory activities of international law will be given legislative articulation. Perhaps in the future it will be recognized as feasible to draft a uniform international contractual instrument that would govern as an aggregate all matters pertaining to ensuring safety of civil aviation, including taking into account appropriate standards and recommendations drawn up by the ICAO.

D. Measures Against Terrorism on the Seas

For a long time the question of international response measures to combat this relatively rare variety of terrorism remained in the background, as it were, while the struggle against piracy—the most widespread manifestation of violence on the high seas—the history of which goes back many centuries, is formally articulated, in particular, in the 1958 Geneva Convention on the High Seas and the 1982 UN Convention on the Law of the Sea. According to these conventions, piracy is defined as an unlawful act of force, detainment, or robbery on the high seas or at a location that is outside the jurisdiction of any state, committed for private aims by the crew or passengers of a privately owned vessel or aircraft, against persons and property on board. The definition of piracy encompasses only a portion of unlawful acts of force at sea, committed on the high seas or beyond the jurisdiction of any state, with private aims by the crew or passengers of one vessel against persons and property aboard another vessel.

However, matters pertaining to combating other unlawful acts on the seas, including terrorist actions, were covered by the Convention on the

Suppression of Unlawful Acts Against the Safety of Maritime Navigation, and by the Protocol on the Suppression of Unlawful Acts Against the Safety of Fixed Platforms Located on the Continental Shelf, drafted within the framework of the IMO and adopted in Rome in 1988.

The Convention applies to any vessel that is not permanently anchored to the seabed, as well as to any other craft. On analogy with conventions dealing with aviation safety, however, it does not apply to warships or vessels belonging to or operated by a state when they are being used as auxiliary ships or for customs or police duties. (Article 2).

Geographically the Convention applies "if the ship is navigating or is scheduled to navigate into, through or from waters beyond the outer limit of the territorial sea of a single State, or the lateral limits of its territorial sea with adjacent States." (Article 4(1)). In other cases the Convention applies when a presumed criminal is located on the territory of another State Party.

States Parties have the obligation to determine punishment for the following unlawful and intentionally committed actions that are specified as an offense in the Convention:

seizure and control of a vessel by force or the threat thereof or by means of any other form of intimidation;

an act of violence against a person on board a vessel if such act may threaten the safe navigation of that vessel;

the destruction of a vessel or doing damage to a vessel or its cargo, which may threaten the safe navigation of that vessel;

placement, or the performance of actions for the purpose of placement, aboard a vessel by any means whatsoever, of a device or substance that can destroy that vessel or cause damage to that vessel or its cargo, that threatens or may threaten the safe navigation of that vessel;

destruction of or serious damage to marine navigation equipment, or creation of serious interference with the operation of such equipment, if any such act may threaten the safe navigation of a vessel;

communication of deliberately false information, by this act threatening the safe navigation of a vessel;

injuring or killing any person in connection with the commission of or attempt to commit any of the above-enumerated crimes.

Also classified as offenses are attempts to commit any of the above-named criminal acts or to incite to such acts, as well as a threat (with or without conditions, as national legislation prescribes) for the purpose of compelling a natural person or legal entity to perform or to refrain from performing any action, to commit any of the listed offenses, if such threat may endanger the safe navigation of the vessel in question. (Article 3).

Proceeding from aims of ensuring inescapable punishment, the Convention obligates States Parties to conduct criminal prosecution of perpetrators, regardless of where an illegal act was committed and regardless of where the persons suspected of committing such act are to be found. A state is obligated either to extradite or to prosecute such persons.

Criteria are prescribed for establishing compulsory jurisdiction over offenses when committed against or on board a vessel sailing under the flag of a given state; on the territory of a given state, including its territorial sea, or by a citizen of a given state. A state may also establish its jurisdiction when an offense has been committed by a stateless person who customarily resides in the state in question; when during the commission of such a crime a citizen of the state in question has been seized, threatened, injured, or killed; when it has been committed in an attempt to compel the state in question to perform or to refrain from performing any action. (Article 6).

The principle "either extradite or prosecute" has been supplemented by a mechanism of transfer of a presumed perpetrator by a vessel's captain over to the proper authorities of a State Party. This mechanism, which enables a vessel's captain to get rid of a "dangerous guest" at the nearest port, is further developed in the Convention than in the 1963 Tokyo Convention.

Other provisions of the Convention are in large measure analogous to counterpart provisions of agreements in the area of aviation safety.

As for the 1988 Rome Protocol, it is optional for the States Parties to the Convention. Its provisions apply to fixed platforms located on the continental shelf, *i.e.*, man-made islands, rigs, and structures that are permanently anchored to the seabed for the purpose of exploration or development of resources and for other economic purposes.

Practical recommendations on combating crime on the high seas are being drafted by the International Maritime Organization. The Committee on Maritime Safety, which functions under the IMO, has drafted a body of measures to prevent unlawful acts against passengers and crews aboard vessels (Annex 14 to the Report of the Committee on Maritime Safety–Document MS 53/24). This document contains recommendations to the IMO member nations on organizing counterpart efforts at the national level, including in particular the devising and implementing of plans for the security of port facilities and vessels, disseminating information on illegal acts and measures and procedures of monitoring and verification of security, and training of appropriate personnel.

Unquestionably the adoption of the 1988 Rome Convention and Protocol gave a certain impetus to efforts in this area being carried out within IMO. At the end of 1988, for example, a special open-membership working group was formed at U.S. initiative, actively supported by the Soviet Union, within the framework of the Committee on Maritime Safety. This group will regularly examine matters pertaining to ensuring safety of international sea lines of communication against criminal acts. Practical seminars on security measures to be implemented at seaports by IMO member states have recently been conducted under IMO auspices, based on recommendations developed by this organization.

At the same time, just as in the area of aviation safety, international legal norms and recommendations on combating unlawful acts at sea do not encompass naval objects or installations, and regulation of cooperation on the part of law enforcement agencies pertaining to effective detection and neutralization of terrorists on the high seas continues to remain outside their domain.

Evidently these questions can be resolved in the future within the context of the increasing potential in the world for confidence and trust and the removal of political and ideological stereotypes and other obstacles in the path of forming a common front of states in combating terrorism.

INDEX—AUTHORITIES CITED